D0936931

ISBN# 0-9646341-0-4	Suggested Retail $19.95	Spiral
ISBN# 0-9646341-2-0	Suggested Retail $24.95	Hardcover
ISBN# 0-9646341-3-9	Suggested Retail $16.95	Paperback

MYKCO Communications, Inc.
4957-B Winters Chapel Rd., Suite 103
Atlanta, GA. 30360

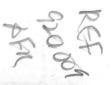

MYKCO COMMUNICATIONS

MAIL ORDER

Send Check or Money Order for appropriate amount (specifying ISBN#) plus $3.50 s/h per book to:

BOOKMASTERS

P.O. Box 388, Dept. 51024, Ashland, OH. 44805

CREDIT CARD ORDERS

Call 800.247.6553, ONLY if you are ready to order

PREPAID VOLUME DISCOUNT & GOVERNMENT / CORPORATE PURCHASE ORDERS

Contact:

MYKCO Communications, Inc.

4957-B Winters Chapel Rd., Suite 103, Atlanta, GA. 30360

770.399.6576 bus 770.698.9009 fax   Email: mwoods366@aol.com

RETAIL ORDERS

Contact:

BAKER & TAYLOR

ONLINE ORDERS

Keyword: AFROMATION

amazon.com   barnesandnoble.com   bookcrafters.com/markplc

ORDER FORM

MYKCO Communications is happy to invite you into the world of AFROMATION. This is a perpetual calendar with the dates serving as a chronological guide to "on this day in history," and as a page reference number for our 366 categorized and alphabetized biographies of notable African-Americans from the past.

The format was designed with education and user friendliness in mind. You can utilize this "book" day-by-day, or refer to the table of contents and index to find that individual or subject that most interests you. However utilized, this is not intended to be the definitive "book" on African-American history, but just a taste of a proud heritage.

The "366" in the subtitle also represents how long it took me to dream, research, organize, and complete this historic project. My reason for wanting to share all of this AFROMATION with you goes back to my grade school days in the Midwest where I was introduced to the proud history of Native Americans and European contributions to America. But every time the subject of black, Negro, and/or colored people came up, all I heard was the word slavery--which made me feel naked. I was never taught that an African-American: drew up plans for Bell's telephone invention; was the first to reach the North Pole; became America's first female self-made millionaire; invented the 3-way stop light; organized the first blood bank; revolutionized the South's farming industry. I hope you get the picture.

Before I began this project, I thought that Black History Month was the best thing since the drive-thru window at McDonald's. But, now I feel like I got home and opened my bag to find no fries--short-changed! To use another analogy, we all celebrate Mother's Day; yet, we don't forget about her the rest of the year. We've integrated schools, public transportation, lunch counters, hospitals, etc.; but, American history is, for the most part, still segregated. Black History Month should be the celebration that it is; however, I have found that there are too many great African-American contributions for us to just wait until February to discuss, inform, and educate...

In conclusion, we hear mostly about Martin and Malcolm who were two great men. However, as you will read, they were not the first and I hope they won't be the last. Like Martin, I too have a dream--that no African-American child will ever again have to grow up feeling naked about his/her heritage, and that every child is introduced to *Ourtruth*.

I welcome your feedback. You will find our address on the last (order form) page.

Michael D. Woods

INDEX

Afromation, as coined by Michael Woods, is Afrocentric information. Affirmation is the declaration of those collected words and works. Afromotion, as coined by yours truly, is the movement of Afromation in the appropriate manner, to the appropriate people, at the appropriate time, using the appropriate vehicle. Another word that I have coined is *Ourtruth*--this is us revealing and reporting the story of a grand and magnificent people.

Whom shall I send and who will go for me; and I answered, here am I, send me. These words as expressed in Isaiah, are appropriate for Michael. The same question was breathed into his nostrils, and he exhaled with the Afromation, the Affirmation, and the Afromotion. The information is not new; but is for far too many. For each heart, soul, and spirit featured herein, there are millions more whose stories we will never hear, for they make up the kingdoms in depths of the sea and castles neath the sands on the Island of Goree, under the Baobob tree.

This book serves as an inspiration and incentive to our children and generations yet unborn. They are in history's arena and research the truth, they must. It is what will set us free. However, it is critical that we write it right. This is the only way that we can right history as it is lived. Our very existence is dependent on the breath and breadth of our commitment to *Ourtruth* and how we confront the challenges of keeping it write and right, as we bequeath it to our young and lead them into tomorrow.

Thank you, Michael, for your actions and motivating us to further seek, share, and support *Ourtruth*.

Rev. LaVerne C. Williams Hall
Mt. Zion Baptist Church, Seattle

FOREWORD

INDEX

The celebration tends not to promote propaganda, but to counteract it by popularizing the truth. It is not interested so much in Negro History as it is in history influenced by the Negro; for what the world needs is not a history of selected races or nations but the history of the world void of national bias, race hate, and religious prejudice. There has been, therefore, no tendency to eulogize the Negro nor to abuse his enemies. The aim has been to emphasize important facts in the belief that facts properly set forth will speak for themselves...

Carter G. Woodson

INDEX

AFROMATION

TABLE OF CONTENTS

WILLIAM WELLS BROWN

Abolitionist, Underground Railroad conductor, reformer, and author.   Born into slavery around 1814 on the John Young Plantation near Lexington, Ky.   Escaped to freedom in Cincinnati (1834); employed on a Lake Erie steamer, where he ferried his Underground Railroad passengers to freedom in Canada; lecturing agent for the Western New York Anti-Slavery Society (1843-1847); became a lecturer in New England for the Massachusetts Anti-Slavery Society and the American Anti-Slavery Societies (1847), working side by side with William Lloyd Garrison and Wendell Phillips. Represented the American Peace Society at the International Peace Conference (Paris, 1849); lectured in Europe (1849-1854), delivering over a thousand anti-slavery lectures and enlisting support from the British for the anti-slavery movement in the U.S.; emancipated (1854); recruited African-American enlistees for the Massachusetts 54th Regiment (1863); became a practicing physician after the war. Author of: *Narrative of William W, Brown, A Fugitive Slave, Written By Himself* (1847), which sold over 10,000 copies; *Three Years in Europe; Or, Places I Have Seen and People I Have Met* (1852), becoming a pioneer as an African-American writer of travel books; *Clotel; Or, The President's Daughter: A Narrative of Slave Life in the United States* (1853), a story about Thomas Jefferson's relationship with his slave mistress Sally Hemings and was considered the **first novel by an African-American**, although not published in the U.S. until 1969; *The Escape; Or, A Leap for Freedom* (1856), the **first drama published by an African-American**; *The Negro in the American Rebellion: His Heroism and His Fidelity* (1867), becoming a **pioneer in writing the military history of African-Americans**. Died on November 6, 1884, in Chelsea, Mass.   Further reading, William Edward Farrison, *William Wells Brown: Author and Reformer* (1969).

---

on this day in history...

1834,	William Wells Brown escaped from slavery in Cincinnati, Ohio.
1863,	President Lincoln issued the Emancipation Proclamation Act.
1916,	The first issue of the *Journal of Negro History* was published with Carter Woodson as editor.
1928,	Christopher Edley, Sr., president emeritus of the United Negro College Fund, was born in Charleston, W.Va.
1942,	Dennis Wayne Archer, Detroit mayor and former Michigan State Supreme Court justice, was born in Detroit, Mich.
1967,	The Black Panther Party opened its first official headquarters on 56th & Grove Street in Oakland, Calif.

JANUARY 1   **ABOLITIONISTS**

INDEX

SAMUEL ELI CORNISH

Missionary, abolitionist, and editor. Born in 1795 in Sussex County, Del. Trained for the ministry by Philadelphia's First African Presbyterian Church pastor John Gloucester; licensed to preach (1819), and served as a missionary to slaves on Maryland's Eastern Shore; **organized and preached at New Demeter Street Presbyterian Church (1821-1828), New York City's first African-American Presbyterian church**; ordained (1822); traveling preacher and missionary to African-Americans in the New York City area (1824-1846); **established, with John Russwurm, *Freedom's Journal* (1827), the nation's first African-American newspaper in the U.S.**; agent of the New York African Free School (1827-1829), pastor of Gloucester's Philadelphia Church (1831-1832); organizer and pastor of Emmanuel Church in New York City. **Founded the American Anti-Slavery Society,** served as executive committee member (1833-1838), agent (1834, 1837, and 1840); helped found the New York Anti-Slavery Society (1833); executive committee member of the New York City Vigilance Committee (1835-1837); vice president of the American Moral Reform Society (1835-1836); manager of the American Bible Society (1835); principal editor of the *Colored American* (1837-1839);executive committee member of the American and Foreign Anti-Slavery Society (1840-1841, 1847-1853); manager of the Union Missionary Society (1842); **founder of the American Missionary Association**, and executive committee member (1846-1855), and vice president (1848-1858). Co-wrote *The Colonization Scheme Considered, in Its Rejection by the Coloured People--in Its Tendency to Uphold Caste--in Its Unfitness for Christianizing and Civilizing the Aborigines of Africa, and for Putting a Stop to the African Slave Trade* (1840), which condemned the American Colonization Society's program. Died on November 6, 1858, in New York City. Further reading, Jane H. Pease and William H. Pease, "Cornish, Samuel E.," *Dictionary of American Biography* (1982).

---

on this day in history...

1831,	*The Liberator*, an abolitionist newspaper, was first published in Boston, Mass.
1911,	St. Clair Drake, pioneering anthropologist of African and African-American studies, was born in Suffolk, Va. (d. 1990).
1915,	John Hope Franklin, the nation's preeminent African-American historian, was born in Rentiesville, Okla.
1965,	The Selma Voters Registration Drive began.

JANUARY 2   ABOLITIONISTS

INDEX

WILLIAM HOWARD DAY

Abolitionist, clergyman, printer, educator, and editor. Born on October 19, 1825, in New York City. Oberlin College (1847). Learned the printing trade while working at the *Northhampton Gazette*; moved to Cleveland and became a crusader against the Black Laws of Ohio (1847), which prohibited African-Americans from settling without proof of freedom and a co-signer, attending common schools, and testifying in any court where a white person was involved; chairman of the group that organized the National Convention of Colored Freemen, with Frederick Douglass presiding (Cleveland, 1848); lobbied the Ohio legislature (1849), contributing to the Ohio Black Law repeal and better educational opportunities for African-American children; compositor and editor of the *Cleveland Daily True Democrat* (1851-1852), editor of *Aliened American* (1853-1854), and librarian of the Cleveland Library Association (1854-1856). Went to Canada (1856); embarked on a tour of England, Ireland, and Scotland (1858-1863), raising funds for a church and school for free Negroes in Buxton, Canada; elected president of the National Board of Commissioners of Colored People of Canada and the U.S. (1858); assigned to the Freedmen's Bureau as an inspector-general of schools in Maryland and Delaware (1865), founding over 100 schools and hiring over 100 teachers. Ordained as a minister in the African Methodist Episcopal Church (1867); organized voters in Wilmington, Del. (1869); clerk in the corporation department of the auditor-general's office of Harrisburg, Pa.; general secretary of the General Conference of the AME Zion Church (1875-1880, 1888-1900); **member of the Harrisburg School Board (1878-1891), president (1891-1893), becoming the nation's first African-American city school board president in a predominately white community**. Died on December 3, 1900, in Harrisburg, Pa. Further reading, Russell H. Davis, *Black Americans in Cleveland* (1974).

---

on this day in history...

1834,   Alonzo Jacob Ransier, former South Carolina congressman (1873-1875), was born in Charleston, S.C. (d. 1882).
1934,   Carla Anderson Hills, first African-American woman assistant U.S. attorney general, was born in Los Angeles, Calif.
1964,   Cheryl DeAnn Miller, Olympic basketball champion and sports broadcaster, was born in Riverside, Calif.
1966,   Floyd McKissick succeeded James Farmer as national director of CORE.
1989,   The *Arsenio Hall Show* premiered.

JANUARY 3   **ABOLITIONISTS**

Herskovits, Melville J.
> played a key role in establishing African-American studies as an acceptable scholarly

Hill, Oliver O.
> Civil War Union general who was the principal founder of Howard University

Humphrey, Hubert H.
> Minnesota U.S. senator who, as Senate majority whip, was mainly responsible for the passage of the Civil Rights Act of 1964

Ickes, Harold L.
> U.S. secretary of the interior who was a watchdog for African-Americans' inclusion within the social and economic programs of FDR's New Deal

Johnson, Frank M.
> U.S. Federal District judge who applied the *Brown vs. Board of Education* decision to the Montgomery bus boycott case

Margold, Nathan R.
> attorney whose work, "The Margold Report," became an intricate part of the NAACP's legal defense campaign

Moore, William L.
> retired postmaster who was murdered while on a solo protest march against segregation from Chattanooga to Jackson, Miss.

Muste, Abraham J.
> Fellowship of Reconciliation head who founded the Congress of Racial Equality (CORE)

Ovington, Mary W.
> socialite who was a founding member of the NAACP

Reeb, James J.
> Unitarian minister who was murdered during civil rights activities in Selma

Rockefeller, John D.
> philanthropist who founded the General Education Board, which helped educate over 1,000,000 southern African-Americans

Rosenwald, Julius
> philanthropist whose gifts led to the construction of over 5,000 schools for southern African-American youths

Schwerner, Michael H.
> CORE field worker who was murdered by Mississippi Klansmen while participating in the Freedom Summer of 1964

Spingarn, Arthur B.
> civil rights attorney who co-founded the NAACP and served as vice president and chairman of the its National Legal Defense Committee

Stevens, Thaddeus
> major force behind the passage of the 13th, 14th, and 15th Amendments

Storey, Moorfield
> attorney who served as the NAACP's first president

Stowe, Harriet Beecher
> abolitionist who wrote *Uncle Tom's Cabin*, which showed the world the atrocities of slavery

Sumner, Charles
> Massachusetts U.S. senator who pressured President Lincoln to emancipate the slaves

Tappan, Lewis
> abolitionist who ran the evangelical wing of the abolitionist movement and helped found the American Missionary Association

Whittier, John G.
> Quaker poet who was powerful voice for abolitionist movement

FOR YOUR AFROMATION

MARTIN ROBINSON DELANEY

Abolitionist, editor, author, physician, Black Nationalist, army officer, and colonizationist. Born into slavery on May 6, 1812, in Charlestown, Va. Harvard College of Medicine. Emancipated (1822); became an officer of the Pittsburgh Anti-Slavery Society; helped organize literary societies; delegate to colored conventions in Philadelphia and New York (1836); **published _The Pittsburgh Mystery_ (1843-1847), first African-American newspaper west of the Allegheny Mountains**, which was devoted to the anti-slavery movement; co-editor, with Frederick Douglass, of the _North Star_ (1847), traveling throughout the eastern U.S. gathering subscribers and news for the weekly; organized resistance against the Fugitive Slave Act of 1850; wrote _The Condition, Elevation, Emigration and Destiny of the Colored People of the United States, Politically Considered_ (1852), the **first full-length draft of Black Nationalism**, in which he criticized abolitionists and recommended emigration out of the U.S. Attended the National Emigration Convention (Cleveland, 1854), where he reported on "The Political Destiny of the Colored Race" and stressed the need for an independent black nation; traveled to Liberia and the Niger Valley (1859), where he negotiated a treaty granting African-Americans the right to establish a self-governing colony in Abbeokuta, which is now Nigeria; wrote his _Official Report of the Niger Valley Exploring Party_ (1861). Recruited African-American soldiers for state regiments (1863); **commissioned as a major in the Army (1865), becoming the first African-American field officer of high rank**, and was sent to Charleston, S.C.; customs inspector in Charleston (1873-1874); supported the Liberian Exodus Joint Stock Exchange Company (1878), which carried emigrants to Liberia. Died January 24, 1885, in Wilberforce, Ohio. Further reading, Victor Ullman, _Martin R. Delaney, The Beginning of Black Nationalism_ (1971).

---

on this day in history...

1935,	Floyd Patterson, boxing champion, was born in Waco, N.C.
1937,	Grace Bumbry, one of the brightest stars of 20th century opera, was born in St. Louis, Mo.
1971,	Melvin H. Evans was sworn in as the Virgin Islands' first elected governor by Thurgood Marshall.
1985,	William Gray of Pennsylvania was elected chairman of House Budget Committee.

JANUARY 4   **ABOLITIONISTS**

FOR YOUR AFROMATION

NON-BLACK ABOLITIONISTS AND CIVIL RIGHTS ADVOCATES

Alexander, Will W.
Methodist minister who founded the Commission on Interracial Cooperation

Allen, Ivan
Atlanta mayor who was the only southern politician to support desegregation of public accommodation

Anthony, Susan B.
abolitionist who spoke out against slavery and spear-headed the fight for women's suffrage

Ashmore, Harry Scott
Arkansas Gazette editor who opposed Governor Faubus' segregationist policies in dealing with the Little Rock Nine

Baldwin, Roger
founder of the American Civil Liberties Union

Blake, Eugene C.
United Presbyterian Church leader who helped organize the 1963 March on Washington

Brown, John
militant abolitionist who was hanged by Confederate soldiers for his lead role in the raid on the Harper's Ferry Arsenal

Brown, John Robert
Fifth Circuit appellate court judge who helped expand the *Brown v. Board* decision to deal with voting and employment

Butler, Benjamin F.
Union Civil War general who refused to return fugitive slaves to their masters, labeling them as "contrabands of war"

Coffin, Levi
abolitionist who was nicknamed "the president of the Underground Railroad"

Daniels, Jonathan M.
clergyman who was murdered in Lowndes County, Ala., while working with the Student Nonviolent Coordination Committee

Durr, Clifford J.
attorney who helped prepare the legal challenge to Montgomery's segregated public transportation system

Garrett, Thomas
Underground Railroad conductor who reportedly aided more than 2,500 slaves in reaching freedom in Canada

Garrison, William Lloyd
one of the nation's most famous abolitionists who published the anti-slavery journal *The Journal*

Goodman, Andrew
college student who was murdered by Mississippi Klansman while participating in the Freedom Summer of 1964

Griffin, John H.
author who journeyed through the South disguised as an African-American and wrote the book *Black Like Me*

Harmon, William E.
philanthropist who promoted and honored African-American achievers in the arts

FREDERICK DOUGLASS

Abolitionist, journalist, and public servant who was called the **"father of the civil rights movement" and became the nation's most famous African-American**.   Born into slavery, as Frederick Washington Bailey, reportedly on February 14, 1817, in Tuckahoe, Md.   Escaped slavery (1838); became an agent and abolitionist lecturer for the Massachusetts Anti-Slavery Society (1841); wrote his autobiography, *Narrative of the Life of Frederick Douglass* (1845); lectured against slavery in Great Britain (1845-1847); founded the anti-slavery weekly newspaper *North Star* in Rochester, N.Y. (1847-1863); used his print shop as an Underground Railroad station; elected president of the Colored Convention Movement (1848); helped found the women's rights movement at the Seneca Falls Convention (New York, 1848). Wrote that the best remedy for the Fugitive Slave Act of 1850, was a "good revolver, a steady hand, and a determination to shoot down any man attempting to kidnap." Supporter of the Free Soil Party (1852), and the new Republican Party (1856); became a recruiter for the Massachusetts 54th and 55th Regiments; chaired the National Convention of Colored Men (Syracuse, 1864); editor of the weekly newspaper *New National Era* (1870-1874), and spoke against convict lease, the crop-lien system, the prevalence of lynching, and the anti-Negro rulings of the U.S. Supreme Court; opposed the "Great Exodus" of African-Americans from the South to Kansas (1870). **Became the first African-American marshal of the District of Columbia** (1877-1881), where he led President Garfield's inaugural procession; recorder of deeds of the District of Columbia (1881-1886); served as minister-resident and consul general to the Republic of Haiti and charge d'affaires for the Dominican Republic (1888-1891). Died on February 20, 1895, in Washington, D.C.   Further reading, Frederic May Holland, *Frederick Douglass: The Orator* (1891).

---

on this day in history...

1869,	Matilda Sissieretta Joyner, world renowned singer known as "Black Patti," was born in Portsmouth, Va.
1911,	Kappa Alpha Psi fraternity was founded at Indiana University.
1912,	John Wheeler, publisher of the *St. Louis Palladium*, died in St. Louis, Mo. (b. 1847).
1926,	Hosea Lorenzo Williams, civil rights leader, was born in Attapulgus, Ga.

JANUARY 5   **ABOLITIONISTS**

71	81,550	Hartford, Conn.	112	36,979	Wichita, Kan.
72	79,770	Jersey City, N.J.	113	36,877	Pine Bluff, Ark.
73	74,257	Phoenix, Ariz.	114	36,805	Alexandria, La.
74	72,254	Austin, Texas	115	36,400	Knoxville, Tenn.
75	70,738	Las Vegas, Nev.	116	35.975	Longview-Marshall, Texas
76	70,670	Middlesex-Somerset, N.J.	117	35,081	Springfield, Mass.
77	70,227	Tallahassee, Fla.	118	35,055	Biloxi-Gulfport, Miss.
78	69,717	Toledo, Ohio	119	34,801	Clarksville-Hopkinsville, Tenn.-Ky.
79	65,091	Akron, Ohio	120	34,771	Lake County, Ill.
80	64,220	New Haven-Meriden, Conn.	121	34,350	Danville, Va.
81	61,481	Trenton, N.J.	122	33,455	Daytona Beach, Fla.
82	59,264	Monmouth-Ocean, N.J.	123	33.423	Fresno, Calif.
83	58,218	Chattanooga, Tenn.-Ga.	124	31,720	Ann Arbor, Mich.
84	58,186	Tulsa, Okla.	125	31,572	Tyler, Texas
85	56,211	San Jose,Calif.	126	31,417	Melbourne-Titus Bay-Palm Bay, Fla.
86	55,893	Pensacola, Fla.	127	31.365	Lansing-E. Lansing, Mich.
87	54,902	Youngstown-Warren, Ohio	128	30,709	Ft. Pierce, Fla.
88	54,385	Lakeland-Winter Haven, Fla.	129	39,526	Providence, R.I.
89	51,522	Albany, Ga.	130	30,380	Ft. Wayne, Ind.
90	51,426	Omaha, Neb.-Iowa	131	30,131	Bakersfield, Calif.
91	51,378	Lafayette, La.	132	30,079	Lynchburg, Va.
92	49,687	Killeen-Temple, Texas	133	29,808	Jacksonville, N.C.
93	48,116	Huntsville, Ala.	134	29,520	Waco, Texas
94	47,043	Vallejo-Fairfield-Napa, Calif.	135	29,003	Athens, Ga.
95	45,826	Bridgeport, Conn.	136	28,593	Colorado Springs, Colo.
96	44,398	Atlantic City, N.J.	137	27,801	Dothan, Ala.
97	44,276	Florence, S.C.	138	27,602	Roanoke, Va.
98	44,096	Monroe, La.	139	27,094	Stockton, Calif.
99	42,681	Anaheim-Santa Ana, Calif.	140	26,735	Houma-Thibodeaux, La.
100	41,671	Portland-Vancouver, Ore.-Wash.	141	26,423	Texarkana, Texas-Ark.
101	41,311	Grand Rapids, Mich.	142	25,875	Honolulu, Hawaii
102	41,112	Albany-Troy-Schenectady, N.Y.	143	25,187	Canton, Ohio
103	39,472	Harrisburg-Lebanon-Carlisle, Penn.	144	25,142	Peoria, Ill.
104	39,377	Tuscaloosa,Ala.	145	24,872	Benton Harbor, Mich.
105	39,095	Syracuse, N.Y.	146	24,844	Ocala, Fla.
106	38,982	Gainesville,Fla.	147	24,190	SouthBend-Mishawaka, Ind.
107	38,810	Saginaw-Bay City-Midland, Mich.	148	24,170	Jackson, Tenn.
108	38,445	Lake Charles, La.	149	24,151	Anderson, S.C.
109	38,382	Joliet, Ill.	150	24,097	Wilmington, N.C.
110	38,154	Galveston-Texas City, Texas	151	23,581	Pascagoula, Miss.
111	37,212	Lexington-Fayette, Ky.			

Source: U.S. Bureau of Census, Department of Commerce

FOR YOUR AFROMATION

JAMES FORTEN, SR.

Businessman, abolitionist, and reformer who became **one of the best known abolitionists of the first half of the 19th century**.   Born in 1766 in Philadelphia, Pa.   Powderboy on a Philadelphia privateer, *Royal Louis*, during the Revolutionary War; apprenticed to sailmaker Robert Bridges, foreman (1786-1798), owner (1798-1842), where he amassed a fortune of over $100,000 and employed over 40 white and African-American workers; promoted women's rights, temperance, peace, and equal rights for Negroes; joined with Richard Allen in circulating a petition calling for the U.S. Congress to emancipate the slaves (1800), which Congress rejected; organized, with the assistance of Richard Allen and Absalom Jones, an African-American volunteer force of 2,500 men for the defense of Philadelphia during the War of 1812. Wrote a pamphlet (1813), protesting against a bill before the Pennsylvania legislature prohibiting the immigration of free Negroes from other states; strongly opposed colonization at a meeting of the Negro Convention (1830), where he supported raising funds for an African-American technical college; credited with persuading William Lloyd Garrison to call for emancipation and equality rather than colonization, and became a major contributor to his *Liberator* publication. Organized the American Anti-Slavery Society at his Philadelphia home on Lombard Street (1833), serving on its board of managers and providing financial assistance; founded and served as president of the American Moral Reform Society (1839), which was established for the "promotion of Education, Temperance, Economy, and Universal Liberty." Died on February 24, 1842, in Philadelphia, Pa.   Further reading, Esther M. Doughty, *Forten the Sailmaker, Pioneer, Champion of Negro Rights* (1968).

---

on this day in history...

1882,	Thomas Boyne, sergeant in Troop C of the 9th U.S. Cavalry, received the Medal of Honor for bravery in two New Mexico battles.
1944,	Van McCoy, Grammy Award-winning composer of *The Hustle*, was born in Washington, D.C. (d. 1979).
1948,	Edith DeVoe became the first African-American nurse to be transferred into the Regular Army.
1971,	The Dance Theater of Harlem, the nation's first all-black classical ballet company, was founded.
1984,	Robert N.C. Nix, Jr., was inaugurated as chief justice of the Pennsylvania State Supreme Court.

JANUARY 6

ABOLITIONISTS

FOR YOUR AFROMATION

AFRICAN-AMERICAN METROPOLITAN POPULATIONS

#	Population	City	#	Population	City
1	2,250,026	New York, N.Y.	36	164,602	Columbus, Ohio
2	1,332,919	Chicago, Ill.-Wis.	37	159,306	San Diego, Calif.
3	1,041,934	Washington, D.C.-Md.-Va.	38	156,509	Baton Rouge, La.
4	992,974	Los Angeles-Long Beach, Calif.	39	153,227	Charleston, S.C.
5	943,479	Detroit, Mich.	40	152,349	Nashville, Tenn.
6	929,907	Philadlephia, Penn.	41	143,850	Ft.Worth, Texas
7	736,153	Atlanta, Ga.	42	137,906	Columbia, S.C.
8	616,065	Baltimore, Md.	43	133,308	Orlando, Fla.
9	611,243	Houston, Tx.	44	130,512	Mobile, Ala.
10	430,470	New Orleans, La.	45	126,238	Dayton-Springfield, Ohio
11	423,182	St. Louis-E. St. Louis, Mo.-Ill.	46	124,761	Louisville, Ky.-Ind.
12	422,802	Newark, N.J.	47	123,482	Augusta, Ga.-S.C.
13	410,766	Dallas, Texas	48	123,266	Seattle-Tacoma, Wash.
14	399,011	Memphis, Tenn.-Ark.-Miss.	49	122,494	San Francisco, Calif.
15	398,093	Norfolk-Virginia Beach-Newport News, Va.	50	117,142	Gary, Ind.
16	397,993	Miami-Hialeah, Fla.	51	116,892	Shreveport, La.
17	355,619	Cleveland, Ohio	52	111,334	Greenville-Spartanburg, S.C.
18	303,826	Oakland, Calif.	53	109.852	Buffalo, N.Y.
19	252,340	Richmond-Petersburg, Va.	54	107,705	W. Palm Beach-Boca Raton-Delray Beach, Fla.
20	245,726	Birmingham, Ala.	55	106,108	Bergen-Passiac, N.J.
21	231,654	Charlotte-Gastonia-Rock Hill, N.C.-S.C.	56	105,196	Montgomery, Ala.
22	209,970	Boston, Mass.	57	101,940	Sacramento, Calif.
23	200,508	Kansas City, Mo.-Kan.	58	101,862	LittleRock-N. Little Rock, Ark.
24	197,183	Milwaukee, Wis.	59	101,082	Oklahoma City, Okla.
25	193,967	Nassau-Suffolk, N.Y.	60	97,294	Macon-Warner Robbins, Ga.
26	193,447	Ft. Lauderdale-Hollywood-Pompano Beach, Fla.	61	95,796	Denver, Colo.
27	190,473	Cincinnati, Ohio-Ky.-Ind.	62	93,819	Rochester, N.Y.
28	185,503	Tampa-St. Petersburg-Clearwater, Fla.	63	91,484	Columbus, Ga.-Ala.
29	183,447	Raleigh-Durham, N.C.	64	89,710	MinneapolisSt. Paul, Minn,-Wis.
30	182,284	Greensboro-Winston Salem-High Point, N.C.	65	88,778	San Antonio, Texas
31	181,265	Jacksonville, Fla.	66	87,496	Fayetteville, N.C.
32	178,525	Riverside-San Bernadino, Calif.	67	86,228	Savannah, Ga.
33	172,326	Indianapolis, Ind.	68	85,641	Wilmingham, Del.-Md.-N.J.
34	168,382	Pittsburgh, Penn.	69	84,665	Beaumont-Port Arthur, Texas
35	167,899	Jackson, Miss.	70	84,257	Flint, Mich.

FOR YOUR AFROMATION

HENRY HIGHLAND GARNET

Abolitionist, clergyman, temperance leader, editor, and diplomat. Born into slavery in 1815 in New Market, Md. Oneida Theological Institute in Whitesboro, N.Y. (1840). Licensed to preach in Troy, N.Y. (1842), and became a pastor of the city's only African-American Presbyterian church; **became one of the nation's most prominent Negro abolitionists (1842-1860)**; co-editor of the *Troy National Watchman* (1842), editor (1843), where he worked for enfranchisement of free Negroes, women's rights, temperance, religious reform, and the world peace movement; delivered his famous "Call to Rebellion" speech at the National Negro Convention (Buffalo, 1843), where he demanded that all African-Americans embrace a "motto of resistance;" called for the establishment of a national African-American press (1847). Delegate to the World Peace Congress (Frankfurt, 1850); sent to Jamaica by the United Presbyterian Church of Scotland (1853-1856), as pastor of the Stirling Presbyterian Church; elected president of the African Civilization Society (1858); became one of the first to demand that President Lincoln permit the enlistment of African-American soldiers (1863); pastor of the 15th Street Presbyterian Church in Washington (1864-1866), where he became the **first African-American to deliver a sermon before the U.S. House of Representatives**; worked for the Freedmen's Bureau; resident minister and consul general of Liberia (1882). Died on February 12, 1882, in Liberia. Further reading, Benjamin Quarles, *Black Abolitionists* (1969).

---

on this day in history...

1890,	William B. Purvis patented a fountain pen.
1917,	Ulysses Simpson Kay, the leading African-American composer of his time, was born in Tucson, Ariz.
1919,	Dorothy L. Brown, the South's first African-American surgeon, was born in Philadelphia, Pa.
1941,	Frederick D. Gregory, first African-American space shuttle commander, was born in Washington, D.C.
1955,	Marian Anderson became the first African-American singer to perform with the New York Metropolitan Opera Company.

JANUARY 7   **ABOLITIONISTS**

1955 Executive Order 10590
    issued by President Eisenhower--established the President's Committee on Government Employment Policy.
1957 Civil Rights Act
    established the Civil Rights Section in the U.S. Department of Justice.
1959 *State Athletic Commission v. Dorsey*, 359 U.S. 533
    extended the inconstitutionality of racial segregation to public athletic contests.
1960 *Bates v. Little Rock*, 361 U.S. 516
    ruled that compulsory disclosure of the Ark. state NAACP membership list was an unconstitutional invasion of freedoms protected in the due process clause of the Fourteenth Amendment.
1960 *Boynton v. Virginia*, 364 U.S. 454
    ruled that racial segregation practiced by a privately operated restaurant in an interstate bus terminal violated the Interstate Commerce Act.
1960 *Gomillion v. Lightfoot*, 364 U.S. 339
    banned racial gerrymandering in state legislative redistricting plans.
1961 Executive Order 10925
    issued by President Kennedy--established the President's Equal Employment Opportunity Commission.
1962 Executive Order 11063
    issued by President Kennedy--prohibited discrimination in federally owned and operated housing, federally assisted public housing, and housing funded through FHA and VA loans.
1963 *Johnson v. Virginia*, 373 U.S. 61
    desegregated southern courtrooms.
1963 *Peterson v. Greenville*, 373 U.S. 244
    ruled that states or communities could not rrquire segregation in a business and use police power to enforce the segregation.
1964 Civil Rights Act
    banned discrimination by businesses offering food, lodging, gasoline, or entertainment to the public, and by employers when hiring, promoting, and dismissing.

1964 *Hamilton v. Alabama*, 376 U.S. 650
    set a precedence for addressing African-Americans during cross-examination as Mr. or Mrs., not "boy" or "nigger".
1964 *NAACP v. Alabama*, 377 U.S. 288
    prohibited the state of Ala. from banning the NAACP from conducting business within its borders.
1964 Twenty-fourth Amendment
    abolished poll taxes, which were used as a criteria for voting.
1965 Executive Order 11246
    issued by President Johnson--distributed authority among federal agencies for enforcing the Civil Rights Act of 1964.
1965 Voting Rights Act
    outlawed educational requirements for voting and empowered the U.S. government to assign federal registrars to enroll voters.
1967 *Loving v. Virginia*, 388 U.S. 1
    abolished state laws prohibiting interracial marriages.
1967 *Walker v. City of Birmingham*, 388 U.S. 307
    used to suppress student protest, ruling that injunctions against protests were to be challenged in the courts and not in the streets.
1968 Civil Rights Act
    prohibited discrimination in the rental or sale of housing.
1970 *Swann v. Charlotte-Mecklenburg Bd. of Education*, 402 U.S. 1
    upheld the nation's first extensive court-orderd use of busing to achieve desegregation in public schools.
1972 Equal Employment Opportunity Act
    provided enforcement powers for the Equal Employment Opportunity Commission.
1980 *Fullilove v. Klutznick*, 448 U.S. 448
    upheld the constitutionality of minority "set-aside" programs.

FOR YOUR AFROMATION

PRINCE HALL

Abolitionist, colonizationist, and **organizer of what is now called The Ancient Egyptian Arabic Order of Nobles of the Mystic Shrine**. Born into slavery around 1732. Emancipated (1770); worked in the leather trade, acquired real estate, and attended night school; became a minister in the Methodist Church; urged the Committee of Safety to enlist slaves in the Colonial armies (1775). Initiated into a British army lodge #441 of Free Masons and was attached to the 38th Foot Regiment near Boston during the Revolutionary War (1775); organized and became master of African Lodge #1 (1775), which was granted a license from the provincial grand master of North America, becoming the first organized body of African-American Masons; granted a charter from the British Grand Lodge (1784), which authorized the organization in Boston of a "regular lodge of Free and accepted Masons, under the title or denomination of the African Lodge," that resulted in the formation of African Lodge #459; granted warrants to establish lodges in Providence and Philadelphia (1797), with Hall serving as grand master. Made the first major statement on colonization in Africa (1787); lobbied the Massachusetts legislature for support in educating African-Americans (1787); signer of a petition seeking to have the Massachusetts State Legislature abolish slavery (1777), and was successful, after one of his Masons was kidnapped, in getting the Commonwealth to pass an act ending the slave trade (1788); **founded the African Society House on Boston's Belkap Street (1806), Boston's first separate schoolhouse for African-American children.** Died on December 4, 1807, in Boston, Mass. Further reading, <u>Charles H. Wesley</u>, *<u>Prince Hall, Life and Legacy</u>* (1977).

---

on this day in history...

1867,   Congress passed legislation giving African-Americans in the District of Columbia the right to vote.

1937,   Shirley Bassey, popular music singer, was born in Cardiff, Wales.

1952,   Mel Reynolds, Illinois 2nd District congressman, was born in Mound Bayou, Miss.

1977,   Pauli Murray was ordained as the first African-American woman priest of the Protestant Episcopal Church.

1990,   Thomas E. Brown, Jr., was appointed the first African-American public safety director of Dekalb County, Ga.

JANUARY 8   **ABOLITIONISTS**

FOR YOUR AFROMATION

ACTS, AMENDMENTS, EXECUTIVE ORDERS, & LANDMARK U.S. SUPREME COURT RULINGS THAT HAVE AFFECTED AFRICAN-AMERICANS

1863 Emancipation Proclamation Act
  signaled the end of slavery in the U.S.

1865 Freedmen's Bureau Act
  was called the nation's first federal civil rights agency.

1865 Thirteenth Amendment
  banned slavery and abolished servitude in the U.S. and its territories.

1866 Civil Rights Act
  declared that all persons, except certain Indians, born in the U.S. were now citizens without regard to race, color, or previous conditions.

1868 Fourteenth Amendment
  gave U.S. citizenship to African-Americans, prohibited states from denying "any person of life, liberty, or property, without due process of law", and guaranteed "equal protection before the law".

1870 Fifteenth Amendment
  gave all U.S. citizens the right to vote.

1890 Morrill Act
  led to the formation of a assortment of institutions of higher education for African-Americans in the South.

1896 *Plessy v. Ferguson*, 163 U.S. 537
  made the "separate but equal" doctrine the law of the land unil the 1954 *Brown v. Board of Education* decision.

1899 *Carter v. Texas*, 177 U.S. 442
  ruled that Seth Carter must be giving a new murder trail because of the state's deliberate exclusion of African-Americans from jury service at the time of his conviction.

1911 *Bailey v. Alabama*, 219 U.S. 219
  helped bring an end to black peonage, an involuntary servitude for debt that was common in the South following Reconstruction.

1917 *Buchanan v. Warley*, 245 U.S. 60
  established a precedence against residential segregation ordinances.

1927 *Nixon v. Herndon*, 273 U.S. 536
  outlawed Texas' all-white primaries.

1940 *Chambers v. Florida*, 309 U.S. 227
  prohibited the introduction of forced confessions as evidence in criminal trails.

1942 Executive Order 8802
  issued by President Roosevelt--prohibited discrimination in government departments and defense industries and established the Fair Employment Practice Committee.

1944 *Smith v. Allwright*, 321 U.S. 649
  ruled that the white primaries of the Texas Democratic party were unconstitutional.

1946 Executive Order 9808
  issued by President Truman--created the President's Committee on Civil Rights.

1948 Executive Order 9981
  issued by President Truman--led to the integration of the armed forces.

1948 *Shelley v. Kraemer*, 334 U.S. 1
  made racially restrictive property deeds unenforceable.

1950 *Sweatt v. Painter*, 339 U.S. 629
  ruled that the University of Texas Law School had to admit Herman Sweatt and became one of the precedence for overturning the 1896 *Plessy v. Ferguson* ruling.

1953 *Avery v. Georgia*, 345 U.S. 559
  helped clarify what constituted racial discrimination in a state's jury selection process.

1954, *Brown v. Board of Education*, 347 U.S. 483
  concurring unanimously that "in the field of public education the doctrine of 'seperate but equal' has no place".

FOR YOUR AFROMATION

CHARLES LANGSTON

Abolitionist, educator, and reformer.   Born into slavery in 1817 in Louisa County, Va.   **Oberlin College preparatory department's first African-American student**.   Emancipated (1834); helped establish and taught in a school for African-American children in Chillicothe, Ohio (1836); member of the executive committee and sales agent for Columbus, Ohio's civil rights-oriented publication, *Palladium of Liberty* (1842-1843); participated in the State Colored Convention (Columbus, 1844), where he proposed the repeal of Ohio's Black Laws, the provision of equal education for African-American children, and the increased opportunity for home ownership; member of the Liberty Party; served on the Business and Organization Committee at the Colored National Convention (Cleveland, 1848), and was appointed to the National Central Committee. Appointed deputy most worthy patriarch for the West of the National Organization of the Sons of Temperance (1848); helped organize the Ohio Colored American League (1850); organizer and worshipful master of the St. Marks Masonic Lodge (1852-1855), and later deputy grand master in the state organization; became principal of the Columbus Colored Schools (1856); member of the Manual Labor Committee of the Colored National Convention (Rochester, 1853), where he was **responsible for the establishment of Wilberforce University** by the Methodist Episcopal Church in Wilberforce, Ohio (1856); recording secretary and business agent of the Ohio Anti-Slavery Society; Lorain County, Ohio Underground Railroad conductor who was convicted in the rescue of a fugitive slave (1858), which brought him national distinction. Moved to Kansas after the Civil War; principal of the Colored Normal School at Quindaro (1872); presided over the Convention of Colored Men (Topeka, 1880); joined the Prohibition Party (1886). Died in 1892 in Lawrence, Kan.   Further reading, Jacob R. Shipherd, *History of the Oberlin-Wellington Rescue* (1859).

---

on this day in history...

1907,   Earl Wiley Renfro, nation's first African-American orthodontist, was born in Chicago, Ill.
1914,   Phi Beta Sigma fraternity was founded at Howard University.
1935,   Earl G. Graves, Jr., publisher of *Black Enterprise* magazine, was born in Brooklyn, N.Y.
1940,   Joseph A. Delpit, Louisiana House of Representative speaker pro-tempore, was born in Baton Rouge, La.

JANUARY 9   ABOLITIONISTS

GEORGE WASHINGTON

Pioneer and town founder. Born into slavery on August 15, 1817, in Frederick County, Va. Raised by foster parents James and Anna Cochran, who educated him at home; became an expert tailor, a superior marksman, and skilled as a miller, distiller, tanner, cook, weaver, and spinner; left for the West with the Cochrans (1850), reaching Oregon City in the Oregon Territory, where he rented a home and began cutting timber. Staked a claim in the Oregon Territory, that was later known as Black George Prairie, at the junction of the Chehalis and Skookumchuck Rivers (1853), which later became the Washington Territory; began clearing part of his land, built a house, started a farm, and operated a ferry service across the Chehalis River; worked out a transfer of land arrangement with the Cochrans, because of a territorial law allowing any land owned by Indians or African-Americans to be fair game for white settlers to file a claim, later buying the land back for five times his selling price; befriended by the Chehalis Indians, while white settlers had to flee to nearby Fort Henness during the Indian War of 1853. **Founded Centerville [now Centralia], Wash.** (1872), after the Northern Pacific Railroad built a line halfway between the Columbia River and Puget Sound passing through his land; sold lots to anyone for $10 a lot, donated land to the First Baptist Church for a new church building and cemetery, set aside property for a public square, built rental units, provided jobs, and sustained the town when the railroad shifted to a new route. Died on August 26, 1905, in Centralia, Wash. Further reading, Herdon Smith, _Centralia: The First Fifty Years, 1845-1900_ (1942).

---

on this day in history...

1900,   Selma Hortense Burke, sculptor whose bust of FDR appears on the dime, was born in Mooresville, Okla.

1908,   Adam Clayton Powell, Sr., became pastor of Abyssinian Baptist Church in N.Y. and built it into the world's largest African-America congregation.

1930,   Odetta Holmes Felious, folklorist, was born in Birmingham, Ala.

1948,   LaDonna Andrea Gaines ("Donna Summers"), "queen of disco," was born in Boston, Mass.

1984,   The United Negro College Fund held its first nationally-televised telethon.

DECEMBER 31   **WESTERN TRAILBLAZERS**

JAMES W.C. PENNINGTON

Clergyman, author, abolitionist, civil rights leader, and educator.   Born in 1807 on the Eastern Shore of Maryland.   Learned the stone mason and blacksmith trades; studied theology; was pastor of African Congregational Churches in Newton, Conn. (1838-1840), and in Hartford (1840-1847), where he served as president of the Hartford Central Association of Congregational Ministers; became president of the Union Missionary Society (1841), where he urged members to boycott slave produced products and oppose colonization; performed the marriage ceremony for Frederick Douglass and his wife (1841). Wrote: *A Text Book of the Origin and History of Colored People* (1841); *Covenants Involving Moral Wrong Are Not Obligatory Upon Man: A Sermon* (1842); *The Fugitive Blacksmith* (1850), a scathing condemnation of slavery in the U.S.; *The Reasonableness of the Abolition of Slavery* (1856). Connecticut delegate to the World's Anti-Slavery Convention (1843), and American Peace Convention delegate to the World's Peace Society (London, 1843); pastor of New York City's First Presbyterian Church (1847-1855); emancipated in Hartford (1851), after fleeing to Europe in response to the Fugitive Slave Act of 1850; traveled to Scotland as a guest of the Glasgow Female Anti-Slavery Society; **helped organize one of the first civil rights organizations, the New York Legal Rights Association (1855)**, whose goals included gaining equal treatment in New York City's transportation system. Died in 1870 in Jacksonville, Fla.   Further reading, Benjamin Quarles, *Black Abolitionists* (1969).

---

on this day in history...

1888,   A.B. Blackburn patented a railway signal.
1915,   Dean Charles Dixon, first African-American to devote his career to symphonic conducting, was born in New York City (d. 1976).
1925,   Max Lemuel Roach, modern jazz drummer, was born in New Land, N.C.

JANUARY 10   **ABOLITIONISTS**

BENJAMIN SINGLETON

"Exoduster" who was nicknamed "Pap."   Born into slavery in 1809 in Nashville, Tenn.   Fled to Canada, living in Detroit until the end of the Civil War; returned to Nashville and became a cabinet maker; formed the Edgefield Real Estate and Homestead Association just outside of Nashville (1874), and guided hundreds of African-American migrants to Kansas; prepared hundreds of flyers advertising the activities of the Exodus and circulated them in Tennessee, Mississippi, Louisiana, Texas, Alabama, North and South Carolina, Georgia, and Virginia; settled in the Dunlap colony of Kansas; testified before a U.S. Senate committee on the Exodus (1880), gaining national attention after claiming to be the cause of the great migration of African-Americans to Kansas from the South, and was giving the title **"father of the Exodus."** Formed the United Colored Links of Topeka (1881), whose goal was race unity for economic reasons; organized the Trans-Atlantic Society (1885) with the goal of migrating to the Mediterranean island of Cyprus. Died in 1892 in St. Louis, Mo.   Further reading, Nell Irvin Painter, *Exodusters: Black Migration to Kansas Following Reconstruction* (1977).

---

on this day in history...

1928,   Elias Bates McDaniel ("Bo Didley"), blues composer, was born in Magnolia, Miss.

1930,   Herman Jerome Russell, founder of H.J. Russell Construction Co. (which was involved in building MARTA subway stations, the Georgia Dome, the New Hartsfield International Airport, Benjamin E. Mays High School, and the Coca Cola Tower), was born in Atlanta, Ga.

DECEMBER 30   WESTERN TRAILBLAZERS

ROBERT PURVIS, SR.

Abolitionist and civil rights leader who was the father of famed surgeon, Charles Purvis. Born on August 4, 1810, in Charleston, S.C. Inherited a small fortune from his father, a cotton broker; lobbied for the establishment of a manual labor school for African-Americans (1831); helped found the Philadelphia Library Company of Colored People (1833); **helped found the American Anti-Slavery Society** in Philadelphia (1833); vice president and corresponding secretary from Pennsylvania of the Colored National Convention (1833); opposed a legislative motion that would have prevented out-of-town free Negroes from locating in Pennsylvania (1833); traveled to England (1834), with letters of introduction from abolitionist William Lloyd Garrison. Fought unsuccessfully for the repeal of a new state law barring African-Americans from voting (1838); chaired a committee that drew up a protest entitled "Appeal of Forty Thousand Citizens Threatened with Disfranchisement, to the People of Pennsylvania;" member of the Pennsylvania Society for Promoting the Abolition of Slavery; president of the Vigilance Committee of Philadelphia (1839-1844), and chairman of the General Vigilance Committee (1852-1857) (whose missions were to assist runaway slaves by providing housing and food). President of the Pennsylvania Anti-Slavery Society (1845-1850); caused his township to reverse a policy of excluding African-American children from public schools (1853), by withholding his substantial tax responsibilities; supported temperance crusade, women's rights, and prison improvements; opposed colonization; criticized President Lincoln for suggesting that African-Americans voluntarily leave the country during the Civil War; presided over the 50th anniversary meeting of the American Anti-Slavery Society (Philadelphia, 1883). Died on April 15, 1898, in Philadelphia, Pa. Further reading, Benjamin Quarles, *Black Abolitionists* (1969).

---

on this day in history...

1900,	Wilbur DeParis, jazz trumbonist, was born in Crawfordsville, Ind. (d. 1973).
1985,	Rueben Anderson became the first African-American to be appointed to the Mississippi State Supreme Court.

JANUARY 11   **ABOLITIONISTS**

JEREMIAH BURKE SANDERSON

Abolitionist, educator, clergyman, and California civil rights leader. Born on August 10, 1821, in New Bedford, Mass. Worked as a barber in New Bedford and Wareham, Mass.; made his first public address as an active abolitionist at a Nantucket anti-slavery meeting (1841), where Frederick Douglass was also making his debut; lectured in Massachusetts and New York State; member of the National Council of the National Colored Convention (Rochester, 1853); left for California (1854). Petitioned for the right of African-Americans to give testimony in California courts (1855); secretary and delegate to the Colored Conventions of California (1955, 1956); taught school in Sacramento, where he lobbied the local school board to grant financial support to the school for African-American children; teacher and principal of a San Francisco school for African-American children (1859-1865); became a pastor in the African Methodist Episcopal Church. Organizer and first president of an African-American cultural and self-education organization in San Francisco, called the Young Men's Union Beneficial Society; founding member of the Franchise League (1862); trustee of San Francisco's Ladies Union Beneficial Society and the Ladies Pacific Accumulating and Benevolent Association; **head of the Stockton school for African-American children (1868-1874), where he established a statewide reputation as an outstanding educator**; helped organize a statewide conference on integrated education (1871); elected to the Republican State Judicial Convention (1873); became head of the Equal Rights League of Oakland (1874); elected secretary of the state conference of the AME Churches of California (1875), and also state delegate to the AME national conference in Atlanta. Killed in a train accident on August 19, 1875, in Oakland, Calif. Further reading, <u>Delilah Beasley</u>, <u>*The Negro Trail Blazers of California*</u> (1968).

---

on this day in history...

1890,	Buffalo Soldiers of the 9th Cavalry, led by First Sergeant George Jordan, rescued the all-white 7th Cavalry from a Sioux ambush on the Pine Ridge, S.D., Indian Reservation a day after the infamous Wounded Knee massacre.
1907,	Robert C. Weaver, U.S. secretary of housing and urban development during the Johnson administration, was born in Washington, D.C.
1917,	Tom Bradley, Los Angeles' first African-American mayor, was born in Calvert, Texas.

DECEMBER 29   WESTERN TRAILBLAZERS

CHARLES LENOX REMOND

Abolitionist, reformer, and **one of America's first great African-American orators.** Born in 1810 in Salem, Mass. **Appointed the Massachusetts Anti-Slavery Society's first African-American lecturer** (1838), speaking in Massachusetts, Rhode Island, Maine, New York, Pennsylvania, and the Midwest; delegate to the World's Anti-Slavery Convention (London, 1840), where he went on to lecture in England, Ireland, and Scotland on anti-slavery topics; became the **first African-American to address the Massachusetts House of Representatives** (1842), where he spoke on "Rights of Colored Persons in Travelling;" addressed a Boston crowd on the topic of ending slavery in the District of Columbia (1842), with a speech entitled "Address from the People of Ireland." Elected a vice president and served on the finance committee of the National Convention of the American Equal Rights Association (1867); opened a Ladies and Gentlemen's Dining Room (1856); recruited for the 54th Massachusetts Regiment (1863), the first northern Negro regiment to see action in the Civil War; became a Boston street light inspector (1865); clerk in the Boston Customs House (1871-1873); advocated equal school rights, universal suffrage, and abolition. Died on December 22, 1873, in Massachusetts. Further reading, Carter G. Woodson, *Negro Orators and Their Orations* (1925).

---

on this day in history...

1944,	Joe Frazier, boxing champion, was born in Beaufort, S.C.
1946,	Andre DeShields, Emmy Award-winning actor, singer, and dancer, was born in Baltimore, Md.
1946,	George Duke, jazz pianist, was born in San Rafael, Calif.
1960,	Dominique Wilkins, Atlanta Hawks All-Star, was born in Sorbonne, France.

JANUARY 12   **ABOLITIONISTS**

MARY ELLEN PLEASANT

Abolitionist, civil rights leader, and entrepreneur. Born around 1814, reportedly on a southern plantation. Married a wealthy abolitionist who died and reportedly left her a large sum of money; set out for California (1849), during the gold rush; arrived in San Francisco (1850), where she was hailed as "one of the great Southern cooks" and a bidding war commenced for her culinary services; decided instead to open a restaurant and boarding house on Washington Street (1849-1858), where she served and housed some of the most important businessmen in California; loaned money to miners and other businessmen at 10 percent interest, and reportedly operated a "matchmaking service." **Credited with winning the right of African-Americans to have their testimonies accepted in California courts** (1863); successfully sued a San Francisco railroad for refusing to let African-Americans ride on the city's streetcars, in the case of *Pleasants vs. North Beach and Mission Railroad* (1868); the California State Supreme Court upheld a lower court decision, which ruled that the railroad had to pay her $500 in damages; the decision led to a California statute prohibiting racial discrimination in places of public accommodations. Died on January 11, 1904, in San Francisco, Calif. Further reading, Delilah Beasley, *The Negro Trail Blazers of California* (1968).

on this day in history...

1816,   The American Colonization Society was formed in Washington to transport free Negroes back to Africa.
1905,   Earl "Father" Hines, "father of modern piano jazz," was born in Duquesne, Pa. (d. 1983).
1940,   Lonnie Liston Smith, jazz keyboardist, was born in Richmond, Va.
1954,   Denzel Washington, Academy Award-winning actor, was born in Mount Vernon, N.Y.
1977,   Karen Farmer became the first African-American member of the Daughters of the American Revolution.

DECEMBER 28   **WESTERN TRAILBLAZERS**

DAVID RUGGLES

Abolitionist, businessman, journalist, and hydropathist. Born in 1810 in Norwich, Conn. Moved to New York City and worked as a grocer (1829-1834); traveling agent for the abolitionist weekly, *Emancipator and Journal of Public Morals* (1833-1842), where he wrote articles, edited newspapers, gathered subscriptions, emphasized the importance of the press, and gave lectures on denouncing slavery and colonization; **became the nation's first African-American bookseller** when he opened and operated a bookstore near Broadway (1834-1835), distributing abolitionist and anti-colonization publications. Wrote the pamphlets, *Extinguisher, Extinguished* (1834), and *Abrogation of the Seventh Commandment, by the American Churches* (1835); Underground Railroad conductor (1835-1838), receiving fugitive slaves from Philadelphia and preparing them to move farther north; aided Frederick Washington Bailey, better known as Frederick Douglass, in his escape to freedom (1838), while he was secretary of the New York Vigilance Committee; publisher and editor of the *Mirror of Liberty* (1838-1841), where he protested against colonization, disenfranchisement, segregation, and slavery. Became a member of the Northhampton Association of Education and Industry (1842); erected the first new building specifically for hydropathy in the U.S., operating from 1846 to 1849, advertising that he could cure headaches, bronchitis, general and nervous debilities, pulmonary affections, liver complaints, jaundice, acute and chronic inflammatory rheumatism, neuralgia, sciatica, lame limbs, paralysis, fevers, salt rheum, and scrofulous and erysipelas humors; treated Sojourner Truth and William Lloyd Garrison, and saved the lives of many people who were diagnosed with incurable diseases. Died on December 26, 1849, in Norwich, Conn. Further reading, Dorothy Porter, *Early Negro Writing* (1971).

---

on this day in history...

1913,	Delta Sigma Theta sorority was founded at Howard University.
1923,	Edward McKnight Brawley, Morris Brown College founder and president, died in Raleigh, N.C. (b. 1851).
1953,	Christopher Edley, Jr., U.S. Office of Management and Budget's first African-American deputy director, was born in Boston, Mass.
1990,	Lawrence Douglas Wilder was sworn in as Virginia's first African-American governor.

JANUARY 13   **ABOLITIONISTS**

BILL PICKETT

Internationally-famed rodeo performer.   Born on December 5, 1870, in Williamson County, Texas.   Worked as a ranch hand in South America and the U.S. Southwest, where he developed his roping and riding skills; **originated a type of steer wrestling known as "bulldogging,"** a method of bringing a steer to submission by seizing it about the horns or neck, and then biting into its upper lip or nose, forcing it to the ground; he used his bulldogging technique in catching wild cattle and performing exhibitions at various stockyards; became a semiprofessional, appearing at county fairs; bulldogged in various Texas towns (1898-1906), receiving national attention in an edition of *Leslie's Illustrated Weekly* (1905). Signed with the Oklahoma Cherokee Strip-based Miller brothers' 101 Ranch Wild West Show (1907-1916), becoming their star performer, achieving international fame, and reaching legendary status; appeared all over the U.S., Canada, Mexico, Argentina, and England; performed in Madison Square Garden, Mexico City bull rings, and before King George V and Queen Mary of England. Retired from the rodeo (1916), and settled on his ranch near Chandler, Okla.; returned to performing (1931-1932), to help out the financially-troubled 101 Ranch and was fatally injured while roping a stallion on foot; he was said to have contributed more to rodeos than any other person. Died on April 2, 1932.   Further reading, Bailey C. Haines, *Bill Pickett, Bulldogger: The Biography of a Black Cowboy* (1977).

---

on this day in history...

1857,   Henry Plummer Cheatham, former North Carolina congressman (1888-1893), was born in Henderson, N.C. (d. 1935).

1892,   The first African-American intercollegiate football game was played between Livingstone College and Biddle College [now Johnson C. Smith University].

1939,   John Amos, actor, was born in Newark, N.J.

DECEMBER 27   **WESTERN TRAILBLAZERS**

WILLIAM STILL

Abolitionist, writer, and businessman.   Born in 1821 in Burlington County, N.J.   Learned to read and write on his own; moved to Philadelphia (1844); worked for the Pennsylvania Society for the Abolition of Slavery (1847-1861); named chairman of a Vigilance Committee (1852), which assisted large numbers of fugitive slaves heading to Canada through Philadelphia after the passage of the Fugitive Slave Act of 1850; aided John Brown's accomplices after the raid on Harper's Ferry; campaigned to end racial discrimination on Philadelphia streetcars (1859-1867), and wrote *A Brief Narrative of the Struggle for the Rights of the Colored People of Philadelphia in the City Railway Cars* (1867). Organized and financed a social, civil, and statistical association to collect data on African-Americans (1861); established a coal business during the Civil War; became post sutler at Camp William Penn (1864); **wrote *The Underground Railroad*** (1872), one of the most comprehensive books on the lives of the courageous fugitive slaves and the African-American and white abolitionists during the days of the Underground Railroad; published a pamphlet entitled *An Address on Voting and Laboring* (1874); helped found a Mission Sabbath School in North Philadelphia; **organized one of the first YWCAs for African-American youths** (1880); member of the Freedmen's Aid Commission and the Philadelphia Board of Trade; helped found and manage an orphanage for African-American youths in Philadelphia. Died in 1902 in Philadelphia, Pa.   Further reading, Lurey Khan, *One Day, Levin...He Be Free, William Still and the Underground Railroad* (1972).

---

on this day in history...

1887,	Henry Arthur Callis, founder of the National Medical Association, was born in Rochester, N.Y. (d. 1974).
1940,	Horace Julian Bond, civil rights leader, was born in Nashville, Tenn.
1943,	Harvey Gantt, Charlotte's first African-American mayor, was born in Charleston, S.C.
1975,	William T. Coleman was named U.S. secretary of transportation by President Ford.
1981,	James Frank of Lincoln University, Mo., became the first African-American president of the NCAA.

JANUARY 14   **ABOLITIONISTS**

EDWARD PRESTON McCABE

Politician, publisher, and "Exoduster" [African-Americans who in a mass migration moved from the South to the Kansas and Oklahoma Territories] who **encouraged thousands of African-Americans to settle in the Oklahoma Territory**. Born on October 10, 1850, in Troy, N.Y. Worked as a clerk and porter for the Wall Street firm of Shreve, Kendrick & Co.; moved to Chicago (1872), and worked for the firm of Potter Palmer and in the treasure's office of the Cook County courthouse; joined the "Exoduster" movement and headed for the Nicodemus colony in northwest Kansas' Graham County (1878), where he assisted other new arrivals and became the principal leader; secretary of the Nicodemus Town Company (1878-1879); appointed Graham County clerk (1880); **served as Kansas' first African-American state auditor (1882-1886), which was the highest state office attained by a non-southern African-American.** Operated as a real estate agent in Topeka; appointed the Washington, D.C., representative of Oklahoma Immigration Association (1889), whose goals were to make the Oklahoma Territory a Negro state; moved to Guthrie, Okla. (1890), and was appointed the first treasurer of Logan County; became involved in the development and establishment of the all-Negro town of Langston, Okla. (1890), which was named after Virginia's first African-American congressman; sold contracts for land in Langston all over the South; acquired interest in the *Langston City Herald* (1891), and used it to promote Negro colonization. Established the town of Liberty, Okla. (1893); elected secretary of the Republican Territorial League (1894), and served as deputy territorial auditor (1897-1907); **successfully lobbied for the establishment of the Colored Normal and Agricultural University (1897), [now Langston University]**; led the fight to abolish Oklahoma's "Jim Crow" laws in the case of *E.P. McCabe vs. Atchinson Topeka and Santa Fe Railroad Company* (1914), with the U.S. Supreme Court affirming the state's constitutional right to mandate "separate but equal" accommodations. Died on March 12, 1920, in Chicago, Ill. Further reading, Kaye M. Teall, *Black History in Oklahoma* (1971).

---

on this day in history...

1849,	David Ruggles, Underground Railroad conductor and hydropathist, died in Norwich, Conn. (b. 1810).
1894,	Nathan Jean Toomer, Harlem Renaissance writer, was born in Washington, D.C. (d. 1967).
1908,	Jack Johnson defeated Tommy Burns for the heavyweight boxing championship.
1931,	La Julia Rhea integrated opera when she performed in the Chicago City Opera Company's production of Verdi's *Aida*.
1954,	Osborne Earl "Ozzie" Smith, St. Louis Cardinal All-Star, was born in Mobile, Ala.
1966,	Kwanzaa (Swahili for first fruit) was first celebrated by Maulana Krenga in Los Angeles, Calif.

DECEMBER 26   **WESTERN TRAILBLAZERS**

SOJOURNER TRUTH

Abolitionist, women's rights activist, lecturer, and religious leader. Born into slavery, as Isabella Baumfree, in 1797 in Ulster County, N.Y. Escaped slavery (1826); emancipated (1827), after passage of the New York State Emancipation Act; worked as a domestic servant and evangelist in New York City; follower of the prophet Matthias (1832-1834), where she was the only African-American member of his religious commune; left her New York City home with 25 cents, a new dress and the name Sojourner Truth, after receiving a religious vision telling her to go out and testify to the sins committed against her people (1843); traveled to rallies on abolition in the Midwest, New England, and Middle Atlantic states, **becoming the first African-American woman to speak out publicly against slavery**; reached the colony of Northhampton in Mass. (1844), where she first encounted Garrisonian abolitionism; joined the anti-slavery lecture circuit; published *The Narrative of Sojourner Truth* (1850), which allowed her to be self-supporting; addressed a women's rights conference in Akron, Ohio (1851), with her famous "Ain't I A Woman" speech; settled in Battle Creek, Mich. (1856); met President Lincoln in Washington (1864); taught housekeeping skills to former women field hands, nursed African-American soldiers at Freedmen's Hospital, and helped disburse relief supplies to ex-slaves in camps around the District of Columbia; worked with the National Freedmen's Relief Association; **credited with inspiring the exodus of African-American families from the South to Kansas** (1879), after campaigning for a "Negro State" in the West while in the District of Columbia. Died on November 26, 1883, in Battle Creek, Mich. Further reading, Hertha Pauli, *Her Name was Sojourner Truth* (1962).

---

on this day in history...

1908,	Alpha Kappa Alpha sorority, the first African-American sorority, was founded at Howard University.
1928,	William Lucas, Republican Party leader, was born in New York City.
1929,	Martin Luther King, Jr., leader of the modern civil rights movement, was born in Atlanta, Ga.
1991,	Roland Burris was sworn in as Illinois' first African-American state attorney general.

JANUARY 15   **ABOLITIONISTS**

BIDDY MASON

Entrepreneur, nurse, philanthropist, and humanitarian. Born into slavery on August 15, 1818, in the South. Her master, Robert Marion Smith, who became a Mormon convert, took her family and other slaves on a cross-country journey to the Utah Territory (1847), with Mason herding oxen, milk cows, and mules that belonged to the party; lived in the Mormon environs (1848-1851), where she was subjected to indignities of the Mormon establishment; her master decided to leave the Salt Lake Valley and move to the newly-established community of San Bernardino, Calif. (1851), taking his slaves with him to a state that ambiguously forbade slavery; her owner became unsettled over California's confused status of slaves and began making preparations to relocate his family and slaves to the slave state of Texas. She solicited the help of three free African-American men, Charles Owens, Manuel Pepper, and Bob Owens, who assisted her in gaining her freedom; served Smith at his Santa Monica Mountains hideout, with the help of sheriffs, with a writ of habeas corpus; Smith failed to appear in court, and Mason and her family were emancipated (1856). Remained in Los Angeles and became a midwife to Anglo immigrants, American Indians, and the wealthy; bought a home on South Spring Street (1866), **becoming the first African-American woman to own property in Los Angeles**; continued purchasing land and built a commercial building with rental space in downtown Los Angeles (1884); performed many charitable and philanthropic works, frequently visited the jails, provided refuge for needy people of all races, and fed the poor; **founded the Los Angeles branch of the First African Methodist Episcopal Church**. Died on January 15, 1891, in Los Angeles, Calif. Further reading, Lonnie G. Bunch, *Black Angelenos: The Afro-American in Los Angeles, 1850-1950* (1988).

on this day in history...

1776,   Oliver Cromwell and Prince Whipple crossed the Delaware River with George Washington to attack the Hessians in New Jersey.

1863,   Robert Blake won the Navy Medal of Honor for distinguished service aboard the *U.S.S. Marblehead*.

1907,   Cabell "Cab" Calloway, first singer to record a million-selling jazz record (*Minnie the Moocher*), was born in Rochester, N.Y.

1932,   Richard Perriman ("Little Richard"), Grammy Award-winning rock'n'roll innovator, was born in Macon, Ga.

1951,   Harry T. Moore, Florida coordinator of the NAACP, was killed when his Mims, Fla., home was bombed.

1958,   Rickey Henderson, major league baseball's "stolen base king," was born in Chicago, Ill.

DECEMBER 25   **WESTERN TRAILBLAZERS**

EDWARD MITCHELL BANNISTER

Painter who became the **first African-American artist to receive a national award** and was the only major African-American artist of the late 19th century who developed his talents without the benefit of European exposure. Born in 1828 in St. Andrews, New Brunswick, Canada. Lowell Institute of Art. Worked at sea before moving to Boston (1848), and becoming a barber; learned to paint at the Boston Studio Building, where he was influenced by the works of William Morris Hunt; produced his first commissioned painting, *The Ship Outward Bound* (1854); moved to Providence (1870), where he became one of their leading painters during the 1870s and 1880s; **helped found the Providence Art Club (1873), which later became the Rhode Island School of Design**; received the first-prize bronze medal at the Philadelphia Centennial Exposition with a painting entitled, *Under the Oaks* (1876), which brought him great fame and numerous commissions allowing him to devote all of his time to painting. Created mostly landscape paintings with tranquil moods, which became one of the hallmarks of the Bannister style; also painted portraits, figure studies, religious scenes, seascapes, still lifes, genre subjects, and was attracted mainly to castles, cattle, cottages, dawns, sunsets, and small bodies of water. Some of his other paintings include: *Newspaper Boy* (1869), one of his few genre subjects; *Tree Landscape* (1877), a tranquil composition; *Woman Walking Down Path* (1882). His works appear in the collections of the Atlanta University, the Howard University Gallery of Art, and the Rhode Island School of Design. Died on January 9, 1901, in Providence, R.I. Further reading, Lynn Moody Igoe, *Two Hundred Fifty Years of Afro-American Art: An Annotated Bibliography* (1981).

---

on this day in history...

1941,	The Tuskegee Training Program and the U.S. Army 99th Pursuit Squadron were established.
1943,	Marcelite Jordan Harris, first African-American woman general in the U.S. Air Force, was born in Houston, Texas
1948,	Fred Conley, Omaha's first African-American city council president and mayor, was born in Jonesboro, Ark.
1950,	Debbie Allen, Emmy Award-winning actress, choreographer, director, and producer, was born in Houston, Texas
1959,	Helen Folsade Adu ("Sade"), recording artist, was born in Ibadan, Nigeria.
1978,	NASA named Frederick Gregory, Guy Bluford, and Ronald McNair to its space shuttle program.

JANUARY 16   **ARTISTS**

NAT LOVE

Cowboy, expert marksman, and **one of the first rodeo champions**.   Born into slavery in 1854 in Davidson County, Tenn.   Worked on his father's small farm and on surrounding plantations; broke in horses; left the destitute conditions of the South for Dodge City, Kan. (1869), where he found no discrimination, as long as one had money; worked for the Duval Ranch of Texas (1869-1872); became an employee of the Peter Gallinger Company in southern Arizona (1872), where his duties included mustang hunts, roundups, horse and cattle drives along the Chisholm Trail; became Gallinger's chief brand reader. Participated in Deadwood, S.D., Fourth of July celebration, competing with the best cowboys in the West (1876); he won the following contests: roping, throwing, tying, bridling, saddling, mounting wild broncos, shooting with a rifle at 100 and 200 yards, and a Colt .45 at 150 yards; the assembled crowd gave **him the nickname of "Deadwood Dick" and proclaimed him the champion roper of the western cattle country.** Hung his saddle up and went to work as a Pullman porter on the Denver & Rio Grande Railroad (1890-1921); wrote his autobiography, *The Life and Adventures of Nat Love, Better Known in Cattle Country as Deadwood Dick* (1907). Died in 1921.   Further reading, Harold Felton, *Nat Love, Negro Cowboy* (1967).

---

on this day in history...

1895,   Marguerite Thomas Williams, first African-American woman to earn a Ph.D. in geology, was born in Washington, D.C.
1936,   Count Basie made his New York City debut at the Roseland Ballroom.
1989,   Thomas W. Cole, Jr., was inaugurated as the first president of the newly-merged Clark Atlanta University.

DECEMBER 24   **WESTERN TRAILBLAZERS**

RICHMOND BARTHE

Artist, educator, and lecturer who became one of the **best-known African-American sculptors of his time**. Born on January 28, 1901, in Bay St. Louis, Miss. Chicago Art Institute; Art Students League in New York City. Began as a painter, then a three-dimensional artist, and finally a modern sculptor; received a Harmon Foundation Award (1928), Rosenwald fellowship (1928-1929), Guggenheim fellowship (1940-1941); cited by the American Academy of Arts and Letters; presented with the Audubon Artists Gold Medal (1945); some of his works were exhibited at the Harmon Foundation shows (1929, 1931, and 1933), Whitney Museum of American Art (1933), World's Fair (1939), and at the Grand Central Gallery (1947). Some of his works included *The Harmonica Player, Shoeshine Boy, Boxer, Mother and Son, Blackberry Woman, African Boy Dancing*, and perhaps his best known, *Feral Benga*. Commissioned by the Haitian government to create a bust of Toussaint L'Ouverture; his works appear in New York City's Metropolitan Museum of Art, Oberlin College's Hackley Museum, the Art Institute of Chicago, the Schomburg Collection of the New York Public Library, the Pennsylvania Academy of Fine Arts, Atlanta University, and in England, Germany, France, Africa, Canada, Haiti, and the Virgin Islands. Died in 1989. Further reading, Richard Bardolph, *The Negro Vanguard* (1961).

---

on this day in history...

1910,	Sidney "Big Sid" Catlett, who was called the greatest jazz drummer of the '30s and '40s, was born in Evansville, Ind. (d. 1951).
1924,	Jewel Plummer Cobb, California State University-Fullerton president, was born in Chicago, Ill.
1931,	James Earl Jones, Tony and Emmy Award-winning actor, was born in Arkabutla, Miss.
1942,	Cassius Marcellus Clay ("Muhammad Ali"), boxing legend known as "the Greatest," was born in Louisville, Ky.

JANUARY 17   **ARTISTS**

WILLIAM ALEXANDER LEIDESDORFF

Merchant, early California settler, government official, and entrepreneur who **became one of San Francisco's most prominent early residents**. Born in 1810 in St. Croix, Danish West Indies. Became a master of vessels sailing between New York and New Orleans; made trips aboard the 160-ton schooner *Julia Anna* between the West Indies, via the southern tip of South America, and California-- which was part of Mexico at the time (1841-1845); secured Mexican land grant for two large lots on the corner of Kearney and Clay Streets in San Francisco (1843); became a Mexican citizen (1844); **acquired the Rancho Rio de los Americanos near Sutter's Mill on the American River (1844), which was worth a fortune after gold was found not far from his claim two months before his death**; served as Mexican consul to the U.S. in Monterrey, Calif. (1845-1846), meeting with American explorers to debate the confiscation of California by the U.S. and continuing to secure land from the Mexican government; settled in San Francisco and built a warehouse at California & Leidesdorff Streets [now in the financial district] (1846), the City Hotel (1846), and a cottage on the corner of California & Montgomery Streets (1847), where he lived the rest of his life. Reportedly launched the first steamer that ever sailed into San Francisco Bay; became a member of the San Francisco City Council, treasurer of the local school committee, and a local political leader; **chairman of the San Francisco School Board (1848), which opened California's first public school**; held California's first formal horse race. Died in 1848 in San Francisco, Calif. Further reading, William Sherman Savage, "The Influence of William Alexander Leidesdorff on the History of California," (*Negro History Bulletin*, July 1953).

---

on this day in history...

1903,   Fredericka Carolyn "Fredi" Washington, founder of the Negro Actors Guild, was born in Savannah, Ga.

DECEMBER 23   **WESTERN TRAILBLAZERS**

ROMARE BEARDEN

Artist. Born in 1912 in Charlotte, N.C. New York University (B.S., mathematics, 1935); Art Students League; the Sorbonne in Paris. Editorial illustrator for the *Baltimore Afro-American*; worked for *Colliers* and the *Saturday Evening Post*; became a professional artist (1935), after attending a meeting of the Harlem Artists Guild; joined the "306" Group (1936), a group of African-American artists in Harlem who met at 306 West 141st Street; began working as a caseworker in the New York City Department of Social Services (1937-1942, 1945-1950, and 1952-1966); served in the U.S. Army (1942-1945); held his first one-man exhibition at the Samuel M. Kootz Gallery (1945); went to Paris (1950-1951), where he visited museums and galleries while traveling to Nice, Florence, Rome, and Venice. **Organized a group of civil rights-conscious African-American artists in New York** (1963), calling themselves the "Spiral" group; created photo projections for a series of exhibitions entitled "Projections;" organized several important exhibitions including "Contemporary Art of the American Negro" in Harlem (1966), "The Evolution of Afro-American Artists: 1800-1950" at City College of New York (1967), "Romare Bearden, Odysseus" at Cordier and Ekstrom Gallery in New York (1977), and received critical acclaim for an exhibition of monoprints entitled "Of the Blues" (1977). Member of the American Academy of Arts and Letters; became a member of the National Institute of Arts and Letters (1966); co-wrote *The Painter's Mind* (1969) and *Six Black Masters in American Art* (1972); received the President's National Medal of Arts (1988); some of his best work included: a watercolor, *Golgotha* (1945); a serigraph, *The Return of Ulysses*; a collage, *Family* (1988); a color lithograph, *Pepper Jelly Lady* (1980). Died in 1988. Further reading, Myron Schwartzman, *Romare Bearden: His Life and Art* (1990).

---

on this day in history...

1941,   David Ruffin, original lead singer of the Temptations, was born in Meridian, Miss. (d. 1991).
1966,   Robert Weaver took the oath of office as U.S. secretary of housing and urban development, becoming the first official African-American cabinet member.

JANUARY 18   **ARTISTS**

GEORGE JORDAN

Buffalo soldier.   Born in 1847 in Williamson County, Ky.   Joined the newly formed 9th Cavalry and was stationed in Texas (1867-1875), participating in conflicts with American outlaws, Mexican raiders, and Indians; stationed in New Mexico and the Indian Territory (1876-1885), where he saw action in the frontier wars in the campaign against Apache Victorio; led an attachment of African-American troopers to an unprotected white settlement near abandoned Fort Tularosa, erected a stockade and moved the scared settlers, organized his modest force for defense and waited for the imminent attack, held off two waves of over 100 charging Apaches, preventing a massacre, and **earning a Congressional Medal of Honor**.   Stationed at Fort Robinson, Neb. (1885-1897), where he took part in a successful rescue attempt of the all-white 7th Cavalry from a Sioux ambush on the Pine Ridge Indian Reservation, S.D., a day following the infamous Wounded Knee massacre (1890).   Retired from the U.S. Army after serving his entire career with the 9th Cavalry; became a **town leader in Crawford, Neb.**, a small African-American town of mostly former Buffalo Soldiers; became critically ill and (regardless of being a career soldier and Medal of Honor winner) was not admitted into Fort Robinson's infirmary, which was only a couple of miles away.   Died on October 25, 1904, in Crawford, Neb. Further reading, William H. Leckie, *The Buffalo Soldiers* (1967).

on this day in history...

1924,   Arthur Allen Fletcher, U.S. Civil Rights Commission chairman, was born in Phoenix, Ariz.
1939,   Jerry Pinkney, illustrator, was born in Philadelphia, Pa.

DECEMBER 22   **WESTERN TRAILBLAZERS**

BEAUFORD DELANEY

Abstract expressionist artist who became the **best-known African-American artist of his time living abroad**. Born in 1901 in Knoxville, Tenn. Massachusetts Normal Art School; South Boston School of Art. Moved to New York City (1929), settling on Greene Street in Greenwich Village; exhibited his work frequently in the Harmon Foundation shows; held his first one-man exhibition at the 135th Street branch of the New York Public Library (1930), and at a Washington gallery (1938); held an exhibition, along with Ellis Wilson, at the Artist's Gallery in New York City (1948), and became a prominent member of the art circles. Sketched many famous African-Americans of the middle 20th century, while living in New York City; taught part-time at a Greenwich Village art school; received a fellowship to the Yaddo Art Colony near Saratoga Springs, N.Y. (1951), where he was inspired to travel to Europe and eventually, move to Paris; received a National Council of the Arts grant (1969). His style was influenced by Vincent Van Gogh, the color of the French Fauves, and the design principles of abstract expressionism; evolved from creating mostly portraits executed in pastels, to painting New York City street scenes and interiors executed in impasto technique. Died on March 26, 1979, in Paris, France. Further reading, Richard A. Long, *Beauford Delaney: A Retrospective* (1978).

---

on this day in history...

1880,   Frederick Madison Roberts, California's first African-American state legislator, was born in Chillicothe, Ohio (d. 1952).

1918,   John Harold Johnson, publisher of *Ebony, Jet,* and *Ebony Man*, was born in Arkansas City, Ark.

1993,   Reginald Lewis, CEO of TLC Beatrice International, the nation's largest African-American business, died in New York City (b. 1943).

JANUARY 19   **ARTISTS**

MIFFLIN WISTAR GIBBS

Politician, government official, abolitionist, lawyer, entrepreneur, and publisher.   Born in 1823 in Philadelphia, Pa. Studied at Philomathean Institute, an African-American literary society.   Became a carpenter's apprentice and a journeyman contractor; active in the Underground Railroad with William Still and accompanied Frederick Douglass and Charles Lenox Redmond on dangerous speaking tours; sailed to San Francisco to seek his fortune (1850), becoming a partner in a clothing import store; became a member of the California State Negro Convention (1854, 1855, and 1857); **founded California 's first African-American newspaper,** *The Mirror of Times* (1855), a weekly abolitionist newspaper. Set out to explore British Columbia (1858), where he reportedly started the first mercantile house outside of the Hudson Bay Company's fort, making a small fortune in sales and real estate; established himself in Victoria, British Columbia (1866), and was elected to the city's Common Council and became director of Queen Charlotte Island Coal Company; read law with an English barrister; moved backed to the U.S. (1869). Established a law practice in Little Rock (1871); appointed county attorney (1873); **elected the nation's first African-American municipal judge** (1873); elected presidential elector for Arkansas (1876); appointed Receiver of the U.S. Land Office for the Little Rock District of Arkansas (1877-1898), where he encouraged thousands of immigrants to move to Arkansas and helped them set up schools; delegate to several Republican Nation Conventions; U.S. consul to Madagascar (1898-1901). Wrote his autobiography (1902); became president of the newly-organized Capital City Savings Bank in Little Rock (1903), and a partner in the Little Rock Electric Company. Died on July 11, 1915, in Little Rock, Ark.   Further reading, <u>Delilah Beasley</u>, <u>*The Negro Trail Blazers of California*</u> (1968).

---

on this day in history...

1936,	Alton Ronald Waldron, Jr., former New York congressman (1986-1987), was born in Lakeland, Fla.
1945,	George William Faison, Tony Award-winning dancer and choreographer, was born in Washington, D.C.
1956,	Montgomery African-Americans called off the year-long bus boycott.
1959,	Delorez Florence Griffith Joyner, Sullivan Award-winning Olympic track and field champion, was born in Los Angeles, Calif.

DECEMBER 21   **WESTERN TRAILBLAZERS**

META VAUX WARRICK FULLER

Sculptor. Born on June 9, 1877, in Philadelphia, Pa. Philadelphia College of Industrial Art (1898); Ecole des Beaux Arts in Paris, studying under Auguste Rodin; Academie Colaroosi in Paris, where she studied sculpting from live models; Pennsylvania Academy of Fine Arts (1907). **Became the first African-American sculptor to express the suffering and toil of slavery, and became known as a "sculptor of horrors;"** created many portrait sculptures, including busts of Charlotte Hawkins Brown, Frederick Douglass, Richard Harrison, Sojourner Truth, and Harriet Tubman; exhibited her *The Impenitent Thief, The Wretched,* and *Man Carrying a Dead Comrade* at the L'Art Nouveau Gallery in Paris (1903); commissioned to produce 150 African-American figures for the Jamestown Tercentennial Exposition (1907), where she won a gold medal for illustrating the progress of African-American since the Jamestown settlement. Exhibited her work at the Harmon Foundation (1931-1933), Howard University (1961), and City College of New York (1967). Married Solomon Fuller (1909), nation's first African-American psychiatrist; created a statute for New York's 50th anniversary celebration of the Emancipation Proclamation (1913); honored at the dedication of Howard University's new Fine Arts Building (1964). Some of her other works include: *Awakening Ethiopia* (1921), done for the "Making of America Exhibit" in New York City; *The Talking Skull* (1939); *Storytime* (1964), a bronze piece done for the Framingham Center Library; *The Crucifixion*, done in memory of the four African-American girls killed in the 1963 Birmingham church bombing. Her style evolved from Gothic, to African-American types, to more realism, to religious subjects; her sculptures appear in the San Francisco Museum of Fine Arts, Howard University, and in the New York Public Library Schomburg Collection. Died on March 13, 1968, in Framingham, Mass. Further reading, James A. Porter, *Modern Negro Art* (1969).

on this day in history...

1788, The first African Baptist Church was organized in Savannah with Andrew Bryan as its minister.

1895, Eva Jessye, choral director who formed the original Dixie Jubilee Singers, was born in Coffeyville, Kan. (d. 1992).

1977, Clifford Alexander was sworn in as the first African-American U.S. secretary of the Army.

1993, Jerry Jewell, Arkansas state senate president *pro tem*, became governor for 96 hours when President Clinton's successor Jim Tucker went to Washington to attend inaugural festivities.

JANUARY 20 ARTISTS

BARNEY LAUNCELOT FORD

Businessman, political leader, and Underground Railroad conductor. Born into slavery around 1824 in Virginia. Escaped to freedom (1848), met Henry O. Wagoner, self-educated himself, and began working with the Underground Railroad; opened the United States Hotel (1851), Hotel William Walker, and the California Hotel. Opened a livery stable business in Chicago and struck out for the gold fields in Colorado; worked as a barber on a wagon train; boarded with Aunt Clara Brown, after being refused hotel accommodations; lost some claims for gold fields to theft and was driven from a Breckenridge, Colo., area hill by white men (1860), but his gold was never found and legend has it that Ford buried the gold on what they then called "Nigger Hill." He and Wagoner **opened barbershops, restaurants, and hotels in Denver**; provided financial assistance, food, and employment to escaped or freed slaves during the Civil War; left Denver and went to Washington, D.C., to lobby against a proposed Colorado bill prohibiting African-American suffrage (1865); returned to Denver and **established in Wagoner's home, Colorado's first adult education classes for African-Americans**; a member of the Arapahoe County, Colo. Republican Central Committee. Operated a restaurant in Cheyenne, Wyo. (1867-1870); **opened and operated the Inter Ocean Hotel in Cheyenne** (1875-1880), proclaiming that it was "the largest and finest hotel between Omaha and San Francisco," with President Grant stopping as a guest; moved to San Francisco (1880); rented a lunch counter and prospected for gold; returned to Denver (1882), where he rebuilt his fortune by opening another series of restaurants and barbershops; became the **first African-American to serve on a Colorado grand jury**; organized a victorious drive for a state public accommodations bill prohibiting discrimination (1885). Died in 1902. Further reading, Forbes Parkhill, *Mister Barney Ford, A Portrait in Bistre* (1963).

on this day in history...

1860, South Carolina succeeded from the Union leading to the Civil War.
1942, Bob Hayes, first African-American to earn the title of "world's fastest human," was born in Jacksonville, Fla.
1981, *Dreamgirls* opened on Broadway.

DECEMBER 20

WESTERN TRAILBLAZERS

PALMER HAYDEN

Painter who focused on African-American themes.   Born Peyton Cole Hedgeman on January 15, 1890, in Widewater, Va.   Cooper Union School of Art in New York; Ecole des Beaux Arts in Paris.   Served in the U.S. Army, at West Point and in the Philippines during World War I; awarded a fellowship to Boothbay Art Colony in Maine (1925-1926), where he devoted most of his time to painting boats and other marine subjects; **won the Harmon Foundation's first Gold Award in art** (1926); went to Paris to study art (1927-1932); held a one-man show at the Galerie Berheim in Paris (1928), the Salon des Tuileries (1930), and the American Legion Exhibition (1931); exhibited at the Harmon Foundation shows (1928-1932); awarded the Rockefeller's prize at the Harmon Show prize for his small still-life composition, *Fetiche et Fleurs* (1933), becoming **one of the first African-American artist to incorporate African imagery**. Worked on the U.S. Treasury Art Project and the WPA Art Project (1934-1940), painting scenes from the New York City waterfront. Some of his other paintings include: *The Janitor Who Paints* (1937), a symbolic self-portrait; *Midsummer Night in Harlem* (1938), which showed Harlem residents outside trying to escape the heat; *The Ballad of John Henry* (1944-1954), a series of 12 paintings depicting scenes from the life of the legendary African-American folk hero. Exhibited his John Henry series at the Countee Cullen Library in Harlem (1952); his work was represented in the large exhibition, "The Evolution of Afro-American Artist," held in the Great Hall of the City University (1967), which was sponsored by the City University of New York, the Urban League, and the Harlem Cultural Council; his style, in his later years, consisted mostly of "consciously naive" vignettes of African-American life. Died in 1973.   Further reading, Cedric Dover, *American Negro Art* (1960).

---

on this day in history...

1938,	Jack and Jill of America, Inc., was founded in Philadelphia, Pa., by Marion Thomas.
1941,	Richie Haven, folk singer, was born in Brooklyn, N.Y.
1963,	Hakeem "The Dream" Olajuwon, Houston Rockets All-Star, was born in Lagos, Nigeria.
1964,	Carl T. Rowan was named the first African-American director of the U.S. Information Agency.

NORRIS WRIGHT CUNEY

Republican politician and businessman who **became one of the most powerful African-American politicians of the post-Reconstruction era and was recognized as the leader of the African-American vote in Texas**, resulting in all-white Democratic primaries in Texas that remained until the 1944 U.S. Supreme Court ruling.   Born into slavery in 1846, on the Sunnyside Plantation, near Hempstead, Texas.   Appointed as first assistant to the 12th Legislature's sergeant at arms (1870); inspector of customs (1872-1877), and collector of customs in Galveston, Texas (1889-1893), which included dispensing patronage; operated a lucrative longshoreman business in Galveston; appointed secretary of the Texas Republican State Executive Committee (1874); appointed delegate to the Republican National Convention (1876), delegate-at-large and one of the vice presidents (1884). Galveston alderman (1881-1883); member of the Texas delegation to a national convention of Negroes (Nashville, 1879), where he opposed the "Great Exodus" led by Pap Singleton; founding member of the Colored Teachers' State Association of Texas; Republican state national committeeman (1885-1896); directly responsible for the presidential nomination of Benjamin Harrison (1888). Died in 1896 in Galveston, Texas.   Further reading, Maud Cuney-Hare, _Norris Wright Cuney: A Tribune of the Black People_ (1913).

---

on this day in history...

1933,	Cicely Tyson, Emmy Award-winning actress, was born in New York City.
1941,	Maurice White, leader of the R&B group Earth, Wind & Fire, was born in Memphis, Tenn.
1963,	Jennifer Beale, actress, was born in Chicago, Ill.

DECEMBER 19   WESTERN TRAILBLAZERS

SARGENT CLAUDE JOHNSON

Educator and artist who became **one of the most important sculptors and printmakers of the 20th century**. Born on October 7, 1887, in Boston, Mass. Worcester Art School; A.W. Best School of Art in San Francisco (1923), where he studied under sculptors Ralph Stackpole and Beniamino Bufano; California School of Fine Arts. Opened and operated a studio in Berkeley (1925-1933), where he worked with terra cotta, wood, beaten copper, marble, terrazzo, ceramics, water colors, and porcelain; **only California artist represented in the Harmon Foundation show at the Oakland Municipal art Gallery** (1931, 1932); won the Robert C. Ogden prize at a Harmon Foundation show (1933), gaining international fame. Some of his original work include: *Mask* (1935), a copper mask of a young African princess on a wood base; *Lenox Avenue* (1938), a two-dimensional cubist-inspired lithograph depicting the metamorphosis of the Harlem Renaissance. Became a **senior sculptor and supervisor for the WPA Art Project**; carved a redwood relief panel for the California School of the Blind in Berkeley (1937); created two eight-foot-high cast stone figures called "Happy Incas Playing the Piper of Pan" for display around the fountain in the Court of Pacifica for the Golden Gate International Exposition held on Treasure Island (1939); designed three figures symbolizing industry, home life, and agriculture for the Alameda-Contra Costa Building at the Exposition. Taught art classes at Mills College for the San Francisco Housing Authority's Junior Workshop Program (1947); commissioned to produce a porcelain enamel mural for a wall in the City Hall Chamber, Richmond, Calif. (1949); his works were influenced by cubism, as well as the art of West Africa, Latin America, and Mexico. Died on October 10, 1967, in San Francisco, Calif. Further reading, Yvonne Greer Theil, *Artists and People* (1959).

---

on this day in history...

1935,   Sam Cooke, one of the first gospel singers to cross over to secular music, was born in Chicago, Ill. (d. 1964).
1945,   Isaiah Jackson, philharmonic orchestra conductor, was born in Richmond, Va.
1948,   Ben Chavis, NAACP executive director, was born in Oxford, N.C.
1981,   Samuel Pierce was named U.S. secretary of housing and urban development.

JAMES PIERSON BECKWOURTH

Western frontiersman, explorer, trader, scout, and trapper. Born in April 6, 1798, in Fredericksburg, Va. Apprenticed to a blacksmith; became a scout for the second and third exposition of William Henry Ashley's Rocky Mountain Fur Company (1823, 1824); worked as a mountain man (1824-1837), becoming a legendary figure and being accepted by the Blackfoot and Crow Indian tribes; served in the Second Seminole War and operated trading posts near the headwaters of the South Platte and Arkansas Rivers; established his own trading post in what is now Taos, N.M., and in Los Angeles (1840). Fought in the California revolution against Mexico (1846), and in the War with Mexico (1846-1848), serving as a guide and dispatch carrier for a U.S. Army general; **became chief scout for the exploring expedition of John Fremont (1848), and discovered a pass between the Feather and Truckee Rivers in California, which became a major route for California emigrants**. Died in 1866. Further reading, Thomas D. Bonner, *The Life and Adventures of James P. Beckwourth* (1969).

---

on this day in history...

1852,	George Henry White of North Carolina, last former slave to serve in Congress, was born in Rosindale, N.C. (d. 1918).
1865,	The 13th Amendment, which abolished slavery, was ratified by Congress.
1898,	Fletcher Hamilton "Smack" Henderson, first band leader to become famous playing jazz, was born in Cuthbert, Ga. (d. 1952).
1917,	Ossie Davis, Emmy Award-winning actor, was born in Cordele, Ga.
1925,	Paul W. Stewart, founder and curator of Denver's Black American West Museum, was born in Clinton, Iowa.
1971,	Jesse Jackson founded Operation PUSH (People United to Save Humanity) in Chicago, Ill.

DECEMBER 18   WESTERN TRAILBLAZERS

MARY EDMONIA LEWIS

Neoclassical artist who became the **first professional African-American sculptor**. Born around 1845 in Albany, N.Y., and was raised by Chippewa Indians who gave her the name "Wildfire." Oberlin College. Moved to Boston (1863), and began studying under portrait sculptor Edward Brackett; began producing medallion portraits of William Lloyd Garrison, Charles Sumner, Wendell Phillips, and other well-known abolitionists; produced portrait busts of abolitionist John Brown and of Robert Gould Shaw, the leader of the all-Negro 54th Massachusetts Regiment; traveled to London, Paris, Florence, and settled in Rome (1865), because of its artistic traditions, abundant marble supply, and inexpensive artisan labor, and rented a studio near the Piazza Barberini; her work focused on slavery and racial oppression. Produced: *The Freed Woman and Her Child* (1866), which captured the strong emotion of emancipation; *Forever Free* (1867), part of Howard University's collection; *Hagar* (1868), the biblical maidservant to Abraham; *Poor Cupid* (1876), her best known work that is now displayed in the National Museum of American Art; *Hiawatha and Minnehaha* (1871), a series of small busts that were inspired by Henry Wadsworth Longfellow's poem "The Song of Hiawatha;" *Old Arrow Maker* (1872), her reaction to the negative stereotypes of Native Americans as murderous savages. Converted to Catholicism in Rome (1868); toured the U.S., exhibiting her work in Chicago, California, Boston, and Philadelphia (1870-1876); produced *The Death of Cleopatra* at the Centennial Exposition (Philadelphia, 1876), where she was awarded a medal; commissioned to make the *Adoration of the Maji* (1883), for a church in Baltimore. Died around 1911. Further reading, Nicola Ciovsky, Jr., *The White, Marmorean Flock: Nineteenth-Century American Women Neoclassical Sculptors* (1972).

---

on this day in history...

1891,	Daniel Hale Williams founded Provident Hospital in Chicago, the nation's first African-American hospital.
1904,	Benjamin Quarles, renowned historian and chairman of Morgan State's history department, was born in Boston, Mass.
1946,	Susan L. Taylor, editor-in-chief of *Essence* magazine, was born in Harlem, N.Y.
1964,	The 24th Amendment, which abolished poll taxes, was ratified.
1977,	The first episode of *ROOTS* was aired on ABC.
1989,	The U.S. Supreme Court ruled in favor of the plaintiff in *J.A. Croson County vs. City of Richmond*.

JANUARY 23   **ARTISTS**

ALLEN ALLENSWORTH

Town founder, businessman, educator, and chaplain.   Born into slavery on April 7, 1842, in Louisville, Ky.   Ely Normal School in Louisville. Escaped to freedom (1862), and joined the 44th Illinois Infantry's hospital corps as a civilian nurse; worked on a hospital ship; enlisted in the Navy (1863), and served on the gunboats *Queen City, Tawah,* and the *Pittsburgh*, rising to the rank of chief petty officer. Operated two restaurants in St. Louis; taught in a Freedmen's Bureau school in Christmasville, Ky. (1868); ordained as a Baptist minister in Louisville (1871); worked as a financial agent of the General Association of the Colored Baptists in Kentucky, superintendent of Sunday schools of the state Baptist convention, and missionary for the American Baptist Publication Society in Philadelphia; attended the Republican National Convention (1880, 1884); lectured in New England; served as pastor of the Joy Street Baptist Church in Boston (1884), and the Union Baptist Church in Cincinnati (1885-1886). Became chaplain of the all-Negro 24th Infantry (1886), stationed in the Indian Territory, New Mexico, Utah, and Montana; established separate school programs for enlisted men and children, which were implemented by other chaplains throughout the Army; addressed the National Education Association Convention (Toronto, 1891), speaking on "The History and Progress of Education in the U.S. Army;" served as a recruiter in Louisville during the Spanish-American War and later rejoined the 24th Infantry in the Philippine Insurrection; retired as a senior chaplain (1906), and was **promoted to lieutenant colonel, the highest rank held by an African-American in the Regular Army** until World War I. Moved to Los Angeles and established a business to aid African-Americans wishing to migrate to the West (1908); **founded and sold lots in Tulare County, California's new community of Allensworth**, a town that became a market center for the area and included a hotel, post office, and railroad station. Died on September 14, 1914, in California.   Further reading, <u>Charles Alexander</u>, <u>*Battles and Victories of Allen Allensworth*</u> (1914).

on this day in history...

1802,	Henry Adams, organizer of Louisville's colored school system, was born in Franklin County, Ga. (d. 1872).
1937,	Calvin Waller, U.S. Army lieutenant general who was second in command of Operation Desert Storm, was born in Baton Rouge, La.
1940,	Edward Kendricks, Grammy Award-winning original member of the Temptations, was born in Union Springs, Ala. (d. 1992).
1991,	Michael Jordan of the Chicago Bulls was named the 1991 *Sports Illustrated* Sportsman of the Year.

DECEMBER 17

WESTERN TRAILBLAZERS

JAMES AMOS PORTER

Educator, writer, and painter who was the **first African-American art historian**. Born in 1905 in Baltimore, Md. Howard University (B.S., art, 1927); Columbia University; Art Students League in New York, where he studied with painter Dimitri Romanwosky. Art instructor and **head of Howard University's art department (1927-1970), where he was credited with establishing the art department gallery, and serving as a mentor to generations of African-American students**; won the Arthur Schomburg Portrait Prize (1933), for his figure painting, *Woman Holding a Jug*; received a fellowship from the Institute of International Education to study medieval archeology at the Sorbonne in Paris (1935); painted a bust-length portrait of a Senegalese soldier called *Colonial Soldier* while in Paris (1937), which showed his familiarity with Fauvism and expressionism; exhibited his work at the American Negro Exposition (Chicago, 1940), and a one-man show at the Barnett-Aden Gallery in Washington, D.C. (1948). **Published *Modern Negro Art* (1943), which was the earliest comprehensive treatment of African-American art** and became a standard reference work for the field; wrote a historical monograph, a catalog-brochure, prize-winning book reviews, and illustrated books for others. Appointed a fellow of the Belgium-American Art Seminar (1955), where he pursued further studies in the history of Flemish and Dutch art of the 16th, 17th, and 18th centuries while in Belgium; conducted research for a book on West African architecture; honored by President Johnson on the 25th anniversary of the founding of the National Gallery of Art (1966), as "one of America's most outstanding men of the arts." Died on February 28, 1970, in Washington, D.C. Further reading, <u>Negro History Bulletin</u> (April 1970).

---

on this day in history...

1865, Congress passed the 13th Amendment abolishing slavery.
1987, Hosea Williams led 20,000 protesters in the "Brotherhood Anti-Intimidation March" on all-white Forsythe County, Ga.

JANUARY 24   **ARTISTS**

JOHN QUINCY ADAMS

Editor and civil rights leader.   Born on May 4, 1848, in Louisville, Ky.   Oberlin College.   Participated in the reconstruction of Arkansas, serving as a schoolteacher and engrossing clerk of the state senate; moved back to Louisville (1874), and continued teaching and being appointed to public office; founder and publisher of the *Bulletin* (1879-1886), a weekly newspaper. Left the South and settled in St. Paul (1886); staff member of the African-American-owned and -edited *Western Appeal* (1886-1887), publisher and editor (1887-1922), condemning segregation by any level of government, attacking Booker T. Washington's "Tuskegee Machine," and criticizing both major political parties for failure to protect the rights of all citizens; served as bailiff of the Municipal Court (1896-1902); active member of the Republican Party; played a key role in the formation of the Minnesota Protective Rights League, the NAACP, and the Equal Rights League. Died on September 3, 1933, in Minnesota.   Further reading, <u>Earl Spangler</u>, *<u>The Negro in</u> <u>Minnesota</u>* (1961).

on this day in history...

1834,   George Ruffin, first African-American Harvard Law School graduate, was born in Richmond, Va. (d. 1886).

1859,   Shields Green, one of John Brown's men at Harper's Ferry, was hanged in Virginia (b. 1825).

1895,   Andreamentania Paul Razafinkeriefo, Songwriters Hall of Fame member, was born in Washington, D.C. (d. 1973).

1934,   John Edward Jacob, National Urban League executive director, was born in Trout, La.

1976,   Andrew Young was appointed ambassador to the U.N. by President Carter.

DECEMBER 16   WESTERN TRAILBLAZERS

AUGUSTA CHRISTINE SAVAGE

Artist and educator.   Born on February 29, 1892, in Green Cove Springs, Fla.   Tallahassee State Normal School [now Florida A&M University]; Cooper Union School of Art (1924).   Became a portrait sculptor in bronze, plaster, and wood; produced busts of W.E.B. DuBois, Marcus Garvey, Frederick Douglass, James Weldon Johnson, and many other African-American leaders; was the **first artist to consistently deal with African-American physiognomy**; exhibited her work at the Philadelphia Sesquicentennial Exposition (1926), and at the Harmon Foundation Exhibitions (1928, 1930, and 1931). Created a life-size bronze bust, *Gamin* (1929), which won her a Rosenwald fellowship to study in Paris with Felix Benneteau at Academie de la Grand Chaumiere (1929-1931); won citations from the Salon d'Atomne and the Salon Printemps in Paris; received a Carnegie Foundation grant to travel in France, Belgium, and Germany. Returned to the U.S. and produced, *Martinisquaise*, *After the Glory*, and *Envy*; established the Savage Studio of Arts and Crafts in Harlem (1932); became the **first African-American member of the National Association of Women Painters and Sculptors** (1934); exhibited at the Architecture League (1934); appointed the first director of the Harlem Community Art Center (1937); commissioned by the New York World's Fair Board of Design to create *The Harp* for the court of the Community Arts Building (1937), a sculpture that symbolized the musical contributions of African-Americans; founder and director of the Salon of Contemporary Negro Art in Harlem (1939); held a one-woman show at the Argent Galleries in New York; retired to the Catskill Mountains of New York (1945). Died on March 26, 1962, in New York City.   Further reading, <u>Romare Bearden</u> and <u>Harry Henderson</u>, <u>"August Savage,"</u> *<u>Six Black Masters of American Art</u>* (1972).

---

on this day in history...

1922,   John W. Blanton, mechanical engineer who helped design the first jet-propelled airplane, was born in Louisville, Ky.
1938,   Etta James, singer, was born in Los Angeles, Calif.
1966,   Constance Baker Motley became the first woman to be named to a federal judgeship.
1972,   Shirley Chisholm began her presidential campaign.
1974,   Nora Holt, founder of the National Association of Negro Musicians, died in Los Angeles, Calif. (b. 1895).
1980,   Black Entertainment Television began broadcasting from Washington, D.C.
1993,   Harold Moss was named Tacoma's first African-American mayor.

JANUARY 25   **ARTISTS**

NOBLE SISSLE

Bandleader, lyricist, actor, and producer.   Born on July 10, 1889, in Indianapolis, Ind.   DePauw University; Butler University.   Toured on the Chautauqua circuit, with the Thomas Hahn Jubilee Singers (1911-1913), and with Joe Porter's Serenaders (1913-1915); became the protege of James Reese Europe, serving as his drum major in the 369th Regiment (1916-1919); teamed up with composer Eubie Blake (1915), touring as the Dixie Duo. Collaborated with Blake and produced the Broadway musical comedy, *Shuffle Along* (1921), which became a huge success, and was credited with sparking the Harlem Renaissance; also collaborated on the musicals, *Elsie* (1923), *Chocolate Dandies* (1924), and *Keep Shufflin* (1928); formed an orchestra and toured Europe; composed with Blake, "I'm Just Wild About Harry," "Love Will Find A Way," and "Boogie-Woogie Beguine." **Founded the Negro Actors Guild** (1937), becoming its first president; wrote columns for the *New York Age* and the *Amsterdam News*; tour with a USO Camp Show that staged *Shuffle Along* (1945-1946); became a disc jockey at New York City's WMGM radio station (1952); managed his own publishing company; honored as the unofficial mayor of Harlem. Died on December 17, 1972, in Tampa, Fla.   Further reading, Robert Kimball and William Bolcom, *Reminiscing wit Sissle and Blake* (1973).

---

on this day in history...

1961,   Reggie Hudlin, Hollywood film producer, was born in Centerville, Ill.
1985,   J. Bruce Llewellyn and Julius Erving became owners of the Philadelphia Coca-Cola Bottling Company.

DECEMBER 15   **STAGE PERFORMERS**

HENRY OSSAWA TANNER

Painter, of mostly landscape and religious themes, who became the **first African-American artist to achieve international acclaim**. Born on June 21, 1859, in Pittsburgh, Pa. Pennsylvania Academy of the Fine Arts, where he was greatly influenced by Thomas Eakins; Academie Julien in Paris. Taught drawing at Clark College in Atlanta (1888-1890); sailed to Europe (1891), and settled in Paris; painted during the summers at Pont-Avon and Concarneau in Brittany (1892, 1893); studied the Old Masters at the Louvre. Painted: *The Banjo Lesson* (1893), *The Thankful Poor* (1894), both depicting African-American subjects; *The Bagpipe Lesson* (1894), *The Young Sabot Maker* (1895), both depicting French peasants; *Daniel in the Lion's Den* (1895), which won an honorable mention in the Paris Salon and silver medals at the Universal Exposition (Paris, 1900), the Pan American Exposition (Buffalo, 1901), and the St. Louis Exposition (1904); *Resurrection of Lazarus* (1897), which was exhibited at the Luxembourg Gallery, became part of the collection of the Louvre, and earned him sponsorship for a trip to the Holy Land; *The Two Disciples at the Tomb* (1906), which was purchased by the Art Institute of Chicago; *Mary* (1914), the mother of Christ. Became the **first African-American artist to be included in the annual exhibition of the Carnegie Institute** (1905); held his first U.S. one-man exhibition of religious paintings at the American Art Galleries in New York City (1908); won a gold medal at the Panama-Pacific Exposition (San Francisco, 1915); served in the American Red Cross as a lieutenant in the Farm Service Bureau during World War I; became the **first African-American full academician of the National Academy of Design** (1927). Died on May 25, 1937, in Paris, France. Further reading, Lynda Roscoe Hartigan, *Sharing Traditions: Five Black Artists in Nineteenth-Century America* (1985).

---

on this day in history...

1896,	James Edwin Campbell, West Virginia State College's first president, died in Pomeroy, W.Va. (b. 1867).
1928,	Eartha Kitt, actress and dancer, was born in North, S.C.
1940,	Sharon Grace Cadoria, U.S. Army brigadier general and the U.S. Armed Forces' highest ranking African-American woman, was born in Marksville, La.
1958,	Anita Baker, Grammy Award-winning recording artist, was born in Toledo, Ohio.
1963,	Ashley L. Totten, who helped organize the Brotherhood of Sleeping Car Porters, died in St. Croix (b. 1884).

JANUARY 26   **ARTISTS**

CANADA LEE

Athlete and actor.   Born Leonard Lionel Cornelius Canegota on May 3, 1907, in New York City.   Studied violin under J. Rosamond Johnson; became a jockey and trainer (1921), racing on the Canadian circuit and at Saratoga, Belmont, and Aqueduct racetracks; became an amateur boxer, winning the Metropolitan Inter-City and Junior National Championships, and the national amateur lightweight title; fought professionally under the name of "Canada Lee," becoming a leading contender for the welterweight crown (1926-1933), only to suffer a career ending blow to one of his eyes.   Worked as a stevedore; made his acting debut in a Work Projects Administration theatrical production of Brother Mose (1934); played "Banquo" in the Federal Theater Negro production of Orson Wells' *Macbeth* (1936), "Jean Christopher" in *Haiti* (1938), "Blacksnake" in the Theater Union Revival of *Stevedore* (1938), and "Draylon" in *Mamba's Daughters* (1939); narrated for radio, "Unofficial Ambassador," "Flow Gently Sweet Rhythm," "Tolerance Through Music," and "New World A-Coming." **Starred in the screen and stage version of Richard Wright's *Native Son*** (1941), which earned him critical acclaim as the best theatrical performance of the year; also appeared in *Across the Board Tomorrow Morning* (1942), *South Pacific* (1943), *Lifeboard* (1944), *The Tempest* (1945), and *Body and Soul* (1947).   Died on May 9, 1952.   Further reading, Edith Isaacs, *The Negro in the Theater* (1947).

---

on this day in history...

1920,   Clark Terry, jazz trumpeter, was born in St. Louis, Mo.
1959,   The "Motown Sound" was born when Berry Gordy founded Motown Records in Detroit, Mich.

DECEMBER 14   **STAGE PERFORMERS**

ALMA THOMAS

Educator and artist.   Born on September 22, 1891, in Columbus, Ga.   Miner Teachers Normal School; **first graduate of Howard University's new art department** (B.A., 1924); Columbia University (M.A., education, 1934); American University in Washington, D.C.   Taught at the Thomas Garret Settlement House in Wilmington, Del. (1915-1921); taught at Shaw Junior High School in Washington, D.C. (1924-1960); studied painting under Joe Summerford, Robert Gates, Jacob Kainen, and was influenced by Washington-based Color Field painters Morris Louis, Kenneth Noland, and Gene Davis; developed an interest in color and abstract art, and later acrylics on canvas; held her first solo exhibit at the Du Pont Theater Art Gallery in Washington, D.C. (1960); honored with a retrospective exhibit at the Corcoran Gallery (1972); **first African-American woman to have a solo exhibition at the Whitney Museum of American Art** in New York City (1972), which brought her national attention. Painted: *The Eclipse* (1970), *Red Sunset, Old Pond Concerto* (1972), *Arboretum Presents White Dogwood* (1972), *Elysian Fields* (1973), and *Red Azaleas Singing and Dancing Rock and Roll Music* (1976). Exhibited her paintings at the Gallery of Art at Howard University, the Carl Van Vetchen Gallery in Nashville, the Martha Jackson Gallery in New York City, North Carolina A&T State University's H.C. Taylor Art Gallery in Greensboro, Philadelphia's Afro-American History and Culture Museum, the Liz Harris Gallery in Boston, and the White House (1969, 1970, and 1977). Died on February 25, 1978.   Further reading, <u>Merry A. Foresta</u>, <u>*A Life in Art--Alma Thomas*</u> (1981).

---

on this day in history...

1930,	Bobby "Blue" Bland, blues great, was born in Rosemark, Tenn.
1952,	Ralph Ellison won the National Book award for his novel, *The Invisible Man*.
1973,	George Forman defeated Joe Frazier for the heavyweight boxing championship.

JANUARY 27   **ARTISTS**

FRANCIS HALL JOHNSON

Musician, conductor, and composer who became **one of the most important choral directors of his time.**   Born on March 12, 1888, in Athens, Ga.   Knox Institute; Allen University; Hahn School of Music in Philadelphia; University of Pennsylvania (B.A., 1910); Juilliard School of Music.   Settled in New York City (1914), becoming a member of the African-American music establishment; played violin in James Reese Europe's Tempo Club Orchestra and in Willima Marian Cook's New York Syncopated Orchestra; performed with theater pit orchestras, including that of the Noble Sissle-Eubie Blake musical, *Shuffle Along* (1921); organized the Negro String Quartet (1923), performing at Carnegie Hall.   Organized the Hall Johnson Choir (1925), debuting at New York City's Pythian Temple, appearing on radio and in theaters, singing with major orchestras, performing on Broadway, and singing in films; arranger and music director for Marc Connolly's Broadway Play *Green Pastures* (1930); began recording with his choir for Victor RCA Records (1930), and singing in films that he scored, such as *Hearts Divided* (1936), *Lost Horizon* (1937), *Way Down South* (1939), and *Cabin in the Sky* (1943). Produced his folk opera, *Run Littl' Chillun*, on Broadway (1933), receiving critical acclaim; organized the 200-voice Festival Choir of Los Angeles (1941), and the Festival Negro Chorus of New York City (1946); inaugurated his annual concert series, "New Artists" (1947); represented the U.S. at the International Festival of Fine Arts (Berlin, 1951), directing his 27-member Hall Johnson Choir; composed "Honor, Honor," "Ride On, King Jesus," and "Crucifixion." Honored with the Simon Haessler prize (1910), Casper Holstein prizes (1925, 1927), Harmon Foundation award (1930), Philadelphia Academy of Music (Ph.D., 1934), and the New York Handel Medal (1970). Died on April 30, 1970, in New York City.   Further reading, <u>Cornelius V. Troup</u>, <u>*Distinguished Negro Georgians*</u> (1962).

---

on this day in history...

1913,	Archibal Lee Wright ("Archie Moore"), boxing champion, was born in Benoit, Miss.
1936,	Charles Adams, Progressive National Baptist Convention president, was born in Detroit, Mich.
1943,	Ferguson Jenkins, Professional Baseball Hall of Famer, was born in Chatham, Ontario, Canada.
1945,	Herman Cain, president and CEO of Godfathers Pizza, was born in Memphis, Tenn.

DECEMBER 13   **STAGE PERFORMERS**

JAMES VAN DER ZEE

Photographer.   Born on June 29, 1886, in Lenox, Mass.   Carlton Conservatory in New York City.   Worked as a busboy, musician, and photographer; became a darkroom assistant for Gertz Department Store in Newark, N.J. (1915); opened and operated his own studio, Guarantee Photos or Gaynella Grenley Greenlee (GGG) Photo Studio, in Harlem at 272 Lenox Ave. (1916-1968), often being sought after to photograph weddings, funerals, and other opportunistic occasions; served as the official photographer for Marcus Garvey's Back to Africa movement. Became known outside of Harlem after his work was featured in the Metropolitan Museum of Art exhibition, *Harlem on My Mind: Cultural Capital of Black America, 1900-1968* (1969); his work is said to have captured the energy and pride of Harlem through his camera's lens.   Honored with: the American Society of Magazine Photographers Award (1969); a Life Fellowship at the Metropolitan Museum of Art (1970); an honorary doctorate from Seton Hall University, Haverford College in Pennsylvania, and Howard University (1976, 1980, and 1983), respectively; the Pierre Toussaint Award for outstanding service to humanity (1978); the International Black Photographers Award (1979); and by President Jimmy Carter with the Living Legacy Award (1979); became known as the **"dean of Harlem photographers."** Died on May 15, 1983, in Washington, D.C.   Further reading, Reginald McGhee, *The World of James Van Der Zee* (1973).

---

on this day in history...

1948,   Bennie Thompson, Mississippi 2nd District congressman, was born in Bolton, Miss.
1986,   Ronald McNair, NASA mission specialist, was killed in the space shuttle *Challenger* explosion.

JANUARY 28   ARTISTS

EVA ALBERTA JESSYE

Choir director, educator, and composer who became the **first African-American woman to gain success as a professional choral conductor.** Born on January 20, 1895, in Coffeyville, Kan. Western University in Quindaro, Kan. (B.A., 1914); Langston University. Taught in the Haskell and Muskogee, Okla., public school systems; instructor at Claflin College; director of the music department at Morgan State College (1919-1920), and a staff member of the Baltimore's *Afro-American* newspaper. Met and became a protege of William Marion Cook (1926), while he was performing at the Capitol Theater in New York City; formed the Original Dixie Jubilee Singers and Eva Jessye Choir (1926), becoming popular in stage appearances and on radio shows, such as *Major Bowes Family Radio Hour* and the *General Motors Hour*; choral director for King Vidor's *Hallelujah* (1929), making her the **first musical director of a motion picture starring African-American actors**; *Paradise Lost and Regained*, her folk oratorio, was broadcasted on NBC radio (1931). Choral director of the V. Thomson and G. Stein opera, *Four Saints in Three Acts* (1934), and of Gershwin's *Porgy and Bess* (1935-1958); creator of "Aunt Mamy's Chillun and Four Dusty Travellers" radio show; featured in the first annual "I Am an American Day" in New York City (1944); **director of the official choir of the 1963 March on Washington**; artist-in-residence at Pittsburgh State University in Kansas (1978-1982). Published *My Spirituals* (1927), *The Life of Christ in Negro Spirituals* (1931), and *The Chronicle of Job* (1936); contributed materials for the establishment of the Eva Jessye Collection of Afro-American Music at the University of Michigan (1972); honored with degrees from Wilberforce, Allen, Eastern Michigan, and Pittsburgh State University (1978-1982). Died on February 21, 1992. Further reading, "What Ever Happened to Eva Jessye?", *Ebony* (May 1974).

---

on this day in history...

1870,   Joseph Rainey of South Carolina was sworn into Congress as the nation's first African-American U.S. congressman.
1899,   George Grant patented a wooden golf tee.
1941,   Dionne Warwick, Grammy Award-winning entertainer and humanitarian, was born in East Orange, N.J.
1943,   Grover Washington, Jr., jazz saxophonist, was born in Buffalo, N.Y.

DECEMBER 12   STAGE PERFORMERS

CHARLES WILBERT WHITE

Painter, graphic artist, and educator who became **one of America's foremost modern contemporary artists**. Born in 1918 in Chicago, Ill.
Art Institute of Chicago; Art Students League in New York City; Taller de Grafica in Mexico. Employed by the Illinois Art Project of the Work
Progress Administration; won a Rosenwald fellowship, a John Hay Whitney fellowship, and a National Institute of Arts and Letters grant; taught
at the Chicago Community Art Center (1941); artist-in-residence at Howard University (1945). Some of his paintings include: *Move On Up A
Little Higher*, which depicts a woman with her palms stretched to the heavens; *Take My Mother Home*, which depicts a young man with one
hand raised in benediction; *Mary, Don't Weep*, which illustrates two women in sorrow; *The Contribution of Negro to American Democracy,*
an 18'x 60' mural commissioned by Hampton Institute; *Wanted Poster #6, Birmingham Totem,* and *Preacher.* His paintings were exhibited
at the World Festival of Negro Arts (Senegal, 1966), Palace of Culture in Poland (1967), Fisk University (1968), Boston Museum of Fine Arts
(1969), and the Metropolitan Museum of Art in New York City (1971); his works can be found in the collections of the Library of Congress, the
Whitney Museum of African Art, Long Beach Museum of Art, the Barnett Aden Gallery in Washington, Atlanta University, Tuskegee Institute,
Howard University; his works also can be found in private collections in France, England, Canada, Switzerland, Italy, Africa, India, and Japan.
Died in 1979. Further reading, Janice Lovoos, "Charles White," (*American Artist: Anniversary Issue, June 1962*).

---

on this day in history...

1837,   Alexander Sergeyevich Pushkin, "the Shakespeare of Russian literature," was killed in a duel (b. 1799).
1889,   Huddie William Ledbetter ("Leadbelly"), blues great, was born in Mooringsport, La. (d. 1949).
1926,   Violette Neatly Anderson became the first woman to practice before the U.S. Supreme Court.
1954,   Oprah Gail Winfrey, Emmy Award-winning talk show host and broadcasting executive who is known as the "queen of talk," was born in
            Kosciusko, Miss.
1967,   Robert W. Clayton was elected the first African-American president of the YMCA.

JANUARY 29   ARTISTS

PAULINE ELIZABETH HOPKINS

Publisher, author, journalist, editor, stenographer, historian, and musician. Born in 1856 in Portland, Maine. Produced "Hopkins' Colored Troubadours in the Great Musical Drama, Escape from Slavery" (1880); lectured on Toussaint L'Ouverture; stenographer in the Bureau of Statistics for the Census; her first novel about the attributes of middle-class African-Americans, *Contending Forces, A Romance Illustrative of Negro Life North and South*, was published by the Colored Cooperative Publishing Company in Boston (1900); she promoted the book by reading sections to women's clubs across the nation. Served as **editor and contributor to the monthly *Colored American Magazine* (1900-1904), the first African-American journal established in the 20th century** and a major source of literature, science, music, art, religions, facts, and traditions of African-Americans; wrote the following serials for the magazine: "Hagar's Daughters, A Story of Southern Caste Prejudice" (1901-1902), "Winona, A Tale of Negro Life in the South and Southwest" (1902), and "Of One Blood; or, the Hidden Self" (1902-1903); wrote sketches about "Famous Men of the Negro Race" and "Famous Women of the Negro Race," which dealt with the biographies of William Wells Brown, Frederick Douglass, Harriet Tubman, Sojourner Truth, Booker T. Washington, Robert Brown Elliott, Lewis Hayden, Charles Lenox Redmond, and later, Leonard Grimes, Henry Highland Garnet, William Lloyd Garrison. Served as a contributor to J. Max Barber's *Voice of the Negro* (1904-1905), where she wrote "The Dark Races of the Twentieth Century;" founded her own publishing company, P.E. Hopkins & Company, and published *A Primer of Facts Pertaining to the Early Greatness of the African Race and the Possibility of Restoration by Its Descendants, with Epilogue* (1905); contributed articles to *New Era* magazine (1916). Died on August 13, 1930, in Massachusetts. Further reading, Dorothy B. Porter, "Hopkins, Pauline Elizabeth," *Dictionary of American Negro Biography* (1982).

---

on this day in history...

1872,	P.B.S. Pinchback of Louisiana became the nation's first African-American governor.
1922,	John Elroy Sanford ("Redd Foxx"), comedian and actor, was born in St. Louis, Mo. (d. 1991).
1932,	Donald Toussaint L'Ouverture Byrd, jazz musician, was born in Detroit, Mich.

DECEMBER 11   **STAGE PERFORMERS**

PAUL REVERE WILLIAMS

Architect.   Born in 1894 in Los Angeles, Calif.   University of California at Los Angeles; Los Angeles School of Art and Design; Beaux-Arts Institute of Design.   Became certified as an architect (1915), initially working as a landscape architect for seven dollars a week, then as a residential architect with Reginald Johnson, and later becoming commercial buildings architect John Austin's chief designer. Opened his own office (1923), and soon earned the respect of the white builder and developer establishment by learning to draw upside down so that clients could see his designs take form right before their very eyes, learning to produce full preliminary plans in 24 hours instead of the usual week, and by accentuating his positives--efficiency and competence. Some of his more notable designs, include the Music Corporation of America (MCA) Building in New York City, Federal Customs and Office Building in Los Angeles, UCLA's Botany Building and Franz Hall, W.J. Sloan and Haggerty Buildings in Beverly Hills, several Los Angeles city and county public school buildings, and scores of expensive Southern California homes; earned the nickname **"architect to the stars,"** for his design work on many of the Hollywood elite's homes. Served as vice president and director of the Broadway Federal Savings & Loan Association in Los Angeles, **president of the Los Angeles Art Commission**, a member of the President's Committee on Housing, and as a member of the California Redevelopment Commission and the California Housing Commission; awarded the NAACP Spingarn Medal (1963), for his contributions to the quality of American life. Died in 1980.   Further reading, <u>Richard Bardolph</u>, <u>*The Negro Vanguard*</u> (1961).

---

on this day in history...

1858,	William Wells Brown published *Leap To Freedom*, the first drama written by an African-American.
1927,	The Harlem Globetrotters were formed by Abe Saperstein.
1928,	Ruth Brown, Tony Award-winning singer nicknamed "Miss Rhythm," was born in Portsmouth, Va.
1944,	Sharon Pratt Dixon, first African-American woman mayor of Washington, was born in Washington, D.C.
1945,	Floyd Harold Flake, New York 6th District congressman, was born in Los Angeles, Calif.
1979,	Franklin A. Thomas became the first African-American to head a major U.S. charitable foundation, the Ford Foundation.

JANUARY 30   ARTISTS

ROLAND W. HAYES

Singer who became the **world's leading concert tenor during the 1920s-'40s.** Born on June 3, 1857, in Curryville, Ga. Fisk University. Joined the Fisk Jubilee Singers for a series of concerts in Boston (1911), where he remained; studied voice with Arthur Hubbard and George Henschel; worked as a messenger for the John Hancock Insurance Company; gave his first recital at Steinhart Hall in Boston (1912); toured the eastern U.S. (1912-1920), performing on the Chautauqua Concert circuit, Booker T. Washington's lecture tour, Walter Craig's concert series, Henry Proctor's Colored Musical Festival Concerts in Atlanta, circuit of African-American churches and colleges, and with Harry T. Burleigh. Became the first African-American soloist to perform at Symphony Hall in Boston (1917); traveled to Europe to study and perform (1920-1923), making his debut concert at London's Aeolian Hall, giving a command performance before King George V of England, and singing in the major capitals of Europe before crown heads and international celebrities; returned to the U.S. as a success and performed at New York City's Town Hall (1923), which was a turning point in his career; became the **first African-American to sing with a major symphony**--Boston Symphony Orchestra (1923), and later with the Philadelphia, Detroit, San Francisco, and New York City Symphony Orchestras. Became the first African-American to sing before mixed audiences in the South; opened doors for African-American singers who followed him; awarded the NAACP Spingarn Medal (1924); published *My Songs: AfroAmerican Religious Folk Songs* (1948); joined the faculty of Boston University (1950); honored with the American Missionary Association's 1st Amistad Award (1962); gave his farewell performance at Carnegie Hall (1962). Died in Brookline, Mass. Further reading, MacKinley Helm, *Angel Mo' and Her Son, Roland Hayes* (1942).

---

on this day in history...

DECEMBER 10   STAGE PERFORMERS

HALE WOODRUFF

Painter, printmaker, and educator who became known as **one of the most talented African-American artists of the Depression era**.   Born in 1900 in Cairo, Ill.   John Herron Art Institute in Indianapolis; Harvard University; Art Institute of Chicago; Academie Moderne and Academie Scandinave in Paris.   Exhibited his work at the Harmon Foundation show (1928, 1931, 1933, and 1935); began teaching art at Atlanta University (1931), later became chairman of the department where he was **credited with AU being designated as the "Ecole des Beaux Art" of the black South**; studied mural painting with Diego Rivera (1938); **painted the *Amistad* murals in the Savary Library at Talladega College** (1939-1940), which were commissioned in celebration of the 100th anniversary of the mutiny by African slaves aboard the slave ship *Amistad*, the trial in New Haven, Conn., and their return to West Africa following their acquittal. Initiated a series of Atlanta University art shows (1941); professor of art education at New York University (1947-1968); influenced by the abstract expressionism and the painters of the New York School, and associated himself with artists Adolf Gottlieb, Mark Rothko, Frank Kline, and Jackson Pollock; co-founded, along with Romare Bearden, the "Spiral" organization (1963), a collaboration of African-American artists working in New York City. Painted: *Shanty-town* and *Mudhill Row*, two paintings for the Work Projects Administration; *Man With a Balloon,* a surrealistic painting of a lynching; an oil portrait of Countee Cullen; *Georgia Landscape* (1935), which was inspired by scenes around his Atlanta home; *Afro Emblems* (1950), which showed his shift to a nonfigural style. Died in 1980 in New York City.   Further reading, Winifred L. Stoetling, *Hale Woodruff, Artist and Teacher: Through the Atlanta Years* (1978).

---

on this day in history...

1925,	Benjamin Lawson Hooks, NAACP executive director, was born in Memphis, Tenn.
1948,	Larry Doby of the Cleveland Indians became the first African-American player to sign with the American League.
1983,	Norman S. Early was appointed Denver's first African-American district attorney.
1988,	Doug Williams became the first African-American quarterback to start and win a Super Bowl--Washington 42, Denver 10.

JANUARY 31   **ARTISTS**

RICHARD BERRY HARRISON

Actor, educator, lecturer, and elocutionist.   Born on September 28, 1864, in London, Ontario, Canada.   Detroit Training School of Art. Studied acting with Edward Weitzel of London; began his first extensive one-man tour of the U.S. (1891); worked for the Santa Fe Railroad in Los Angeles (1891-1892); toured on the Chautauqua Circuit (1892-1896), giving recitations from Dunbar, Kipling, Poe, and Shakespeare; gained a national reputation in the African-American community as a dramatic reader; founder of North Carolina A&T University's Dramatic School (1922-1929), where he also taught drama and elocution; organized festivals for African-American schools and churches. Appeared in Frank Wilson's play, *Pa William's Gal*, at the Lafayette Theater in New York City (1923); accepted the role of "de Lawd" in Marc Connelly's *Green Pastures*, which opened at the Mansfield Theater in New York City (1930), bringing him his greatest triumph, after 1,657 performances, in a musical play about a white writer's version of another white writer's version of one African-American minister's version of religion; **received the NAACP Spingarn Medal (1931), for his years of interpreting English drama to African-Americans.** Died on March 14, 1935, in New York City.   Further reading, Marc Connelly, *Voice Offstage* (1968).

---

on this day in history...

1931,   Hugh D. Milligan, first African-American manager of a federally-operated airport, was born in Washington, D.C.
1933,   Clerow "Flip" Wilson, Grammy Award-winning comedian, was born in Jersey City, N.J.
1939,   Jerry Butler, singer known as the "Iceman," was born in Sunflower, Miss.

DECEMBER 9   STAGE PERFORMERS

ROBERT REED CHURCH, SR.

Businessman and philanthropist who was known as **the richest African-American in the South**. Born into slavery on June 18, 1839, in Mississippi. Emancipated (1865); invested in a saloon, billiard room, and real estate; was shot during race riots in Memphis (1866), but recovered; expanded his holdings during a yellow fever epidemic, which brought death, evacuation, and inexpensive property prices in Memphis (1878-1879); bought a substantial amount of municipal bonds after the State of Tennessee revoked Memphis' charter, earning the title of **"founding father" of Memphis** for his financial role in saving the city from the brink of bankruptcy; toured Europe with his daughter Mary Church Terrell (1888); delegate to the Republican National Convention (1900). Helped finance the official Confederate Reunion (Memphis, 1901); developed a park for African-Americans on Beale Street because of the "Jim Crow" atmosphere of the South; built a large auditorium that served as a site for graduations, political rallies, African-American road shows, and an annual Thanksgiving dinner for the poor; founded the Solvent Savings Bank & Trust Company of Memphis (1906). Died on August 2, 1912, in Memphis, Tenn. Further reading, Annette E. Church, _The Robert Churches of Memphis_ (1975).

---

on this day in history...

1865,	John Sweat Rock became the first African-American to practice before the U.S. Supreme Court.
1885,	Jonathan Jasper Wright became South Carolina's first African-American state Supreme Court justice.
1936,	Azie Taylor Morton, first African-American woman treasurer of the U.S., was born in Dale, Texas.
1938,	Sherman Hemsley, actor, was born in Philadelphia, Pa.
1960,	Four North Carolina A&T students held a sit-in at a downtown Greensboro Woolworth lunch counter, ushering in the civil rights movement of the '60s.

FEBRUARY 1   **BUSINESS LEADERS**

LORRAINE VIVIAN HANSBERRY

Playwright who became the **first African-American woman to have a play open on Broadway.**   Born on May 19, 1930, in Chicago, Ill.   University of Wisconsin; Art Institute of Chicago; New York School for Social Work.   Moved to New York City (1950), working as a waitress, sales clerk, associate editor of Paul Robeson's Harlem-based *Freedom* newspaper, and as a theatrical producer's assistant; began writing short stories, poetry, and plays.   Playwright of a three-act drama (whose title came from Langston Hughes' famous poem, "Harlem") inspired by her childhood experiences with racism and discrimination--*A Raisin in the Sun* (1959), which premiered in New Haven, opened on Broadway at the Ethel Barrymore Theater, ran for 538 performances, **ushered in a new era for the role of the African-American artist during the modern civil rights movement,** opened the doors for African-American artists, like Ruby Dee, Lou Gossett, Sidney Poitier, and Lloyd Richards, began an unprecedented rise in the African-American theater, and became a full-length motion picture.   Became a spokeswoman for African-Americans in life and art; wrote the text for a collection of photographs entitled *The Movement: Documentary of a Struggle for Racial Equality in the USA* (1964); opened her second Broadway play, *The Sign in Sidney Brustein's Window*, at the Longacre Theater (1964); some of her other works include, *To Be Young, Gifted, and Black: Lorraine Hansberry in Her Own Words* (1969), and *Les Blancs: The Collected Last Plays of Lorraine Hansberry* (1972).   Winner of the New York Drama Critics Circle Award for Best Play of the Year (1960), Cannes Film Festival Award (1961), and posthumously inducted into the Black Filmmakers Hall of Fame; inspired many African-American writers, such as Pulitzer Prize-winner Charles Gordone.   Died on January 12, 1965, in New York City.   Further reading, Darlene C. Hine, *Black Women in America: An Historical Encyclopedia* (1993).

---

on this day in history...

1964,   Martin Luther King, Jr., received the Nobel Peace Prize.
1967,   Otis Redding was killed when his plane crashed in Madison, Wis.

DECEMBER 8   STAGE PERFORMERS

ALEXANDER G. CLARK

Businessman, religious leader, lawyer, politician, diplomat, and civil rights advocate. Born in 1826 in Washington County, Pa. University of Iowa Law School (1884). Learned the barber trade; moved to Muscatine, Iowa (1842), and opened a barbershop, supplied wood to steamboats, acquired real estate, and became a very prosperous man. Founder of Muscatine's African Methodist Episcopal Church (1849), serving as trustee, steward, and Sunday school superintendent; attended the AME General Conference (St. Louis, 1880), and served as a lay delegate to the Methodist Ecumenical Conference (London, 1881). Joined St. Louis' Prince Hall Lodge #1 (1851); elected deputy grand master of the Grand Lodge of Missouri (1868); organized the Hiram Grand Lodge of Iowa (1884), and later organized and served as president of the United Grand Lodge of Iowa. In response to his daughter being denied admission into the Muscatine public schools (1868), successfully persued a law suit all the way to the Iowa State Supreme Court, which ruled that all state public schools were opened to everyone of school age; was chairman and spokesman for the committee that organized Iowa's First Colored Convention (1868), where he became **known as the "colored orator of the West**;" served as a vice president of the Republican State Convention of Iowa (1869); delegate-at-large from Iowa to the Republican National Convention (Philadelphia, 1872). Represented Iowa at the Centennial exposition (Philadelphia, 1876); owner of the *Conservative* (1882-1887), a protest journal; opened a Chicago law office (1884); elected treasurer and appointed chairman of the executive committee of the National Press Association (1887); minister and consul general to Liberia (1890-1891). Died on May 31, 1891, in Monrovia, Liberia. Further reading, Leola Nelson Bergmann, "The Negro in Iowa," (*Iowa Journal of History and Politics*, February 1969).

---

on this day in history...

1847,	Robert Morris, Sr., was admitted to the Suffolk County, Mass., bar, becoming the first African-American lawyer in the U.S.
1924,	"Sonny" Stitt, a leading jazz saxophonist of the 1940s and '50s, was born in Boston, Mass. (d. 1982).
1938,	Simon Lamont Estes, operatic baritone, was born in Centerville, Iowa.
1989,	Evelyn Fields, U.S. Navy lieutenant commander, became the first African-American woman to command a naval ship.

CHARLES SIDNEY GILPIN

Vaudeville performer and dramatic actor. Born on November 20, 1878, in Richmond, Va. Performed with: Brown's Big Spectacular Log Cabin Company (1896), his first professional acting job; Perkus and Davis' Great Southern Minstrels (1896), Carey and Carter Canadian Jubilee Singers (1903-1905); Bert Williams and George Walker's Company (1905-1906), working as a baritone soloist in *Abyssinia*; Gus Hill's Original *Smart Set* (1906-1907); Pekin Stock Company of Chicago (1907-1911), where he first performed as a dramatic actor, winning critical acclaim for his role in *The Mayor of Dixie*; Pan American Octette on a transcontinental tour (1911-1914); Anita Bush Players at the Lincoln Theater in Harlem (1914-1916), appearing in *The Girl at the Fort*. **Organized New York City's first African-American dramatic stock company, the Lafayette Theater "Players"** Stock Company (1916), starring in the company's first production, *Across the Footlights*; played the role of "preacher William Custin" in John Drinkwater's British biographical drama *Abraham Lincoln* (1919), appearing in his first Broadway play; offered the lead role in Eugene O'Neill's *The Emperor Jones* (1920), while working as an elevator operator at Macy's. Starred in *The Emperor Jones* at the Provincetown Theater, Broadway's Princess Theater, and on a road tour (1920-1924), playing the role of "Brutus Jones," becoming an overnight success and the **first African-American actor to play a major role in an American tragedy,** being reviewed as the greatest artist of the American stage, and helping the play win a Pulitzer Prize (1921); honored by the Drama League (1921), as one of ten people who had contributed the most to the American theater; awarded the NAACP Spingarn Medal (1921). Died on May 6, 1930, in Eldridge Park, N.J. Further reading, Loften Mitchell, *Black Drama: The Story of the American Negro in the Theater* (1967).

---

on this day in history...

1931,   Comer Cottrell, first African-American to own part of a Major League Baseball team (the Texas Rangers), was born in Mobile, Ala.

1940,   Carol Simpson, network broadcaster who was Chicago's first African-American woman TV reporter, was born in Chicago, Ill.

1941,   Dorie Miller downed three Japanese planes during the attack on Pearl Harbor, becoming the first hero of World War II, which earned him the Navy Cross.

1972,   Sterling Cary was elected the first African-American president of the National Council of Churches.

1981,   John E. Jacob replaced Vernon Jordan as president of the National Urban League.

DECEMBER 7   **STAGE PERFORMERS**

PAUL CUFFE

Shipowner, businessman, colonizationist, and humanitarian.   Born in 1759 in Massachusetts.   Became a master of his own ship (1784), and owned interest in the schooner *Ranger,* the brigs *Traveller* and *Hero,* and the ship *Alpha*; **amassed a fortune obtained from whaling, costal shipping, and trade with Europe and the Caribbean**; purchased a farm on the East Branch of Massachusetts' Westport River (1797), and later established a school for African-American children on the property; donated half the money needed to build the Friends Meeting House in Westport (1797); joined with Dartmouth Negroes in petitioning the state, county, and local governments to grant relief from paying taxes until African-Americans and Indians were given the right to vote. Became associated with the Society of Friends (1808), which convinced him that he was God's representative for the conversion of Africans and that colonization in Africa would bring about the abolishment of slavery in the U.S.; set out to establish missionary activities in Sierra Leone, with the support of the Westport Friends, the African Institution in London, and the Quakers in Philadelphia; traveled to Sierra Leone first on an exploratory mission and founded the Friendly Society for the emigration of free Negroes from America (1810-1812), and later with close to 40 settlers (1815); added to his fortune by trading with Europe, Asia, and the West Indies. Died in 1817.   Further reading, <u>George Salvador</u>, <u>*Paul Cuffe, the Black Yankee, 1759-1817*</u> (1969).

---

on this day in history...

1874,	Blanche Kelso Bruce of Mississippi became the first African-American elected U.S. senator.
1939,	The U.S. attorney general established the Civil Rights Division within the Department of Justice.
1948,	Laura Wheeler Waring, organizer of Cheyney State's art and music department, died in Pennsylvania (b. 1887).
1956,	Autherine Lucy became the first African-American student at the University of Alabama.
1989,	Bill White was named president of Major League Baseball's National League.

FEBRUARY 3   BUSINESS LEADERS

LILLIAN EVANTI

Soprano and composer nicknamed "Madame Evanti," who became the **first African-American woman to sing in an opera anywhere in the world.** Born Lillian Evans on August 12, 1890, in Washington, D.C. Miner Teachers College; Howard University (B.Mus., 1917), where she became a protege of Howard University School of Music founder Lulu Childers. Performed with violinist Felix Weir (1915), where she first attracted attention; studied voice with Frank LaForge in New York City; studied voice, French, and acting with Madame Ritter Ciampi in Paris, Rosa Stochia in Italy, and with M. Gaston Dupins (1925-1928); made her operatic debut in Europe, because of racism in the U.S., in the title role of Delibes's *Lakme* (1925), at the Casino Theater in Nice, France; repeated the performance at the Trianan Lyrique in Paris (1927), which brought her heralded attention back to Washington, D.C., as an "American" opera star. Performed a recital at the International House in New York City (1925), which was sponsored by Harry Burleigh and Peter M. Murray; sang at the Town Hall in New York City (1932); gave a recital at the only prestigious stage in D.C., the Belasco Theater (1932); invited to sing at the White House for President and Mrs. Roosevelt (1934); toured the U.S., Europe, and Latin America; traveled to Argentina and Brazil with Artura Toscanini and the NBC Orchestra as a goodwill ambassador of the U.S. State Department (1940); **co-founder of the National Negro Opera Company** (1941), with whom she performed the role of "Violetta" in Verdi's *La Traviata* at the Watergate in Washington, D.C. Composed the songs, "Himno Panamericano," "Salute to Ghana," "On Furlough Manana," "23rd Psalm," "My Little Prayer," and "Mighty Rapture;" some of her repertoire, along with her ability to sing in five different languages, included *Rigoletto*, *Barber of Seville*, *Romeo and Juliette*, *Boheme*, *Carmen*, and *Hamlet*; cited by General Eisenhower and Admiral Nimitz for concerts at military installations during World War II. Died on December 6, 1967, in Washington, D.C. Further reading, Rosalyn Story, *And So I Sing* (1990).

---

on this day in history...

1877, Caspar Holstein, Harlem businessman who created the "numbers game," was born in the Virgin Islands (d. 1944).

1932, R.B. Spikes patented an automatic gear shift.

DECEMBER 6   STAGE PERFORMERS

HOWARD NAYLOR FITZHUGH

Pioneering marketing and corporate relations consultant who was known as the **"dean of Black business."** Born on October 31, 1909, in Washington, D.C. Harvard University *cum laude* (B.S., 1930; M.B.A., 1933), becoming the **first African-American to receive a Harvard M.B.A.;** Columbia University; American University; Virginia State College (LL.D., 1971). Assistant professor of marketing at Howard University (1934-1965), where he developed Howard's marketing program and organized its Small Business Center; chairman of the advisory committee of the Howard University Business School (1965-1972). Became **one of the earliest authorities on African-American consumer marketing** and pioneered segmented marketing techniques; vice president of special marketing for Pepsi-Cola Company (1974); vice president of public policies and the issues division of the American Marketing Association (1970-1971); expert consultant for the U.S. Bureau of the Census' Minority Statistics Program (1975-1981). Executive director and president of the National Association of Market Developers (1967-1968, 1976-1977); visiting committee chairman of the Harvard Business School Black Alumni Association (1977-1978), and chairman emeritus (1978-1992); author and developer of the Pepsi/DECA Learn and Earn High School Project (1972). Named Newsmaker of the '60s by *Advertising Age* (1969); honored with an award in his name by the National Black MBA Association (1979); named Man of the Year by *Excel Magazine* (1986); received the Harvard Business School Distinguished Service Award (1987); honored with degrees from Howard University (LL.D., 1987), and Livingstone College (D.H.L., 1988). Died on July 26, 1992, in New York City. Further reading, Iris Cloyd, *Who's Who Among Black Americans* (1991).

---

on this day in history...

1913,	Rosa Louise Parks, "mother of the civil rights movement," was born in Tuskegee, Ala.
1922,	Herman M. Holloway, Sr., Delaware's first African-American state senator, was born in Wilmington, Del.
1947,	Sanford Bishop, Georgia 2nd District congressman, was born in Mobile, Ala.
1959,	Lawrence J. Taylor, New York Giants' "Lawrence of the Meadowlands," was born in Williamsburg, Va.

FEBRUARY 4   BUSINESS LEADERS

THEODORE DRURY

Tenor who **organized one of the first African-American opera companies and was regarded as the first highly trained African-American male singer.** Born in the 1860s. Studied acting, voice, and the piano, and became fluent in French and German; toured the Northeast and accompanied artists on productions of the Grand Star Concerts in New York City; organized the Drury Comic Opera Company, later to be called the Theodore Drury Opera Company (1889), making his debut in Brooklyn with costumes, decorations, pianist, scenery, singers and Drury as musical director; toured over 100 U.S. cities given solo recitals (1895-1896). Produced Bizet's *Carmen* (1900), which was reviewed as the **first successful operatic performance by a predominately African-American company;** also produced Gomez's *Il Guarany* (1901), Gounod's *Faust* (1902), Verdi's *Aida* (1903), Mascagni's *Canalleria Rusticiana* (1904), Leoncavallo's *I Pagliacci* (1904), and another production of *Carmen* (1906), playing to audiences in New York City, Philadelphia, Providence, and Boston. Settled in Boston, where he organized the Drury Musical Arts Club and produced Handel's *Messiah* (1911); made his concert debut as tenor at the Palm Garden in Boston (1912); studied abroad (1912-1918), returning to the U.S., for a national tour; opened a voice studio in Boston, and began coaching professional singers; presented *Faust* with his Drury Opera Company in Providence, R.I. (1928); served as a judge for the Wannamaker Music Contests (1930). Died around 1944. Further reading, Eileen Southern, *Biographical Dictionary of Afro-American and African Musicians* (1982).

---

on this day in history...

1895,	Elbert Frank Cox, nation's first African-American to earn a Ph.D. in mathematics, was born in Evansville, Ind.
1931,	James Cleveland, founder of the Gospel Workshop of America, was born in Chicago, Ill. (d. 1991).
1935,	The National Council of Negro Women was founded in New York City by Mary McLeod Bethune.
1946,	President Truman issued Executive Order 9809, creating the President's Committee on Civil Rights.
1955,	The Montgomery bus boycott began.

DECEMBER 5   STAGE PERFORMERS

ARTHUR G. GASTON, SR.

Self-made millionaire, civil rights activist, and **Birmingham community leader and philanthropist**. Born on July 4, 1892, in Demopolis, Ala. Tuggles Institute in Birmingham. Worked as a subscription collector for the *Birmingham Reporter*, and as a bellhop at Mobile's Battle House Hotel; served as a sergeant with the all-Black unit, 317th Ammunition Train of the 92nd Division, during World War I; began working for $3.10 a day at the Tennessee Coal and Iron Co., in Birmingham (1918), where he started a burial society for co-workers and friends; acquired the mortuary that later became the home of Smith & Gaston Funeral Directors (1923). Incorporated the burial society as Booker T. Washington Insurance Co. (1932), which served Birmingham's African-American community at a time when white insurers would not and became the seed capital for the acquiring and/or launching of the following ventures: BTW Jr. College of Business (1939); Brown Belle Bottling Co. (1946); New Grace Hill Cemeteries, Inc. (1947); A.G. Gaston Motel in downtown Birmingham (1954), serving African-American travelers barred from segregated lodging, and as Martin Luther King, Jr.'s headquarters during the 1963 Birmingham "Confrontation;" Zion Memorial Gardens; Vulcan Realty & Investment Co. (1955); Citizens Federal Savings & Loan Assoc. (1957), filling a need for more African-American homeowners; A.G. Gaston Home for Senior Citizens (1963); Citizens Drugstore; A.G. Gaston Boys Club (1966), with a $50,000 contribution; a new Citizens Federal Building (1970); BTW Broadcasting Services (1975), which includes WENN/WAGG radio stations; A.G. Gaston Construction Co. (1986). Worked behind the scenes during Alabama's civil rights movement, providing lodging for demonstrators, putting up their bail, providing financial support to anyone being pressured by white banks during economic boycotts, and serving as a middle-man between civil rights activists and white businessmen; created an employee stock option plan (1987), selling BTW Insurance Co. to his employees for less than $4 million; honored by *Black Enterprise* as the **"Entrepreneur of the Century."** Further reading, A.G. Gaston, *Green Power* (1968).

---

on this day in history...

1884,	Willis Johnson patented an egg beater.
1934,	Henry "Hank" Aaron, baseball's "home run king" and Atlanta Braves vice president, was born in Mobile, Ala.
1950,	Stephanie Natalie Maria Cole, Grammy Award-winning singer, was born in Los Angeles, Calif.
1954,	Linda Dianne Johnson, Mississippi's first African-American woman optometrist, was born in Richland, Miss.
1958,	Clifton W. Wharton, Sr., became the first African-American U.S. ambassador to a European country (Romania).

FEBRUARY 5   BUSINESS LEADERS

ANITA BUSH

Actress who was called "the little mother of drama." Born around 1883 in Washington, D.C. Toured with Bert Williams and George Walker's Williams and Walker Players (1903-1910), appearing in *In Dahomey*, *Abyssiania*, *Mr. Lode of Koal*, and performed in *In Dahomey* before King Edward VII of England; organized her own vaudeville touring act, "The Hula Hula Dancers" (1910); formed a group of Harlem's favorite actors to perform in serious drama at New York City's Lincoln Theater, and the Anita Bush Players (1915), which included Charles Gilpin, Dooley Wilson, Andrew Bishop, and Carolotta Freeman. Moved the company to New York City's Lafayette Theater, becoming the Lafayette Players (1916), appearing in *The Girl at the Fort*, introducing legitimate theater to over 25 cities across the U.S., performing over 250 dramas never presented by a completely African-American company, and becoming a training ground for hundreds of African-American thespians; starred in the first all-black Western movie, *The Crimson Skull* (1921), and in *The Bulldogger* (1922); featured in the Work Projects Administration Federal Theater Project's *Swing It* (1938), and the WPA's *Androcles and the Lion* (1939). Served as executive secretary of the Negro Actors Guild; became a **pioneer in the development of the African-American theater;** credited with launching the professional careers of scores of successful African-American performers and changing the face of the American theater forever. Died on February 16, 1974, in New York City. Further reading, Edward Mapp, *Dictionary of Blacks in the Performing Arts* (1974).

---

on this day in history...

1874,　John Anderson Lankford, nation's first African-American architect, was born in Potsoi, Mo.

1906,　Alpha Phi Alpha Fraternity Inc. was organized on the campus of Cornell University.

1950,　Jesse Leroy Brown became the first African-American naval officer to lose his life in combat.

1958,　Terdema Ussery, Jr., first African-American head of a professional sports league (CBA), was born in Los Angeles, Calif.

1969,　Fred Hampton and Mark West, Illinois Black Panther Party members, were killed in a police raid in Chicago, Ill.

DECEMBER 4　　　　　　　　　　　　　　　　　　　　**STAGE PERFORMERS**

REGINALD LEWIS

Attorney, Wall Street financier, and philanthropist who became **CEO of the nation's largest black-owned company-- TLC Beatrice International.**   Born on December 7, 1942, in Baltimore, Md.   Virginia State College (A.B., 1965); Harvard Law School (LL.B., 1968).   Attorney with the New York City law firm of Paul, Weiss, Rofkind, Wharton & Garrison (1968-1970); partner in Wall Street's first African-American firm, Murphy, Thorpe & Lewis (1970-1973); established his own corporate law firm, Lewis & Clarkson (1973), specializing in venture capital. Started TLC Group Ltd. (1983), and struck a $22-million leveraged buyout deal of McCall Pattern Co.; sold McCall for $90 million (1987); orchestrated a $985-million leveraged buyout of Beatrice International Food Cos., an ice cream, snack, and food distribution concern (1987), which became the largest leveraged buyout ever of overseas assets by a U.S. company, and made TLC Beatrice the **first black-owned company to break the $1-billion-in-revenues barrier.** Member of the American Bar Association, National Bar Association, and the National Conference of Black Lawyers; served as a director of the North St. Capital Corp., members of the board of trustees of Antioch University, and as a member of the board of directors of the New York City Off-Track Betting Corp., and Central Park Conservancy; member of Kappa Alpha Psi fraternity. **Gave a $3-million grant to Harvard Law School, the largest gift in Harvard's history** (1992), which was used to establish Harvard's first building named after an African-American, the Reginald F. Lewis International Law Center; contributed $1 million to Howard University. Died January 19, 1993, in New York City.   Further reading, Iris Cloyd, *Who's Who Among Black Americans* (1991).

---

on this day in history...

1882,   Anne Spencer, Harlem Renaissance poet, was born in Henry County, Va. (d. 1975).
1900,   Melvin Beaunorus Tolson, author of *Libretto for the Republic of Liberia*, was born in Moberly, Mo.
1933,   Walter Edward Fauntroy, former District of Columbia congressional delegate (1971-1991), was born in Washington, D.C.
1945,   Robert Nestam "Bob" Marley, legendary reggae singer, was born in St. Ann, Jamaica (d. 1981).
1956,   Robert Townsend, actor, producer, writer, and director, was born in Chicago, Ill.

FEBRUARY 6   **BUSINESS LEADERS**

MARIAN ANDERSON

Contralto who was called one of the **greatest singers of the 20th century.** Born on February 17, 1902, in Philadelphia, Pa. Studied voice and music privately in Philadelphia, New York City, and Europe with masters, such as Giuseppe Boghetti, Raimund Von Zur Muhlen, Michael Rauscheisen, and the Philadelphia Choral Society; began touring African-American colleges and churches and in theaters and school auditoriums; made her debut as a concert contralto at Town Hall in New York City (1922); won first place in a New York Philharmonic Symphony's summer concert series' singing competition (1925), winning critical acclaim; toured Europe extensively, singing for crown heads of state. Performed at Carnegie Hall (1936); became one of Columbia Records' top-selling artists and the **nation's highest paid concert singer**; denied the use of Constitution Hall by the Daughters of the American Revolution for a Howard University sponsored concert because she was an African-American (1939), resulting in Eleanor Roosevelt resigning from the organization and arranging for Anderson to perform on the steps of the Lincoln Memorial on Easter Sunday before 75,000 people; **became a symbol of triumph over discrimination in the arts.** Made her television debut on the *Ed Sullivan Show* (1952); became the **first African-American to perform with the New York Metropolitan Opera Company** (1955), singing the role of "Ulrica" in Verdi's *Un Ballo in Maschera*; toured the Far East as a U.S. State Department goodwill ambassador (1957); performed in a farewell concert with the Philadelphia Symphony Orchestra at Carnegie Hall (1965). Awarded the NAACP Spingarn Medal (1939); established the Marian Anderson Fellowship (1942); honored with the Presidential Medal of Freedom (1963), Kennedy Center Performing Arts award (1978), and the National Medal of Arts (1986). Died on April 8, 1993, in Portland, Ore. Further reading, Marian Anderson, *My Lord, What a Morning* (1956).

on this day in history...

1847,	Frederick Douglass and Martin Delaney began publishing the abolitionist newspaper, the *North Star*.
1851,	Myrtilla Miner established what is now the University of the District of Columbia.
1855,	John Wesley Bowen, first African-American professor at Gammon Seminary in Atlanta, was born in New Orleans, La.
1880,	Walter Gilbert Alexander, physician who served on the New Jersey State Board of Health, was born in Lynchburg, Va.

DECEMBER 3   **STAGE PERFORMERS**

JOHN MERRICK

Durham businessman, fraternal leader, and insurance pioneer who became the **business community leader of one of the most progressive cities in the South for African-Americans**.   Born into slavery in 1859 in Clinton, N.C. Worked as a hod carrier in Raleigh and helped build the first building on the campus of Shaw University; learned the barbering trade, became owner of five barbershops for whites and African-Americans in Durham; became well-known for his Merricks Dandruff Cure, and attended to tobacco magnate James B. Duke, politician William Jennings Bryan, and many other prominent white men; joined with six other African-American businessmen in purchasing a mutual aid society called the Royal Knights of King David (1883), becoming supreme grand treasurer of a 21,000-member organization; president and chairman of the board member of Lincoln Hospital in Durham (1901-1919), where he helped develop it into one of the better private hospitals for African-Americans in the South. Co-founder, along with A.M. Moore, P.W. Dawkins, D.T. Watson, W.G. Pearson, E.A. Johnson, and J.E. Shepard, and president of North Carolina Mutual Life Insurance Company (1899-1919), which later became the nation's largest African-American business; **founder and vice president of Mechanics & Farmers Bank of Durham** (1907); founded the Bull City Drug Company (1908), the Merrick-Moore-Spaulding Real Estate Company (1910), and the Durham Textile Mill (1914). Died on August 6, 1919, in Durham, N.C.   Further reading, <u>William J. Kennedy</u>, <u>*The North Carolina Mutual Story*</u> (1970).

---

on this day in history...

1883,	James Hurbert "Eubie" Blake, ragtime and musical comedy composer, was born in Baltimore, Md. (d. 1983).
1914,	Charles Kenzie Steele, civil rights leader of the 1956 Tallahassee Bus Boycott, was born in Gary, W.Va. (d. 1980).
1923,	Harvey Washington Banks, first African-American to earn a Ph.D. in astronomy, was born in Atlantic City, N.J.
1926,	The first Negro History Week began, coinciding with President Lincoln's birthday.

IRA FREDERICK ALDERIDGE

Actor who was called **the greatest Shakespearean actor of his time.** Born reportedly on July 24, 1807, in New York City. African Free School in New York City (1824); University of Glasgow. Debuted as an actor in August von Kotzebue's *Pizarro* in the role of "Rolla" at the African Theater in New York City (1824); left for London on a ship working as a steward (1824); opened at the Royal Coburg, London, in *A Slave's Revenge* (1825); played in Thomas Morton's *The Ethiopian*, H.M. Milner's *The Negro's Curse*, and J.H. Armherst's *The Negro's Curse*; toured England appearing in Edinburgh, Halifax, Lancaster, Liverpool, Manchester, Newcastle, Sheffield, and Sunderland (1827), performing Shakespeare's *Othello*, E. Young's *The Revenge*, I. Bickerstaff's *The Padlock*, Southerne's *Oroonoko*, and Morton's *The Slave*, and *Titus Andronicus*. Debuted at London's Theater Royal Covent Garden in the role of "Othello" (1833), where from then on he was referred to as "The African Roscius" or "The Celebrated African Tragedian;" embarked on his first European tour (1852), performing in the roles of "Lear," "MacBeth," "Mungo," "Othello," "Richard III," and "Shylock," and praised by critics as the greatest actor that Europe has ever seen. Honored by the Republic of Haiti as **"the first man of color in the theater"** (1827), with the Golden Cross of Leopald by the Czar of Russia, by Frederick William IV with the Prussian Academy of Arts and Sciences' Large Gold Medal (1853), with the White Cross of Switzerland (1854), by Duke Bernhard with Verdienst Medal of Order (1858), and with Russia's Imperial Jubilee de Tolstoy Medal (1858); became a citizen of Great Britain (1863). Died on August 7, 1867, in Lodz, Poland. Further reading, Herbert Marshall and Mildred Stock, *Ira Aldridge: The Negro Tragedian* (1955).

---

on this day in history...

1866,   Harry Thacker Burleigh, first African-American to serve on the board of directors of the American Society of Composers, was born in Erie, Pa. (d. 1949).

1891,   Charles Harris Wesley, historian and president emeritus of Central State University, was born in Louisville.

1922,   Charles Coles Diggs, Jr., Michigan's first African-American U.S. congressman, was born in Detroit.

1935,   Eddie Bernice Johnson, Texas 13th District congresswoman, was born in Waco, Texas.

1955,   A. Phillip Randolph and Williard Townsend were elected vice presidents of the AFL-CIO.

DECEMBER 2   STAGE PERFORMERS

JOHN R. MITCHELL, JR.

Journalist, politician, and banker. Born into slavery in 1863, outside of Richmond, Va. Richmond Normal & High School valedictorian (1881). Correspondent for the *New York Globe*; assumed ownership of the *Richmond Planet* (1884), and turned it into one of the nation's leading African-American newspapers; became an anti-lynching crusader who wrote "the best remedy for a lyncher or a cursed midnight rider is a 16-shot Winchester rifle in the hands of a Negro who has nerve enough to pull the trigger." President of the Afro-American Press Association (1890-1894); **Richmond city councilman** (1888-1896); fought against the Spanish-American War and became one of the nation's most outspoken African-American opponents of imperialism; **founder of the Mechanics Savings Bank of Richmond** (1902); served as grand chancellor of the Virginia Knights of Pythias, where he invested in real estate, buying a movie theater, cemetery, and other Richmond property; became the **first African-American member of the American Bankers Association** (1904); led a boycott of Richmond's segregated streetcars (1904); lobbied for a Richmond ordinance against residential segregation. Died on December 3, 1929, in Richmond, Va. Further reading, Abram L. Harris, *The Negro Capitalist* (1936).

---

on this day in history...

1876,	Crawford Goldsby ("Cherokee Bill"), Oklahoma bandit, was born in Fort Concho, Texas (d. 1896).
1900,	Roscoe Lewis McKinney, first African-American to earn a Ph.D. in anatomy, was born in Washington, D.C.
1924,	Joe Black, Negro League baseball champion and Greyhound vice president, was born in Plainfield, N.J.
1944,	Harry S. Alpin of the *Atlanta Daily World* became the first African-American accredited White House correspondent.
1968,	Thirty S.C. State College students were shot, and three were killed by police, in what was called the Orangeburg Massacre.

ALVIN AILEY

Dancer, choreographer, educator and actor. Born on January 5, 1931, in Rogers, Texas. University of California at Los Angeles; Los Angeles City College; San Francisco State College. Studied dance at the Lester Horton Theater in Los Angeles (1949-1953), where he debuted as a choreographer; also studied dance under Hanya Holm (1949-1955), Martha Graham (1956), and Anna Sokolow (1956); studied acting with Stella Adler (1960-1962). Performed at the Jacobs Pillow Dance Festival (1954, 1959-1960); **formed the Alvin Ailey American Dance Theater Company** (1958); performed at the Boston Arts Festival (1961), on a U.S. State Department tour of Australia, Southeast Asia, and Africa (1962), at the International Music Festival (Brazil, 1963), on a tour of the Soviet Union (1970), at President's Carter's inauguration (1977), and on a tour of Latin America. **Founded the American Dance Center** (1975); choreographed and danced for the Harkness Ballet Company; became a distinguished professor at Borough of Manhattan Community College of the City University of New York (1985-1989); appeared in the movie *Carmen Jones* (1954); choreographed and danced in the television specials, *Alvin Ailey: Memories and Vision* (1971), *Ailey Celebrates Ellington: Festival of Arts for Young People* (1974), and *Great Performances* (1987); choreographed the plays *Creation of the World* (1960), *After Eden* (1966), *The River Carmen* (1972), and *For Bird--With Love* (1985). Held membership in the Actors Equity Association, American Federation of Television and Radio Artists, American Guild of Musical Artists, and the American Guild of Variety Artists; honored with an Alvin Ailey Day in Atlanta (1975), *Dance Magazine* award (1975, 1982), UN Peace medal (1982), and the Samuel H. Scripps American Dance Festival award (1987). Died on December 1, 1989, in New York City. Further reading, <u>John Willis</u>, <u>*Dance World*</u> (1990).

---

on this day in history...

1871,	Arthur Craig, nation's first African-American electrical engineer graduate (University of Kansas), was born in Weston, Mo.
1935,	Louis Allen Rawls, Grammy Award-winning host of the annual UNCF Telethon, was born in Chicago, Ill.
1940,	Richard Pryor, Grammy and Emmy Award-winning comedian, actor, and producer, was born in Peoria, Ill.
1949,	Kurt Schmoke, Baltimore's first African-American mayor, was born in Baltimore.
1955,	Rosa Parks was arrested for refusing to give up her seat to a white person, which sparked the Montgomery bus boycott.
1992,	Pearl Stewart of the *Oakland Tribune* became the nation's first African-American woman editor-in-chief of a major daily paper.

DECEMBER 1   **STAGE PERFORMERS**

JAMES CARROLL NAPIER

Lawyer, politician, government official, banker, and civic leader. Born on June 9, 1845, in Nashville, Tenn. Wilberforce University; Oberlin College, Howard University (LL.B., 1872). Commissioner of refugees and abandoned lands for the Freedmen's Bureau in Davidson County, Tenn. (1867-1868); became the **first African-American clerk for the U.S. State Department**; set up a Nashville law practice (1872), and held patronage appointments under Presidents Grant, Hayes, Garfield, and Arthur; **Nashville city councilman (1878-1885), and became Tennessee's ranking African-American Republican**; served on the State Republican Executive Committee and represented the state at six Republican National Conventions. Brought the National Business League national meeting to Nashville (1903), and succeeded Booker T. Washington as president (1915); registrar in the U.S. Treasury Department (1911-1913); was **primary initial investor and nonsalaried cashier at the One-Cent Savings Bank in Nashville** (1903-1940) [later called Citizens Savings Bank]; member of the board of directors of the Jeanes Fund, Meharry Medical College, and Fisk and Howard Universities; helped found Tennessee Agricultural & Industrial State Normal School [now Tennessee State University]. Died on April 21, 1940, in Nashville, Tenn. Further reading, Cordell Hull Williams "The Life of James Carroll Napier from 1845 to 1940," (M.A. thesis, Tennessee State University, 1954).

---

on this day in history...

1944,   Alice Malsenior Walker, Pulitzer Prize-winning author of *The Color Purple*, was born in Eatonton, Ga.

1953,   Gary A. Franks, Connecticut 5th District congressman, was born in Waterbury, Conn.

1960,   One hundred Johnson C. Smith University students staged sit-ins at downtown Charlotte lunch counters.

FEBRUARY 9   BUSINESS LEADERS

MAJOR TAYLOR

Cyclist who became **one of the most glorified African-American athletes in history.**   Born Marshall W. Taylor on November 16, 1878, in Indianapolis, Ind.   Began as a trick rider and soon established an early reputation as a racer, which earned him support from the leading sports' managements; unofficially beat champion cyclist Walter Sanger's mark of 2:18 at the Capital City track in Indianapolis (1888), turning in a 2:11 mile after the competition was over because of the track's "color" bar against African-Americans racing whites; established a Capital City track record, 23.6 seconds in the 1/5-mile oval, which lasted as long as the track did; finished one hour ahead of the nearest competing cyclist in a 75-mile road race between Indianapolis and Matthews, Ind., a race where he had to hide in woods until the race began. Moved to Worcester, Mass., to escape the racial climate of Indianapolis, and trained to eventually become the **fastest cyclist in the world;** U.S. national sprint champion (1898), defeating all of the previous champions, finishing first in 21 races, second 13 times, and third 11 times; U.S. national sprint champion (1899), finishing first in 23 races, second 3 times, and in the top three all but twice; U.S. national sprint champion (1890), finishing with twice as many points as the nearest competitor. Traveled to Europe (1901), competing in France, Belgium, Italy, Switzerland, Denmark, and Germany, defeating their national champions; honored many times by royal families of Europe; traveled to Australia (1902), where he received a hero's welcome when he sailed in the Sydney Harbor, and duplicated his European success; honored by President Theodore Roosevelt for his achievements as a professional bicycle rider, which was one of the most popular sports in America at the time. Retired in 1910. Died on June 21, 1932, in Chicago, Ill.   Further reading, <u>Edina</u> and <u>Art Rust, Jr.</u>, <u>*Art Rust's Illustrated History of the Black Athlete*</u> (1985).

---

on this day in history...

1868,	William Henry Lewis, first African-American assistant U.S. attorney general, was born in Berkeley, Va. (d. 1949).
1912,	Gordon Alexander Parks, Sr., photo-journalist, was born in Fort Scott, Kan.
1924,	Shirley Anita Chisholm, nation's first African-American congresswoman, was born in Brooklyn, N.Y.
1953,	Albert Mike Espy, first African-American U.S. agriculture secretary, was born in Yazoo City, Miss.
1962,	Vincent Edward "Bo" Jackson, 1985 Heisman Trophy winner, was born in Bessemer, Ala.

NOVEMBER 30   *SPORTS LEGENDS*

CHARLES CLINTON SPAULDING

Businessman who was called **"Mr. Negro business."** Born on August 1, 1874, in Columbus County, Ga. Whitted School (1898). Worked as a dishwasher and bellboy, and managed a Durham African-American grocery store. Met John Merrick and Aaron Moore (1898), and joined the staff of their fledgling North Carolina Mutual Life Insurance Company, serving as their sole initial employee, custodian, bookkeeper, agent, marketing director, and as general manager (1898-1919); became a pioneer in saturation marketing, distributing matchbooks, fans, calendars, pens, paper weights, and advertising in African-American newspapers. Also served as a North Carolina Mutual Life Insurance Company: Board of Directors member (1900-1952), helping to launch two newspapers, a drugstore, the Mechanics & Farmers Bank, the Merrick-Moore-Spaulding Real Estate Company, a hosiery mill, and developing markets in 12 states and the District of Columbia; secretary-treasurer (1919-1923); president (1923-1952), guiding the insurance company through the Great Depression, and **building North Carolina Mutual into the nation's largest owned and operated African-American business**. Helped **organize the National Insurance Association (1921), making it the first African-American organization of its kind**; president of the National Negro Business League (1926); received the Harmon Foundation Gold Medal for distinguished achievement (1926); addressed the annual meeting of the Association for the Study of Negro Life and History (1932), where he stated that the business world offered many opportunities for economic advancement of African-Americans. Died on August 1, 1952, in Durham, N.C. Further reading, Walter Weare, _Black Business in New South, A Social History of North Carolina Mutual Life Insurance Company_ (1973).

---

on this day in history...

1854,	Joseph Charles Price, Livingstone College president, was born in Elizabeth City, N.C. (d. 1893).
1907,	Grace Towns Hamilton, Georgia's first African-American woman state legislator, was born in Atlanta, Ga. (d. 1992).
1907,	William "Chick" Webb, jazz musician, was born in Baltimore, Md.
1927,	Mary Leontyne Price, Grammy Award-winning opera diva, was born in Laurel, Miss.
1939,	Roberta Flack, Grammy Award-winning singer, was born in Asheville, N.C.
1989,	Ronald Brown became the first African-American chairman of the Democratic National Committee.

FEBRUARY 10　　　　　　　　　　　　　　　　　　　　　　　**BUSINESS LEADERS**

WENDELL OLIVER SCOTT

Pioneer African-American stock car racer.   Born on August 29, 1921, in Danville, Va.   Served in the U.S. Army as a paratrooper with the 101st Airborne unit; hauled moonshine from the hideaway stills to the Danville Fairgrounds; began stockcar racing at the Danville Fairgrounds (1947), finishing third and winning a purse of $50 in his first race, and going on to win 80 Sportsman and 40 Modified stock car races; entered a Sportsman event at Atlanta's Lakewood Speedway, but was not permitted on the track until an ambulance for African-Americans arrived (in case Scott wrecked, the ambulance for whites could not take him to the hospital); won the Virginia State Championship (1959), in a car named "Old Rusty." Made his Winston Cup Grand National debut at the Spartanburg Fairgrounds (1961), gaining sponsorship and support from automobile companies, but rarely driving the best cars and constantly being harassed by spectators and promoters; became the **first African-American to win a National Association for Stock Car Auto Racing (NASCAR) sponsored race** at a Jacksonville, Fla., racetrack (1963), where he won the 100-mile contest and had to file a protest to receive his $1,000 purse from the promoter, who had given it to the second place finisher--white driver Buck Baker; finished sixth in the NASCAR points standing (1966), tenth (1967), ninth (1968), and handing in his best year with earnings of over $27,000 (1969). Finished in the top ten 147 times throughout his career; retired from racing after breaking his pelvic bone in a crash during the Winston 500 (1973); portrayed by Richard Pryor in the biographical film, *Grease Lightning*. Died on December 22, 1990, in Detroit, Mich.   Further reading, *The African-American Encyclopedia* (1990).

---

on this day in history...

1919,   Pearl Primus, "queen of black dance," was born in Trinidad, West Indies.

NOVEMBER 29   SPORTS LEGENDS

ELLA PHILLIPS STEWART

Pharmacist, entrepreneur, editor, and clubwoman. Born on March 6, 1893, in Stringtown, Va. Storer College in Harper's Ferry, W.Va. (B.A., 1910); **first African-American woman graduate of the University of Pittsburgh School of Pharmacy** (Ph.D., 1916); University of Toledo. Worked as a bookkeeper and cashier for the Lincoln Drug Company in Pittsburgh, assistant pharmacist for Mendeleson Drug Company, and manager of Howard's Drugstore in Braddock, Penn; founded and operated Myers Pharmacy in Pittsburgh (1918-1920); moved to Ohio and worked as a pharmacist and purchasing agent for Youngstown City Hospital (1920-1922); **founded and operated Stewart's Pharmacy on City Park and Indiana Avenues in Toledo** (1922-1945), which became a gathering place and center of activities in the African-American community; entertained distinguished visitors to Toledo, such as Marian Anderson, Mary McLeod Bethune, W.E.B. DuBois, Carter Woodson, Benjamin O. Davis, and Rayford Logan; became an adviser on Negro affairs to First Lady Eleanor Roosevelt. Served as chaplain and president of the Ohio Association of Women's Clubs; national treasurer, editor-in-chief of *National Notes*, and president of the National Association of Colored Women (1936-1952), where she established a voucher system, a budget for officers and chairpersons, the Hallie Quinn Brown Scholarship Fund, a youth organization, a national life-membership drive, and began preserving historical records from local archives for deposit in the NACW headquarter files; goodwill ambassador for the U.S. State Department's Education Exchange Service (1954), studying conditions in Pakistan, India, Ceylon, Indonesia, and the Philippines; appointed to the executive board of the U.S. Commission of UNESCO. Died on November 27, 1987, in Toledo, Ohio. Further reading, Charles Harris Wesley, *The History of the National Association of Colored Women's Clubs* (1984).

on this day in history...

1945,	August Wilson, playwright of *Fences* and *Piano Lessons*, was born in Pittsburgh, Pa.
1990,	James "Buster" Douglas defeated Mike Tyson for the heavyweight boxing championship.
1990,	Nelson Mandela was released from a South African prison after nearly 27 years.

FEBRUARY 11   BUSINESS LEADERS

SUGAR RAY ROBINSON

Boxer who was called **"pound for pound the greatest fighter in the world."**   Born Walker Smith on May 3, 1920, in Detroit, Mich.   Began boxing at the Salem-Cresent Athletic Club in Harlem; obtained the name Ray Robinson from a retired boxer, and "Sugar" from his manager's "sweet as sugar" response to a New York sports writer; turned in 69 KO's in 85 amateur bouts; won the Golden Gloves featherweight title (1939), and the lightweight title (1940). Won his first professional fight with a second round KO of Joe Escheveria in New York City (1940); defeated the lightweight champion Sammy Angott, in a ten-round nontitle bout (1941); served in the U.S. Army during World War II; became the undisputed welterweight champion of the world (1946), after winning a 15-round decision over Tommy Bell at Madison Square Garden. Defended his welterweight title by defeating Jimmy Doyle, Chuck Taylor, Bernard Docusen, Kid Gavilan, and Charlie Fusari; won the middleweight championship by defeating Jake La Motta in Chicago (1951), vacating his welterweight crown; lost his middleweight belt to European champion Randy Turpin (1951), winning it back two months later in a rematch at the Polo Grounds in New York City; announced his retirement (1952), and became an actor. Announced his return to the ring (1954); KO'd Bobo Olson in the second round at Chicago Stadium (1955), regaining the middleweight crown; lost the title to Gene Fullmer in New York City (1957), winning it back five months later in a rematch at Chicago Stadium to become the **first fighter in the history of the middleweight division to win the title four times;** lost the title again, regaining it in a rematch against Carmen Basilio (1958), for an unprecedented fifth middleweight title; fought his last bout against Joey Archer in Pittsburgh (1965). Died on April 12, 1989.   Further reading, Arthur R. Ashe, Jr., *Hard Road to Glory* (1988).

---

on this day in history...

1929,   Berry Gordy, Jr., founder of Motown Records, was born in Detroit, Mich.
1950,   Frederick M. Jones patented a two-cycle gasoline engine.
1981,   Pam McAllister Johnson became the editor of the *Ithica Journal*.

NOVEMBER 28   *SPORTS LEGENDS*

MADAME C.J. WALKER

Entrepreneur, socialite, and philanthropist who became the **nation's first self-made woman millionaire.** Born Sarah Breedlove on December 23, 1867, in Delta, La. Moved to St. Louis (1887), gaining employment as a washwoman; invented a hair softener and a special straightening comb for African-American women (1905), calling it the "Walker System" of treating hair; relocated to Denver (1906), where she demonstrated her method door-to-door, organized her agents into clubs, trained operatives for her system, allocated franchises and provided all relevant cosmetics and equipment, and eventually reached an annual payroll of over $200,000 with some 3,000 mostly women employees; opened a second office in Pittsburgh (1908), with her daughter A'Lelia as manager; moved both Denver and Pittsburgh offices to Indianapolis (1910), where she had built a factory to manufacture her facial creams, Madame C.J. Walker Hair Grower, pomade, and other products. Arrived in New York City (1913), where she became one of the foremost social leaders of her time; built Villa Lewaro at Irvington-on-Hudson (1917), a mansion designed by the African-American architect Vertner Tandy; established Lelia College to train young women in the "Walker System," which turned into a chain of salons; contributed to the NAACP, St. Louis and Indianapolis nursing homes, Palmer Memorial Institute, a Tuskegee Institute scholarship fund for young women, private colleges, African-American YWCA branches, and orphanages; founded an academy for girls in West Africa. Died on May 25, 1919, in New York City. Further reading, Russell L. Adams, *Great Negroes Past ant Present* (1991).

on this day in history...

1909,	The National Association for the Advancement of Colored People was formed.
1919,	Eddie Robinson of Grambling University, college football's winningest football coach, was born in Jackson, La.
1934,	William Felton Russell, first African-American to coach a major sports team (Boston Celtics), was born in Monroe, La.
1948,	Nancy C. Leftenant, U.S. Army first lieutenant, became the first African-American nurse in the Regular Army Nurse Corps.
1955,	Arsenio Hall, first successful African-American late night talk show host, was born in Cleveland, Ohio.
1989,	Barbara Clementine Harris became the first woman Anglican bishop.

FEBRUARY 12   **BUSINESS LEADERS**

JACKIE ROBINSON

Athlete who **broke major league baseball's color barrier.** Born Jack Roosevelt Robinson on January 31, 1919, in Cairo, Ga. Pasadena Junior College; University of California at Los Angeles, where he lettered in baseball, basketball, track, and football. Worked as an assistant athletic director for the National Youth Administration; played professional football for the Los Angeles Bulldogs (1941); entered Officers' Candidate School at Fort Riley, Kan. (1941), and served in the U.S. Army as a first lieutenant during World War II. Coached basketball at Sam Houston College in Austin, Texas (1944-1945); signed with the Kansas City Monarchs of the National Negro Baseball League (1945); met Brooklyn Dodgers President Branch Rickey (1945), and signed with the Dodgers farm team in the International League, the Montreal Royals, for a signing bonus of $3,500 and a $600-a-month salary; hit three singles, smashed a three-run homer, stole two bases and scored four runs in the Royals opening day 14-1 victory over the Jersey City Giants (1946), and led his team to the 1946 International League pennant, batting .349 driving in 66 runs, stealing 40 bases, scoring 113 runs, and fielding .985 at second base. Opened the season, playing the first base with the Brooklyn Dodgers, against the Boston Braves at Ebbets Field (1947), becoming the first African-American baseball player with the majors in modern times; selected by the Baseball Writers Association as National League Rookie of the Year (1947), after batting .297, stealing 29 bases, scoring 125 runs, and helping the Dodgers get to the World Series; won the National League's MVP award (1949), with a .342 average, 37 stolen bases, 122 runs, and 124 RBIs; led the Dodgers to six pennants; became the **first African-American to be inducted into the Baseball Hall of Fame** (1962). Died on October 24, 1972, in Stamford, Conn. Further reading, Columbus Salley, *The Black 100* (1993).

---

on this day in history...

1942,   Jimi Hendrix, pioneering rock guitarist, was born in Seattle, Wash. (d. 1970).
1944,   George Thomas "Mickey" Leland, former Texas congressman (1979-1989), was born in Lubbock, Texas (d. 1989).
1957,   Dorothy I. Height was elected president of the National Council of Negro Women.
1990,   Charles R. Johnson won the National Book Award for his novel *Middle Passage*.

NOVEMBER 27   *SPORTS LEGENDS*

MAGGIE LENA WALKER

Businesswoman, civil rights activist, and lecturer who became **one of the nation's wealthiest and most influential women of the early 20th century**. Born on July 15, 1867, in Richmond, Va. Armstrong Normal School (1883). Taught public school in Richmond and worked as an agent for the Woman's Union Insurance Company; became executive secretary-treasurer of the Independent Order of St. Luke (1902), a fraternal business organization that was created for African-Americans to help the sick and bury the dead during the post-Civil War period and to encourage self-help and racial solidarity; kept the Order's books, verified claims, collected dues, and built the membership to over 100,000; began publishing the *St. Luke Herald* (1902), to provide increased communication between the community and the order; **founder and president of the St. Luke Penny Savings Bank** (1903-1932), whose motto was "Bring It All Back Home;" started a department store called the St. Luke Emporium. Organized the Richmond Council of Negro Women (1912), where she raised funds for the Piedmont Tuberculosis Sanitarium for African-Americans in Burkeville, Va., a community center, and a visiting nurse program for African-Americans; co-founder of the Richmond branch of the NAACP and later became president of the state branch; served as vice president of the Negro Organization Society of Virginia, trustee of Virginia Union University and the National Training School in Washington. Died on December 15, 1934, in Richmond, Va. Further reading, Sadie I. Daniels, *Women Builders* (1931).

---

on this day in history...

1907,	William P. Dabney founded the *Cincinnati Union* weekly newspaper.
1920,	Rube Foster founded the Negro Baseball League.
1970,	Joseph L. Searles became the first African-American member of the New York Stock Exchange.

FEBRUARY 13 BUSINESS LEADERS

PAUL BUSTILL ROBESON

Athlete, singer, actor, scholar, author, spokesman, Black Nationalist, and civil rights activist.   Born on April 9, 1898, in Princeton, N.J.   Rutgers University Phi Beta Kappa and valedictorian (A.B., 1919), winning 13 varsity letters in sports and a spot on the **Walter Camp's All-American college football team his junior and senior year**; Columbia University (LL.B., 1923).   Became a professional football player, playing with the Hammond Pros (1920), Akron (1921), and the Milwaukee Badgers (1922); admitted to the New York bar, obtained a position with a New York law firm, but left the bar after a stenographer refused to take down a memorandum for a him because of his race (1923). Began acting and appeared: in Torrences' *Simon the Cyrenian* at the Harlem YMCA (1921), making his acting debut; as "Jim" in Wilborg's *Taboo, or The Voodoo* in London (1922); with the Provincetown Players as "Jim Harris" in O'Neill's *All God's Chillun Got Wings* (1924), which caused a controversy when Robeson acted opposite of white actress Mary Blair; as "Brutus Jones" in the revival of *The Emperor Jones* (1924, 1925), which brought him international critical acclaim; as "Crown" in *Porgy and Bess* (1928); as "Joe" in the musical production of *Show Boat* (1928), singing "Ol' Man River;" in the title role in Shakespeare's *Othello* (1930, 1943), *Toussaint L'Ouverture* (1936), and *John Henry* (1940). Used elements of African-American culture, such as spirituals, folk songs, and dialect as his weapons to inform whites of unjust conditions among African-Americans; learned 20 different languages and spent most of his time in Europe (1927-1939), making several trips to Russia, speaking out against the Nazis, entertained Loyalist troops during the Spanish Civil War, supporting the Committee to Aid China and **co-founding the Council of African Affairs for the "struggle of the African masses..."**.   Honored with the American Academy of Arts and Letters Medal (1944), NAACP Spingarn Medal (1945), Ira Alderidge Award from the Association for the Study of Afro-American Life and History (1970), and the National Urban League's Whitney M. Young, Jr., National Memorial Award (1972); member of Alpha Phi Alpha fraternity. Died on January 23, 1967, in Philadelphia, Pa.   Further reading, Paul Robeson, *Here I Stand* (1971).

---

on this day in history...

1866,	Rust College was founded in Holly Springs, Miss.
1890,	Savannah State College was founded in Savannah, Ga.
1933,	William Lucy, Coalition of Black Trade Unionist president, was born in Memphis, Tenn.
1969,	Shawn Kemp, Seattle Supersonics All-Star, was born in Elkhart, Ind.

EARTHA M.M. WHITE

Businesswoman, community leader, educator, and social worker.   Born on November 8, 1876, in Jacksonville, Fla. Madam Thurber's National Conservatory of Music; Florida Baptist Academy.   Toured with the nation's first African-American opera company (1895-1896), traveling throughout the U.S., Europe, and Asia; taught at the Stanton School located just outside of Jacksonville; worked as a secretary for the Afro-American Life Insurance Company, saving the company's records from the great fire that destroyed Jacksonville; opened a department store that catered to African-Americans (1904), and later owned a dry-goods store, a general store, an employment agency, a janitorial service, a real estate business, and a steam laundry; eventually **built her investment portfolio to over one million dollars**. Became **Jacksonville's first African-American social worker and census taker**; a charter member of the National Business League (1900); established the Boy's Improvement Club (1904); conducted Bible studies at the Duval County prison; established a mission on Jacksonville's West Ashley Street, which served as a haven for transients and the homeless and hungry. Directed the War Camp Community Services in Savannah during World War I; the only African-American woman to attend the White House meeting of the Council of National Defense; **helped A. Phillip Randolph organize the March on Washington to protest employment discrimination** (1941), which led to Executive Order 8802 banning discrimination in employment in the federal government and to the Fair Employment Practices Committee; initiated the building of the 120-bed Eartha M. White Nursing Home; honored as the official historian of the National Negro Business League (1973), with the Booker T. Washington Symbol of Service Award. Died on January 18,1974, in Jacksonville, Fla. Further reading, Lawrence E. Gray, "Eartha M. White," *Dictionary of Social Welfare in America* (1986).

on this day in history...

1936,	William R. Norwood, United Airlines' first African-American pilot, was born in Centralia, Ill.
1939,	Leroy Keith, Morehouse College president, was born in Chattanooga, Tenn.
1946,	Gregory Oliver Hines, Tony Award-winning dancer and actor, was born in New York City.
1967,	Lyda Moore Merrick, founder of *Negro Braille Magazine*, died in Durham, N.C. (b. 1890).

FEBRUARY 14   **BUSINESS LEADERS**

JESSE OWENS

Olympic track and field champion, who was known as the "ebony antelope."   Born James Cleveland Owens on September 12, 1913, in Danville, Ala.   Ohio State University.   Grew up in Cleveland, and worked his way through college as an elevator operator; competed in the Big Ten championships in Ann Arbor, Mich. (1935), where he made track and field history by long-jumping 26'8-1/4"--a world record, sprinting 100 yards in 9.4 seconds--tying his own world record, running the 200-yard clash in 20.3 seconds--another world record, and winning the 220-low hurdles in 22.6 seconds--another world record, which became known as **"the greatest single day in the history of man's athletic achievement."** Won four gold medals in the 1936 Summer Olympics at Berlin, Germany, winning: the 100-meter dash in world record time--10.3 seconds; the broad jump in Olympic record time--26'5-1/4"; the 200-meter dash in Olympic record time--20.7 seconds; the 400-meter relay, where the American team of Ralph Metcalfe, Foy Draper, and Frank Wykoff set a world record--39.8 seconds. Held 11 world records throughout his career; **selected as the greatest track and field athlete of the first half century** by the Associated Press (1950); awarded an honorary doctorate from Ohio State University (1972); presented with the Theodore Roosevelt Award (1974), for his collegiate athletic contributions; named a member of the U.S. Olympic Committee (1976); awarded the Presidential Medal of Freedom (1976). Died on March 30, 1980.   Further reading, James A. Page, *Black Olympian Medalists* (1991).

---

on this day in history...

1901,	Howard Hamilton Mackey, Sr., Howard University School of Architecture and City Planning founder and president, was born in Philadelphia, Pa. (d. 1987).
1912,	John H. Sengstacke, founder of the Negro Newspapers Publishers Association, was born in Savannah, Ga.
1941,	Annie Marie Bullock ("Tina Turner"), Grammy Award-winning recording artist, was born in Nutbush, Tenn.
1955,	The Interstate Commerce Commission banned segregation in all buses, waiting rooms, and travel coaches involved in interstate travel.

NOVEMBER 25   *SPORTS LEGENDS*

RICHARD ROBERT WRIGHT, SR.

Educator, politician, editor, and banker.   Born into slavery in 1855 in Dalton, Ga.   Valedictorian of the first graduating class of Atlanta University (B.A., 1876); University of Pennsylvania Wharton School of Finance.   Escaped slavery and joined the Union Army during the Civil War; principal of an elementary school in Cuthbert, Ga.; **organized farmers cooperatives and Georgia's first African-American county fair**; organizer and first president of the Georgia State Teachers Association (1878), and began publishing its *Weekly Journal of Progress* and *Weekly Sentinel*; represented Georgia African-Americans at the First National Conference of Colored Men of the U.S. (Nashville, 1879), where he planted the seeds for his later participation in politics. Founded Ware High School in Augusta (1880), Georgia's first public high school for African-Americans; delegate to the Republican National Convention (1880-1896), and became a member of Georgia's Republican State Central Committee; special agent of the U.S. Interior Department for land development in Alabama (1885); served as paymaster in the Army, during the Spanish-American War, with a rank of major; president of the State College of Industry for Colored Youth in Savannah (1891-1921); organized the Negro Civic Improvement League in Savannah (1893). **Co-founded the Citizens & Southern Bank & Trust Company in Philadelphia** (1921); organized the Haitian Coffee & Products Trading Company (1935); president of the National Association of Presidents of A&M Colleges (1906-1919), and of the National Association of Teachers in Colored Schools (1908-1912); helped establish the National Freedom Day Association and a commemorative stamp honoring Booker T. Washington. Died on July 2, 1947, in Philadelphia, Pa.   Further reading, Elizabeth Ross Haynes, *The Black Boy of Atlanta* (1952).

---

on this day in history...

1924,	Angela Dorothea Ferguson, sickle cell anemia researcher, was born in Washington, D.C.
1968,	Henry Lewis of the New Jersey Symphony became the first African-American to lead a symphony orchestra in the U.S.
1978,	Leon Spinks defeated Muhammad Ali for the heavyweight boxing championship.

FEBRUARY 15   BUSINESS LEADERS

ISAAC MURPHY

Three-time Kentucky Derby-winning jockey. Born Isaac Burns on January 1, 1861, in Lexington, Ky. Worked for the Owings and Williams Stable, galloping horses; rode in his first race in Louisville (1875), and won his first race on Glentina, at Crab Orchard Park in Lexington (1876), which was during a period of time when African-American jockeys were the norm. Won 49 out of 51 starts at Saratoga, N.Y. (1882); won the Hindoo Stakes (1883, 1885, and 1886), four of the first five runnings of the American Derby (1884, 1885, 1886, and 1888), and the Latonia Derby (1887); won a record three Kentucky Derbys, riding to the winner's circle on (Buchanan, 1884; Riley, 1890; Kingman, 1891), a record that was not surpassed until 1948, when Eddie Arcaro won his fourth on Citation; also won the Swift, Travers, and the Saratoga Cup. Won his most memorable race by a head at the Coney Island Jockey Club, Sheepshead Bay, New York City (1890), while riding Salvator, he defeated jockey Snapper Garrison in what became known as the "Garrison finish;" won almost 45 percent of his starts during his horse racing career; became the **first jockey to be voted into the Jockey Hall of Fame** at the National Museum of Racing, Saratoga Springs, N.Y. (1955). Died on February 12, 1896, in·Lexington, Ky. Further reading, Jack Orr, _The Black Athlete: His Story in American History_ (1969).

---

on this day in history...

1883,   Edwin Bancroft Henderson, "father of black sports," was born in Washington, D.C.
1920,   Pierre Sutton, entrepreneur and civic leader, was born in San Antonio, Texas.
1935,   Ronald Vernie Dellums of California, chairman of the U.S. House Armed Services Committee, was born in Oakland, Calif.
1938,   Oscar Palmer Robertson, first African-American to lead the NBA in assists, was born in Charlotte, Tenn.

NOVEMBER 24   *SPORTS LEGENDS*

MARIA LOUISE BALDWIN

Educator, elocutionist, and community worker nicknamed "Mollie," who became **New England's first African-American woman school master**. Born on September 13, 1856, in Cambridge, Mass. Cambridge Training School for Teachers (1875); Harvard University; Boston University. Taught in Chestertown, Md.; primary grade teacher at Agassiz Grammar School in Cambridge, Mass. (1881-1889), principal (1889-1915), and school master (1915-1922); instructor in summer normal classes at Hampton Institute and the Institute for Colored Youth in Cheyney; developed a large private library; held weekly reading classes in her home for African-American students at Harvard University, who included W.E.B. DuBois; lectured throughout the country on such notables as Paul Laurence Dunbar, George Washington, Abraham Lincoln, Ulysses Grant, Thomas Jefferson, and James Madison, and on such topics as women's suffrage, poetry, and history. Worked with: the Women's Era Club; the Boston Banneker Club, a scholarly literary society where she served as president; the Omar Circle; the Twentieth Century Club of Boston; Cantabrigia Club; the Boston Ethical Society; the Teacher's Association, for whom she lectured throughout New England; the League of Women for Community Service, an organization that she organized and served as president. **Gave the Washington Birthday Memorial Address before the Brooklyn Institute of Arts and Science on "The Life and Services of the late Harriet Beecher Stowe" (1897), becoming the first woman invited to deliver the annual address**; became a member of the Church of the Disciples in Boston (1907); addressed the council of the Robert Gould Shaw House Association at the Copley Plaza Hotel in Boston (1922). Died on January 9, 1922, in Boston, Mass. Further reading, Benjamin G. Brawley, *Negro Builders and Heroes* (1937).

---

on this day in history...

1904,   James Baskett, Special Academy Award-winning actor from *Song of the South,* was born in Indianapolis, Ind. (d. 1948).

1957,   Levar Burton, actor, was born in Landsthul, Germany.

1972,   Wilt Chamberlain became the first NBA player to score 30,000 points.

FEBRUARY 16   **CIVIC LEADERS**

RALPH HAROLD METCALFE

Olympic track and field champion and U.S. congressman (92nd-95th). Born on May 29, 1910, in Atlanta, Ga. Marquette University (1936); University of Southern California (1939).   NCAA and AAU 100 and 200-meter champion (1932-1936), earning him the title of the "world's fastest human;" competed in the Olympics, winning a silver medal in the 100-meter run in Olympic-record time, 10.38 seconds (Los Angeles, 1932), a bronze medal in the 200-meter run, 21.51 seconds (Los Angeles, 1932), a **gold medal along with Jesse Owens in the 4x 100-meter relay in the world record time**, 39.8 seconds (Berlin, 1936), and a silver medal, second to Jesse Owens, in a 10.4 second 100-meter run (Berlin, 1936). Political science teacher and track coach at Xavier University in New Orleans (1936-1942); served in the U.S. Army Transportation Corps during World War II as a first lieutenant (1942-1945); director of the Chicago Commission on Human Relations' civil rights department (1945-1949); **Illinois State Athletic commissioner** (1949-1952); elected Third Ward Democratic committeeman (1952); Chicago city councilman (1955-1970), where he chaired the housing committee. Illinois 1st District Democratic (1971-1978), serving on the Merchant Marine and Fisheries and on the Interstate and Foreign Commerce Committees; fought for the improved safety of residents in public housing projects, to expand the availability of home improvement loans, to eliminate the practice of "redlining," to improve the climate for minority-owned business, for legislation to bring minority firms into the revitalization projects of the nation's railroads, for passage of the Panama Canal treaty, and for better airline safety; broke from the Chicago Democratic machine (1972), over the issue of police brutality in the African-American community; member of the board of directors of the U.S. Olympic Committee (1969-1975). Died on October 10, 1978, in Chicago, Ill.   Further reading, Patrick Griffin, *The Black Olympians* (1986).

---

on this day in history...

1897,	John Lee Lowe patented a pencil sharpener.
1946,	Bobby Rush, Illinois 1st District congressman, was born in Albany, Ga.
1965,	Mike Garrett, University of Southern California athletic director, was named the Heisman Trophy winner.

NOVEMBER 23   *SPORTS LEGENDS*

EVA D. BOWLES

Educator and organizational worker.   Born on January 24, 1875, in Albany, Ohio.   Ohio State University; Columbia University.   Became the first African-American teacher at Chandler Normal School in Lexington, Ky.; taught in St. Augustine, Fla., Raleigh, N.C., and at St. Paul's Normal and Industrial Institute in Lawrenceville, Va. **Director of a project for young African-American women at Harlem's 137th Street Branch of the YWCA (1906-1908), which became the nation's largest African-American YWCA**; appointed the first African-American caseworker in Associated Charities of Columbus, Ohio (1908-1913); secretary of a subcommittee on Negro work for the national board of the YWCA (1913-1917). **Director of the Colored Work Committee of the YWCA's War Work Council** (1917-1932), where she set up many recreational facilities in industrial centers throughout the nation, in communities near Army camps, and employed a number of prominent African-American women, including Crystal Bird, Sara Brown, Iona Whipper, and Ruth Fisher; established 15 hostess houses in Army camps during World War I, including Camp Upton, N.Y. Supported an interracial movement in the YWCA; served as an executive of the National Colored Merchants Association, acting secretary of the West End Branch of the Cincinnati YWCA (1934-1935), and as a Harlem organizer for the Wendell Willkie Republicans. Died on June 14, 1943, in Richmond, Va.   Further reading, Jean Blackwell Hutson, "Eva del Vakia Bowles," *Notable American Women: 1607-1950* (1971).

on this day in history...

1936,   James Nathaniel Brown, professional football legend, was born in St. Simon's, Ga.
1938,   Mary Francis Berry, the nation's first African-American chief educational officer (deputy secretary of the Department of Health, Education and Welfare), was born in Nashville, Tenn.
1941,   Wellington Webb, Denver's first African-American mayor, was born in Chicago, Ill.
1942,   Huey P. Newton, co-founder of the Black Panther Party, was born in Monroe, La. (d. 1989).
1949,   Dennis Green, Minnesota Vikings head coach, was born in Harrisburg, Pa.
1963,   Michael Jeffrey Jordan, NBA superstar, was born in Brooklyn, N.Y.

FEBRUARY 17   **CIVIC LEADERS**

JOE LOUIS

Boxing champion, nicknamed the "Brown Bomber," who became the **first African-American to become an idol to all Americans, regardless of color.** Born Joe Louis Barrow on May 13, 1914, in Lexington, Ala. Started boxing at Brewster's East Side Gym in Detroit (1930); boxed as an amateur, while working for the Ford Motor Company (1930-1934); won the National Amateur Athletic Union light-heavyweight title in St. Louis (1934); defeated Jack Kracken in his first professional fight, in a first round KO in St. Louis (1934), going on to defeat Davis, Udell, Kranz, Everett, Borchuk, Wiater, Sykes, O'Dowd, Poreda, Massera, Ramage, Perroni, Birkie, Ramage, Barry, Brown, Lazer, Benton, Toles, Davis, Stanton, Carnera, and Levinsky. Fought Max Bear (on his wedding day) in front of 95,000 people at Yankee Stadium, knocking him out in the fourth round (1935), making him the most famous African-American in the world, and a symbol of African-American triumph over white domination and supremacy; defeated Paolino Uzcudun (1935), becoming the **first African-American to fight in a main event at Madison Square Gardens;** took a 27-0 record into the much anticipated bout against German Max Schmeling (1936), losing in the 12th round KO. Defeated Jimmy Braddock in the eighth round TKO at Comiskey Park in Chicago for the heavyweight championship of the world (1937); destroyed the pride of Nazi Germany, Max Schmeling, in front of 70,000 spectators in New York City (1935), avenging his only professional loss; successfully defended his crown until his retirement (1949), defeating Abe Simon, Buddy Bear, Billy Conn, and Jersey Joe Walcott; came out of retirement (1950), losing his last professional fight to Rocky Marciano; became a professional wrestler, and later worked as a greeter at Caesar's Palace in Las Vegas. Died on April 12, 1981, in Las Vegas, Nev. Further reading, Arthur R. Ashe, Jr., _Hard Road to Glory_ (1988).

---

on this day in history...

1930,	The Nation of Islam was founded in Detroit, Mich.
1942,	Guion S. Bluford, first African-American in space, was born in Philadelphia, Pa.
1942,	Harry Edwards, renowned sociologist, was born in St. Louis, Mo.
1962,	Cleo Fields, Louisiana 4th District congressman, was born in Baton Rouge, La.
1986,	George Branham won the Brunswick Memorial World Open, becoming the first African-American bowler to win a PBA title.
1988,	Bob Watson was named assisted general manager of the Houston Astros.

NOVEMBER 22   *SPORTS LEGENDS*

FANNIE JACKSON COPPIN

Educator, civic leader, and religious activist. Born into slavery in 1837 in Washington, D.C. Rhode Island State Normal School; Oberlin College (B.A., 1865), where she was elected class poet and to the nation's oldest women's club--the Young Ladies Literary Society. Established evening classes in Oberlin, Ohio (1863), where she taught illiterate newly-freed slaves; became the first African-American teacher in the preparatory department at Oberlin College (1865); principal of the female department of the Institute for Colored Youth in Philadelphia (1865-1869), principal of the entire school (1869-1902); **responsible for the establishment of Philadelphia's first trade school for African-Americans**. Began writing a regular column entitled "Women's Department" for the *Christian Recorder*, in which she reported on the achievements of women in education, employment, and on cases of discrimination against African-American women; organized a World's Fair in Philadelphia (1879), to keep the *Christian Recorder* from dissolving; elected president of the local Women's Mite Missionary Society (1881); became **national president of the Women's Home and Foreign Missionary Society of the AME Church** and represented the organization at the Centenary of Missions Conference in London; opened a home for needy young women in Philadelphia (1888); established the Women's Exchange and Girls' Home (1894), which provided housing for students and gave instruction in cooking, dressmaking, and home economics; founding member and a vice president of the National Association of Colored Women (1897). Died on January 21, 1913, in Philadelphia, Pa. Further reading, Linda M. Perkins, *Fanny Jackson Coppin and the Institute for Colored Youth, 1865-1902* (1987).

---

on this day in history...

1867,	Augusta Institute [now Morehouse College of Atlanta] was founded in Augusta, Ga.
1894,	Paul Revere Williams, "architect to the stars," was born in Los Angeles, Calif. (d. 1980).
1924,	Vel Rogers Phillips, Wisconsin's first African-American secretary of state, was born in Milwaukee, Wis.
1931,	Toni Morrison, first African-American Nobel Prize for Literature winner, was born in Lorain, Ohio.
1941,	Emma C. Chappell, founder and CEO of United Bank of Philadelphia, was born in Philadelphia, Pa.
1965,	Jimmie Lee Jackson, a civil rights movement martyr, was fatally shot while on a voter registration drive in Alabama.

FEBRUARY 18   **CIVIC LEADERS**

WILLIAM HENRY LEWIS

Athlete, attorney, politician, and government official.   Born in November 20, 1868, in Berkeley, Va.   Virginia Normal and Industrial Institute; Amherst College (B.A., 1892), where he was elected class orator, and became captain of the football team, the games first "roving lineman," and the **first African-American to be named a college football All-American**; Harvard Law School, where he became the first African-American to play on the Harvard football team. Cambridge, Mass., city councilman (1899-1903); Massachusetts state representative (1902-1903); assistant U.S. attorney for the Boston area (1903-1906); head of the Naturalization Bureau for New England (1907); assistant U.S. attorney for New England (1907-1911); served as the **first African-American assistant U.S. attorney general of the United States** (1911-1913), making him the highest appointed African-American federal official up to that time; became **one of the first African-American to be admitted to the American Bar Association;** operated a private practice (1913-1949), where he earned a reputation as one of Boston's leading criminal lawyers. Died in 1949 in Boston, Mass.   Further reading, Harold Wade, Jr., _Black Men of Amherst_ (1976).

---

on this day in history...

1841,	John Francis Cook founded the First Colored Presbyterian Church (15th Street) in Washington, D.C.
1865,	Shaw University was founded in Raleigh, N.C.
1882,	Lawrence C. Jones, founder of Piney Woods Country Life School in Mississippi, was born in St. Joseph, Mo. (d. 1975).
1904,	Coleman Hawkins, first jazz musician to gain fame on the saxophone, was born in St. Joseph, Mo. (d. 1969).
1936,	James DePriest, Oregon Symphony Orchestra musical director, was born in Philadelphia, Pa.
1969,	George Kenneth Griffey, Jr., Seattle Mariners All-Star known as "The Kid," was born in Donora, Pa.

NOVEMBER 21   SPORTS LEGENDS

JOHN CAMPBELL DANCY, JR.

Community leader nicknamed **"Mr. Urban League."** Born in 1888 in Salisbury, N.C. University of Pennsylvania (B.A., 1910). Worked as a waiter on boats on the Great Lakes during the summers; served as a school principal in Clairmount, W.Va.; secretary of the Negro YMCA in Norfolk (1911-1916); probation officer in the Children's Court of New York City (1916), where he became active in the Urban League and Big Brother Movements. Served as **executive director of the Detroit Urban League (1918-1960)**, where he convinced the United Community Services to hire an African-American stenographer, helped break Detroit's residential segregation policies, introduced hundreds of African-Americans to art and music, established the Green Pastures Camp, and was said to have had the greatest impact of any individual on race relations in Detroit. Served as a member of the Detroit House of Corrections Commission, secretary-treasurer of the Parkside Hospital, director of the United Community Services, member of the Metropolitan Planning Commission, president of the Detroit Library Commission, patron of the Detroit Symphony Orchestra, and as a member of the Governor's Commission on Youth Problems. Honored by the mayor of Detroit with "John C. Dancy Day" (1960), at his retirement dinner; given the annual Amity Day Award (1963), by the Women's Division of the American Jewish Congress; awarded the John Phillips Award (1967), by the trustees of the Phillip-Exeter Academy. Died on September 10, 1968, in Detroit, Mich. Further reading, William J. Walls, _The African-Methodist Episcopal Zion Church, Reality of the Black Church_ (1974).

---

on this day in history...

1902, John William Sublett Bubbles, "father of tap soul," was born in Louisville, Ky. (d. 1986).
1919, The First Pan-African Congress, organized by W.E.B. DuBois, met at the Grand Hotel in Paris, France.
1920, Eileen Southern, African-American music historian, was born in Minneapolis, Minn.
1940, William "Smokey" Robinson, Grammy Award-winning singer and songwriter, was born in Detroit, Mich.
1992, John Singleton became the first African-American director to be nominated for an Academy Award (for the _Boyz N The Hood_).

FEBRUARY 19   **CIVIC LEADERS**

JACK JOHNSON

Boxer who became the **first person of African descent to gain worldwide distinction in athletics**. Born John Arthur Johnson on March 31, 1878, in Galveston, Tex. Began boxing, not for sport, but for survival purposes; gained a reputation as a fighter, while working on the Galveston docks; turned pro (1897), fighting in Illinois, Pittsburgh, New York City, Boston, Galveston, and eventually became a contender for the heavyweight championship. Pursued the heavyweight champion half-way around the world before he could obtain a title match, finally catching up with him in Australia; defeated Tommy Burns in the 14th round of a heavyweight title bout in Sidney, Australia (1908), becoming the **first world heavyweight boxing champion of African descent**, sending a shockwave throughout "white America" that launched an immediate search for a "great white hope" to regain the title. Defeated former heavyweight champion James Jefferies in the 15th round of a $100,000 title bout in Reno (1910), causing race riots across the U.S.; sentenced to a year in prison for violating the Mann Act, commonly known as the "White Slave Law", after charges were pressed by the mother of one of his secretaries (1913), prompting him to flee the country to France; fought to a 10-round draw with American heavyweight Jim Johnson in Paris (1913), which was the first all-Black heavyweight title bout; lost his title to Kansas native Jess Willard in the 26th round in front of 30,000 spectators at an Havanna racetrack infield (1915), with Johnson later claiming to have thrown the fight to appease certain "powers that be" and ease his entrance back into the U.S., only to serve a year in Leavenworth anyway (1920); became a lecturer at Times Square's Hubert Museum in New York City. Died on June 11, 1946, in Raleigh, N.C. Further reading, Ocania Chalk, *Pioneers of Black Sports* (1975).

---

on this day in history...

1962, President Kennedy issued Executive Order 11063, banning racial discrimination in federally-assisted housing.
1963, Mike Powell, Sullivan Award-winning Olympic track and field champion, was born in Philadelphia, Pa.
1981, The Negro Ensemble Company's production of Charles Fuller's *A Soldier's Play* won a Pulitzer Prize.

NOVEMBER 20   *SPORTS LEGENDS*

OPHELIA SETTLE EGYPT

Social worker, educator, and author of children's books. Born on February 20, 1903, in Clarksville, Texas. Howard University (B.A., 1925); University of Pennsylvania (M.A., 1928); Columbia University School of Social Work (M.S., 1944); University of Pennsylvania. Taught at the Orange County Training School in Chapel Hill, N.C. (1925-1926); **chief field researcher at Fisk University (1928-1933), where she helped Charles S. Johnson build the school's social science department**; conducted research on the African-American in Tennessee, which resulted in the publication of *Shadow of the Plantation* and *The Negro Graduate*; published *Unwritten History of Slavery* (1945), which contained a compilation of interviews with over 100 former slaves from Tennessee and Kentucky; directed a research study on African-American sharecroppers in South Georgia and Macon County, Ala. Became a social worker for a St. Louis relief agency during the Great Depression; head of social services at Flint Goodridge Hospital in New Orleans (1934-1939); moved to Washington to work with E. Franklin Frazier at Howard University (1939), where she served as professor in the School of Social Work; probation officer in the Juvenile Court of Washington (1950-1952); executive director of the Iona R. Whipper Home for unmarried African-American mothers in the Washington (1952-1954); caseworker for the Family and Child Services (1954-1956); **founder and director of the Planned Parenthood of Metropolitan Washington's Parklands Neighborhood Clinic** (1956-1968); family planning consultant for the U.S. Department of Health, Education, and Welfare's Office of Economic Opportunity (1968-1970). Served as a member of the National Association of Social Workers, Black Writers' Workshop of Washington, and as president of the Garfield-Douglass Civic Association. Died on May 25, 1984, in Washington, D.C.   Further reading, Special Collections, Fisk University Library.

---

on this day in history...

1924,	Sidney Poitier, first African-American to win an Oscar for best actor (for *Lillies of the Fields*), was born in Miami, Fla.
1931,	Emmett Paige, Jr., U.S. Army Signal Corps' first African-American general, was born in Jacksonville, Fla.
1936,	Sharpe Jones, Newark mayor, was born in Jacksonville, Fla.
1937,	Nancy Wilson, Emmy and Grammy Award-winning singer, was born in Chillicothe, Ohio.

FEBRUARY 20   CIVIC LEADERS

NELL CECILIA JACKSON

A pioneer in women's track and field.   Born on July 1, 1929, in Athens, Ga.   Tuskegee Institute (B.A., 1951); Springfield College (M.A., 1953); University of Iowa (Ph.D., 1962).   Member of the Tuskegee Institute Track and Field Club; set an American record time of 24.2 seconds in the 200-meter relay; became an All-American sprinter and a member of the 1948 U.S. Olympic team; placed second in the 200-meter relay and first as a member of the 400-meter relay (1951), during the Pan-American games. Taught physical education and coached track at Tuskegee Institute, Illinois State University, University of Illinois, and Michigan State University; served as **Michigan State University women's athletic director** and was appointed professor and director of athletics and physical education at State University of New York at Binghamton; author of *Track and Field for Girls and Women* (1968). Became the **first African-American head track coach of an Olympic team** (Melbourne, 1956); head U.S. Olympic women's track coach (Munich, 1972); attended the International Olympic Academy in Olympia, Greece (1980); manager of the U.S. women's track team that competed in the Pan-American games (1987); served on the board of directors of the U.S. Olympic Committee, as vice president and secretary of The Athletic Congress, and as a member of the NCAA; inducted into the Black Athletes Hall of Fame. Died on April 1, 1988, in Binghamton, N.Y.   Further reading, Arthur Ashe, Jr., *A Hard Road to Glory: A History of the African-American Athlete Since 1946* (1988).

---

on this day in history...

1915,   William "Swee Pea" Strayhorn, composer of "Satin Doll" and "Take the A Train," was born in Dayton, Ohio (d. 1967).
1921,   Roy Campanella, major league baseball's first African-American catcher, was born in Homestead, Pa. (d. 1993).

NOVEMBER 19   *SPORTS LEGENDS*

ARNA ARNOLD HEDGEMAN

Social worker, writer, lecturer, and consultant. Born on July 5, 1899, in Marshalltown, Iowa. **First African-American graduate of Hamline College** in St. Paul, Minn. (B.A., 1922); University of Minnesota. Taught ancient and modern history, logic, methodology, and English at Rust College in Holly Springs, Miss.; worked with the African-American branch of the Springfield (Ohio) YWCA (1924-1926); executive director of an African-American branch YWCA in Jersey City (1927-1929); responded to the Great Depression by organizing employment programs, establishing vocational training workshops, and manning soup kitchens; executive director of Philadelphia's Catherine Street Branch of the YWCA (1933-1934); supervisor and consultant to the Department of Welfare (1934-1938); served as executive director of the African-American branch of the Brooklyn YWCA. Executive director of the National Council for Fair Employment Practices Commission (1944-1946); sworn in as assistant to the administrator of the Federal Security Agency (1949), now called the U.S. Department of Health, Education, and Welfare; **cabinet member of New York City Mayor Robert Wagner** (1954-1958); joined the African-American owned Fuller Products Company as public relations director (1958); helped plan the March on Washington (1963). Keynote speaker at the first Conference of the Women of Africa and of African Descent (Ghana, 1960); member of the NAACP and National Urban League; author of *The Gift of Chaos* (1977). Died on January 17, 1990, in Harlem, N.Y. Further reading, <u>Arna Hedgeman</u>, <u>*The Trumpet Sounds*</u> (1964).

---

on this day in history...

1905, Samuel M. Nabrit, Morehouse College biology professor, was born in Macon, Ga.
1933, Eunice Kathleen Waymon ("Nina Simone"), jazz singer, was born in Tryon, N.C.
1936, Barbara Charline Jordan, Texas' first African-American congressperson, was born in Houston, Texas.
1940, John R. Lewis, Georgia 5th District congressman, was born in Troy, Ala.
1965, Malcolm X was assassinated at the Audubon Ballroom in Harlem.

FEBRUARY 21   **CIVIC LEADERS**

FLO HYMAN

Athlete who was called the **best known volleyball player in the world.**   Born on July 31, 1954, in Los Angeles, Calif.   University of Houston. Member of the U.S. National Volleyball team (1975-1984); named Tournament MVP at the NORCECA Championship (1979); member of the U.S. Olympic Volleyball team (1980), but missed the trip to Moscow because of the U.S. boycott; selected to the All-World Cup team, which consisted of the top six women volleyball players in the world, after competing in the World Cup Games in Tokyo (1981). Earned the nickname "Stuff" for her hard-hitting spiking ability; led the U.S. women's volleyball team to a silver medal at the Olympics in Long Beach (1984); credited with being a major force in turning the U.S. women's team from a recreational sport into an internationally-competitive program; played in a Japanese women's league for Daiei, Inc. (1984-1986), fatally collapsing during a match with Hitachi, Ltd.; played a guerrilla warrior in the movie, *Order of the Black Eagle* (1985); honored on National Women in Sports Day with the first annual Flo Hyman Memorial Award (1987). Died on January 24, 1986, in Matsue City, Japan.   Further reading, *Los Angeles Times* obituary (January 25, 1986).

on this day in history...

1900,	Howard Thurman, theologian, was born in Daytona Beach, Fla. (d. 1981).
1956,	David Adkins ("Sinbad"), comedian and actor, was born in Benton Harbor, Mich.
1956,	Warren Moon, Houston Oilers All-Pro, was born in Los Angeles, Calif.
1978,	Over 900, mostly African-American, cult members of the People's Temple committed a mass suicide in Jonestown, Guyana.

ADDIE D. HUNTON

Organizational official, educator, clubwoman, and suffragist. Born on July 11, 1875, in Norfolk, Va. **First African-American woman graduate of Spencerian College of Commerce** in Philadelphia (1889); Kaiser Wilhelm University; College of the City of New York. Served as lady principal at State Normal and Agricultural College in Normal, Ala.; wrote the essay "Negro Womanhood Defended" (1904), which was published in *Voice of the Negro*; appointed by the national board of the YWCA as secretary for Negro work (1907), as such she toured the South and Midwest conducting surveys; **national organizer for the National Association of Colored Women** (1906-1910), where she wrote "The National Association of Colored Women: Its Real Significance" for *The Colored American Magazine*. Volunteered for YWCA services during World War I (1918-1919), and was sent to France as one of only three African-American women assisting over 200,000 segregated African-American troops, taught literacy courses, held Sunday evening discussion programs, organized religious activities, helped establish a library; addressed the Pan-African Congress (Paris, 1919); returned to the U.S. after the war and co-authored *Two Colored Women with the American Expeditionary Forces* (1920). Served on the Council on Colored Work of the national board of the YWCA, as president of the International Council of the Women of Darker Races and the Empire State Federation of Women's Clubs, and as vice president of and field secretary of the NAACP; was principal organizer of the 4th Pan-African Congress (New York City, 1927). Died on June 21, 1943, in Brooklyn, N.Y. Further reading, <u>Charles H. Wesley</u>, *<u>The History of the National Association of Colored Women's Clubs</u>* (1984).

---

on this day in history...

1881,   James Reese Europe, organizer of the first African-American musicians' union (The Clef Club) and of the U.S. Army's 369th "Hellfighters" Band, was born in Mobile, Ala. (1919).

1928,   Conrad Mallett, Michigan State Supreme Court justice, was born in Ames, Texas.

1932,   Gil Noble, network broadcaster, was born in New York City.

1950,   Julius Winfield Erving ("Dr. J"), ABA and NBA legend, was born Roosevelt, N.Y.

FEBRUARY 22   **CIVIC LEADERS**

RUBE FOSTER

First great African-American pitcher who became a driving force behind the founding of Negro baseball. Born Andrew Foster on September 17, 1879, in Calvert, Texas. Organized a baseball team in Calvert, while still in grammar school; became a star pitcher with the Waco Yellowjackets (1897); joined Chicago Union Giants (1902), pitching a shutout in his first game; played with the Cuban Giants of Philadelphia (1902), where he out-pitched Philadelphia A's pitcher Rube Waddell, earning him the nickname "Rube;" pitched in the first Negro world championship for the Cuban X-Giants (1903), winning four games in a five games to two victory over the Philadelphia Giants. Hired by the New York Giants as a pitching coach; joined the Lelands of Chicago (1907), leading them to 48 straight victories; formed the Chicago American Giants as a player/manager (1911), which won over 95 percent of their games in the first year, became the first Negro team to play in a major league ball park, outdrew the Chicago Cubs and White Sox at the gate, and defeated the Brooklyn Royals for the Negro world championship. **Founder and president of the first Negro league, the National Negro Baseball League** (1920-1930), which consisted of the American Giants, Cuban all-stars Chicago Giants, Detroit Giants, Indianapolis ABCs, Kansas City Monarchs, and the St. Louis Stars, with his American Giants winning the first three pennants; credited with saving Negro baseball and paving the way for the Jackie Robinsons to enter the major leagues. Died on December 9, 1930, in Chicago, Ill. Further reading, Ocania Chalk, *Pioneers of Black Sport* (1974).

---

on this day in history...

1879,   Mary W. Stewart, nation's first African-American political writer, died in Washington, D.C. (b. 1803).
1945,   Elvin Hayes, basketball great, was born in Rayville, La.
1955,   James Price Johnson, musician who recorded the first jazz piano solo ("Carolina Shout"), died in New Brunswick, N.J. (b. 1894).
1979,   Arthur Lewis was named the recipient of the Nobel Prize for Economics.
1980,   The nation's first African-American-owned public broadcasting station, Howard's WBMM-TV, began operations in Washington, D.C.

NOVEMBER 17   SPORTS LEGENDS

WILLIAM ALPHEUS HUNTON

YMCA secretary who was referred to as a "**pioneer prophet of young men**." Born in 1863 in Chatham, Ontario, Canada. Wilberforce Institute of Ontario (1884). Taught public school and worked for the YMCA in Dresden, Canada; probationary officer in the Department of Indian Affairs in Ottawa, Canada (1885-1888); **secretary of the Norfolk YMCA (1888-1891), where he became the first African-American employee of the YMCA** and established literary and debating societies, educational and athletic programs, a library and choral club, and a Bible study class; served as the **first African-American secretary of the International YMCA** (1891-1914); married Addie D. Waites (1893); wrote the pamphlet *The First Step* (1893), which defined methods for groups seeking to organize local YMCA branches; member of the U.S. delegation to the Golden Jubilee of the YMCA (London, 1894), where he also toured Glasgow, Paris, Brussels, and Antwerp. **Helped organize the Colored Men's Division of the YMCA** (1896), where he became senior secretary; helped recruit Jesse Moorland, George Edmund Haynes, Channing Tobias, and Max Yergan to assist in organizing African-American YMCA branches in the cities and on college campuses; attended the World's Student Christian Federation Conference (Tokyo, 1907), traveling also to Shanghai, Peking, Tientsin, and Korea; addressed nonsegregated Tennessee State YMCA Convention (1910). Died in 1916 in Brooklyn, N.Y. Further reading, Addie W. Hunton, *William Alphaeus Hunton, A Pioneer of the Young Men* (1938).

---

on this day in history...

1927,	Charles Z. Smith, Washington State Supreme Court justice, was born in Lakeland, Fla.
1955,	Rodney Slater, the nation's first African-American Federal Highway Administrator, was born in Tutwiler, Miss.
1960,	Frederick M. Jones patented a thermostat and temperature control system.
1979,	Frank E. Peterson was named the first African-American general in the U.S. Marine Corps.

FEBRUARY 23   CIVIC LEADERS

ARTHUR R. ASHE, JR.

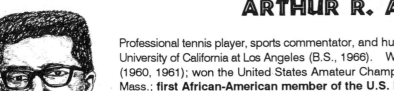

Professional tennis player, sports commentator, and human rights advocate.   Born on July 10, 1943, in Richmond, Va. University of California at Los Angeles (B.S., 1966).   Won the Junior Singles title at the National Junior Championships (1960, 1961); won the United States Amateur Championship tournament at the Longwood Cricket Club in Brookline, Mass.; **first African-American member of the U.S. Davis Cup** (1963-1970, 1972, 1976, and 1978), and became the first African-American Davis Cup team captain (1981-1985); U.S. Men's Clay Court Champion (1967); defeated Tom Okker of the Netherlands for the U.S. Open title at the West Side Tennis Club in Forest Hills, N.Y. (1968), becoming the first amateur American in 13 years and African-American to win the Open (which showcased the world's greatest professional tennis players).   Victorious in 30 consecutive matches (1968), and became the **first African-American to be ranked #1 by the United States Lawn Tennis Association**; won his opening match against Australia to help the U.S. team win the title (1968), and again the following year, after sweeping both of his singles match against Romania; Australian Open champion (1970); barred from competing in the South African Open (1970), resulting in South Africa being barred from the 1970 Davis Cup competition; French Open Doubles title (1972); World Champion Tennis Singles title (1975); defeated Jimmy Connors to become the **first African-American Wimbledon Men's Singles champion** (1975); Australian Open Doubles title (1977).   ATP Player of the Year (1975); honored with the Jefferson Award (1982), Kappa Alpha Psi's Laurel Wreath Award (1986), and honorary doctorates from Dartmouth, Virginia Union, St. John's, and Princeton Universities; served in the U.S. Armed Forces during the Vietnam War.   Died on February 6, 1993, in New York City.   Further reading, Arthur R. Ashe, Jr., _A Hard Road to Glory: A History of the African-American Athlete, Vol I-III_ (1988).

---

on this day in history...

1943,	Dick Griffey, recording industry executive, was born in Nashville, Tenn.
1963,	Zina Garrison, tennis champion, was born in Houston, Texas.
1964,	Dwight Gooden, New York Mets All-Star, was born in Tampa, Fla.
1967,	Lisa Michelle Bonet, actress, was born in San Francisco, Calif.

NOVEMBER 16   *SPORTS LEGENDS*

MOLLIE LEWIS MOON

Organization founder, pharmacist, and civic worker who became a pioneer in race relations.   Born on July 21, 1912, in Hattiesburg, Miss. Meharry Medical College (Phr.C., 1929); Columbia University Teachers College; New School of Social Research in New York City; University of Berlin.   Worked as a pharmacist in New Orleans' Douglas Pharmacy (1933-1934), Schultz's Pharmacy (1934-1937), and in New York City's La Morrell's Drug Store (1937-1938); social worker with the Department of Social Services in New York City (1938-1972). Recruited by Lester Granger, National Urban League executive director, to help the league overcome its financial problems by organizing fundraisers; **founder and president of the Council of Urban League Guilds** (1942-1990); co-sponsored a benefit called the Victory Cocktail Party in New York City (1942), which was so successful that it became the New York City tradition known as the annual black tie Beaux-Arts Ball. Secretary of the board of directors of the National Urban League (1955-1962); member of the U.S. Department of Health, Education and Welfare's Food and Drug Committee national advisory board (1972-1976); chaired a fundraising committee for the Henry Lee Moon Civil Rights Library located at the NAACP's national headquarters in Baltimore. Honored by the National Association of Negro Business and Professional Women's Clubs with the Scroll of Honor (1975), the American Cancer Society with the Robert Kitchen Award (1983), and the National Urban League with the Whitney M. Young, Jr., and Equal Opportunity Awards; member of the board of directors of the Coalition of 100 Black Women, Arthur Mitchell's Dance Theater of Harlem, and the Sickle Cell Foundation of New York. Died on June 24, 1990, on Long Island, N.Y.   Further reading, Stephen Birmingham, _Certain People_ (1977).

---

on this day in history...

1980,	Willie Davenport and Jeff Gadley became the first African-American athletes to participate in the Winter Olympics.
1992,	Edward Perkins was nominated as U.S. ambassador to South Africa by President Bush.

FEBRUARY 24   **CIVIC LEADERS**

CHARLES HENRY TURNER

Zoologist and educator.   Born on February 3, 1867, in Cincinnati, Ohio.   University of Cincinnati (B.S., 1891; M.S., 1892); University of Chicago (Ph.D., 1907), dissertation title: "The Homing of Ants: An Experimental Study of Ant Behavior." Assistant instructor in the biology laboratory at the University of Cincinnati (1892-1893); professor of biology at Clark College (1893-1895), Haines Normal Industrial Institute in Augusta, Ga. (1907-1908), and at St. Louis' Sumner High School (1908-1923), where he carried out his insect and animal behavior research; taught in the Evansville and Cincinnati public schools; principal of College Hill High School in Cleveland (1906). Contributed many scholarly papers, such as "Psychological Notes on the Gallery Spider," "Habits of Mound-Building Ants," "Experiments on the Color Vision of the Honey Bee," "Behavior of a Parasitic Bee," "Hunting Habits of an American Sand Wasp," and "Do Ants form Practical Judgement;" published research appeared in *Biological Bulletin, Journal of Comparative Neurology, Zoological Bulletin, Journal of American Behavior,* and *Psychological Bulletin*; **first to prove that insects can hear and distinguish pitch** and that roaches learn by trial and error. Died in 1923 in St. Louis, Mo.   Further reading, Robert C. Hayden, *Seven Black American Scientists* (1970).

---

on this day in history...

1887,   Granville T. Woods patented an electric railway telegraphy.
1992,   The Birmingham Civil Rights Institute officially opened.

NOVEMBER 15

SCIENTISTS

JESSE EDWARD MOORLAND

Clergyman and YMCA secretary, who was nicknamed **"the Dean."** Born on September 10, 1863, in Coldwater, Ohio. Northwest Normal University in Ada, Ohio; Howard University class salutatorian (1891). Organized and developed Negro YMCAs on black college campuses and in large cities (1888-1898); ordained as a Congregational minister (1891); secretary of the Washington YMCA (1891-1893), nation's oldest Negro YMCA; pastor of Howard Chapel in Nashville (1893-1896), and of Mount Zion Congregational Church of Cleveland (1896-1898); **senior secretary of the Colored Men's Department of the YMCA** (1898-1923). Became a member of the board of trustees of Howard University (1907), where he encouraged instruction and research on Africa and African-Americans, recruited Carter Woodson and William Hansberry to the history department, and helped establish Founders Library; wrote an essay entitled *The Demand and the Supply of Increased Efficiency in the Negro Ministry* (1909), which was published by the American Negro Academy; **donated his private library, which was called "The Moorland Foundation," to Howard University (1914), creating the nation's first research library devoted fully to materials on African-Americans**; incorporator, Executive Council member, and secretary-treasurer of the Association of the Study of Negro Life and History. Helped organize the Manual Training School for Colored Youth at Bordentown, N.J. (1924), a training center for YMCA secretaries, whose staff included Channing Tobias, Mordecai Johnson, John Hope, Charles Wesley, Robert Moton, William Trent, Sr., and W.E.B. DuBois; served as president of the National Health Circle for Colored People (1926); was Thirty-third Degree Mason; member of the Alpha Phi Alpha fraternity, and trustee of the Frederick Douglass Home Association. Died on March 20, 1939, in Brooklyn, N.Y. Further reading, Jesse Moorland Papers, Moorland-Spingarn Research Center.

on this day in history...

1870,	Hiram B. Revels was sworn in as the nation's first African-American U.S. senator.
1895,	George Samuel Schuyler, *Pittsburgh Courier* editor and author of *Black No More*, was born in Providence, R.I. (d. 1977).
1925,	Louis Stokes, Ohio 11th District congressman, was born in Cleveland, Ohio.
1928,	A. Leon Higginbotham, Jr., 3rd U.S. Circuit appellate judge, was born in Trenton, N.J.
1964,	Muhammad Ali defeated Sonny Liston for the heavyweight boxing championship.
1991,	Adrienne Mitchell was killed in the Persian Gulf War, becoming the first African-American woman to die in combat.

FEBRUARY 25   **CIVIC LEADERS**

FRANCIS CECIL SUMNER

Psychologist.   Born on December 7, 1895, in Pine Bluff, Ark.   Lincoln University in Pennsylvania *summa cum laude* (B.A., 1915; M.A., 1917); Clark University in Massachusetts (Ph.D., 1920), becoming the **first African-American psychology Ph.D.**; dissertation title: "Psychoanalysis of Freud and Adler."   Served in the U.S. Army infantry in France during World War I; taught at Wilberforce University (1920-1921), and West Virginia State College (1921-1928); published *The Nature of Education* (1924), and *Hygiene of the Mind* (1933); professor and chairman of the department of psychology at Howard University (1928-1954), which has been the main source of African-American Ph.D. degrees in psychology. Delivered a paper at the International Congress of Religious Psychology on "The Mental Hygiene of Religion" (Vienna, 1931); fellow of the American Psychological Association and the American Association for the Advancement of Science; member of Kappa Alpha Psi fraternity. Died on January 11, 1954, in Washington, D.C.   Further reading, Robert Vs. Guthrie, *Even the Rat Was White: A Historical View of Psychology* (1976).

---

on this day in history...

1900,   The Washington Society of Colored Dentists was organized.

1945,   Norman Early, Denver's first African-American district attorney, was born in Washington, D.C.

NOVEMBER 14   SCIENTISTS

JOSEPHINE ST. PIERRE RUFFIN

Clubwoman, civic leader, and civil rights activist who **founded both African-American and white civic organizations in Boston**. Born in 1842 in Boston, Mass. Married George Ruffin (1858), who became Boston's first African-American municipal judge; helped recruit soldiers for the 54th and 55th Massachusetts Negro Regiments, during the Civil War, and worked for the U.S. Sanitary Commission; organized the Boston Kansas Relief Association (1879), after African-Americans from the South were no longer welcomed in Boston; served: on the executive board of the Massachusetts Moral Education Association and General Federation of Women's Clubs, as a charter member of the Massachusetts School Suffrage Association and the NAACP, as a volunteer visitor for the Associated Charities, as an editor of the *Boston Courant*, as a member of the New England Women's Press Association, and as a vice president of the National Association of Colored Women. Helped **organize the Women's Era Club** (1894), whose goal was to further the interest of African-Americans, especially African-American women; **called for a convention of African-American women in Boston (1895), which led to the formation of the National Federation of Afro-American Women**; organized the Northeastern Federation of Women's Clubs (1896). Helped establish the Association for the Promotion of Child Training in the South, the Boston branch of the NAACP, and the League of Women for Community Service; co-founded the American Mount Coffee School Association (1902), for the betterment of the Jennie Sharpe School in Liberia. Died on March 13, 1924, in Boston, Mass. Further reading, <u>Alice Dunbar Nelson</u>, <u>*Masterpieces of Negro Eloquence*</u> (1974).

---

on this day in history...

1844,	James Edward O'Hara, former North Carolina congressman (1883-1887), was born in New York City (d. 1905).
1899,	Alexander Pierre Tureaud, one of Louisiana's top civil rights attorneys, was born in New Orleans, La. (d. 1972).
1923,	Dexter Gordon, tenor saxophonist, was born in Los Angeles, Calif. (d. 1990).
1928,	Antoine "Fats" Domino, pioneer R&B pianist, was born in New Orleans, La.
1933,	Godfrey Cambridge, actor, was born in New York City.
1966,	Andrew Brimmer became the first African-American governor of the Federal Reserve Board.

FEBRUARY 26   **CIVIC LEADERS**

ESLANDA GOODE ROBESON

Anthropologist, chemist, civil rights activist, author, and business manager.   Born on December 15, 1896, in Washington, D.C.   University of Chicago; Columbia University (B.S., 1923); London School of Economics; Hartford Seminary Foundation (Ph.D., anthropology, 1945).   Business manager for her entertainer husband Paul Robeson (1921-1965), accompanying him on most of his trips and standing by him during the Congressional hearings on communism in the U.S.; became the **first African-American to obtain employment as an analytical chemist and technician in the surgery and pathology department at Columbia Presbyterian Hospital** (1918-1925); published *African Journey* (1945); observer for the Council of African Affairs at the San Francisco Conference, which led to the establishment of the U.N.; traveled to China (1949); attended the Afro-Asian Conference (Indonesia, 1955). Died on December 13, 1965, in New York City.   Further reading, Robert E. Skinner, "Robeson, Eslanda Goode," *Notable Black American Women* (1992).

---

on this day in history...

1837,   James Thomas Rapier, former North Carolina congressman (1873-1875), was born in Florence, Ala. (d. 1883).
1949,   Caryn Johnson ("Whoopi Goldberg"), Academy Award-winning actress, was born in New York City.
1992,   Riddick Bowe defeated Evander Holyfield for the heavyweight boxing championship.

NOVEMBER 13   SCIENTISTS

CHANNING HEGGIE TOBIAS

YMCA secretary, religious leader, and organization executive.   Born on February 1, 1882, in Augusta, Ga.   Paine Institute (B.A., 1902); Drew University in Madison, N.J. (B.D., 1905).   Taught biblical literature at Paine Institute (1905-1911); secretary of the National Council of the YMCA in Washington, D.C. (1911-1923); **senior secretary of the Colored Department of the YMCA National Council** in New York City (1923-1946); delegate and speaker at the World Conference of the YMCAs (Finland, 1926); received the Harmon Award for Religious Services (1928); met Ghandi while at the World Conference of the YMCAs (India, 1936); member of the board of trustees of Howard University (1931-1953). Member of the National Advisory Committee on Selective Service, Joint Army Committee on Welfare and Recreation during World War II, Civilian Committee of the U.S. Navy (1946), President Truman's Committee on Civil Rights (1946, 1947), and the Mayor's Committee on Survey Management of New York City. Served on the editorial board of the *Protestant Voice*; U.S. delegate to the 6th General Assembly of the U.N. in Paris (1951-1952); chairman of the board of trustee of Hampton Institute (1946); **first African-American director of the Phelps-Stokes Fund**, a foundation devoted to the improvement of educational opportunities for African-Americans; director of the Jesse Noyes and Marshall Field Foundations; **member of the board of trustees of the NAACP (1943-1953), chairman (1953-1959), and chairman emeritus (1959-1961)**; awarded the NAACP Spingarn Medal (1948), for his role in defending fundamental American liberties. Died on November 5, 1961, in New York City.   Further reading, Channing Tobias, *Thirteen Americans: Their Spiritual Biographies* (1953).

on this day in history...

1853,   The first African-American YMCA was organized in Washington, D.C.

1924,   Samella Sanders Lewis, prominent African-American art historian, was born in New Orleans, La.

1942,   Charlayne Hunter-Gault, University of Georgia's first African-American student and Emmy Award-winning journalist, was born in Due West, S.C.

1988,   Debi Thomas became the first African-American to win a medal (bronze in figure skating) in the Winter Olympics.

FEBRUARY 27   **CIVIC LEADERS**

FLEMMIE PANSY KITTRELL

Educator, home economist, and nutritionist.   Born on December 25, 1904, in Henderson, N.C.   Hampton Institute (B.S., 1928); Cornell University (M.A., 1930; Ph.D., 1938), **first African-American women to earn a Ph.D. in nutrition**; dissertation title: "A Study of Negro Infant Feeding Practices in a Selected Community in North Carolina."   Teacher and director of nutrition at Bennett College (1928-1940); dean of women and chairman of the department of home economics at Hampton Institute (1940-1944); head of the department of home economics at Howard University (1944-1973), and professor emeritus of nutrition (1973-1980). Conducted a nutritional survey of Liberia (1947), under the auspices of the U.S. State Department and found that 90 percent of the Liberian people suffer from "hidden hunger" from subsisting largely on diets of rice and cassava dishes; her findings were published in the booklet, *Preliminary Food and Survey of Liberia* (1947). Helped organize India's Baroda University College of Home Economics (1950); helped organize the Congo Polytechnic Institute's School of Home Economics (1952); studied home economic extension methods in Japan and Hawaii (1957); led three cultural tours for the U.S. Department of State to West Africa (1957), West and Central Africa (1959), and Guinea (1961); fought for the building of the School of Home Ecology at Howard (1963); Cornell Visiting Senior fellow (1974-1976). Died on October 3, 1980, in Washington, D.C.   Further reading, Harry Washington Greene, *Holders of Doctorates Among American Negroes: An Educational and Social Study of Negroes Who Earned Doctoral Degrees in Course, 1876-1943* (1946).

---

on this day in history...

1882,	Lane College was founded in Jackson, Tenn.
1900,	Thomas Campbell became the first African-American U.S. Department of Agriculture demonstration agent.
1922,	Sigma Gamma Rho sorority was founded in Indianapolis, Ind.
1933,	Diane Watson, California state senator, was born in Los Angeles, Calif.
1938,	Delano E. Lewis, first African-American head of National Public Radio, was born in Arkansas City, Kan.
1941,	The Negro Opera Company was founded in Pittsburgh, Pa., by Mary Caldwell and Lillian Evanti.

NOVEMBER 12   SCIENTISTS

FANNIE BARRIER WILLIAMS

Civic leader, lecturer, journalist, and a **pioneer in the women's club movement**. Born on February 12, 1855, in Brockport, N.Y. State Normal School in Brockport (1870); New England Conservatory of Music; School of Fine Arts in Washington. Assisted Daniel Hale Williams in founding Provident Hospital in Chicago (1891); addressed the World's Congress of Representative Women at the Columbian Exposition (Chicago, 1893), on "The Intellectual Progress of the Colored Women of the United States since the Emancipation Proclamation" and "Religious Duty of the Negro;" worked as a journalist for the *New York Age* and the *Chicago Record-Herald.* Helped found the National League of Colored Women (1893); became the **first African-American member of the Chicago Women's Club** (1895); **co-founded, along with Mary Church Terrell, the National Association of Colored Women** (1896). Active in the Illinois Women's Alliance; co-authored, with Booker T. Washington, *A New Negro for a New Century* (1900), which showed her transformation from militancy to conciliation; elected corresponding secretary at the Afro-American Council Conference (St. Paul, 1902); became a director of Southside Chicago's Frederick Douglass Center (1905); served as corresponding secretary of the board of directors of the Phillis Wheatley Home for Girls. Served as Booker T. Washington's primary contact in Chicago; began working with W.E.B. DuBois and the newly-formed NAACP (1912); served as the **first woman and African-American on the Library Board of Chicago** (1924-1926). Died on March 4, 1944, in Brockton, N.Y. Further reading, Elizabeth Davis, *Lifting as They Climb* (1933).

---

on this day in history...

1921, Paul Stephens, first African-American president of the Academy of General Dentistry, was born in Muskogee, Okla.

1928, Gladys McCoy (Portland, Ore.), Multnomah County Commission's first African-American chairperson, was born in Atlanta, Ga. (d. 1993).

1984, Michael Jackson won a record eight Grammy Awards for his best-selling album *Thriller.*

FEBRUARY 28   **CIVIC LEADERS**

ERNEST EVERETT JUST

Zoologist, biologist, physiologist, and research scientist known as the **"Black Apollo."** Born on August 14, 1883, in Charleston, S.C. Dartmouth College *magna cum laude* (B.A., 1907); University of Chicago (Ph.D., zoology and physiology, 1916), dissertation title: "Studies of Fertilization in Platynerois megalops" (1916); studied at the Woods Hole Marine Biological Lab (1909-1915, 1920-1933). Organized the first drama group at Howard University (1908), the College Dramatic Club; instructor in English at Howard University College of Arts and Science (1907-1908), instructor of zoology (1909-1938, 1940-1941), assistant professor and head of the department of physiology (1912-1920). Published his first paper, "The Relation of the First Cleavage Plane to the Entrance Point of Sperm," in the *Biological Bulletin* (1912), and published 47 research papers on fertilization. Researched in the field of experimental embryology (1912-1930), and conducted research abroad in Europe (1929-1935, 1938-1940); **awarded the first NAACP Spingarn Medal (1915), for his research in biology**; became able to reproduce all the histological characteristics of human cancer (1925), and was said to be the first person to have increased the number of chromosomes in an animal. Became the **first American invited to conduct research at the Kaiser Wilhelm Institut for Biolegie** in Germany (1929), considered by most scientists as "the greatest research laboratory;" addressed the General Session of the Eleventh International Congress of Zoologists (Italy, 1930); elected vice president of the American Society of Zoologists (1930); became a member of the Washington Academy of Sciences (1936), and the New York Academy of Sciences (1941); member of the editorial boards of biology-oriented journal; awarded research grants from the Rosenwald Fund (1920-1925, 1928-1933), National Research Council (1920-1933), and the Rockefeller Foundation (1925-1930). Died on October 27, 1941, in Chicago, Ill. Further reading, Kenneth R. Manning, *Black Apollo of Science; the Life of Ernest Everett Just* (1983).

---

on this day in history...

1831,   Richard DeBaptiste, lead organizer of the first national association of African-American Baptists, Consolidated American Baptist Convention, was born in Frederickburg, Va.

1936,   Norma Quarles, network broadcaster, was born in New York City.

1946,   Corrine Brown, Florida 3rd District congresswoman, was born in Jacksonville, Fla.

1984,   Martin Luther King, Sr., "Daddy King," died in Atlanta, Ga. (b. 1899).

NOVEMBER 11   SCIENTISTS

JAMES FINLEY WILSON

Editor, politician, and fraternal leader who was known as "the Grand." Born in 1881 in Dickson, Tenn. Fisk University. Traveled throughout the U.S. and Canada, spending time in New York City, the Klondike, and Utah; worked as a miner along with Buffalo Bill in Arizona, editor of the *Plaindealer* in Salt Lake City, sanitary inspector in Denver, cowboy in Wyoming, reporter for the *Baltimore Times*, editor of the *Washington Eagle*, and as a staff member of T. Thomas Fortune's *New York Age*;member of the Masons, Odd Fellows, Knights of Pythias, and the Order of St. Luke's. Elected as the **Grand Exalted Ruler of the Improved Benevolent Protective Order of the Elks of the World,** or IBPOEW (1922-1948), which he built into the largest African-American social welfare and fraternal organization, launching a scholarship program and the Elks Oratorical Contest, initiating the first systematic health survey of African-Americans, assisting in drives for Allied War Relief funds and in campaigns for buying defense bonds, and contributing books to servicemen in the Elks' Victory Book campaign during World War II. Took the Elks from 30,000 members to over half a million members with 900 lodges worldwide; became a powerful member of the Republican Party and served as president of the Negro Newspaper Association. Died on February 18, 1952, in Washington, D.C. Further reading, Charles H. Wesley, *History of the Benevolent and Protective Order of Elks of the World, 1888-1954* (1955).

---

on this day in history...

1920, LeGree Daniels, U.S. Postal commissioner, was born in Barnwell, S.C.

1940, Hattie McDaniel became the first African-American to receive an Academy Award (best supporting actress for her role in *Gone With the Wind*).

FEBRUARY 29   **CIVIC LEADERS**

HENRY AARON HILL

Scientist and chemist. Born on May 30, 1915, in St. Joseph, Mo. Johnson C. Smith University (B.A., 1936); Massachusetts Institute of Technology (Ph.D., 1942), dissertation title: "Test of Van't Hoff's Principle of Optical Superposition." Rosenwald fellow; research chemist for Atlantic Research Associates (1942-1943), director of research (1943-1944), and vice president in charge of research (1944-1946); civilian employee for the Office of Scientific Research and Development (1944); supervisor of research for Dewey & Almy Chemical Company (1946-1952); assistant manager of National Polychemicals (1952-1962); founder and president of Riverside Research Laboratory (1962-1979); director of Rohm & Hass Company (1976); conducted research in fluorocarbons and became the **first African-American president of the American Chemical Society.** Died in 1979. Further reading, Julius Taylor, *The Negro in Science* (1955).

---

on this day in history...

1930,	Clarence Pendleton, first African-American chairman of the U.S. Civil Rights Commission, was born in Louisville, Ky.
1957,	Charlie Sifford became the first African-American to win a PGA championship (the Long Beach Open).
1960,	Andrew Hatcher was named associate press secretary in the Kennedy administration.

NOVEMBER 10   SCIENTISTS

RALPH DAVID ABERNATHY

Minister, civil rights leader, and top aide to Martin Luther King, Jr. Born on March 11, 1926, in Linden, Ala. Alabama State College (B.S., 1950); Atlanta University (M.A., sociology, 1951). Appointed Dean of Men at Alabama State College (1951); pastor of the First Baptist Church in Montgomery (1951-1961); **co-founded the Southern Christian Leadership Conference (SCLC) in 1957, secretary/treasurer (1961-1968), president (1968-1977), president emeritus** (1977-1990). Directed the Poor People's March on Washington (1968); launched the building of Resurrection City, U.S.A., a site of tents that remained in the center of Washington for over a month and became the last major civil rights demonstration for the next 10 years; led demonstrations at the Republican National Convention (Miami, 1968); helped organize the Atlanta sanitation workers' strike (1968); organized the SCLC's Operation Breadbasket, in which economic pressure by means of selective buying was brought against companies that had refused equal opportunities to African-Americans. Founded the Foundation for Economic Enterprises Development; served as pastor of West Hunter Street Baptist Church in Atlanta (until 1983); published *And the Walls Came Tumbling Down* (1989), an autobiographical account of the civil rights movement. Died on April 17, 1990, in Atlanta, Ga. Further reading, A. John Adams and Joan Martin Burke, *A CBS News Reference Book: Civil Rights, A Current Guide to the People, Organizations and Events* (1970).

on this day in history...

1896,	Over 300 African-Americans emigrated to Liberia from Savannah aboard the steamship *Laurada*.
1914,	Ralph Waldo Ellison, National Book Award-winning author of *Invisible Man*, was born in Oklahoma City, Okla.
1927,	Harry George Belafonte, first African-American Emmy Award winner, was born in New York City.

MARCH 1   **CIVIL RIGHTS LEADERS & BLACK NATIONALISTS**

ELIZABETH ROSS HAYNES

Social scientist, organization official, and author.   Born on July 30, 1883, in Lowdnes County, Ala.   State Normal School [now Alabama State University] valedictorian (1900); Fisk University (A.B., 1903); University of Chicago; Columbia University (A.M., sociology, 1923). Taught school in Alabama, Missouri, and Texas; appointed the **first African-American YWCA national secretary**, responsible for activities among colleges, as well as supervisory responsibility in cities with African-American YWCAs; became the **first African-American to be elected to the national board of the YWCA** (1924-1934), where she helped build the national YWCA movement. Petitioned the First International Congress of Working Women (D.C., 1919); published "Two Million Negro Women at Work" (1922), in which she reported that the three types of occupations that most African-American women were involved in were domestic and personal service, agriculture, and manufacturing and mechanical industries. Moved to New York and became involved in the New York Planning Commission and the Harlem Better Schools Committee; chair of the Industry and Housing Department of the National Association of Colored Women; elected co-leader of the 21st Assembly District, New York County (1935), where her work was mostly economic, social, and educational; superintendent of the Junior Department of Abyssinian Baptist Church in Harlem; secretary of the board of managers of the Adam Clayton Powell Home for the Aged; member of Alpha Kappa Alpha sorority. Died on October 26, 1953, in New York City.   Further reading, Paula Giddings, *When and Where I Enter* (1984).

---

on this day in history...

1867,   Arthur McKimmon, first African-American officer commissioned in the Regular Army, was born in Raleigh, N.C. (d. 1939).

1923,   Alice Coachman-Davis, first African-American woman to win an Olympic gold medal, was born in Albany, Ga.

1935,   Bob Gibson, World-Series, Cy Young, and MVP-winning member of the Hall of Fame, was born in Omaha, Neb.

NOVEMBER 9   **SCIENTISTS**

ELLA JO BAKER

Community organizer, civil rights activist, and education consultant. Born on December 18, 1903, in Norfolk, Va. Shaw University valedictorian (B.A., 1927). Editor of *The American West Indian News* and the *Negro National News*; organizer and national director of the Young Negro Cooperative League in New York City (1931-1935), a successful organization whose goal was to promote consumer cooperatives; director of the Consumer Education Project in the Work Projects Administration (1935-1938). NAACP field secretary (1938-1942), making over 300 trips throughout the South, focusing on membership recruiting, establishing new chapters, fundraising, and consciousness raising; national director of NAACP branches (1943-1946); president of the New York City NAACP branch (1954-1957), becoming the highest ranking woman in the organization. Founded the first office of the American Cancer Society in Harlem; founding member and "interim executive secretary" of the SCLC (1957-1960), responsible for the organizational structure and organized the 1958 Citizenship Crusade; persuaded the SCLC to arrange a conference (Raleigh, 1960), for which she **organized college students into the Student Nonviolent Coordinating Committee (SNCC)**, which sponsored sit-ins, wade-ins, kneel-ins, voter registration drives, and boycotts of retail establishments; helped organize the "Mississippi Freedom Summer" of 1964, which led to the establishment of the Mississippi Freedom Democratic Party (1964). Died on December 18, 1986, in New York City. Further reading, <u>Gerda Lerner</u>, <u>*Black Women in White America: A Documentary History*</u> (1973).

---

on this day in history...

1807,	Congress outlawed the importation of slaves into the jurisdiction of the U.S.
1867,	Congress chartered Howard University in Washington, D.C.
1867,	The first Reconstruction Act was passed dividing the South into five military districts.
1917,	Janet Collins, first African-American to perform at New York's Metropolitan Opera House, was born in New Orleans. La.
1921,	Pace Phonograph Corp., first African-American owned and operated record company, was established by Harry Pace.
1944,	Elaine R. Jones, director-counsel of the NAACP Legal Defense Fund, was born in Norfolk, Va.

MARCH 2   **CIVIL RIGHTS LEADERS & BLACK NATIONALISTS**

EDWARD FERGUSON, JR.

Biologist and zoologist. Born on January 6, 1907, in Dawson, Ga. University of Illinois (B.A., 1929; M.S., 1933; Ph.D., 1942), dissertation title: "Studies on the Seasonal Life History of Three Species of Fresh Water Ostracods." Professor of biology at South Carolina State College (1929-1936), professor and head of the biology department (1951-1956); associate professor at Southern University and A&M College (1936-1940); instructor at Sumner High School in St. Louis (1940-1941); professor at Tennessee State College (1946-1948); professor and chairman of the Division of Arts & Sciences at Maryland State College (1948-1951); professor and head of the biology department at Grambling College (1956-1960), Lincoln University in Missouri (1960-1968). Member of the American Society of Zoology; National Science Foundation fellow (1963-1966). Died in 1968. Further reading, Julius Taylor, *The Negro in Science* (1955).

on this day in history...

1922,	Esther Rolle, Emmy Award-winning actress, was born in Pompano Beach, Fla.
1938,	Crystal Bird Faucet of Pennsylvania became the first African-American woman to be elected to a state legislature.
1953,	Alfre Woodard, Emmy Award-winning actress, was born in Tulsa, Okla.
1966,	Edwin Brooks of Massachusetts became the first African-American to be elected to the U.S. Senate since Reconstruction.
1983,	Harvey Gantt of Charlotte, W. Wilson Goode of Philadelphia, and James A. Sharp, Jr., of Flint became the first African-American mayors of their respective cities.

NOVEMBER 8   SCIENTISTS

MEDGAR WILEY EVERS

Civil rights martyr who became a **central figure in Mississippi's civil rights struggle.** Born on July 2, 1925, in Decatur, Miss. Alcorn A&M College (B.A., business administration, 1952). Served in the U.S. Army during World War II (1943-1946), fought in France and Germany; sold insurance in the Mississippi Delta, where he employed economic boycotts to mobilize African-Americans against inequality; joined the NAACP (1952), organizing chapters and revitalizing branch chapters throughout the state. Mississippi state field secretary for the NAACP (1954-1963), where he served the organization by: monitoring, collecting, and publicizing data concerning civil rights violations; organizing campaigns against racial injustices in Jackson; leading meetings, economic boycotts, marches, prayer vigils, and picket lines; bailing out demonstrators arrested by all-white police forces; participating in sit-ins and lunch counter demonstrations; unifying the Jackson African-American community; delivering radio addresses; initiating mass direct action; speaking constantly of the need to overcome hatred and to promote understanding and equality between the races; going to jail and being beaten frequently; living with death threats 24 hours a day. Awarded the NAACP Spingarn Medal, posthumously (1963). Assassinated on June 12, 1963, in Jackson, Miss. Further reading, Jack Mendelson, *The Martyrs: Sixteen Who Gave Their Lives for Racial Justice* (1966).

on this day in history...

1821, Thomas Jennings, inventor of a clothes dryer, became the first known African-American to receive a patent.

1865, Congress established the Bureau of Freedmen, Refugees, and Abandon Lands.

1962, Jackie Joyner-Kersee, "world's greatest female athlete," was born in East St. Louis, Ill.

1988, Juanita Kidd Stout of Pennsylvania became the first African-American woman to serve on a state supreme court.

1989, The Georgia State Supreme Court unanimously declared the nation's oldest affirmative action plan, Atlanta Minority-Female Business Enterprise Program, unconstitutional.

MARCH 3   CIVIL RIGHTS LEADERS & BLACK NATIONALISTS

LEWIS KING DOWNING

Engineering educator and administrator. Born on January 2, 1896, in Roanoke, Va. Biddle University [now Johnson C. Smith University] (B.A., 1916); Howard University (B.S., civil engineering, 1921); M.I.T. (B.S., engineering administration, 1923); University of Michigan (M.S., highway transport and traffic control, 1923). **Helped set up Howard University's School of Engineering and Architecture** (1934); dean of the School (1936-1964), dean emeritus (1964-1967), and was credited with saving the program during the Depression years; wrote the articles "The Negro in the Professions of Engineering and Architecture" (*Journal of Negro Education.* January 1935), "Howard Engineers" (*Howard University Alumni Journal*, 1923), and "The Civil Engineer" (*Beta Kappa Chi Bulletin*, June 1943). Co-author of the *Howard University Professional Guidance Bulletin*, published by the School of Engineering and Architecture (1930); editor of the *Yearbook of National Technical Association* (1936-1937, 1942, and 1948-1949); fellow in the American Society of Civil Engineers; member of Beta Kappa Chi Science Honor Society; member of the D.C. Commissioners Traffic Advisory Board (1958-1967), and chairman of the D.C. Engineering Commission. Died on October 19, 1967, in Washington, D.C. Further reading, Frederick D. Wilkinson, *50 Years of Engineering and Architecture--The School of Engineering and Architecture, Howard University, 1910-1960.*

---

on this day in history...

1950,	Alexa Canady, neurosurgeon, was born in Lansing, Mich.
1967,	Rufus Earl Clements, Atlanta University president, died in New York City (b. 1900).
1967,	Richard Hatcher of Gary and Carl Stokes of Cleveland became the first African-American mayors of major U.S. cities.
1972,	Barbara Jordan became the first African-American to be elected to Congress from Texas.
1989,	Michael White of Cleveland, Chester Jenkins of Durham, and John Daniels of New Haven were elected mayors of their respective cities.

MARCUS MOSIAH GARVEY

Pan-Africanist and leader of the most powerful movement of African-Americans of the early 20th century. Born on August 17, 1887, in St. Ann's Bay, Jamaica. Migrated to England (1911), and studied at Birbeck College in England. **Launched the Universal Negro Improvement and Conservation Association** (UNIA) and African Communities League in Jamaica (1914), its main purpose being "to draw the peoples of the race together;" arrived in the U.S. (1916), and went on a year-long speaking tour of 38 states; organized the first U.S. UNIA branch in New York City, and published the *Negro World* (1917); presided over a UNIA, which stressed the need for real economic opportunities and the uniting of persons of African descent, with dozens of chapters and thousands of supporters around the world. Operated the Black Star Steamship Line (1919-1922), established to foster trade by linking black enterprises into a worldwide economic network and to provide transportation to Africa; sold titles [lord, duke, lady, countess] to well-to-do African-Americans; declared himself "Provisional President of Africa" at a UNIA convention (1920), started his own army called the African Legion, and a medical corps. Convicted of mail fraud and sentenced to the Atlanta Federal Penitentiary (1925); returned to Jamaica (1932), and published *The New Jamaican* and *The Black Man's Magazine*; sailed to England (1935), where he lived out the rest of his life. Died on June 10, 1940, in London, England. Further reading, David E. Cronon, *Black Moses: The Story of Marcus Garvey and the Universal Negro Improvement Association* (1955).

---

on this day in history...

1911, Clarence M. Mitchell, Jr., nation's top civil rights lobbyist, was born in Baltimore, Md. (d. 1984).
1924, Isaiah Thorton Montgomery, founder of the all-black town of Mound Bayou, Miss., died in Mound Bayou, Miss. (b. 1841).
1930, Joseph Jerome Ferris, 9th U.S. Circuit appellate judge, was born in Birmingham, Ala.
1944, Robert Dwayne Womack, R&B recording artist, was born in Cleveland, Ohio.
1991, Walter Massey was named the first African-American director of the National Science Foundation.

MARCH 4   CIVIL RIGHTS LEADERS & BLACK NATIONALISTS

ALBERT IRVIN CASSELL

Architect, engineer, planner, entrepreneur, and educator. Born in 1895 in Towson, Md. Cornell University College of Architecture (B.A, 1919). Served as a second lieutenant training officer in heavy field artillery in the U.S. and France during World War I (1917-1918); **faculty member of the Howard University (1920-1921), associate professor and head of the department of architecture (1921-1928); helped develop Howard's College of Engineering.** Co-planned the initial architectural and structural design of five trade buildings at Tuskegee (1919); worked in the office of Howard J. Wiegner in Bethlehem, Pa. (1920), designing silk mills industrial plants; architect for the construction of the Home Economics Building at Howard University (1921), gymnasium, armory, and athletic field (1924), College of Medicine Building (1926-1927), three dormitories, alterations to the Art Gallery and School of Religion, and the heat, light, and power requirements of Freedmen's Hospital; head of Howard's maintenance department (1929-1932). Architect, structural designer, and supervisor for the construction and interior facilities for Howard's Chemistry Building (1935), Frederick Douglass Memorial Hall (1935), and Founders Library (1938); constructed over 500 dwellings on his own land in Northeast D.C. (1942-1946), becoming part owner and vice president of Mayfair Mansions (1948-1952); creator and architect for a proposed a 192-million-dollar bomb shelter in northeast D.C. (1951-1954); senior member of Cassell, Gray & Sultan (1961-1969) and participated in the construction of the U.S. Army installation at Washington National Airport (1963), the Pentagon (1964), Kimball School in D.C., and St. Paul Baptist Church in Baltimore (1966). Died on November 11, 1969, in Washington, D.C. Further reading, Frederick D. Wilkinson, *50 Years of Engineering and Architecture--The School of Engineering and Architecture, Howard University, 1910-1960*.

---

on this day in history...

1930,	Derrick Bell, Harvard's first African-American tenured professor, was born in Pittsburgh, Pa.
1941,	Joan Murray, first African-American woman to report the news on television, was born in Ithaca, N.Y.
1973,	Coleman Young was elected Detroit's first African-American mayor.
1976,	Benjamin Hooks succeeded Roy Wilkins as executive director of the NAACP.

FRANCIS JAMES GRIMKE

Minister, author, and civil rights leader known as **"the Black Puritan."** Born on November 4, 1850, near Charleston, S.C. Lincoln University, Pa. (B.A., 1870); Howard University School of Law; Princeton Theological Seminary (1878). Escaped to the Confederate Army to avoid enslavement (1861), serving as a valet to an officer; enslaved (1863), as a servant to another Confederate officer; emancipated (1865). Ordained by the Presbytery of Washington (1878); pastor of the 15th Street Presbyterian Church in Washington, D.C. (1878-1885, 1889-1937), where from the pulpit he denounced the hypocrisy of American churches and gave full support to civil rights organizations; Howard University board of trustees (1880-1925); pastor of the Laura Street Presbyterian Church in Jacksonville, Fla. (1885-1889); charter member of the Afro-Presbyterian Council (1893); founding member of the American Negro Academy (1897), the nation's first African-American learned society; chairman of the Committee of Religion and Ethics of the Hampton Negro Conference (1898-1902); joined the movement that called for the Springfield, Ill., meeting, which led to the formation of the NAACP. Died on October 11, 1937, in Washington, D.C. Further reading, Clifton E. Olmsted, _Sons of the Prophets_, (1963).

---

on this day in history...

1770,	Crispus Attucks became the first person to give his life for America when he was killed in the Boston Massacre.
1897,	The American Negro Academy, nation's first African-American learned society, was organized.
1920,	Leontine T.C. Kelly, first African-American woman bishop of a major religious organization, was born in Washington, D.C.
1925,	George Washington Collins, Illinois congressman (1970-1972), was born in Chicago, Ill. (d. 1972).
1939,	Charles H. Fuller, Jr., Pulitzer Prize-winning playwright of _A Soldier Play_, was born in Philadelphia, Pa.
1969,	President Nixon established the Office of Minority Enterprise within the U.S. Department of Commerce.

MARCH 5   CIVIL RIGHTS LEADERS & BLACK NATIONALISTS

GEORGE WASHINGTON CARVER

Agriculturist, inventor, and botanist known as the "**Wizard of Tuskegee.**" Born in 1864 near Diamond Grove, Mo. Simpson College; **first African-American graduate of Iowa Agricultural College [now Iowa State University]** (B.S., 1894; M.S., 1896), where he was also a faculty member in charge of laboratory work in systematic biology. Became head of Tuskegee Institute's department of Agriculture (1896-1943), after being persuaded by Booker T. Washington to leave the money and position in Iowa; became director of the experimental station "Branch Agricultural Experiment Station and Agricultural School for the Colored Race" at Tuskegee (1897). Gave lectures at Tuskegee Agricultural Farmers' Institute's monthly meetings; published bulletins communicating scientific discoveries and concepts to the farmers of Macon County, Ala. (1898-1942); drove a mule-drawn wagon known as the "Movable School" throughout impoverished farmlands (1899-1906), bringing the experiment station straight to the farmers; developed over 300 different products from peanuts and appeared in front of the U.S. House Ways and Means Committee to convince them that cotton should not remain the dominate crop of the South (1921), which brought him worldwide fame. Pioneer in the new science of chemurgy--the industrial utilization of agricultural products; produced 118 products and over 500 dyes from 28 kinds of plants; elected fellow of the Royal Society of Arts of Great Britain in 1916; awarded the NAACP Spingarn Medal (1923), for his outstanding work in agricultural chemistry; received patents for producing cosmetics, paint and stains, and a process of producing paints and stains; appointed collaborator for the Mycology and Plant Survey, U.S. Department of Agriculture (1935). Died on January 5, 1943, in Tuskegee, Ala. Further reading, Lawrence Elliott, _George Washington Carver: The Man Who Overcame_ (1971).

---

on this day in history...

1974,	George Brown and Melvin Dymally were elected Colorado and California's first African-American lieutenant governors, respectively.
1974,	Shirley Chisholm of New York became the first African-American woman elected to Congress.
1974,	Harold Ford was elected Tennessee's first African-American congressman.
1974,	Walter Washington became first elected African-American mayor of Washington, D.C.
1989,	The first memorial to the civil rights movement was dedicated in Montgomery, Ala.

NOVEMBER 5   SCIENTISTS

FANNIE LOU HAMER

Political and civil rights leader. Born on October 6, 1917, in Montgomery County, Miss. Joined the Student Nonviolent Coordinating Committee in Ruleville, Miss. (1962), and became SNCC field secretary and a registered voter (1963); helped start the Delta Ministry, an extensive community development program; **helped found the Mississippi Freedom Democratic Party;** addressed the Democratic National Convention (1964), which was televised to a national audience; became the first African-American woman (along with Victoria Gray and Annie Devine) to ever sit, although temporarily, on the floor of the U.S. House of Representative (1965), after unsuccessfully challenging the seating of the regular Mississippi congressmen; delegate to the Democratic National Convention (Chicago. 1968); founded the Freedom Farms Corporation, a nonprofit venture conceived to help needy families raise food and livestock. Died on March 14, 1977, in Mound Bayou, Miss. Further reading, Jerry DeMuth, "Tired of Being Sick and Tired," *Nation* (1 June 1964).

---

on this day in history...

1857, The U.S. Supreme Court ruled against Dred Scott in the case of *Scott vs. Sandford*, stating that slaves were property, not citizens.

1901, Virginia State University was founded in Petersburg, Va.

1925, John Leslie "Wes" Montgomery,"world's greatest jazz guitarist," was born in Indianapolis, Ind. (d. 1968).

1931, Carmen Paula de Lavallade, dancer and actress, was born in Los Angeles, Calif.

1961, President Kennedy issued Executive Order 10925, creating the Equal Employment Opportunity Commission (affirmative action).

MARCH 6   CIVIL RIGHTS LEADERS & BLACK NATIONALISTS

WILLIAM WARRICK CARDOZO

Physician and pioneer sickle cell anemia researcher. Born on April 6, 1905, in Washington, D.C. Ohio State University (B.A., 1929; M.D., 1933); interned at Cleveland City Hospital (1933-1934), and was resident in pediatrics at Chicago's Provident Hospital (1934-1935). Served as General Education Board fellow in pediatrics at Chicago's Children's Memorial Hospital and Provident Hospital (1935-1937), where he became a **pioneer in the research on sickle cell anemia** with the aid of a grant from the Alpha Phi Alpha fraternity; his pioneer study, "Immunologic Studies in Sickle Cell Anemia" (1937), was published in the *Archives of Internal Medicine*. Associate professor of Pediatrics at Howard University College of Medicine and Freedmen's Hospital (1937-1962); certified by the American Board of Pediatrics (1942), and became a fellow of the American Academy of Pediatrics (1948); school medical inspector for the Washington, D.C., Board of Health (1937-1962). Founder of the Alpha Omega Alpha Honorary Society at Howard University College of Medicine; co-author of "Hodgkin's Disease with Terminal Eosinophilia" (*Journal of Pediatrics*, February 1938), and "Growth and Development of Negro Infants. III. Growth During the First Year of Life" (1950). Died on August 11, 1962, in Washington, D.C. Further reading, Vivian Sammons, *Blacks in Science and Medicine* (1990).

on this day in history...

1950,	Jacqueline Harrison Barrett, first woman sheriff of Fulton County, Ga., was born in Charlotte, N.C.
1969,	Howard N. Lee was elected Chapel Hill's first African-American mayor.
1988,	Bill and Camille Cosby announced their intentions to donate $20,000,000 to Spelman College.

JAMES WELDON JOHNSON

Lawyer, poet, lyricist, author, editor, and civil rights leader.   Born on June 17, 1871, in Jacksonville, Fla.   Atlanta University (A.B., 1894; A.M., 1904); Columbia University.   Admitted to the Florida bar (1898), becoming **Jacksonville's first African-American lawyer**; founded the *Daily American* (1895); wrote the lyrics for "Lift Every Voice and Sing" (1900), which later became "The Negro National Anthem;" wrote musical comedies and light operas (1901-1906), with his brother J. Rosamond Johnson; appointed U.S. consul at Puerto Cabello, Venezuela (1906); member of the diplomatic corps (1909-1912). Published: *The Autobiography of an Ex-Colored Man* anonymously (1912), inspired by his law partner, Douglas Wetmore, who passed for white during a year at the University of Michigan Law School; *Fifty Years and Other Poems* (1917), a collection of some of his best works; *God's Trombones: Seven Negro Sermons in Verse* (1927), buried with a copy in his hand; *Black Manhattan* (1930), a guide to African-American life, theater, and biographies from 1626 to 1930; *Along the Way* (1933), which was viewed as a standard in American biographies. Became editor of the *New York Age* (1914); NAACP field secretary (1916-1920) and investigated the U.S. occupation of Haiti; organized a silent protest march in New York City against lynching and racial oppression (1917); originated the phrase "Red Summer," after race riots in Washington, Chicago, Knoxville, Omaha, and Charleston, S.C.; **NAACP's first African-American executive secretary (1920-1930), becoming most effective defender of equal rights for African-Americans during the 1920s**; charter member of the American Society of Composers, Authors, and Publishers; visiting professor at New York University; chair in creative literature and writing at Fisk University (1930-1938). Died on June 26, 1938, in Wiscasset, Maine. Further reading, <u>Eugene Levy</u>, *James Weldon Johnson: Black Leader, Black Voice* (1973).

---

on this day in history...

1919,	Juanita Kidd Stout of Pennsylvania, first African-American woman state supreme court justice, was born in Wewoka, Okla.
1942,	The first African-American cadets graduated from Tuskegee Flying School.

MARCH 7   CIVIL RIGHTS LEADERS & BLACK NATIONALISTS

SOLOMON G. BROWN

Scientific technician and lecturer. Born on February 14, 1829, in Washington, D.C. Worked in the D.C. post office under the Assistant Postmaster Samuel Morse (1844-1845); as a technician, he **aided in the installation of wiring poles between Washington and Baltimore for the nation's first successful electromagnetic telegraph system experiment**, which used the dot-and-dash alphabet known as Morse Code to transmit a message over a 40-mile distance. Became a battery packer with the newly formed Morse Telegraph Company (1845); assistant packer in the laboratory of Callman & Brothers, a chemical manufacturer; worked in the foreign exchange division of the new Smithsonian Institute (1852-1864), museum assistant (1864-1869), and as a registrar in charge of transportation, registry, and storage of animal specimens and materials received by the institution (1869-1903), preparing most of the illustrations used for scientific lectures by Smithsonian scholars; gave his first public lecture (1855), on the characteristics and social habits of insects; lectured on telegraphs, plants, food, minerals, and geology. Served as trustee of Wilberforce University; elected president of the National Union League (1866); member of the District of Columbia legislature (1871-1879); director of the Industrial Savings Building Association of D.C.; Washington correspondent to the *Anglo-African Christian Recorder*. Died in 1903. Further reading, William J. Simmons, *Men of Mark: Eminent, Progressive and Rising* (1970).

---

on this day in history...

1882,	John Baxter "Doc" Taylor, first African-American Olympic gold medal winner, was born in Washington, D.C. (d. 1908).
1933,	Louis Wade Sullivan, Morehouse School of Medicine dean and U.S. secretary of health and human services (1989-1993), was born in Atlanta, Ga.
1949,	Larry Holmes, heavyweight boxing champion, was born in Cuthbert, Ga.
1992,	Carol Moseley Braun of Illinois was elected the nation's first African-American woman U.S. senator.
1992,	Ralph Campbell became North Carolina's first African-American state auditor.
1992,	Pam Carter of Indiana became the nation's first African-American woman to be elected a state attorney general.

NOVEMBER 3   **SCIENTISTS**

MARTIN LUTHER KING, JR.

Minister, author, and **"leader of the modern civil rights movement."** Born Michael King on January 15, 1929, in Atlanta, Ga. Morehouse College (B.A., sociology, 1948); Crozer Theological Seminary in Chester, Pa. (B.D., 1951); Boston University (Ph.D., systematic theology, 1955), dissertation title: "A Comparison of the Conceptions of God in the Thinking of Paul Tillich and Henry Nelson Weiman." Accepted first pastorate at Dexter Street Baptist Church in Montgomery (1954-1959); drafted as the leader of the Montgomery Improvement Association in (1955), during the time of the Montgomery bus boycott, which became his launching pad to international fame. Awarded the NAACP Spingarn Medal (1957); published *Stride Toward Freedom* (1958), an account of the boycott that explained his philosophy of nonviolent resistance; returned to Atlanta and became the first president of the SCLC (1959-1968), and co-pastor of his father's church, Ebenezer Baptist Church (1959-1968); traveled to India, the home of Ghandi (1959); began a campaign against segregation in Albany, Ga. (1961); launched a series of successful nonviolent demonstrations in Birmingham that led to his arrest and confinement in the Birmingham jail (1963), where he wrote, with a smuggled pen on toilet and newspaper, "Letter from Birmingham Jail." Delivered his famous "I Have A Dream" speech during the March on Washington (1963), to over 250,000 people; received the Nobel Peace Prize (1964); led protests against voting discrimination in Selma, Ala. (1965), which led to the Voting Rights Act of 1965; opened the "northern phase" of the civil rights movement in Chicago (1966). Assassinated on April 4, 1968, in Memphis, Tenn. Further reading, <u>Taylor Branch</u>, <u>*Parting the Waters: American in the King Years,1954-1968*</u> (1988).

---

on this day in history...

1876,	Edward A. Bouchet became the first African-American to receive a Ph.D. from a major university (Yale).
1910,	William Johnson Trent, Jr., first executive director of United Negro College Fund, was born in Asheville, N.C.
1924,	Addie Wyatt, first woman executive board member of the Amalgamated Meat Cutters Union, was born in Brookhaven, Mass.
1971,	Joe Frazier defeated Muhammad Ali for the heavyweight boxing championship in "the Fight of the Century."
1972,	The Equal Employment Opportunity Act was passed.
1977,	Henry Marsh was elected first African-American mayor of Richmond, Va.

MARCH 8   CIVIL RIGHTS LEADERS & BLACK NATIONALISTS

BENJAMIN BANNEKER

Inventor, surveyor, astronomer, mathematician, and almanac maker who was called the **"first Negro American man of science."** Born on November 9, 1731, in Ellicott's Mills, Md. Attended a Quaker School in Joppa, Md.; self-taught in literature, history, and mathematics; studied astronomy under George Ellicott and began making astronomical calculations for almanacs (1773); accurately predicted an eclipse with the use of borrowed text, instruments, and a table; learned to calculate an ephemeris and to make projections for lunar and solar eclipses. **Helped plan the city of Washington, D.C.** (1791), where he made and recorded astronomical observations, maintained the field astronomical clock, and compiled other data as required by the surveyor; computed the cycle of the 70-year locust; **invented a wooden striking clock, the first of its kind built in the U.S.** (it was accurate from 1761 until the time of his death). Published an annual almanac for farmers (1792-1797), the first being titled, *Benjamin Banneker's Pennsylvania, Delaware, Maryland, and Virginia Almanack and Emphemeris, for the Year of Our Lord, 1792; Being Bissextile, or Leap Year, and the Sixteenth Year of American Independence, Which Commenced July 4, 1776.* Died on October 9, 1806, in Baltimore County, Md. Further reading, Silvio A. Bedoni, *The LIfe of Benjamin Banneker* (1972).

---

on this day in history...

1943,	Bernie Bickerstaff, Denver Nuggets general manager, was born in Benham, Ky.
1983,	President Reagan signed a bill establishing the Martin Luther King, Jr., National Holiday.
1993,	Sharon Sayles-Belton was elected Minneapolis' first woman and African-American mayor.

NOVEMBER 2   **SCIENTISTS**

DAISY LAMPKIN

Civil rights reformer, suffragist, organization official, and the **NAACP's most successful fundraiser**. Born on August 9, 1888, in Reading, Pa. NAACP field secretary (1927-1935), national field secretary (1935-1947), member of the board of directors (1947-1965), and served on the Budget, Life Membership, National Nominating, Public Relations, and Branches Committees; vice president of the *Pittsburgh Courier* (1929-1965); president of the Lucy Stone Civic League; national organizer, vice president, and chairperson of the executive board of the National Association of Colored Women. Helped establish the National Council of Negro Women; **first African-American woman alternate delegate to the Republican National Convention** (1933); responsible for bringing Thurgood Marshall to the NAACP's Legal Defense Committee; led Delta Sigma Theta's national headquarter fundraising campaign (1952). Died on March 10, 1965, in Pittsburgh, Pa. Further reading, *In Sisterhood: Delta Sigma Theta and the Challenge of the Black Sorority Movement* (1988).

---

on this day in history...

1891,   North Carolina Agricultural & Technical University was founded in Greensboro, N.C.

1953,   Larry Doby signed a contract with the Cleveland Indians, becoming the first African-American to play in Major League Baseball's American League.

1963,   Carl Thomas Rowan was appointed U.S. ambassador to Finland.

MARCH 9   CIVIL RIGHTS LEADERS & BLACK NATIONALISTS

ARCHIE ALPHONSO ALEXANDER

Engineer and government official. Born on May 14, 1888, in Ottumwa, Iowa. University of Iowa (B.S., civil engineering, 1912); University of London. Became a designer for Marsh Engineering Company (1912), and built the Tidal Basin Bridge and The K Street Freeway in Washington, D.C.; co-founded the general contracting business, Alexander & Higbee, specializing in the design and construction of steel bridges, highways, municipal power and sewer plants, tunnels, and hydraulic plants. **First Republican governor of the Virgin Islands** (1954-1955); received an honorary degree from Howard University (honorary Ph.D., civil engineering, 1946); founding member of Omega Chapter of Kappa Alpha Psi fraternity and awarded its "Laurel Wreath" (1926), given to the member who had the most outstanding accomplishment of that year; trustee of Tuskegee Institute. Died in 1958. Further reading, Harrie Carwell, *Blacks in Science: Astrophysicists to Zoologist* (1977).

---

on this day in history...

1910,	The first issue of *Crisis* magazine was published by the NAACP.
1917,	Margaret Burroughs, founder and curator of Chicago's DuSable Museum, was born in St. Rose, La.
1929,	Grambling State University was founded in Louisiana.
1945,	The first issue of *Ebony* magazine, the nation's largest African-American publication, was published by JPC in Chicago.
1951,	The first issue of *Jet* magazine was published by JPC.
1988,	Lenora Fulini became the first African-American woman to appear on presidential ballots in all 50 states.

NOVEMBER 1   SCIENTISTS

HUEY PERCY NEWTON

Co-founder of the Black Panther Party.   Born on February 17, 1942, in Monroe, La.   Merritt College in Oakland (A.A., social science, 1965); University of San Francisco Law School; University of California at Santa Cruz (Ph.D., social philosophy, 1980), dissertation title: "War Against the Panthers: A Study of Repression in America."   Co-founded with Bobby Seale, the Black Panther Party, in Oakland (1966), following the doctrines of Malcolm X, Mao Tse-Tung, and W.E.B. DuBois; sought racial equality in areas of education, employment, housing, the exemption of African-American men from the Vietnam War, the end of police brutality, and to secure the African-American community against oppression; served as Black Panther Party minister of defense and chief theoretician (1966-1989), patrolling the Oakland African-American neighborhoods (armed with a shotgun, which was legal under California law, and a law book), explaining their legal rights to African-American suspects who had been stopped by police. Protested a proposed gun control law, by leading 30 armed Black Panthers to the California state assembly in Sacramento to disrupt the session (1967); stopped by Oakland police officers (1967), resulting in the death of one of the officers, Newton's arrest for first-degree murder, the polarization of the U.S., the initiation of a "Free Huey" movement, a dramatic increase in the party membership across the U.S. (with chapters in 45 cities), and the overturning of his conviction by the California State Supreme Court. Emerged from prison as the leader of the para-military organization; **developed a nationwide children's breakfast program**, an accredited grammar school, voter registration campaigns, and free health clinics for the African-American community; led the BPP through the decline of the organization, due mainly to an all-out national campaign by the FBI to disrupt the party; exiled to Cuba (1974-1977). Died on August 22, 1989, in Oakland, Calif.   Further reading, Anthony Earl, _Spitting in the Wind_ (1990).

---

on this day in history...

1863,   AME Bishop Daniel A. Payne purchased the future site of Wilberforce University for $10,000 and became the first African-American president of an institute of higher education.

1913,   Harriet Tubman, Underground Railroad leader, died in Auburn, N.Y. (b. 1823).

MARCH 10   CIVIL RIGHTS LEADERS & BLACK NATIONALISTS

WILLIAM SANDERS SCARBOROUGH

Philologist and university president. Born into slavery on February 16, 1852, in Macon, Ga. Atlanta University; Oberlin College (B.A., 1875; M.A., 1878). Emancipated (1865); taught at Lewis High School in Macon (1875-1876); professor of Latin and Greek at Wilberforce University (1876-1892), vice president (1897-1908), and president (1908-1920); published the textbook, *First Lessons in Greek* (1881), and *Birds of Aristophanes* (1886); elected to membership in the American Philological Association (1882), becoming the **first African-American to achieve scholarly distinction as a student of classical philology**. Professor in the Payne Seminary (1892-1897); assistant in farm studies in the Department of Agriculture (1921-1924), where he became an expert on African-American farmers in the South; president of the Afro-American League of Ohio; challenged Booker T. Washington's model of industrial education, arguing that classical studies should be open to everyone regardless of race. Died September 9, 1926, in Wilberforce, Ohio. Further reading, William J. Simmons, *Men of Mark* (1887).

---

on this day in history...

1870,   John Manuel Gandy, Virginia State University president emeritus, was born in Oktibbeha, Miss. (d. 1947).

1950,   Earl Lloyd of the Washington Capitols became the first African-American to play in the NBA.

1953,   John Lucas, San Antonio Spurs head coach and owner of the CBA Miami Tropics, was born in Durham, N.C.

OCTOBER 31   **SCHOLARS**

MARY BURNETT TALBERT

Educator and civil rights activist. Born on September 17, 1866, in Oberlin, Ohio. Oberlin College (S.P., 1886; B.A., 1894). Taught algebra, geometry, Latin, and history in Little Rock; assistant principal of Bethel University (1887-1888), becoming the first woman in the state to hold the position; principal of Union High School in Little Rock (1888-1891); charter member of the Phyllis Wheatley Club (1899); parliamentarian and chair of the executive committee of the National Association of Colored Women's Clubs of New York (NACW) (1910-1912), president of NACW of New York (1911-1916), and vice president-at-large (1914), and president of the national organization (1916-1920). Member of the Women's Committee on National Defense during World War I; appointed to the League of Nations' Women's Committee on International Relations (1920); **attended the International Council of Woman's Conference (Norway, 1920), as the first African-American delegate**; spearheaded the purchase and restoration of Frederick Douglass' home in Washington; served as NAACP vice president; helped establish NAACP chapters in the South and led anti-lynching drives, which were crucial in their NAACP fundraising efforts; **first woman to be awarded the NAACP Spingarn Medal** (1922), in recognition of her efforts to preserve Douglass' house and the contributions she made to advancing human rights. Died on October 15, 1923, in Buffalo, N.Y. Further reading, Marianna W. Davis, _Contributions of Black Women to America_ (1982).

---

on this day in history...

1922,	Vinnette Justine Carroll, Emmy Award-winning jazz artist, was born in New York City.
1950,	Bobby McFerrin, Grammy Award-winning musician, was born in New York City.
1959,	Lorraine Hansberry's _A Raisin in the Sun_ became the first play written by an African-American woman to open on Broadway.

MARCH 11   **CIVIL RIGHTS LEADERS & BLACK NATIONALISTS**

KELLY MILLER

Educator, essayist, and intellectual leader nicknamed **"philosopher of race questions**." Born on July 18, 1863, in Winnsboro, S.C. Howard University (B.A., 1886); **first African-America student at John Hopkins University**. Served as clerk in the U.S. Pension Office (1884-1886); teacher at the M Street School in Washington, D.C., (1889-1890); professor of mathematics at Howard University (1890-1895), professor of mathematics and sociology (1895-1907), dean of the College of Arts and Sciences (1907-1919), professor and head of the department of sociology (1915-1925), and professor of sociology (1925-1934). Some of his writings included, *As to the Leopard's Spots: An Open Letter to Thomas Dixon* (1905), *The Disgrace of Democracy: An Open Letter to President Woodrow Wilson* (1917), *Race Adjustments* (1908), *Out of the House of Bondage* (1914), *An Appeal to Conscience* (1918), and *The Everlasting Stain* (1924). Wrote articles for over a hundred newspapers in a column called "Kelly Miller Says," "Kelly Miller Writes," and "From the Pen of Kelly Miller;" contributed "Education of the Negro" for *U.S. Bureau of Education Report* (1901), and "Enumerations of Errors in Negro Population" for *Scientific Monthly* (February, 1922). Died on December 29, 1939, in Washington, D.C. Further reading, Horace M. Bond, *Black American Scholars: A Study of Their Beginnings* (1972).

---

on this day in history...

1925,   Gus Savage, former Illinois congressman (1981-1993), was born in Detroit, Mich.
1933,   Wallace D. Muhammad ("Iman Warith Deen"), leader of the Black Muslims, was born in Detroit, Mich.
1954,   The Department of Defense announced elimination of all segregated units in the Armed Forces.
1974,   Muhammad Ali defeated George Forman for the heavyweight boxing championship.

OCTOBER 30   SCHOLARS

MARY CHURCH TERRELL

Educator, author, and civil rights leader. Born on September 9, 1863, in Memphis, Tenn. Attended Antioch College's "Model School," forerunner of the nation's kindergarten program; Oberlin College (B.A., 1884; A.M., 1888). Instructor at Wilberforce University (1885-1887); began teaching Latin at M Street High School [now Dunbar High School] in Washington, D.C. (1887); president of the Bethel Literary & Historical Association (1892-1893); appointed to the Board of Education in Washington, D.C. (1895-1901, 1906-1911), reportedly the **nation's first woman schoolboard member**. Formed the Colored Women's League of Washington, D.C.; charter member and president of the National Association of Colored Women (1896-1901); International Council of Women of Darker Races' second vice president; charter member of the NAACP (1909); gained membership in the Washington chapter of the American Associations of Universities (1949), which ended the policy of excluding African-Americans; chairman of the newly-organized Coordinating Committee for the Enforcement of the D.C. Anti-Discrimination Laws (1953), which **led to the integration in the public accommodations of the nation's capitol**. Died on July 24, 1954, in Annapolis, Md. Further reading, Gladys B. Sheppard, *Mary Church Terrell: Respectable Person* (1959).

---

on this day in history...

1791,	Benjamin Banneker was commissioned to help layout the District of Columbia.
1888,	Francis Hall Johnson, one of America's best known choral directors, was born in Athens, Ga. (d. 1970).
1926,	The Savoy Ballroom, "the home of happy feet," opened on Lenox Avenue in New York City.
1932,	Andrew Young, first African-American U.S. ambassador to the U.N., was born in New Orleans, La.
1940,	Al Jarreau, Grammy Award-winning singer and composer, was born in Milwaukee, Wis.
1964,	Malcolm X announced his withdrawal from the Nation of Islam.

MARCH 12   CIVIL RIGHTS LEADERS & BLACK NATIONALISTS

ALAINE LEROY LOCKE

Philosopher, educator, and critic. Born on September 13, 1885, in Philadelphia, Pa. Philadelphia School of Pedagogy (B.A., 1904); Harvard University Phi Beta Kappa and *magna cum laude* (B.A., 1907; Ph.D., 1918), dissertation title: "The Problem of Classification in Theory Value;" **first African-American Rhodes scholar**, Hertford College in England, where he studied philosophy, Greek, and *Literae Humananiores* (1907-1910). Became a symbol of African-American intellectual achievement, a pioneer among American scholars in the field of comparative race studies, a guiding force of the Harlem Renaissance, and one of the nation's best known African-American scholars. Counseled the Harmon Foundation as it began giving annual awards (1926), for literature, music, fine arts, industry, science education, and race relations to African-American artists, writers, and professionals. Assistant professor of philosophy and education at Howard University (1912-1916, 1918-1925), and professor and chairman of the philosophy department (1928-1953); secured a chapter of Phi Beta Kappa at Howard University (1953); professor of philosophy at City College of New York (1948-1953). Organizer and editor of the special Harlem edition of *Survey Graphic*, "Harlem: Mecca of the New Negro" (1925); established the Howard Players; wrote *The New Negro* (1925), and *The Negro in America* (1933). Served as chairman of the Conference on Science, Philosophy and Religion (1945), member of the editorial board of *American Scholar,* Phi Beta Kappa's *Key Reporter* philosophy editor, and president of the American Association for Adult Education (1945), **first African-American national level-president of a predominately white national education association**. Died on June 9, 1954, in New York City. Further reading, Margaret Just Butcher, *The Negro in American Culture* (1972).

---

on this day in history...

1870,   Martha M. Franklin, founder of the National Association of Colored Graduate Nurses, was born in New Milford, Conn. (d. 1968).

1923,   Georgia Montgomery Powers, Kentucky's first African-American woman state senator, was born in Springfield, Ky.

1933,   Thirman L. Milner, Hartford's first African-American mayor, was born in Hartford, Conn.

1945,   Beatrice Moorman ("Melba Moore"), Tony Award-winning entertainer, was born in New York City.

1949,   Alonzo G. Moron became Hampton Institute's first African-American president.

OCTOBER 29   **SCHOLARS**

WALTER FRANCIS WHITE

Author and civil rights leader. Born on July 1, 1893, in Atlanta, Ga. Atlanta University (1916). Led efforts to form an Atlanta branch of the NAACP, while employed at Standard Life Insurance Company; NAACP assistant executive secretary at its national headquarters in New York City (1918-1929), where he investigated race riots and lynching; awarded a Guggenheim fellowship for creative writing; author of *Rope and Faggot: A Biography of Judge Lynch* (1920), which became required reading during the anti-lynching crusades; delegate to the Pan-African Congress (1921); published two novels during the Harlem Renaissance, *The Fire in Flint* (1924), and *Flight* (1926). As acting NAACP executive secretary (1929-1931), he led the fight against the confirmation of North Carolina Judge John Parker, who openly supported African-American disfranchisement, for a seat on the U.S. Supreme Court; **NAACP executive secretary** (1931-1955), transforming the organization into the major civil rights organization of the 1930s, '40s, and '50s, attacking the doctrines of "separate but equal," hiring Charles Houston for the NAACP's Legal Defense Fund, pushing out W.E.B. DuBois as editor of *Crisis* magazine, and shifting the power from whites, who dominated NAACP policies, to African-American professionals and himself. Awarded the NAACP Spingarn Medal (1937), for his work in leading the fight for the passage of federal anti-lynching bills; guided the NAACP through the economic crisis of the Depression years; served as adviser to the U.S. delegation to the U.N. at San Francisco (1945), and at Paris (1948). Died on March 12, 1955, in New York City. Further reading, Walter White, *A Man Called White* (1948).

---

on this day in history...

1918,   John Rhoden, sculptor, was born in Birmingham, Ala.

MARCH 13   CIVIL RIGHTS LEADERS & BLACK NATIONALISTS

MOZELL CLARENCE HILL

Sociologist and educator.   Born on March 27, 1911, in Anniston, Ala.   University of Kansas sociology degrees (B.A., 1933; M.A., 1937); University of Chicago (Ph.D., 1946).   Researched and prepared a critical analysis of social organization, social stratification, personality development, and racial attitudes in all-African-American communities; teacher at Langston University in Oklahoma (1937-1946); wrote *Culture of Contemporary Negro Communities* (1943). Visiting professor, professor of sociology, and **chairman of the department of sociology at Atlanta University** (1946-1958); special research consultant to the Ashmore Project (1953-1955); helped the Unitarian Service Committee establish an organization to expedite school desegregation (1955-1956); served as co-director of the Georgia Council on Human Relations (1955-1957). Held posts at Columbia University, University of Nigeria, and Washington University; planned and conducted pioneering studies on southern race relations; assisted New York area communities in developing and implementing school integration plans (1964-1965); professor of educational sociology and anthropology in the Department of Administration and Supervision, School of Education, New York University. Died on March 26, 1969, in New York City.   Further reading, *Dictionary of American Negro Biography* (1982).

---

on this day in history...

1862,	The first all-Negro unit in the Civil War fights a victorious skirmish at Island Mound, Mo.
1914,	Omega Psi Phi fraternity was incorporated with the help of Ernest E. Just.
1928,	Roscoe Robinson, Jr., U.S. Army's first African-American four-star general, was born in St. Louis, Mo.
1937,	Lenny Wilkens, Atlanta Hawks head coach, was born in Brooklyn, N.Y.
1981,	Edward M. McIntyre was elected first African-American mayor of Augusta, Ga.

OCTOBER 28   *SCHOLARS*

ROY WILKINS

Editor and civil rights leader. Born on August 30, 1901, in St Louis, Mo. University of Minnesota (B.A., sociology, 1923). Editor of the *St Paul Appeal*, an African-American weekly newspaper; newspaperman with the *Kansas City (Mo.) Call* in Missouri (1923-1931). NAACP assistant executive secretary (1931-1949); substantiated charges of discrimination on a federally-financed flood control project in Mississippi, and played a key role in getting Congress to take action to curb its practice there; editor of the NAACP's *Crisis* magazine (1934-1949); joined a picket march in Washington, protesting the failure of the U.S. attorney general to include lynching on the agenda of a national conference on crime, suffering the first arrest of his career; consultant to the American delegation at the U.N. conference in San Francisco; chairman of the National Emergency Civil Rights Mobilization (1949-1955), a pressure group that sent numerous lobbyists to Washington to campaign for civil rights and fair employment legislation; as **executive secretary of the NAACP** (1955-1977), he testified before Congressional hearings, conferred with Presidents, and wrote extensively for a variety of publications. Participated in the March on Washington (1963), the Selma to Montgomery March (1965), and the Meredith March (1966); served as chairman of the Leadership Conference on Civil Rights. Died on September 9, 1981, in New York City. Further reading, <u>Joan M. Burke</u>, <u>*Civil Rights: A Current Guide to the People, Organizations, and Events*</u> (1974).

---

on this day in history...

1919,	Luther Henderson, Jr., Juilliard School of Music-educated composer, was born in Kansas City, Mo.
1933,	Quincy Delight Jones, Grammy and Academy Award-winning musician, was born in Chicago, Ill.
1946,	Wes Unseld, Washington Bullets head coach, was born in Louisville, Ky.
1947,	William J. Jefferson, Louisiana 2nd District congressman, was born in Lake Providence, La.
1961,	Kirby Puckett, Minnesota Twins All-Star, was born in Chicago, Ill.

MARCH 14   CIVIL RIGHTS LEADERS & BLACK NATIONALISTS

GEORGE EDMUND HAYNES

Social scientist. Born on May 11, 1880, in Pine Bluffs, Ark. Fisk University *Herald* editor and valedictorian (B.A., 1903); Yale University (M.A., 1904); **New York School of Philanthropy's first African-American graduate** (1910); **Columbia University's first African-American Ph.D.** (1912), dissertation title: "The Negro at Work in New York City." Became secretary of the Colored Men's Department of the YMCA (1905); became involved with the Association for the Protection of Colored Women (1905), Committee for Improving the Industrial Conditions of Negroes in New York (1906), and Committee on Urban Conditions Among Negroes (1910); professor of sociology at Fisk University (1910-1918, 1921-1947). **Served as first executive secretary of the National Urban League** (1910-1917); director of the Division of Negro Economics in the U.S. Department of Labor (1918-1921), where he conducted a study *The Negro at Work During the World War and During Reconstruction* (1921); directed a survey of African-American churches (1921). **First executive secretary of the Department of Race Relations of the Federal Council of the Churches of Christ in America** (1921-1947); co-author of the article on African-Americans for *Encyclopedia Britannica* (1929, 1941-1942); consultant on Africa for the World Committee of YMCAs (1948-1955); member of the board of trustees of the State University of New York (1948-1953); taught at City College of New York (1950-1959); wrote *Africa, Continent of the Future* (1950). Died on January 8, 1960, in New York City. Further reading, Nancy Weiss, *The National Urban League* (1974).

---

on this day in history...

1927,	(Ruby "Dee") Ann Wallace, Emmy Award-winning actress, was born in Cleveland, Ohio.
1954,	Benjamin O. Davis, Jr., became the U.S. Air Force's first African-American general.
1975,	Oliver Edward Nelson, Grammy Award-winning jazz musician, died in Los Angeles, Calif. (b. 1932).
1987,	John Oliver Killens, founder of the Harlem Writers Guild, mentor to important African-American writers, and author of *Youngblood*, died in Brooklyn, N.Y. (b. 1916).

OCTOBER 27   *SCHOLARS*

MALCOLM X

Minister, Black Nationalist, and civil rights leader. Born Malcolm Little on May 19, 1925, in Omaha, Neb. Released from prison (1952), where he had discovered the Lost-Found Nation of Islam, the Black Muslim religion led by Elijah Muhammad; replaced his "slave name" Little with an "X"; established a mosque in Philadelphia, and secured official orthodox recognition for the sect; **minister of Harlem's Temple #7** (1954-1964); organized mosques all over the U.S.; started the Black Muslim's official newspaper, *Muhammad Speaks* (1961); spoke on behalf of the movement spreading the messages of racial separation, black self-defense, nonparticipation in white society or religion, and western decadence and immorality. Resigned from the Black Muslims (1964); journeyed on a pilgrimage to Mecca where he met non-blacks whom he found not to be racists, and modified his views to encompass the possibility that not all whites were evil; changed his name to El-Hajj Malik El-Shabazz, founded the Muslim Mosque, Inc., and the Organization of Afro-American Unity (1965), "to unite Afro-Americans and to cooperate with sympathetic whites to arrest its pestilence." Assassinated on February 21, 1965, in New York City. Further reading, Malcolm X, *The Autobiography of Malcolm X* (1965).

---

on this day in history...

1842,	Robert Carlos DeLarge, South Carolina congressman (1871-1873), was born in Aiken, S.C. (d. 1874).
1938,	Emilio Cruz, abstract painter, was born in New York City.
1944,	Sylvestor Stewart ("Sly Stone"), recording artist, was born in Dallas, Texas.
1947,	John Lee became the first African-American naval commissioned officer to be assigned to duty.

MARCH 15   **CIVIL RIGHTS LEADERS & BLACK NATIONALISTS**

ABRAM LINCOLN HARRIS

Economist.   Born on January 17, 1899, in Richmond, Va.   Virginia Union University (B.S., 1922; LL.D.); University of Pittsburgh (M.A., 1924); Columbia University (Ph.D., economics, 1931).   Faculty member at West Virginia State College (1924-1925); executive secretary of the Minneapolis Urban League (1925-1926); instructor at Howard University (1927-1945), and **chairman of the department of economics** (1936-1945). Wrote *The Black Worker*, *The Negro and the Labor Movement* (1931), and *The Negro as Capitalist* (1936); served on the Consumer Advisory Board of the National Recovery Administration (1934); professor in the department of philosophy at the University of Chicago (1946-1963); member of the Executive Committee of the American Economics Association (1959-1962). Died on November 16, 1963, in Chicago, Ill.   Further reading, Abram Harris, *The Negro as Capitalist* (1936).

---

on this day in history...

1919,	Edward William Brooke, former Massachusetts U.S. senator (1967-1979), was born in Washington, D.C.
1944,	Emanuel Cleaver, first African-American mayor of Kansas City, Mo., was born in Waxahachie, Texas.
1990,	Evander Holyfield defeated Buster Douglas for the undisputed heavyweight boxing championship.
1992,	Jim Hayes of Fairbanks was sworn in as the first African-American mayor in the state of Alaska.

BLANCHE KELSO BRUCE

U.S. congressman (44th-46th), businessman, and farmer. Born into slavery on March 1, 1841, near Farmville, Va. Oberlin College. Escaped slavery at the beginning of the Civil War; **organized Kansas and Missouri's first schools for African-Americans** in Lawrence and Hannibal; Tallahatchie County, Miss., supervisor of elections, and Bolivar County, Miss. tax assessor, sheriff, tax collector, and supervisor of education. **Mississippi Republican U.S. senator, nation's first elected African-American U.S. senator** (1875-1881), serving on the Pensions, Manufacturers, and Education and Labor Committees; introduced a bill calling for the desegregation of the U.S. Army; supported aid to African-American migrants during the "Great Exodus" from the South to the Midwest; named as head of an committee investigating the bankrupted Freedmen's Savings and Trust Company (1879), a bank of 70,000, mostly ex-slave, depositors that had over 57 million dollars in deposits. **First African-American registrar of the U.S. Treasury** (1881-1885, 1897-1898); superintendent of the exhibit on black achievements at the World's Cotton Exposition in New Orleans (1884-1885); recorder of deeds for the District of Columbia (1889-1893); awarded an honorary degree from Howard University (LL.D., 1893); member of the board of trustees of Howard University (1894-1898); trustee of the public schools in the District of Columbia (1893-1897). Owned 3,000 acres of Mississippi Delta land; made speeches for fees of $100-$150; operated a successful investment, claims, insurance, and real estate agency in Washington. Died on March 17, 1898, in Washington, D.C. Further reading, William C. Harris, "Blanche K. Bruce of Mississippi: Conservative Assimilationist," *Southern Black Leaders of the Reconstruction Era* (1982).

---

on this day in history...

1827,   The first African-American newspaper, *Freedom's Journal*, was published.
1934,   John Brooks Slaughter, first African-American chancellor of the University of Maryland-College Park, was born in Topeka, Kan.
1960,   Abbie Mitchell, dramatic and concert soprano, died in New York City (b. 1884).
1962,   Dwayne M. Brown, first African-American clerk of the Indiana State Supreme Court, was born in Indianapolis, Ind.

MARCH 16   **CONGRESSMEN**

RICHARD THEODORE GREENER

Educator, lawyer, and reform movement leader. Born on January 30, 1844, in Philadelphia, Pa. **Harvard University's first African-American graduate** (B.A., 1870). Served as principal at the Institute for Colored Youth in Philadelphia (1870-1872), and Sumner High School in Washington (1873); professor of metaphysics, Latin, Greek, international law, and U.S. constitutional history (1873-1877), and librarian at the University of South Carolina (1877). Completed a law degree and was admitted to the South Carolina bar (1876), and the District of Columbia (1877); instructor in the law department of Howard University (1877-1879), and dean (1879-1880); advocated migration of the freedman from the South to western states; served as a law clerk and practiced law in Washington, D.C. (1880-1882). Campaigned for the Republican Party; appointed as secretary of the Grant Monument Association in New York state (1885-1892), and as chief examiner of the municipal civil-service board for New York City (1885-1889). Served in the Spanish-American War as a commissioned naval officer, and as the first U.S. consul to Vladivostok, Russia (1898-1905); decorated by the Chinese government for his role in famine relief in North China during the Boxer Rebellion. Died on May 2, 1922, in Chicago, Ill. Further reading, Frank Mather, _Who's Who of the Colored Race_.

---

on this day in history...

1897,   The Afro-American Historical Society was organized by Robert Adger in Philadelphia, Pa.

1904,   George Jordan, Medal of Honor-winning Buffalo Soldier, died in Crawford, Neb. (b. 1847).

1935,   Langston Hughes' _Mulatto_ became the first full-length play by an African-American writer to open on Broadway.

OCTOBER 25   SCHOLARS

WILLIAM LEVI DAWSON

U.S. congressman (78th-91st). Born on April 4, 1886, in Albany, Ga. Fisk University (B.A., 1909); Kent College of Law in Chicago; Northwestern University (LL.B., 1920). First lieutenant, 365th Infantry of the American Expeditionary Force (1917); admitted to the bar (1920); Chicago City Council (1933-1939); 2nd Ward Democratic committeeman (1939-1942); Illinois 1st District Democratic congressman (1943-1970); became the **first African-American to chair a major congressional committee** (Expenditures in the Executive Department) (1949); **served in Congress longer than any other African-American representative.** Died on November 9, 1970, during his final term, in Chicago, Ill. Further reading, Bruce A. Ragsdale and Joel D. Treese, *Black Americans in Congress, 1870-1989* (1990).

---

on this day in history...

1891,   West Virginia State College was founded in Institute, West Virginia.

1896,   Charles Brooks patented the street sweeper.

1940,   Carole Woods Harris, Nebraska's first African-American woman elected county official (Douglas County Commissioner), was born in Omaha, Neb.

1944,   Clarence Edwin "Cito" Gaston, first African-American manager to win the World Series, was born in San Antonio, Texas.

1955,   Cynthia McKinney, Georgia's first African-American congresswoman, was born in Atlanta, Ga.

MARCH 17   CONGRESSMEN

SOLOMON CARTER FULLER

Clinician, researcher, educator, neurologist, and who was **acknowledged as the first African-American psychiatrist**. Born on August 11, 1872, in Monrovia, Liberia.   Livingstone College (B.A., 1893); Long Island College Hospital; Boston University School of Medicine (M.D., 1897); Pathologist Institute of the University of Munich; interned at Westborough State Hospital in Mass. (1897-1899).   Appointed pathologist at Westborough State Hospital (1899), later becoming head pathologist; professor of pathology, neurology, and psychiatry at Boston University School of Medicine (1899-1937), and professor emeritus (1937-1953). Married sculptor Meta Warrick (1909), an internationally-known sculptor; practiced medicine in Boston and Framington; studied under Dr. Alzheimer in Germany (1904), and the Nobel Prize-winning immunology researcher Paul Ehrlich (1905); became editor of the *Westborough State Hospital Papers* (1913), a publication specializing in mental disease; **a pioneer Alzheimer's disease and dementia researcher**. Died in 1953 in Framingham, Mass.   Further reading, W. Montague Cobb, "Solomon Carter Fuller," (*Journal of the National Medical Association, 1954*).

---

on this day in history...

1942,   *Billboard* magazine created *The Harlem Hit Parade*, the first ratings chart devoted to African-American music,

1948,   Frizzell Gray ("Kweisi Mfume"), Maryland 7th District congressman, was born in Baltimore, Md.

1992,   Cito Gaston of the Toronto Bluejays became the first African-American manager to lead his team to a World Series title.

OCTOBER 24   **SCHOLARS**

OSCAR STANTON DE PRIEST

U.S. congressman (71st-73rd), bookkeeper, plasterer, house painter, and businessman. Born on March 9, 1871, in Florence, Ala. Salina Normal School in Kansas. Elected to the Cook County, Ill., Board of Commissioners (1904); **first African-American member of the Chicago City Council** (1915-1917,1943-1947), where he led the fight for fair employment standards; 3rd Ward committeeman (1924-1928). Illinois 3rd District Republican congressman, **first African-American elected to Congress from outside the South** (1929-1935), serving on the Enrolled Bills, Indian Affairs, and Invalid Pensions Committees; secured a $220,000 increase in an appropriation for a Howard University power plant; introduced an amendment prohibiting discrimination in the Civilian Conservation Corps because of race, color, or creed, and the employment of slave labor (1933); initiated an unsuccessful anti-lynching bill (1934), and attempted to integrate the House dining restaurant; obtained the reputation as a "Red hunter" for his condemnation of communism. Died on May 12, 1951, in Chicago, Ill. Further reading, Bruce A. Ragsdale and Joel D. Treese, *Black Americans in Congress, 1870-1989* (1990).

---

on this day in history...

1922,	Fred Lee Shuttlesworth, Alabama Christian Movement for Human Rights president, was born in Mt. Meigs, Ala.
1933,	Unita Blackwell, Mississippi's first African-American woman mayor, was born in Lula, Miss.
1939,	Charlie Pride, first African-American member of the Grand Ole Opry, was born in Sledge, Miss.
1947,	Louis R. Lautier became one of the first African-Americans admitted to the Congressional Press Gallery.
1959,	Irene Cara, Grammy Award-winning entertainer, was born in New York City.
1963,	Vanessa Williams, first African-American Miss America, was born in New York City.

MARCH 18   **CONGRESSMEN**

EDWARD FRANKLIN FRAZIER

Educator and sociologist. Born on September 24, 1894, in Baltimore, Md. Howard University *cum laude* (B.A., 1916); Clark University in Worcester, Mass. (M.A., sociology, 1920); New York School of Social Work; University of Copenhagen; University of Chicago (Ph.D., 1931), dissertation title: *The Negro Family in Chicago* (1932). Taught mathematics at Tuskegee Institute (1916-1917), English and history at St. Paul's Normal and Industrial School in Lawrenceville, Va. (1917-1918), and French and mathematics at Baltimore High School (1918-1919); director of the Atlanta University School of Social Work and instructor in sociology at Morehouse College (1922-1927). His article "The Pathology of Race Prejudice" was published in *Forum Magazine* (1927); research professor of sociology in the department of social sciences at Fisk University (1932-1934); professor and head of the department of sociology at Howard University (1934-1959), and professor emeritus (1959-1962). Director of Howard University's program in social work (1935-1943); wrote *The Negro Family in the United States* (1939), which won him the John Anisfield Award; resident fellow of the Library of Congress (1942); elected president of the American Sociological Society (1948), becoming the **nation's first African-American head of a predominately white professional organization**; instructor at the John Hopkins School of Advanced International Studies (1957-1962), and Howard's Program of African Studies (1959-1962). Died on May 17, 1962, in Washington, D.C. Further reading, G. Franklin Edwards, *The Black Sociologists: Historical and Contemporary Perspectives* (1974).

on this day in history...

1940,   Pele, soccer champion, was born in Tres Coracoes, Brazil.
1945,   Jackie Robinson signed with the Brooklyn Dodger organization.
1948,   Jessie Leroy Brown became the U.S. Navy's first African-American aviator.

OCTOBER 23

SCHOLARS

MELVIN HURBERT EVANS

Virgin Islands delegate to the U.S. Congress and physician.   Born on August 7, 1917, in Christiansted, St. Croix.   Howard University (B.S., 1940); Howard University's College of Medicine (M.D., 1944).   Health commissioner of the Virgin Islands (1959-1967); **first popularly elected governor of the Virgin Islands** (1968-1975); became a Republican National Committeeman and chairman of the board of trustees of the College of the Virgin Islands (1974); U.S. Republican delegate to Congress from the Virgin Islands (1979-1981), serving on the Armed Services, Interior and Insular, and Merchant Marine and Fisheries Committees; U.S. ambassador to Trinidad and Tobago (1981-1984). Died on November 27, 1984, in Christiansted, St. Croix.   Further reading, Bruce A. Ragsdale and Joel D. Treese, *Black Americans in Congress, 1870-1989* (1990).

on this day in history...

1890,   Nancy Elizabeth Prophet, sculptress who helped build Atlanta University's art department, was born in Warwick, R.I. (d. 1960).

MARCH 19   **CONGRESSMEN**

WILLIAM HENRY FERRIS

Intellectual, editor, author, and Pan-Africanist. Born on July 20, 1874, in New Haven, Conn. Yale University (1899); Harvard University Divinity School (M.A., 1900). Called for the meeting of the Afro-American League (1898), which became the National Afro-American Council, a forerunner of the Niagara Movement and the NAACP; member of the American Negro Academy; argued that blacks are not naturally inferior. *Literary Digest* published his article on "Negro Religion" (1904); editor of *The Champion* in Chicago (1916-1917). Teacher, writer, lecturer, preacher, writer, and **vice president of the Universal Negro Improvement Association**; general literary assistant for the UNIA's *Negro World* (1917-1919). Literary editor of *The Spokesman* (1925-1927); wrote *The African Abroad; or His Evolution in Western Civilization, Tracing His Development under the Caucasian Milieu* (1913); advocated black assimilation into the dominant American culture. Died on August 23, 1941, in New York City. Further reading, Wilson J. Moses, *The Golden Age of Black Nationalism, 1850-1925* (1978).

on this day in history...

1854,	James Bland, songwriter of the Virginia state song (*Carry Me Back To Old Virginny*) was born in Flushing, N.Y. (d. 1911).
1936,	Bobby Seale, co-founder of the Black Panther Party, was born in Dallas, Texas.
1952,	Frank E. Petersen, Jr., U.S. Marine Corps' first African-American general, became their first African-American flyer.
1955,	Willa B. Player became the first African-American woman president of Bennett College.
1963,	250,000 people boycotted the Chicago schools to protest segregation.

JOHN ADAMS HYMAN

U.S. congressman (44th), farmer, and political rights advocate who **became North Carolina's first African-American congressman**. Born into slavery on July 23, 1840, near Warrenton, N.C. Emancipated (1865); delegate to the North Carolina Republican state convention (1867), and named to the Republican Party state executive committee; elected a delegate to the North Carolina constitutional convention and state senator (1867); North Carolina 2nd District Republican congressman (1876-1877), serving on the Manufacturers Committee; North Carolina Colored Masons leader; Warrenton Colored Methodist Church sunday school superintendent; mail clerk's assistant in Maryland (1879-1889); U.S. Department of Agriculture seed dispensary (1889-1891). Died on September 14, 1891, in Washington, D.C. Further reading, George W. Reid, "Four in Black: North Carolina's Black Congressman, 1871-1901," (*Journal of Negro History*, 64 summer 1979).

---

on this day in history...

1934,   Willie L. Brown, Jr., first African-American speaker of the California State Assembly, was born in Mineola, Texas.
1950,   Ralphe Bunche became the first African-American Nobel Peace Prize winner.
1957,   Shelton Jackson "Spike" Lee, director, writer, actor, producer, cinematographer, was born in Atlanta, Ga.
1987,   Robert Townsend's independently-produced film, *Hollywood Shuffle*, premiered.

MARCH 20   CONGRESSMEN

W.E.B. DuBOIS

Educator, author, editor, scholar, and Pan-Africanist. Born William Edward Burghart DuBois on February 23, 1868, in Great Barrington, Mass. Fisk University (B.A., 1888); **Harvard University's first African-American Ph.D.** (B.A., *cum laude*, 1890; M.A., 1891; Ph.D., 1895). Taught Latin, Greek, German, and English at Wilberforce University (1895-1897); instructor at University of Pennsylvania and conducted a survey of Philadelphia African-Americans (1897), **the first sociological survey of an African-American community**; taught economics and history at Atlanta University (1897-1910), and served as chairman of the department of sociology (1934-1945). Secretary of the Pan-African Conference (London, 1900); published *Souls of Black Folk* (1903); **founder and general secretary of the Niagara Movement** (1905-1909); founder and editor of *Moon* (1906), *Horizon* (1907-1910), and *The Brownies Book* (1920-1921). **Founding member and incorporator of the NAACP** (1909-1910), director of publicity and research, member of the board of directors, editor of *Crisis* (1910-1934), director of special research (1944-1948), and consultant to the San Francisco Conference, which founded the U.N. (1945). Joined the Socialist Party (1911); **chief organizer of the First Pan-African Congress** (Paris, 1919), the Second (London, Brussels, and Paris, 1921), the Third (London and Lisbon, 1923), the Fourth (New York City, 1927), and the Fifth (Manchester, 1945); co-chairman of the Council on African Affairs (1948-1951); helped organize the Cultural and Scientific Conference for World Peace (New York City, 1949); chairman of the Peace Information Center; joined the Communist Party of the U.S. and migrated to Ghana. Died on August 27, 1963, in Accra, Ghana. Further reading, W. Manning Marable, *W.E.B. DuBois* (1986).

---

on this day in history...

1929,   Walter F. Broadnax, U.S. deputy secretary of health and human services for the Clinton administration, was born in Seabord, N.C.
1979,   Louis Alexander opened the first African-American fashion museum in Harlem, N.Y.

OCTOBER 21   *SCHOLARS*

JOHN MERCER LANGSTON

U.S. congressman (51st), educator, and diplomat who **became Virginia's first African-American congressman**. Born on December 14, 1829, in Louisa County, Va. Oberlin College (B.A., 1849; M.A., 1852). Admitted to the Ohio bar (1854); elected clerk of Brownheim Township (1855), reportedly becoming the **first person of African descent to be elected to public office in the U.S.**; declined to accompany John Brown on his mission to Harper's Ferry (1859); elected to the Oberlin (Ohio) Board of Education (1860, 1865); recruiter of Negro soldiers during the Civil War; elected leader of the National Equal Rights League (1864), a forerunner to the Niagara Movement; member of the Oberlin City Council (1865-1867); recruited African-American soldiers for the 54th and 55th Massachusetts and 5th Ohio Regiments during the Civil War. Inspector-general of the Freedmen's Bureau (1868-1869); **founder and organizer of Howard University's Law School**, where he served as dean (1868-1875); vice president and acting president of Howard University (1873-1875). Addressed the Colored National Labor Convention (Washington, 1869); counsel and member of the District of Columbia Board of Health (1871-1877); member of the Finance Committee and board of trustees of Freedmen's Savings and Trust Company (1872-1874); resident minister and counsel-general to Haiti and charge d'affairs in Santa Domingo (1877-1885); president of Virginia Normal & Collegiate Institute in Petersburg (1885-1887). Virginia 4th District Republican congressman (1890-1891), serving on the Education Committee. Died on November 15, 1897, in Washington, D.C. Further reading, John Mercer Langston, _From the Virginia Plantation to the National Capitol_ (1894).

---

on this day in history...

1934,   Albert Cornelius Freeman, Jr., Emmy Award-winning actor, was born in San Antonio, Texas.

1957,   Martin Luther King, Jr., leading 25,000 demonstrators, began the Selma Freedom March to Montgomery, Ala.

MARCH 21   CONGRESSMEN

ALEXANDER CRUMMELL

Educator and missionary. Born in 1819 in New York City. Queen's College in Cambridge, England (A.B., 1853). Active in the Negro Convention Movement (Albany, N.Y., 1840; Troy, N.Y., 1847); ordained as a priest in Philadelphia (1844); migrated to Liberia as a missionary of the Episcopal Church (1853); master of Mount Vaughan High School at Cape Palmas (1858-1861); published books of sermons and addresses--*The Relations and Duties of Free Colored Men in America to Africa* (1861), *The Future of Africa* (1862), *The Greatness of Christ* (1882), and *Africa and America* (1891); faculty member of the new Liberia College (1862-1866); worked closely with the American Colonization Society. Moved to Washington (1873), and later founded St. Luke's Church; called for the founding of the Conference of Church Workers among Colored People (1883); instructor at Howard University (1895-1897); **organized the American Negro Academy (1897), the nation's first African-American learned society**; lecturer whose message was always "the need for educated Negroes to lead in the redemption of the race." Died on September 10, 1898, in New York City. Further reading, W.E.B. DuBois, "Of Alexander Crummell," *The Souls of Black Folks* (1903).

OCTOBER 20　　　　　　　　　　　　　　　　　　　　　　　**SCHOLARS**

JEFFERSON FRANKLIN LONG

U.S. congressman (41st) and merchant tailor who **became Georgia's first African-American congressman**.   Born into slavery on March 3, 1836, in Crawford County, Ga.   Active in the Georgia Education Association; Georgia State Republican Party organizer, central committeeman, and convention chairman (Macon, 1869); Georgia 4th District Republican congressman (1871), where he opposed removing Confederate sanctions because their leaders publicly stated that they would then again assume control; became the **first African-American to deliver a speech in the House** (1871); participated in the southern Republican convention (Chattanooga, 1874); elected delegate to the Republican National Convention (1880). Died on February 5, 1900, in Macon, Ga.   Further reading, Maurine Christopher, *America's Black Congressmen* (1971).

---

on this day in history...

1492,   Pedro Alonzo Nino, who sailed with Columbus from Spain, reportedly discovered the "New World" while landing on Walting Island in the Bahamas.

1943,   George Benson, Grammy Award-winning jazz guitarist, was born in Pittsburgh, Pa.

1946,   Don Chaney, Detroit Pistons head coach, was born in Baton Rouge, La.

1959,   Stephanie Mills, Grammy and Tony Award-winning entertainer, was born in New York City.

MARCH 22   **CONGRESSMEN**

WILLIAM HENRY CROGMAN

Educator and Greek scholar. Born on May 5, 1841, Philipsburg, St. Martin, Leeward Islands. Pierce Academy in Middleboro, Mass. (1868); **Atlanta University's first graduating class** (B.A., 1873). Served as seaman (1855-1866); **English teacher at Claflin College** in Orangeburg, S.C. (1868-1870), becoming the **first African-American English teacher at Claflin College**; professor of classics at Clark College in Atlanta (1873-1903, 1910-1921), elected the **first African-American secretary of the board of trustees of Clark College** (1885-1922) and served as president (1903-1910); trustee of Gammon Theological Seminary. Lay delegate to the General Conference of the Methodist Church (1880, 1884, 1888), becoming the first African-American secretary (1888); became member of the University Senate of the Methodist Episcopal Church (1892); addressed the National Education Association (Madison, Wis., 1884); commissioner for the Cotton States Exposition (Atlanta, 1885), mainly responsible for the large and credible African-American exhibit; a strong believer that a good education could be found only in the study of the classics. Died on October 16, 1931, in Philadelphia, Pa. Further reading, A.A. McPheeters, *History of Clark College* (1944).

on this day in history...

1934, Richard Arrington, Birmingham's first African-American mayor, was born in Livingston, Ala.

1936, James Bevels, an initiator of the Selma to Montgomery March, was born in Itta Bena, Miss.

1936, Johnetta Betch Cole, first African-American woman president of Spelman College, was born in Jacksonville, Fla.

1960, Jenifer Holiday, Tony and Grammy Award-winning actress and singer, was born in Riverside, Texas.

1962, Evander Holyfield, heavyweight boxing champion, was born in Atmore, Ala.

OCTOBER 19   *SCHOLARS*

JOHN ROY LYNCH

U.S. congressman (43rd, 44th, and 47th), photographer, lawyer, and army officer who **became Mississippi's first African-American member of the U.S. House of Representatives**.   Born into slavery on September 10, 1847, in Concordia Parish, La.   Emancipated (1863); appointed justice of peace (1869); elected to the Mississippi State House of Representatives (1869), where he was responsible for the redistricting of the state; elected speaker of the house (1872); elected Mississippi 6th District Republican congressman (1873-1877, 1882-1883), serving on the Mines and Mining, Expenditures in the Interior Department, Education and Labor, and Militia Committees and worked for the passage of the Civil Rights Bill of 1875. Chairman of the Mississippi Republican State Committee (1881-1892), member of the Republican National Committee (1884-1889); temporary chairman of the Republican National Convention (Chicago, 1884), becoming the **first African-American to deliver a keynote address**; delegate to the Republican National Convention (1884, 1888, 1892, 1900); fourth auditor of the treasury for the Navy Department (1889-1893); admitted to the Mississippi bar (1896), and opened a Washington law office. Major and additional paymaster of the volunteers during the Spanish-American War (1898-1901), U.S. Army paymaster and captain (1901-1906); U.S. Army major (1906-1911), stationed in Cuba, Omaha, San Francisco, and the Philippines; opened a Chicago law office (1912); published *The Facts of Reconstruction* (1913). Died on November 2, 1939, in Chicago, Ill. Further reading, John Hope Franklin, "John Roy Lynch: Republican Stalwart from Mississippi," (*Southern Black Leaders of the Reconstruction Era*, 1982).

---

on this day in history...

1938,	Maynard Holbrook Jackson, Jr., Atlanta's first African-American mayor, was born in Dallas, Texas.
1953,	Yvette Marie Stevens ("Chaka Khan"), Grammy Award-winning singer, was born in Chicago, Ill.
1955,	Moses Malone, professional basketball champion, was born in Petersburg, Va.

MARCH 23   CONGRESSMEN

MARY EDWARD CHINN

Physician and scholar. Born on April 15, 1896, in Great Barrington, Mass. Columbia University (B.S., 1921; M.S., public health, 1933), **first African-American woman graduate of University of Bellevue Medical Center [now New York University Medical College]** (1926). **First African-American woman to intern at Harlem Hospital** (1926); studied with George Papanicolaou (1928-1933), the father of the "Pap" smear; physician to a group of African-American nuns at the Catholic convent Francian Handmaids of Mary (1928-1976); staff member at the Strang Clinic of Memorial Hospital (1945-1974), and New York Infirmary for Women and Children in New York City (1945, 1960-1965). Studied exfoliative cytology at Cornell University Medical School (1948-1955); clinician with the Department of Health Day Care Centers in New York City (1960-1977); consultant to the Phelps-Stokes Fund; founding member of the Susan Smith McKinney Steward, M.D., Society (1975), "for the expressed purpose of aiding Negro women in medical school and to document the achievements of African-American women in medicine over the years;" honorary doctorates from Columbia University (1979), and New York University (1980). Died on December 1, 1980, in New York City. Further reading, Charlayne Hunter-Gault, "Black Women M.D.'s," (*New York Times,* 11-16-1977).

---

on this day in history...

1948, Paulette Williams ("Ntozake Shange"), playwright of *for colored girls...*, was born in Trenton, N.J.
1951, Terri McMillian, author of *Waiting to Exhale*, was born in Port Huron, Mich.
1958, Thomas "Hit Man" Hearns, boxing champion, was born in Grand Junction, Tenn.
1961, Wynton Marsalis, Juilliard School of Music-educated jazz musician, was born in New Orleans, La.

ARTHUR WERGS MITCHELL

U.S. congressman (74th-77th), lawyer, and real estate businessman who **became the first African-American Democrat elected to Congress**.   Born on December 12, 1883, near Lafayette, Ala.   Tuskegee Institute; Columbia University Law School; Harvard University Law School.   Founder and president of Armstrong Agricultural School in West Butler, Ala.; admitted to the bar (1927), practicing in Washington and Chicago; Illinois 1st District Democratic congressman (1934-1942), serving on the Post Office and Post Roads Committee. Sued the Chicago, Rock Island, & Pacific Railway and filed a complaint with the Interstate Commerce Commission (1937), after being forced out of a Pullman car into a "Jim Crow" car when his train crossed into Arkansas; *Mitchell vs. United States et al* (1941), U.S. Supreme Court unanimously held in favor of Mitchell that African-American passengers had the right to receive the same accommodations and treatment as did whites, overturning the segregation policies of the Interstate Commerce Commission. Died on May 9, 1968, in Petersburg, Va.   Further reading, <u>Bardolph Richard</u>, *The Negro Vanguard* (1961).

on this day in history...

1912,   Dorothy Irene Height, National Council of Negro Women president, was born in Richmond, Va.

1968,   Bob Foster defeated Dick Tiger for the light heavyweight boxing championship.

MARCH 24   CONGRESSMEN

EDWARD ALEXANDER BOUCHET

Educator and scholar.   Born on September 15, 1852, in New Haven, Conn.   Yale University Phi Beta Kappa (B.A., 1874; Ph.D., 1876), **first African-American graduate of Yale, first African-American Phi Beta Kappa**, and the **first African-American to earn a Ph.D. from an American university**; dissertation title: "Measuring Refractive Indices."   Instructor of physics and chemistry at the Institute for Colored Youth [now Cheyney State College] (1876-1902); science teacher at Sumner High School in St. Louis (1902-1903); business manager at Provident Hospital in St. Louis (1903-1904); U.S. inspector of customs at the Louisiana Purchase Exposition (1904-1905); director of academics at St. Paul's Normal and Industrial School in Lawrenceville, Va.; principal of Lincoln High School in Gallipolis, Ohio (1908-1913); faculty member at Bishop College in Marshall, Texas (1913-1916). Died on October 28, 1918, in New Haven, Conn.   Further reading, Harry Washington Greene, _Holders of Doctorates Among American Negroes_ (1946).

on this day in history...

1711,	Jupiter Hammon, first published African-American poet, was born in Lloyd's Neck, N.Y.
1864,	Halle Tanner Johnson, first woman to practice medicine in Alabama, was born in Pittsburgh, Pa. (d. 1901).
1928,	Lerone Bennett, Jr., historian and _Ebony_ senior editor, was born in Clarksdale, Miss.
1933,	Richard H. Jackson, Boeing 747 landing gear designer, was born in Detroit, Mich.
1951,	Howard Rollins, actor, was born in Baltimore, Md.
1956,	Mae C. Jemison, first African-American woman in space, was born in Decatur, Ala.

OCTOBER 17   *SCHOLARS*

ROBERT N.C. NIX, SR.

U.S. congressman (88th-95th) and lawyer who **became Pennsylvania's first African-American congressman**. Born on August 9, 1905, in Orangeburg, S.C. Lincoln University (B.A., 1921); University of Pennsylvania School of Law (LL.B., 1924); Temple University. Practiced law in Philadelphia; elected committeeman for the 44th Ward (1932); special deputy attorney general for the Commonwealth of Pennsylvania in the revenue department and special assistant deputy attorney general (1934-1938); Pennsylvania Democratic congressman (1958-1979), serving on the Veterans' Affairs, Foreign Affairs, Merchant Marine and Fisheries Committees, and as chairman of the Post Office and Civil Service Committee; assured the House of his belief that the 1963 March on Washington would be a peaceful one; privately sought to prevent the House from denying Representative Adam Clayton Powell, Jr., his seat in the 90th Congress. Died on June 22, 1987, in Philadelphia, Pa. Further reading, Bruce A. Ragsdale and Joel D. Treese, *Black Americans in Congress, 1870-1989* (1990).

---

on this day in history...

1847,	Theodore Sedwick Wright, nation's first African-American theology graduate, died in New York City (b. 1797).
1942,	Aretha Franklin, Grammy Award-winning singer who is known as the "queen of soul," was born in Memphis, Tenn.
1967,	Debi Thomas, first African-American world figure skating champion, was born in Poughkeepsie, N.Y.
1991,	Whoopi Goldberg won an Academy Award as best supporting actress for her role in *Ghost*.
1991,	Russell Williams, Hollywood sound editor, became the first African-American to win two Oscars.

MARCH 25   CONGRESSMEN

EDWARD WILMOT BLYDEN

Scholar, diplomat, journalist, and educator. Born on August 3, 1832, in St. Thomas, West Indies. Alexander High School in Monrovia, Liberia. Migrated to the U.S. (1950), Liberia (1851); ordained as a Presbyterian minister; editor of *Liberia Herald*; published the pamphlets, *A Voice from Bleeding Africa* (1856), and *A Vindication of the African Race* (1857); commissioned by the Liberian government to interest British and American philanthropists in Liberian education (1861), and to encourage African-Americans to return to Africa (1862). Professor of classics (1862-1871), and president of Liberia College (1862-1871); Liberian secretary of state (1864-1866), minister to Britain (1877-1878, 1892), minister of the interior (1880-1882), and minister plenipotentiary to London and Paris over the country's disputed northern boundary (1905). Wrote the book, *Christianity, Islam and the Negro Race* (1887); agent for the British government in Lagos for native affairs (1896-1897); teacher, writer, and director of Moslem education in Sierra Leone (1901-1906); wrote the pamphlet, *African Life and Customs* (1908), which was called **"the first important attempt at a sociological analysis of African society as a whole,"** became known as "the prophet of the renaissance of the Negro race." Died on February 7, 1912, in Freetown, Sierre Leone. Further reading, Edith Molden, *Blyden of Liberia* (1966).

---

on this day in history...

1922, Leon H. Sullivan, founder of Opportunity Industrialization Center, was born in Philadelphia, Pa.

1940, Benjamin O. Davis, Sr., became the first African-American brigadier general in the Regular U.S. Army.

1951, Alan Dupree Wheat, Missouri 5th District congressman, was born in San Antonio, Texas.

1973, Maynard Jackson was elected Atlanta's first African-American mayor.

OCTOBER 16   SCHOLARS

ADAM CLAYTON POWELL, JR.

U.S. congressman (79th-90th, 91st), minister, publisher, and civil rights leader who was called **"the most powerful African-American politician in the U.S."** Born on November 29, 1908, in New Haven, Conn.   City College of New York; Colgate University (A.B., 1930); Columbia University (M.A., 1932); Shaw University in Raleigh, N.C. (D.D., 1935). Assistant minister, business manager, and **pastor of Harlem's Abyssinian Baptist Church--the nation's largest African-American congregation** (1930-1970); organized mass meetings, rent strikes, and public campaigns to force Harlem business to hire and/or begin promoting African-American employees; **first African-American New York City councilman** (1941-1944); publisher and editor of *The People's Voice* (1941-1945); member of the New York State Office of Price Administration (1942-1944), and Manhattan Civil Defense (1942-1945). New York 22nd / 18th District Democratic congressman, **first African-American elected to Congress from the East** (1945-1967, 1969-1971), serving on the Indian Affairs, Invalid Pensions, Labor, Interior, Insular Affairs Committees and chairman of the Education and Labor Committee. Died on April 4, 1972, in Miami, Fla.   Further reading, Adam Clayton Powell, Jr., *Adam by Adam* (1971).

---

on this day in history...

1833,   James Carter Corbin, Arkansas state superintendent of public instruction, was born in Chillicothe, Ohio (d. 1911).

1913,   John Frederick Burton, first African-American forensic pathologist, was born in Nashville, Tenn.

1925,   Joseph Jacob Simmons, Interstate Commerce Commission vice chairman, was born in Muskogee, Okla.

1939,   Franklyn Jenifer, Howard University president, was born in Washington, D.C.

1944,   Dianna Ross, Grammy Award-winning singer, was born in Detroit, Mich.

1991,   Emanuel Cleaver was elected first African-American mayor of Kansas City, Mo.

MARCH 26   **CONGRESSMEN**

JAMES VARICK

Founder and first bishop of the African Methodist Episcopal Zion Church. Born into slavery in 1750 in Orange County, N.Y. Learned the trade of shoemaking; joined the John Street Methodist Episcopal Church in New York City, where he was licensed to preach; led some 30 African-Americans out of the segregated John Street Church (1796), and **formed the first African-American church in New York City**; dedicated Zion Church (1800), which was located in the vicinity of Wall Street; incorporated his organization as The African Methodist Episcopal Church in New York (1801); **became one of the first three deacons ordained in New York State**. Worked as a shoemaker and tobacco cutter; ran a classroom in the family home and in the Zion Church; became the first chaplain in the New York African Society for Mutual Relief; active in the first African Masonic lodge in New York State, Boyer Lodge No. 1; served as a vice president of the New York Bible Society. **Established the African Methodist Episcopal Zion Church in New Haven (1818), and was elected the first bishop (1822, 1824)**; member of a committee that petitioned the New York State Constitutional Convention (1821), to grant African-Americans the right to vote; helped Alexander Crummell, Samuel Cornish, John B. Russwurm, and Richard Allen in establishing the *Freedom's Journal* (1827); celebrated Thanksgiving at his Zion Church (1827), after New York State emancipated all the slaves in the state. Died on July 22, 1827, in New York City. Further reading, William J. Walls, *The African Methodist Episcopal Church* (1974).

---

on this day in history...

1957, The Sickle Cell Research Foundation opened in Los Angeles, Calif.
1966, Huey Newton and Bobby Seale finalized a draft of a 10-point program and founded the Black Panther Party of Self Defense.
1993, Nelson Mandela was named as co-winner, along with F.W. de Klerk, of the Nobel Peace Prize.

OCTOBER 15   **RELIGIOUS LEADERS**

JOSEPH HAYNE RAINEY

U.S. congressman (41st-45th), barber, and banker who **became the first African-American to be elected and seated in the House of Representatives**.   Born into slavery on June 21, 1832, in Georgetown, S.C.   Emancipated in the 1840s; pressed into the Confederate Army, escaped to Bermuda (1862), and returned to South Carolina (1865). Republican county chairman (1868-1876); member of the executive committee of the South Carolina Republican Party; delegate to the South Carolina Constitutional Convention (1868); state senator (1868-1870), chairman of the finance committee (1870). South Carolina 1st District Republican congressman (1870-1879), serving on the Freedmen's Affairs and Invalid Pensions Committees. Became the **first African-American to preside over a House session** (1874); supported general amnesty, the Civil Rights Bill of 1875, the integration of public schools, enforcement of the 14th Amendment and the Ku Klux Klan Act. Internal revenue agent in South Carolina (1879-1881); broker (1881-1886). Died on August 2, 1887, in Georgetown, S.C.   Further reading, Cyril Outerbridge Packwood, *Detour--Bermuda, Destination--U.S. House of Representatives; The Life of Joseph Hayne Rainey* (1977).

---

on this day in history...

1784,	Tom Molineaux, America's first boxing champion, was born in Washington, D.C. (d. 1818).
1944,	Jesse Brown, first African-American U.S. secretary of veteran's affairs, was born in Detroit, Mich.
1963,	Randall Cunningham, Philadelphia Eagles quarterback, was born in Santa Barbara, Calif.

MARCH 27   **CONGRESSMEN**

HENRY McNEAL TURNER

Chaplain, politician, editor, bishop, college president, and colonizationist. Born in 1834 near Abbeville, S.C. Self-taught in reading, writing, and arithmetic; worked for a law firm; joined the Methodist Episcopal Church (1851); licensed to preach (1853), becoming an itinerant minister in the South; moved to St. Louis (1857), and joined the African Methodist Episcopal Church; studied Latin, Greek, and Hebrew; ordained as a deacon in Baltimore (1860); served as elder and pastor of Israel Church in Washington (1862-1863). **Became the first African-American chaplain in the Army** (1863), attached to the 1st Regiment, U.S. Colored Troops; appointed chaplain in the Regular Army (1865), assigned as an agent of the Freedmen's Bureau in Georgia; elected a Republican member of the Georgia Constitutional Convention (1867), during which he sponsored proposals saving the land of owners with outstanding tax bills, providing relief for banks, the pardon of Jefferson Davis, and educational qualifications for voting; member of the Georgia state legislature (1868-1870); served as postmaster in Macon (1869), and as a customs inspector. Manager of the AME Book Concern in Philadelphia (1876-1880); bishop of the AME Church (1880-1892); served as **president of Morris Brown College**; wrote *The Genius and Theory of Methodist Policy* (1885); founded the *Southern Christian Recorder* (1889), the *Voice of Missions* (1892), and *The Voice of the People* (1901); served as historiographer of the AME Church; elected vice president of the American Colonization Society (1876); **advocated the federal government aid African-Americans in returning to Africa and pay reparations for their labor as slaves**; lectured in Europe and Africa. Died on May 8, 1915, Windsor, Ontario. Further reading, Edwin Redkey, *Black Exodus, Black Nationalist and Back-to-Africa Movements 1890-1910* (1969).

---

on this day in history...

1834,   Henry Blair, inventor of a corn planter, became the first African-American to receive a U.S. patent.

1902,   William Allison Davis, social anthropologist, was born in Washington, D.C. (d. 1983).

1915,   William E. Benson, founder of the Kowaliga Industrial Community, died in Tallapoosa County, Ala. (b. 1876).

OCTOBER 14   RELIGIOUS LEADERS

HIRAM RHODES REVELS

U.S. congressman (41st), minister, army recruiter, and college president who **became the nation's first African-American U.S. senator**. Born on September 27, 1827, in Fayetteville, N.C.   Quaker Seminary in Liberty, Ind.; Drake County, Ohio Seminary; Knox Academy in Galesburg, Ill. (1857).   Ordained as an AME minister (1845); **first African-American pastor of the Madison Street Presbyterian Church in Baltimore** (1858-1863); recruited colored regiments in Maryland during the Civil War, and served as a chaplain in the Union Army. Alderman in Natchez, Miss. (1868-1869); Mississippi state senator (1869-1870); Mississippi Republican U.S. senator (1870-1871), serving on the Education & Labor and District of Columbia Committees. Supported the readmission of Texas under a Republican government and enforcement of the 15th Amendment; introduced bills to repair and build levees in Mississippi, to grant lands and right of way to aid the New Orleans & Northeastern Railroad, to abolish the franking privilege, and to enforce the federal election law. **First president of the nation's first land-grant school for African-Americans**, **Alcorn University** in Mississippi (1872-1874; 1876-1882); Mississippi secretary of state (1873); professor of theology at Shaw [now Rust] University in Holly Springs, Miss. Died on January 16, 1901, in Aberdeen, Miss.   Further reading, Elizabeth Lawson, *The Gentleman from Mississippi* (1960).

---

on this day in history...

1925,   Ed Wilson, Carnegie Foundation Award-winning sculptor, was born in Baltimore, Md.

MARCH 28   **CONGRESSMEN**

HOWARD THURMAN

Theologian, scholar, author, mystic, educator, who was called a leader of leaders, preacher of preachers, and teacher of teachers.   Born on November 18, 1900, in Daytona Beach, Fla.   Morehouse College (B.A., 1923); Colgate-Rochester Divinity School class president (B.D., 1926); Oberlin College; Haverford College.   Ordained a Baptist minister (1925); pastor of Oberlin's (Ohio) integrated Mt. Zion Baptist Church (1926-1928), which was practically unheard of in the U.S.; studied with Quaker philosopher and mystic Rufus Jones in Haverford, Pa. (1929), where he gained his religious insights into social problems; professor of religion at Spelman and Morehouse College (1929-1931). Professor of religion, instructor in social ethics, and dean of Rankin Chapel (1932-1943), joining a faculty that included Ralph Bunche, Benjamin Mays, and Carter Woodson; traveled to India as a delegate of the World Student Christian Federation during India's struggle against British colonialism (1935), where he met Ghandi; returned to Howard and began preaching and teaching Ghandi's philosophy of nonviolent resistance to oppression. Co-founder and co-pastor of the nondenominational and interracial Church for the Fellowship of All Peoples in San Francisco (1944-1953); professor of spiritual resources and disciplines at Boston University (1953-1965), becoming the **first African-American dean of a predominately white university's chapel**, March Chapel; director of the Howard Thurman Educational Trust in San Francisco (1965-1981). Author of *Deep River: An Interpretation of Negro Spirituals* (1945); named by *Life* as one of the 12 great preachers of the 20th century (1953); became a leading African-American intellectual and **helped define the role of the African-American church during the civil rights movement.** Died on April 10, 1981, in San Francisco, Calif.   Further reading, <u>Howard Thurman</u>, <u>*With Head and Heart*</u> (1980).

---

on this day in history...

1825,	John Sweat Rock, first African-American to argue before the U.S. Supreme Court, was born in Salem, N.J. (d. 1866).
1915,	Meharry Medical School opened in Nashville, Tenn.
1936,	Donald McHenry, U.S. career diplomat, was born in St. Louis, Mo.
1939,	Shirley Caesar, Grammy Award-winning gospel singer, was born in Durham, N.C.
1951,	Beverly Johnson, first African-American model to appear on the cover of *Vogue*, was born in Buffalo, N.Y.
1962,	Jerry Rice, San Francisco 49ers All-Pro wide receiver, was born in Starksville, Miss.

OCTOBER 13   **RELIGIOUS LEADERS**

BENJAMIN STERLING TURNER

U.S. congressman (42nd), farmer, merchant, and livery stable owner who **became Alabama's first African-American congressman**. Born into slavery on March 17, 1825, in Halifax County, N.C. Tax collector for Dallas County, Ala. (1867-1869); Selma, Ala., city councilman (1869-1870). Alabama 1st District Republican congressman (1871-1873), serving on the Invalid Pension Committee; introduced a bill to restore political and legal rights to ex-Confederates; spoke on refunding 250 million dollars worth of cotton taxes collected from southern states between 1866 and 1868, and land for freedmen; secured passage of two private pensions. Delegate to the Republican National Convention (Chicago, 1880). Died on March 21, 1894, in Selma, Ala. Further reading, Rayford W. Logan and Michael R. Winston, "Turner, Benjamin Sterling," *Dictionary of American Negro Biography* (1982).

on this day in history...

1945,   Walt Frazier, basketball champion, was born in Atlanta, Ga.

MARCH 29   CONGRESSMEN

WILLIAM J. SIMMONS

Soldier, minister, educator, and biographer.   Born into slavery on June 26, 1849, in Charleston, S.C.   Howard University (B.A., 1873; M.A., 1881).   Became the principal of Hillsdale Public School in Washington; moved to Florida (1874), where he served as principal of Howard Academy; became an ordained minister; served as deputy county clerk and county commissioner; taught school in Washington (1877-1879). Moved to Lexington, Ky., (1879), and became pastor of the First Baptist Church; president of the Normal and Theological Institution in Louisville (1880-1890); editor of the *American Baptist* (1882-1890); founded a school for industrial training at Cane Spring, Ky.; **first president of the American National Baptist Convention**; author of *Men of Mark: Eminent, Progressive, and Rising* (1887), to show friends and oppressors "that the Negro race is still alive, and must posses more intellectual vigor than any other section of human family." Died on October 30, 1890, in Cane Spring, Ky.   Further reading, William J. Simmons, *Men of Mark* (1887).

---

on this day in history...

1904, William Montague Cobb, Howard University professor emeritus who's known as the "principal historian of the Negro in medicine," was born in Washington, D.C.

1932, Richard Claxton ("Dick") Gregory, civil rights and nutrition advocate, was born in St. Louis, Mo.

1935, William Raspberry, syndicated columnist, was born in Okolona, Miss.

1941, Craig Anthony Washington, Texas 18th District congressman, was born in Longview, Texas.

JOSIAH THOMAS WALLS

U.S. congressman (42nd-44th), soldier, and farmer who **became Florida's first African-American congressman**. Born on December 30, 1842, in Winchester, Va. Pressed into the Confederate Army and captured (1862); corporal in the Union Army 3rd Infantry Regiment, U.S. Colored Troops at Philadelphia (1863-1865), where he saw action in the assault on Fort Wagner, S.C.; Florida state representative (1868), state senator (1869-1871, 1876-1879); attended the Southern States Convention of Colored Men (1871). Florida 1st District Republican congressman (1871-1873, 1873-1875, 1875-1876), serving on the Militia, Mileage, and Expenditures in the Navy Committees; supported Cuba in its struggle for freedom, foresaw Florida as a tourist mecca; favored a Florida ship canal, and advocated a national education fund; introduced bills for private pensions, internal improvements of waterways and harbors, establishing mail routes, relief for men who had served in the Seminole Wars and for Florida citizens who had lost property during the Civil War, and general amnesty. Served as superintendent of farms at State Normal and Industrial College for Colored Students [now Florida A&M University]. Died on May 15, 1905, in Tallahassee, Fla. Further reading, Peter D. Klingman, *Josiah Walls: Florida's Black Congressman of Reconstruction* (1976).

---

on this day in history...

1923,	Zeta Phi Beta sorority was incorporated.
1948,	Naomi Sims, supermodel and beauty company executive, was born in Oxford, Miss.

MARCH 30   CONGRESSMEN

ADAM CLAYTON POWELL, SR.

Clergyman and author who was called the one of **"greatest preachers and leaders of his time."** Born on May 5, 1865, in Soak Creek, Va.   Wayland Seminary and College in Washington (1892); Yale University Divinity School (1896). Worked in the coal mines of West Virginia and at the Howard House Hotel in Washington; pastor of Ebenezer Baptist Church in Philadelphia (1893); pastor of Immanuel Baptist Church in New Haven, Conn. (1893-1908); awarded an honorary degree from Virginia Union University (D.D., 1904). **Pastor of Abyssinian Baptist Church on West 40th Street in New York City (1908-1937), which he built into the world's largest African-American congregation**; moved the church to Harlem and for $334,000 built the Abyssinia Baptist Church and Community House Recreation Center on West 138th Street (1923); launched a social and religious education program; dedicated the A. Clayton Powell Home of the Abyssinian Baptist Church (1926), a home for aged members on Nicholas Street in Harlem; sent by his congregation on a trip to Europe, Egypt, and the Holy Land; pastor emeritus (1937-1953). Honored by the Harmon Foundation (1929), for his work in developing Abyssinian Baptist Church; opened food kitchens to feed the poor and campaigned for better jobs during the Depression; lectured on race relations at Colgate University, College of the City of New York, and the Union Theological Seminary; served as an editorial writer for the *Christian Review* and vice president of the NAACP; author of *Saints in Caesar's Household* (1939), *Picketing Hell* (1942), and *Riots and Ruins* (1945). Died on June 12, 1953, in New York City.   Further reading, Adam Clayton Powell, Sr., *Against the Tide* (1938).

---

on this day in history...

1882,	Robert N. Dett, one of the nation's first African-American classical music composer, was born in Canada (d. 1943).
1887,	A. Miles patented an elevator.
1910,	J. Rupert Picott, educator who lobbied both state and federal governments to proclaim February as Black History Month, was born in Suffolk, Va.
1914,	Daisy Bates, Arkansas NAACP president who led the fight to integrate Little Rock Central High School, was born in Huttig, Ark.
1939,	Charles Houston organized the NAACP Legal Defense and Educational Fund.

OCTOBER 11   RELIGIOUS LEADERS

HAROLD WASHINGTON

Congressman and mayor.   Born on April 15, 1922, in Chicago, Ill.   Roosevelt University (B.A., 1949); Northwestern University (J.D., 1952). Attached to the U.S. Army Air Corps Engineers in the Pacific (1942-1946); admitted to the Illinois bar (1953); assistant prosecutor of the city corporation counsel's office in Chicago (1954-1958); became precinct captain in the 3rd Ward regular Democratic organization (1954); arbitrator for the Illinois State Industrial Commission (1960-1964); Illinois state representative (1965-1976); Illinois state senator (1976-1980); Illinois 1st District Democratic congressman (1980-1983), serving on Education and Labor, Government Operations, and Judiciary Committees; **first African-American mayor of Chicago** (1983-1987). Died on November 25, 1987 in Chicago, Ill.   Further reading, <u>Florence Hamlish Levinsohn</u>, <u>*Harold Washington: A Political Biography*</u> (1983).

---

on this day in history...

1891,	George Dixon, first recognized African-American world boxing champion, defeated Cal McCarthy for the featherweight boxing championship.
1939,	Kenneth Edelin, Planned Parenthood of America board chairman, was born in Washington, D.C.
1980,	Larry Holmes defeated Leroy Jones for the heavyweight boxing championship.
1988,	Toni Morrison won the Pulitzer Prize for her novel *Beloved*.

MARCH 31   CONGRESSMEN

DANIEL ALEXANDER PAYNE

Clergyman, educator, civic leader, and church historian.   Born in 1811 in Charleston, S.C.   Tutored in English, mathematics, French, Latin, and Greek by Thomas S. Conneau; Lutheran Theological Seminary in Gettysburg, Pa.   Joined the Methodist Episcopal Church (1826); opened and operated a school for adult slaves (1828-1835), until it was outlawed by the South Carolina state legislature; licensed to preach (1837); ordained by the Frackean Synod of the Lutheran Church (1839); opened a school in Philadelphia (1840). Joined the African Methodist Episcopal Church (1841); received as a minister by its Philadelphia Conference (1842), and appointed to its traveling ministry; **organized the nation's first African-American ministers association** in Washington and founded a school for young preachers; helped organize the Home and Foreign Mission Society. Selected by the General Conference (1848), to prepare a history of the AME Church and published *Semi-Centenary and the Retrospection of the AME Church in the United States of America* (1866); elected bishop of the AME Church at the General Conference (1852); traveled extensively setting up schools, organizing mothers for home training education, and preaching the need for literary and historical societies. Worked with Charles Sumner in urging President Lincoln to emancipate the slaves; purchased the Wilberforce University from the Methodist Episcopal Church in Xenia, Ohio (1863); became the **nation's first African-American head of an institute of higher education as president of Wilberforce University** (1863-1876), and chancellor and dean of its theological seminary (1876-1893); elected president of the Methodist Pastors Association (1868); **founded the Bethel Literary and Historical Association in Washington** (1881). Died on November 21, 1893, in Jacksonville, Fla.   Further reading, Josephus R. Coan, *Daniel Alexander Payne, Christian Educator* (1935).

---

on this day in history...

1866,   Henry Alexander Hunt, Fort Valley State College president, was born in Hancock County, Ga. (d. 1938).

1894,   Macon B. Allen, nation's first licensed African-American attorney, died in Washington, D.C. (b. 1816).

1901,   Frederick Douglas Patterson of Tuskegee Institute, founder of the United Negro College Fund and the nation's only African-American school of veterinary medicine, was born in Washington, D.C. (d. 1988).

1917,   Thelonious Sphere Monk, jazz pianist and composer known as the "high priest of bop," was born in Rocky Mount, N.C. (d. 1982).

1946,   Ben Vereen, Tony Award-winning entertainer, was born in Miami, Fla.

OCTOBER 10   **RELIGIOUS LEADERS**

MARGUERITE ROSS BARNETT

Educator.   Born on May 22, 1942, in Charlottesville, Va.   Antioch College (A.B. political science, 1964); University of Chicago (M.A., 1966; Ph.D., 1972).   Lecturer in political science at the University of Chicago (1969-1970), assistant professor of political science (1970-1976); a James Madison Bicentennial Preceptor at Princeton University (1974-1976); professor of political science at Howard University (1976-1977), chairwoman of the department of political science (1977-1980). Co-director of the Ethnic Heritage Project: Study of an Historic Black Community, Gum Springs, Va., which was funded by the Ethnic Heritage Program, U.S. Department of Education; received the American Political Science Association's top book prize (1981), for her book on ethnic and cultural pluralism, *The Politics of Cultural Nationalism in South India*; investigator on the Constitution and American Culture and the Training Program for Special Project Directors, sponsored by the National Endowment for the Humanities. Professor of politics and education, professor political science, and director of the Institute for Urban and Minority Education at Columbia University (1980-1983); professor of political science and vice chancellor for academic affairs at the City University of New York (1983-1986), which had 21 colleges serving 180,000 students; professor of political science and chancellor at the University of Missouri-St. Louis (1986-1990); **first African-American president of the University of Houston** (1990-1992). Member of the boards of the Monsanto Company, Educational Testing Services, and the Student Loan Marketing Association. Died on February 24, 1992, in Wailuku, Hawaii.   Further reading, Jessie Carney Smith, "Marguerite Ross Barnett," *Notable Black American Women* (1992).

---

on this day in history...

1854,	Augustine Tolton, one of the nation's first Negro priests, was born in Ralls County, Mo. d.1897).
1868,	Hampton University was founded in Hampton, Va.
1905,	Clara McBride Hale, founder of Hale House in Harlem, was born in Philadelphia, Pa. (d. 1992).
1910,	Harry Howell Carney, first baritone saxophone jazz performer, was born in Boston, Mass. (1974).

APRIL 1   **EDUCATORS**

PAULI MURRAY

Lawyer, poet, religious leader, legal scholar, author, educator, and civil rights advocate. Born on November 20, 1910, in Baltimore, Md. Hunter College (B.A., 1933); **Howard University Law School class president (1944), where she was one of the first to argue against the "separate but equal" doctrine**; University of California at Berkeley (LL.M., 1945), where her master's thesis, "The Right to Equal Opportunity in Employment," was the first definitive law review article on this matter; **Yale University's first African-American recipient of a D.J.S. degree** (1965); General Theological Seminary (M.D., 1976). Worked as a teacher for the Work Projects Administration's Remedial Reading Project and Education Project; became a pioneer in the struggle for equal opportunity in higher education; field secretary for the Workers Defense League, where she led a fight against poll taxes; worked with the NAACP and joined CORE; admitted to the California bar (1945), and became the **first African-American deputy attorney general of California**; moved to New York, passed the bar, and opened a law practice. Published her first book, *State's Laws on Race and Color* (1951), which Thurgood Marshall called the Bible for civil rights lawyers fighting segregation; an associate in the law firm of Paul, Weiss, Rifkind, Wharton and Garrison in New York (1956-1960); senior lecturer in constitutional and administrative law at the Ghana Law School (1960-1961); member of the Committee on Civil and Political Rights; vice president of Benedict College (1966-1967); professor of American Studies at Brandeis University (1968-1972), and law professor (1972). **Ordained the first African-American woman priest of the Protestant Episcopal Church at the National Cathedral in Washington.** Died on July 1, 1985, in Pittsburgh, Pa. Further reading, Pauli Murray, *Song in a Weary Throat: An American Pilgrimage* (1987).

---

on this day in history...

1894,   Eugene Jacques Bullard, world's first black combat aviator, was born in Columbus, Ga. (d. 1961).

OCTOBER 9   RELIGIOUS LEADERS

MARY MCLEOD BETHUNE

Educator, civil rights leader, government official, and **chairperson for FDR's Federal Council of Negro Advisers, the "Black Cabinet."** Born on July 10, 1875, in Mayesville, S.C. Scotia Seminary [now Barber-Scotia College] in Concord, N.C.; Moody Bible Institute in Chicago (1895). Teacher at Haines Institute in Augusta, Ga., and Palatka Mission School in Fla.; **founder and president Daytona Normal & Industrial School [now Bethune-Cookman College]** (1904-1947); received major contributions for the college from James Gamble, of Proctor & Gamble, and Thomas White, of White Sewing Machine Company; organized a hospital for Daytona Beach African-Americans after her students were refused service by white hospitals. Became vice president of the National Urban League (1920); president of the National Association of Colored Women (1924-1928); **founder and president the National Council of Negro Women** (1935-1949), an umbrella organization of African-American women organizations; received NAACP Spingarn Medal (1935), for her founding of Bethune-Cookman College against great difficulties; special adviser of minority affairs in the Roosevelt administration (1935-1936); director of the Division of Minority Affairs (1936-1943), in the New Deal's National Youth Administration and one of the few African-Americans who had access to the president; special representative of the U.S. State Department (1945), at the conference that established the U.N. **Formed the Women's Army Corps** (1942); special assistant to the U.S. secretary of war (1945); considered to be one of the most influential women in the U.S. between 1945 and 1955; awarded the Frances Drexel Award for Distinguished Service (1937), the Thomas Jefferson Award for outstanding leadership (1942), the Medal of Honor and Merit from the Republique d'Haiti (1949), and the Star of Africa from the Republic of Liberia (1952). Died on May 18, 1955, in Daytona Beach, Fla. Further reading, Catherine Owens Peare, *Mary McLeod Bethune* (1951).

---

on this day in history...

1855, John Mercer Langston was elected clerk of Brownheim Township, Ohio, reportedly becoming the nation's the first African-American public office holder.

1911, Charles "Honi" Coles, Tony Award-winning entertainer, was born in Philadelphia, Pa.

1939, Marvin Pentz Gaye, Grammy Award-winning singing legend, was born in Washington, D.C. (d. 1984).

APRIL 2   **EDUCATORS**

ELIJAH MUHAMMAD

Spiritual leader of the Nation of Islam.   Born Elijah Poole on October 10, 1897, in Sandersville, Ga.   Worked as a laborer and bricklayer in Sandersville and Macon; converted to Christianity and became a Baptist; moved to Detroit and worked in an automobile plant (1923-1929); met W. Farad Muhammad, the leader of the Lost and Found Nation of Islam in the Wilderness of North America, who had just established the first University of Islam and Temple #1 (1930), which led to Poole denouncing Christianity and becoming a disciple of Farad; anointed as the leader of the Nation of Islam by Farad, who mysteriously disappeared (1934). Officially changed his name to Elijah Muhammad (the "Prophet"), moved to Chicago, founded Temple #2, and assumed control of the Black Muslims (1934-1975); built the Chicago-based religious-nationalist organization's following to over 200,000 people; preached a doctrine of a "separate nation within a nation," racial segregation, self-defense, self-help, self-love, and racial dignity; established over 150 temples in North America and over 40 universities of Islam; operated banks, drycleaners, newspapers (*Muhammad Speaks*), restaurants, and supermarkets in almost every major U.S. city. Converted thousands of African-Americans to Islam, including Malcolm X (1952), and Louis Farrakhan (1955), "rescuing" them from the "mud" of the street corners, prisons, back alleys, and poolhalls, and instilling Black pride and a religious sense of purpose; published his *Message to Black Men* (1965); became a powerful symbol of Black Nationalism during the '60s, and **played a major role in the Black Power movement.** Last seen on February 25, 1975, in Chicago, Ill.

---

on this day in history...

1930,   Faith Ringgold, artist, was born in New York City.
1941,   Jesse Louis Jackson, founder of the Rainbow Coalition and D.C. "shadow senator," was born in Greenville, S.C.

OCTOBER 8   **RELIGIOUS LEADERS**

CHARLOTTE HAWKINS BROWN

Educator and civil rights advocate who was known as a "social dictator." Born in 1883 in Henderson, N.C. Massachusetts State Normal School in Salem (1901); Harvard University; Simmons College; Temple University. Began teaching at Bethany Institute in N.C. (1901); **founder and president of Palmer Memorial Institute** in Sedalia, N.C. (1902-1952), one of the nation's oldest African-American preparatory school whose principal objective was to teach the African-Americans improved methods of agricultural and industrial pursuits; organizer of the North Carolina State Federation of Negro Women's Clubs (1909), and president (1915-1936); founder of the Colored Orphanage at Oxford, N.C.; helped found the Commission on Interracial Cooperation (1919); vice president of the National Association of Colored Women; financial director at Palmer Memorial Institute (1952-1955). Died on January 11, 1961 in Greensboro, N.C. Further reading, Constance H. Marteena, *The Lengthening Shadow of a Woman: A Biography of Charlotte Hawkins Brown* (1977).

on this day in history...

1838,	John Willis Menard, first African-American to be elected to Congress (but was never seated), was born in Kaskaska, Ill. (d. 1893).
1918,	Mabel Smythe-Haithe, former U.S. ambassador to Cameroon and Guinea, was born in Montgomery, Ala.
1938,	Katie Beatrice Hall, Indiana's first African-American U.S. congressperson, was born in Mound Bayou, Miss.
1961,	Eddie Murphy, Grammy Award-winning comedian, actor, singer, and producer, was born in Brooklyn, N.Y.
1963,	Civil rights forces, led by Martin Luther King, Jr., and F.L. Shuttlesworth launch a drive against discrimination in Birmingham.
1984,	John Thompson of Georgetown became the first African-American coach to win the NCAA men's basketball championship.

ABSALOM JONES

Abolitionist, Masonic leader, and clergyman.   Born into slavery in 1746 in Sussex, Del.   Taught himself to read; worked as a handyman and clerk at his master's store; emancipated (1784); met Richard Allen (1786), and became a lay preacher among the African-American congregation at St. George's Methodist Episcopal Church in Philadelphia, increasing the number of African-American members by tenfold; led the entire African-American congregation out of St. George (1786), after being segregated to an upstairs gallery. Helped organize an independent beneficial and mutual aid society called Free African Society (1787), which denounced slavery, gambling, drunkenness, and adultery and was the first such African-American organization in the U.S.; collected dues, along with Richard Allen, administered burial expenses, sick relief, and aid to widows and fatherless children; became sole leader of The African Church (1794), which later became St. Thomas African Episcopal Church and was received into the Diocese of Pennsylvania (1794). Ordained as a deacon (1794); elected most worshipful master of the African Masonic Lodge (1798); **ordained into the priesthood (1804), becoming the first African-American priest of the Protestant Episcopal Church**; founded a school for African-Americans at St. Thomas (1804). Established the Female Benevolent Society and the African Friendly Society; helped in the recruiting of the "Black Legion" during the War of 1812; helped consecrate Richard Allen as the first African-American bishop of the African Methodist Episcopal Church (1816); helped organize a convention of African-American men opposed to the American Colonization Society (1817). Died on February 13, 1818, in Philadelphia, Pa. Further reading, George Freeman Bragg, *The Story of the First of the Blacks, The Pathfinder Absalom Jones* (1929).

---

on this day in history...

1800,   Gabriel Prosser, slave revolt leader, was hanged in Richmond, Va. (b. 1775).

1889,   Clarence E. Muse, co-founder of the Lafayette Players, was born in Baltimore, Md. (d. 1979).

1934,   Leroi Jones ("Imamu Amiri Baraka"), poet, author, and playwright who was a leading spokesman for Black Nationalism, was born in Newark, N.J.

1993,   Toni Morrison was named the first African-American winner of the Nobel Prize for Literature.

OCTOBER 7   **RELIGIOUS LEADERS**

JOSEPH SAMUEL CLARK

College president.   Born in 1871 in Bienville Parish, La.   Bishop College; Leland College in New Orleans (B.A., 1901); Selma University (M.A., 1913); Harvard University; University of Chicago.   Appointed president of Baton Rouge College in Louisiana (1901); **president of Southern University and Agricultural and Mechanical College** (1913-1938), which he expanded from two buildings to 40 buildings on 500 acres, 139 teachers, and 1500 students. President of the Louisiana Colored Teachers Association (1908-1915), National Association of Colored Teachers (1916-1917), and of the National Survey Committee (1928-1930), which was comprised of 22 of the nation's leading educators. Appointed to President Hoover's White House Commission on Child Welfare and Protection (1930); member of the President's Conference on Home Ownership; member of the Commission of Interracial Cooperation (1932-1943), one of the most effective organizations for promoting the advancement of southern African-Americans; president of New Capital Insurance Company of New Orleans. Received honorary degrees from Leland College (Ph.D., 1914), and Arkansas Baptist College (Ph.D., 1921). Died in 1944.   Further reading, John Brother Cade, _The Man Christened Josiah Clark, Who, As J.S. Clark Became President of a Louisiana State Land Grant College_ (1966).

on this day in history...

1899,	B.F. Jones patented a gas burner.
1915,	McKinley Morganfield ("Muddy Waters"), Grammy Award-winning blues great, was born in Rolling Fork, Miss. (d. 1983).
1928,	Marguerite Johnson ("Maya Angelou"), poet, author, dancer, producer, and educator, was born in St. Louis, Mo.
1936,	Julia Wheeler, Mechanics & Farmers Bank president, was born in Durham, N.C.
1938,	Walter Massey, University of California provost and vice president for academic affairs, was born in Hattiesburg, Miss.
1968,	Martin Luther King, Jr., leader of the civil rights movement, was assassinated at the Loraine Motel in Memphis, Tenn.

APRIL 4

EDUCATORS

MAHALIA JACKSON

Singer who was called the **"world's greatest gospel singer"**. Born on October 26, 1912, in New Orleans, La. Madame C.J. Walker and the Scott Institute of Beauty Culture in Chicago. Opened a beauty shop; won an audition for the Work Projects Administration Federal Theater production of *Hot Mikado*, but declined the role; met composer Thomas Dorsey in Chicago (1929); began performing for church programs and conventions with Dorsey as Jackson's musical adviser, songwriter, and accompanist (1937-1946), with "Precious Lord Take My Hand" becoming her signature performance; recorded Memphis preacher W. Herbert Brewster's "Move On Up A Little Higher" (1946), which sold over two million copies for Apollo Records. Became the official soloist of the National Baptist Convention (1947); recorded Chicago songwriter Kenneth Mooris' "I Can Put My Trust in Jesus" and "Let the Power of the Holy Ghost Fall On Me," which earned her the French Grand Prix du Disque (1949); became the **first gospel singer to perform at Carnegie Hall (1950), and at the Newport Jazz Festival (1958)**; featured on Studs Terkel's Chicago television program; opened a flower shop and was given her own radio and television show; toured Europe (1952, 1962, and 1963-1964), where she was called the "Angel of Peace." Signed a profitable record deal with Columbia Records (1954), and recorded "Down By the Riverside," "Joshua Fought the Battle of Jericho," "He's Got the Whole World in His Hands," and "When the Saints Come Marching In." Strong supporter of the SCLC and Chicago mayor Richard Daley; sang at President Kennedy's inauguration (1961), and "How I Got Over" at the 1963 March on Washington; established the Mahalia Jackson Scholarship Foundation; received the Silver Dove Award. Died on January 27, 1972, in Chicago, Ill. Further reading, <u>Larraine Goreau</u>, <u>*Just Mahalia, Baby*</u> (1975).

---

on this day in history...

1871,	The Fisk Jubilee Singers began a fundraising tour for its school and became one of the most popular African-American folk-singing group of the 19th century.
1896,	W.R. Davis patented a riding saddle.
1921,	Joseph Echols Lowery, SCLC president, was born in Huntsville, Ala.
1993,	Michael Jordan of the Chicago Bulls announced his retirement from the NBA.

OCTOBER 6   **RELIGIOUS LEADERS**

SEPTIMA CLARK

Educator, humanitarian, and civil rights activist called the "Mother Conscience" and **"Queen Mother" of the civil rights movement**. Born on March 3, 1898, in Charleston, S.C. Benedict College (B.A.); Hampton Institute (M.A.). Taught at Promise Land School in Johns Island, S.C., Avery Institute, and in Columbia, S.C. (1916-1954); lost her teacher's position in Columbia, because she refused to disassociate herself from the NAACP; director of Highlander Folk School near Chattanooga, Tenn. (1954-1961), where she directed a workshop on the U.N. and sponsored a citizenship school on Johns Island, S.C. (1957); worked with the SCLC (1961-1970), and was presented the Martin Luther King, Jr., Award "for Great Service to Humanity;" set up training sessions at Dorchester Cooperative Community Center in McIntosh, Ga. (1962-1970), and drove throughout the South bringing busloads of students to the center to educate them in mathematics, literacy, and citizenship; elected to the Charleston School Board (1976); received the Living Legacy Award from President Carter (1979); awarded South Carolina's highest civilian award, the Order of the Palmetto (1982); received an American Book Award for her autobiography *Ready from Within: Septima Clark and the Civil Rights Movement* (1987). Died on December 15, 1987. Further reading, Carl Tjerandsen, *Education for Citizenship: A Foundation's Experience* (1980).

---

on this day in history...

1856,	Booker Taliaferro Washington, founder of Tuskegee Institute, was born in Franklin County, Va. (d. 1915).
1934,	Stanley Turrentine, jazz saxophonist, was born in Pittsburgh, Pa.
1937,	Colin L. Powell, first African-American chairman of the Joint Chiefs of Staff, was born in New York City.
1993,	A record six minority Major League Baseball managers opened the season: Cito Gaston, Bluejays; Hal McRae, Royals; Felipe Alou, Expos; Don Baylor, Rockies; Tony Perez, Reds; Dusty Baker, Giants.

PATRICK FRANCIS HEALY

Clergyman and college president. Born into slavery on February 27, 1834, in Jones County, Ga. Holy Cross College in Worcester, Mass. (B.A., 1850); University of Louvain in Belgium (Ph.D., philosophy, 1865), becoming the **first African-American to earn a doctorate**; enrolled in a novitiate at Frederick, Md. (1850-1852). Taught at St Joseph's College in Philadelphia and Holy Cross College (1852-1858); ordained to the Catholic priesthood in Liege, Belgium (1864); prayer and spiritual training at the tertianship in Laon, France (1865-1866). Appointed professor of philosophy at Georgetown University (1866), appointed dean of the college (1868), vice president of Georgetown (1869-1873), vice rector (1873), and president of Georgetown, becoming the **first African-American president of a major university** (1874-1882). Pronounced his final vows as a Jesuit (1867), becoming **first African-American Jesuit**; assistant pastor at St. Joseph's Church in Providence (1891-1894), and St. Lawrence Church in New York City (1895-1906); spiritual father at St. Joseph's College in Philadelphia (1906-1908); headed the Catholic Commission on Indian Affairs. Died in 1910 in Washington, D.C. Further reading, Albert S. Foley, *God's Men of Color* (1970).

---

on this day in history...

1929,   Autherine Lucy Foster, University of Alabama's first African-American student, was born in Shiloh, Ala.

1932,   Yvonne Braithwaite-Burke, Los Angeles County supervisor and California's first African-American congresswoman, was born in Los Angeles, Calif.

1940,   Acel Moore, Pulitzer Prize-winning journalist, was born in Philadelphia, Pa.

OCTOBER 5   RELIGIOUS LEADERS

GEORGE WILLIAM COOK

Civic leader and college administrator. Born into slavery on January 7, 1855, in Winchester, Va. Howard University valedictorian (B.A., 1881; M.A., 1886; LL.B., 1898; LL.M., 1899). Emancipated (1862); **Howard University faculty member (1881-1931)**, where he served as mathematics tutor in the normal department (1881-1887), assistant principal of the normal department (1881-1889), mathematics tutor in the college department (1887-1899), principal of the normal department (1889-1899), dean of the English department (1899-1903), professor of civics and commercial law (1902-1928), dean of Howard's commercial department (1903-1905), and was appointed business manager and acting secretary (1908), secretary of the university and board of trustees (1909), and secretary of the General Alumni Association (1928-1931); elected an alumni trustee (1931). Treasurer of the District of Columbia branch of the NAACP (1912-1931), and member of the NAACP national board of directors (1914-1931); organizer of the Central Committee of Negro College Men; responsible for the establishment of Howard University's Student Army Training Camp during World War I; gave a Charters Day Address (1925), where he stated, "There can be no Howard University without equal rights and highest culture for all, based upon merit and capacity. To be plain, we know of no Negro education. Political rights and civic privileges are accompaniments of citizenship and are therefore part of the warp and woof of Howard University's curricula." Died on August 20, 1931, in Philadelphia, Pa. Further reading, Walter Dyson, *Howard University, The Capstone of Negro Education: A History, 1867-1940* (1941).

---

on this day in history...

1909,	Matthew Henson becomes the first person to reach the North Pole.
1926,	Dorothy Donegan, one of America's great piano virtuosos, was born in Chicago, Ill.
1936,	Marion S. Berry, SNCC's first national chairman and Washington mayor, was born in Itta Bena, Miss.
1937,	William December ("Billy Dee") Williams, actor, was born in Harlem, N.Y.
1968,	Bobby Hutton, Black Panther Party charter member, was killed by Oakland police.
1993,	Freeman Bosley, Jr., was elected St. Louis' first African-American mayor.

APRIL 6   **EDUCATORS**

JAMES AUGUSTINE HEALY

Catholic priest. Born into slavery on April 6, 1830, in Jones County, Ga. Holy Cross University (B.A., 1849; M.A., 1851); Grand Seminary in Montreal; Sulpician Seminary in Paris (1854). **Ordained as the first African-American Roman Catholic priest** at the Cathedral of Notre Dame (1854); served as secretary and chancellor in the Diocese of Boston; appointed pastor of the Cathedral of the Holy Cross during the Civil War; **pastor of St. James, the largest church in Boston** (1866-1875). Became the bishop's deputy for social action; helped in the development the Home for Destitute Catholic Children, in the establishment of the House of Good Shepard, and in promoting and financing the St. Ann's Foundling Home; active in the organization of the first Catholic Union of Boston, helping delinquent boys, the poor, orphans, recent immigrants, farmers, and the sick; fought to allow Catholic clergymen to minister to inmates; appeared before special committees in the Statehouse as a proponent of the immunity of the church from taxation. **Served as the nation's first African-American Roman Catholic bishop** (1875-1900), after being named by Pope Pius IX as bishop of Portland, Maine, where he headed a diocese comprised of Maine and New Hampshire, built churches, schools and convents, and administered to a Catholic population of over 100,000; **became known as "The Children's Bishop,"** because of his social work on behalf of widows and children of the Civil War dead, building orphanages and foundling homes and battling child labor abuses. Proposed three major pieces of church legislation, which were passed by the assembly; member of the commission that established Catholic University of Washington and the permanent commission on Negro and Indian Missions; appointed by Pope Leo XIII as assistant to the papal throne. Died on August 5, 1900, in Portland, Maine. Further reading, William L. Lucey, *The Catholic Church in Maine* (1957).

---

on this day in history...

1919,	C. David Coleman, AME Church senior bishop, was born in Pickens, S.C.
1927,	C. Delores Tucker, Pennsylvania's first African-American secretary of state, was born in Philadelphia, Pa.
1942,	Bernice Johnson Reagan, first African-American curator of the National Museum of American History, was born in Albany, Ga.
1943,	H. Rap Brown ("Jamil Abdullal Alamin"), revolutionary civil rights leader, was born in Baton Rouge, La.
1945,	Clifton Davis, actor and ordained minister, was born in Chicago, Ill.

OCTOBER 4   **RELIGIOUS LEADERS**

ANNA JULIA COOPER

Pioneer in secondary education and civil rights.   Born on August 10, 1858, in Raleigh, N.C.   Oberlin College (A.B., 1884; A.M.1887), becoming the **first African-American woman to earn a bachelor's degree from a major college**; Columbia University (1913-1916); University of Paris (Ph.D., 1925).   Member of Alpha Kappa Alpha sorority; teacher of mathematics and ancient and modern languages at Wilberforce University and St. Augustine's Institute (1885-1887), M Street Preparatory School [now Dunbar High School] in Washington, D.C. (1887-1906, 1910-1930), and Lincoln University, Mo. (1906-1910). Principal of M Street Preparatory School (1901-1906); president of Frelinghuysen University (1930-1940), a group of evening schools for African-Americans in Washington, D.C.; registrar of Frelinghuysen University (1940-1950). Died on February 29, 1964, in Washington, D.C.   Further reading, Mary Gibson Hundley, *The Dunbar Story 1870-1895* (1965).

---

on this day in history...

1867,	Johnson C. Smith University was founded in Charlotte, N.C.
1915,	Eleanor Fagan ("Billie Holiday"), blues singer known as "Lady Day," was born in Baltimore, Md. (d. 1959).
1938,	Freddy Dewayne Hubbard, Grammy Award-winning jazz trumpeter, was born in Indianapolis, Ind.
1940,	The first U.S. stamp ever to honor an African-American (Booker T. Washington) was issued.
1963,	Bull Conner set Birmingham police attack dogs on civil rights marchers, gaining national attention.

APRIL 7   **EDUCATORS**

NANNIE HELEN BURROUGHS

School founder, civil rights advocate, and religious leader. Born on May 2, 1879, in Orange, Va. Bookkeeper and editorial secretary of the Foreign Mission Board of the National Baptist Convention in Louisville (1900-1909); organized a women's industrial club, which taught domestic science and secretarial courses; addressed the Negro Young People's Christian and Educational Congress (Atlanta, 1902); **founding member and corresponding secretary of the National Baptist Convention's auxiliary Women's Convention (1900-1947), president (1948-1961)**, and editor of its quarterly journal, *The Worker* (1944-1961); founder and president of the National Training School for Women and Girls in Washington (1909-1961), which housed and trained girls from the U.S., Africa, and the Caribbean, and was known as the "School of the 3 B's--the Bible, bath, and broom." Founder and president of the National Association of Wage Earners, which served to draw public attention to African-American women; life member of the Association for the Study of Negro Life and History, where she shared the platform on the final day of the 12th Annual Meeting of the association (Pittsburgh, 1927), with Carter G. Woodson and Alain L. Locke introducing her paper, "The Social Value of Negro History;" worked to restore and memorialize the home of Frederick Douglass and served as secretary of the Frederick Douglass Memorial Association. Member of the Women's Division of the Commission on Interracial Cooperation; member of the National Association of Colored Women; author of *Grow: A Handy Guide for Progressive Church Women, Making Your Community Christian,* and *Words of Light and Life Found Here and There* (1948); wrote the syndicated column "Nannie Burrough Says;" worked with the Baptist World Alliance, serving as a member-at-large of the Executive Committee (1950-1955). Died in May 1961 in Washington, D.C. Further reading, Sadie I. Daniels, *Women Builders* (1931).

---

on this day in history...

1900,	Isom Dart, cowboy and alleged cattle rustler, was gunned down in Brown's Hole, Wyo.
1904,	Daytona Normal and Industrial School [now Bethune-Cookman] opened in Daytona Beach, Fla.
1941,	Ernest Evans ("Chubby Checker"), Grammy Award-winning singer, was born in Philadelphia, Pa.
1945,	Ervin C. Mollison was appointed to the U.S. Customs Court, becoming the first African-American lifetime federal judge.
1949,	The nation's first African-American-owned radio station, WERD-AM in Atlanta, was founded by Jesse Blanton, Sr.
1974,	Frank Robinson of the Cleveland Indians became major league baseball's first African-American manager.

JOHN HOPE

Teacher and college president.   Born on June 2, 1868, in Augusta, Ga. Brown University (B.A., 1894).   Teacher at Roger Williams University in Nashville (1894-1898); teacher, bookkeeper, and football coach, and **first African-American president at Atlanta Baptist College [now called Morehouse College]** (1906-1929), where he laid the foundation for the its reputation as "the college of presidents;" alumni member of Phi Beta Kappa at Brown University (1919). **First president of the new Atlanta University** (1929-1936), first institution for African-Americans offering only graduate courses; **organized the cooperative consortium known as the Atlanta University System** (1929), which was designed to coordinate the six denominational schools competing for African-American students in Atlanta--Morehouse, Spelman, Clark, Morris Brown, and Gammon Theological Seminary [now called the Interdenominational Theological Center]. Only college president to attend the Harper's Ferry meeting of the Niagara Movement (1906), and the protest meeting in New York City (1909), which led to the founding of the NAACP; president of the National Association of Teachers of Colored Schools; member of the advisory board of the NAACP and the executive committee of the National Urban League; served as president of the Association for the Study of Negro Life and History. Received a Harmon Award (1929), for distinguished achievement in education; awarded the NAACP Spingarn Medal (1936), posthumously, for his success in the field of education. Died on February 20, 1936, in Atlanta, Ga.   Further reading, Ridgely Torrence, *The Story of John Hope* (1948).

on this day in history...

1922,   Carmen McRae, jazz vocalist, was born in New York City.

1974,   Hank Aaron broke Babe Ruth's home run record by hitting his 715th against the Dodgers in Atlanta's Fulton County Stadium.

1990,   Percy Julian and George Washington Carver became the first African-Americans to be inducted into the National Inventors Hall of Fame.

APRIL 8   **EDUCATORS**

GEORGE BAKER

Religious leader and cultist better known as "Father Divine," who became **one of the nation's best known religious leaders and most powerful African-Americans of his day**. Born around 1880 on Hutchinson Island, Ga. Worked in Baltimore as a garden laborer and preacher; apprenticed under St. John the Divine Hickerson and Samuel Morris who anointed Baker as the "Messenger" and "God in the Sonship Degree;" moved to Brooklyn (1915), where he established his own church, proclaimed himself the only living God, demanded absolute loyalty from his disciples, forbade sexual relations, and preached peace, brotherhood, cleanliness, and honesty. Formally took the name "Father Divine" (1930), and **founded the Father Divine Peace Movement, which was the largest movement of its kind during the Great Depression**, attracting both sexes, illiterate domestics, middle-class and professional workers, some millionaires, the devout, and the hungry as his followers. Sentenced to the maximum time in prison for disorderly conduct, after a noisy demonstration in a white community, by a judge who died of a heart attack four days later (1931), thus convincing his followers and previous doubters that the death was Divine retribution; released and was greeted by 7,000 followers at a "Monster Glory to Our God" reception in Harlem (1932); became one of the largest landlords in Harlem, owning restaurants, barbershops, grocery stores, huckster wagons, hotels, moving firms, and a coal business; began acquiring property in Newark, Jersey City, Bridgeport, and Baltimore and expanding his kingdom across the U.S. and Europe, with a following of over two million. Published *New Day*, a weekly newspaper; provided nutritious meals, housing, and found jobs for his followers; supported Communists in pursuing international peace and the eradication segregation and discrimination. Died on September 10, 1965. Further reading, Rayford Logan, "Father Divine," *Dictionary of American Negro Biography* (1982).

---

on this day in history...

1800,   Nat Turner, slave revolt leader, was born in Southhampton County, Va. (d. 1831).

1935,   Robert Henry Lawrence, Jr., first African-American astronaut chosen to go to the Moon, was born in Chicago, Ill. (d. 1967).

1947,   Michael Lomax, Fulton County (Ga.) Commission chairman, was born in Los Angeles, Calif.

1951,   Dave Winfield, baseball great, was born in St. Paul, Minn.

1959,   Freddie Jackson, R&B recording artist, was born in New York City.

OCTOBER 2   RELIGIOUS LEADERS

CHARLES SPURGEON JOHNSON

Educator, social scientist, and editor. Born on July 24, 1893, in Bristol, Tenn. Virginia Union University (B.A., 1916); University of Chicago (Ph.D., 1918). Director of research and records of the Chicago Urban League (1917-1919); associate executive director of the Chicago Commission on Race Relations (1919-1921); director of the Department of Research and Investigation for the National Urban League in New York City (1921-1928); co-founder and editor of the National Urban League's new publication, *Opportunity: A Journal of Negro Life* (1923-1928), an African-American literary outlet of the Harlem Renaissance. Chairman of the social science department at Fisk University (1928-1946); research secretary for the National Interracial Conference (Washington, 1928), which led to the publication of his book, *The Negro in American Civilization: The Study of Negro Life and Race Relations in the Light of Social Research* (1930); received the Harmon Foundation gold medal (1930); editor of *A Monthly Summary of Events and Trends in Race Relations* (1943-1948). Adviser on the reorganization of the Japanese school system (1946); U.S. delegate to the First UNESCO Conference (Paris, 1946; Mexico City, 1947), World Council of Churches in Amsterdam (1948), and Conference on Indian-American Relations (New Dehli, 1949); **first African-American president of Fisk University** (1946-1956). Died on October 27, 1956, in, Louisville, KY. Further reading, James Blackwell and Morris Janowitz, *Black Sociologists, Historical and Contemporary Perspectives* (1974).

---

on this day in history...

1816,	Richard Allen and Daniel Coker met in Philadelphia and established the African Methodist Episcopal Church.
1866,	Congress passed the Civil Rights Bill of 1866, granting Negroes the rights and privileges of any American citizen.
1942,	Earl Patrick Hilliard, Alabama 7th District congressman, was born in Birmingham, Ala.
1948,	Jeffrey Linton Osborne, R&B recording artist, was born in Providence, R.I.
1950,	Juanita Hall became the first African-American to win a Tony Award (for her role in the musical *South Pacific*).
1991,	The first African-American Summit was held in Abijan, Ivory Coast.

APRIL 9

EDUCATORS

RICHARD ALLEN

Abolitionist, church founder, and the **first major leader of African-Americans in the U.S.** Born into slavery on February 14, 1760, in Philadelphia, Pa. Emancipated (1783); converted to Christianity and served in the Revolutionary War; preached in Delaware, West Jersey, and eastern Pennsylvania; attended the first organizing conference of the general Methodist Church (1784). **Helped organize the independent Free African Society of Philadelphia (1787), the first official organization for African-Americans in the U.S.** (which extended mutual aid; disallowed drunkenness, disorderly conduct, loose marriage ties; denounced slavery; and encouraged other similar organizations in Newport, Boston, and New York); helped organize the nondenominational "African Church" (1791); completed the building of the Bethel Church in Philadelphia (1794), **established the African Methodist Episcopal Church** (1816), and was **consecrated as the first bishop of the AME Church** (1816). Opened a day school (1795); was ordained as a deacon (1799), and later as an elder; led African-Americans communities in petitioning state legislatures and Congress for the abolition of slavery (1799-1800); organized a "Society of Free People of Color for Promoting the Instruction and School Education of Children of African Descent" (1804). Led African-Americans in building a defense of Philadelphia during the War of 1812; helped organize a convention of African-American men who opposed the American Colonization Society (1817); aided the *Freedom's Journal* (1827), the first African-American newspaper in the U.S.; key organizer and president of the "American Society of Free Persons of Colour, for improving their Condition in the United States; for Purchasing Lands; and for the Establishing of a Settlement in the Province of Upper Canada" (1830). Died in 1831 in Philadelphia, Pa. Further reading, Carol George, *Segregated Sabbaths: Richard Allen and the Emergence of Independent Black Churches 1760-1840* (1973).

---

on this day in history...

1886,	Kentucky State College was founded in Frankfort, Ky.
1887,	Henry Francis Downing became U.S. consul to Angola.
1939,	George R. Carruthers, astrophysicist who invented a lunar surface ultraviolet light, was born in Cincinnati, Ohio.
1943,	Willie Williams, Philadelphia and Los Angeles' first African-American police chief, was born in Philadelphia, Pa.
1945,	Rodney Cline Carew, five-time American League batting champion, was born in Gatun, Panama.
1945,	Donny Hathaway, singer, composer, and arranger, was born in Chicago, Ill. (d. 1979).

OCTOBER 1   RELIGIOUS LEADERS

MORDECAI WYATT JOHNSON

Educator, administrator, and public speaker.   Born on January 12, 1890, in Paris, Tenn.   Atlanta Baptist College [now Morehouse College] (B.A., 1911); University of Chicago (B.A., 1913); Rochester Theological Seminary (B.D., 1916); Harvard University School of Divinity (M.A., theology, 1922), where he gave the commencement speech entitled "The Faith of the American Negro," which attracted national attention; Howard University (D.D., 1923); Gammon Theological Seminary (D.D., 1928).   Pastor of Baptist churches in Mumford, N.Y., and Charleston, W.Va.; founded the Charleston, W.Va., branch of the NAACP; student secretary at the YMCA national office, traveling throughout the country making studies of African-American schools and colleges; teacher of English, history, and economics at Atlanta Baptist College; **first African-American president of Howard University** (1926-1956), attracting some of the world's most distinguished African-American academics and scholars, including Edward Frazier, Charles Houston, Alain Locke, Benjamin Mays, and Carter Woodson. Died on September 10, 1976, in Washington, D.C.   Further reading, Rayford W. Logan, *Howard University: The First Hundred Years 1867-1967* (1969).

---

on this day in history...

1943,   Arthur Ashe, tennis legend and humanitarian, was born in Richmond, Va. (d. 1993).

1968,   Congress passed the Civil Rights Act of 1968, banning discrimination in the sale or rental of about 80 percent of the nation's housing.

1993,   Ben Chavis was named executive director of the NAACP, replacing the retiring Ben Hooks.

APRIL 10   **EDUCATORS**

WILLIAM GRANT STILL

Musician who was known as the **"dean of Afro-American composers."** Born on May 11, 1895, in Woodville, Miss. Wilberforce University; Oberlin Conservatory of Music; New England Conservatory of Music. Played the oboe and violin; made his first band arrangements for W.C. Handy's "Beale Street" and "St. Louis Blues" (1916), and became a band member and road manager; served in the U.S. Navy during World War I; became an arranger and recording manager for Harry Pace's Phonograph Company (1921). Composed: the songs, "Breath of a Rose," "Levee Land," and "Kaintuck;" the ballet scores, *Sahdji*(1930), and *La Guiablesse* (1927); the first symphony by an African-American to be played by a major orchestra (the Rochester Philharmonic Orchestra), *Afro-American* (1931); the first opera to be composed by an African-American and performed by a major company (the New York Opera Company), *Troubled Island* (1941). Conductor of the Los Angeles Philharmonic (1936), becoming the **first African-American to lead a major symphony;** wrote the music for the films, *Pennies From Heaven* (1936), and *Stormy Weather* (1943), and for the TV shows, *Gunsmoke* and the original *Perry Mason*; commissioned by the New York World's Fair Committee to write the music for their theme, "The City of Tomorrow" (1939); became the first composer to use a blues melody as the thematic basis for a symphony and the first to employ the banjo as a symphonic instrument. Awarded the Harmon Foundation award (1928); received a Rosenwald and Guggenheim fellowship (1934, 1935); won the Cincinnati Symphony Orchestra's competition contest First Prize (1944); honored with degrees from Howard University (Ph.D., 1941), and UCLA (Ph.D., 1975); cited by the governor of Mississippi as "a distinguished Mississippian" (1974). Died on December 3, 1978, in Los Angeles, Calif. Further reading, <u>Robert B. Hass</u>, <u>*William Grant Still and the Fusion of Cultures in American Music*</u> (1972).

---

on this day in history...

1935,   Johnny Royce Mathis, balladeer, was born in San Francisco, Calif.

1962,   James H. Meredith became the University of Mississippi's first African-American student, after a U.S. Supreme Court ruling ordering his admission.

SEPTEMBER 30   **MUSICIANS**

VIRGINIA LACY JONES

Librarian and educator known as the **"dean of library school deans."** Born on June 25, 1912, in Cincinnati, Ohio. Hampton Institute (B.A., library science, 1933; B.S., 1936); University of Illinois (M.A., 1938); University of Chicago (Ph.D., 1945). Assistant librarian of Louisville Municipal College, the Negro branch of the University of Louisville; organized the librarians' section of the Kentucky Negro Education Association; director of Prairie View A&M's librarianship degree program; participated in protest movement led by the Chicago NAACP against racism, while attending the University of Illinois. Protested to publishers about children's books, seeking a change in the demeaning images of African-Americans in literature; visited libraries in the South offering to assist in the organization or reorganization of library service and the provision of bibliographical assistance in the area of collection development (1942), financed by the Carnegie Corporation of N.Y.; sponsored leadership conferences in the areas of public libraries, African-American bibliographies, and undergraduate library education. Taught cataloging and classification, school library service, and children's literature courses at Atlanta University; **dean of the School of Library Service at Atlanta University** (1945-1981), dean emeritus (1983-1984); director of the Atlanta University Center's Robert W. Woodruff Library (1981-1983). Elected president of the Association of American Library Schools (1967); appointed by President Johnson as a member of the President's Advisory Committee on Library Research and Training Projects (1967); member of the Georgia State Board for the Certification of Librarians (1975-1980); cited by the American Library Association Black Caucus (1976), for 30 years of service to African-American librarians. Died on December 3, 1984, in Atlanta, Ga. Further reading, Casper LeRoy Jordan, "Virginia Lacy Jones," _Notable Black American Women_ (1992).

---

on this day in history...

1883,	Spelman College was founded in Atlanta, Ga.
1908,	Jane M. Bolin, nation's first African-American woman judge, was born in Poughkeepsie, N.Y.
1933,	Tony Brown, Emmy Award-winning producer, was born in Charleston, W.Va.
1955,	Roy Wilkins succeeded Walter White as NAACP executive director.
1963,	The home of Alfred Daniel King, the younger brother of Martin Luther King, Jr., was bombed in Birmingham.
1972,	Benjamin Hooks became the first African-American to be named to the Federal Communications Commission.

APRIL 11   **EDUCATORS**

CHARLIE PARKER

Jazz musicians nicknamed "Bird." Born Charles Christopher Parker on August 29, 1920, in Kansas City, Kan. Played the alto saxophone; co-founder of "The Bop" movement of the '40s with Dizzy Gillespie; became a member of an informal jazz session group of Minto's Playhouse in Harlem, which included Thelonious Monk and Dizzy Gillespie; joined Early "Fatha" Hines' Orchestra (1942), which was later recognized as the "incubator of bop;" played with Noble Sissle (1942), Billy Eckstine (1944), and Dizzy Gillespie (1944-1946). Formed the Charlie Parker Quintet (1947), which included Miles Davis, Duke Jordan, Tommy Potter, and Max Roach; played at the International Paris Jazz Festival (1944); honored by the naming of a new New York City nightclub, Birdland (1949); recorded *Charlie Parker with Strings* (1950), making history as the first jazz group to record with a chamber orchestra. Recorded, "In the Still of the Night" (1953), "Lover Man" (1946), and "Relaxin at Camarillo" (1947); became one of the most imitated and influential of all jazz musicians during the '40s and '50s, and was **one of the largest contributors to the movement that changed jazz from a dance music to chamber music demanding serious listening**; participated in the Newport Jazz Festival; inducted into the Downbeat Hall of Fame (1955); posthumously won a Grammy Award for best jazz soloist (1974). Died on March 12, 1955, in New York City. Further reading, Ross Russell, *Bird Lives* (1973).

---

on this day in history...

1948,   Bryant Charles Gumbel, Emmy Award-winning sportscaster and first African-American anchor of a national network morning news program (*The Today Show*), was born in New Orleans, La.

SEPTEMBER 29   **MUSICIANS**

BENJAMIN ELIJAH MAYS

Minister, educator, and administrator who was called the last of the great schoolmasters.   Born on August 1, 1895, in Epworth, S.C.   Bates College in Lewiston, Maine (B.A., 1920), Phi Beta Kappa; University of Chicago Divinity School (M.A., 1925; Ph.D., 1935).   Ordained a Baptist minister (1921), later serving as pastor of Shiloh Baptist Church in Atlanta; instructor of mathematics and English at Morehouse College (1921-1924), and at South Carolina State (1925-1926); served as an Urban League official (1926-1928), and as a national student secretary of the YMCA (1928-1930). **Director of the first scientific sociological study of the status of African-American churches** (1930-1932), which resulted in the publication, *The Negro's Church*; dean of Howard University School of Religion (1934-1940), becoming one of the most influential African-American religious leaders of his time; served as vice president of the Federal Council of Churches.   President of Morehouse College (1940-1967), where he **helped shape the lives of thousands of "Morehouse Men,"** educate a disproportionate share of African-American college presidents, educators, lawyers, ministers, movement leaders, Ph.D.'s, physicians, and politicians, and built the institution into the "Black Oxford of the South." Served as ministerial mentor and senior advisor to Martin Luther King, Jr., delivering his eulogy (1968); **Atlanta School Board member who became their first African-American president** (1969-1981), where he vigorously sought the cooperation of African-American churches and organizations in helping to solve the societal ills affecting public schools. Died on March 28, 1984, in Atlanta, Ga.   Further reading, Benjamin E. Mays, *Born to Rebel: An Autobiography* (1971).

---

on this day in history...

1787,	Richard Allen, Absalom Jones, and James Forten, Sr., organized the Free African Society of Philadelphia.
1825,	Richard Harvey Cain, South Carolina congressman (1873-1875, 1877-1879), was born in Greenbrier County, Va. (d. 1887).
1940,	Herbie Jeffrey Hancock, Grammy and Academy Award-winning musician and composer, was born in Chicago, Ill.
1966,	Emmett Ashford became the first African-American umpire in the major leagues.
1983,	Harold Washington was elected Chicago's first African-American mayor.
1990,	August Wilson won his second Pulitzer Prize for Drama with *The Piano Lessons*.

APRIL 12   **EDUCATORS**

JELLY ROLL MORTON

Ragtime, blues, and jazz pianist and composer who became **the first great composer of jazz** and the first to write down his jazz arrangements in notation.   Born Ferdinand Joseph LaMenthe on September 20, 1885, in Gulfport, Miss.   St. John's University.   Began playing with the great pianists of New Orleans (1902), where he claimed to have **invented the word jazz** and composed "New Orleans Blues," "King Porter Stomp," and "Alabama Bound;" played in Tulsa, Mobile, Chicago, and New York City; toured with the Memphis-based Benbow circuit (1909-1911), performing in Baltimore, Chicago, Kansas City, Jacksonville, Louisville, St. Louis, and Washington; **composed "Jelly Roll Blues" (1915), making it the first published jazz arrangement.** Played at the San Francisco Exposition (1915); operated a dance hall and hotel in Los Angeles (1917-1923), also performing in Vancouver, San Diego, and Denver; made his first recordings with the New Orleans Rhythm Kings (1918); toured out of Chicago (1923-1928), recording extensively with the Red Hot Peppers, making piano rolls for the Melville Clark Piano Company, serving as a staff arranger for the Melrose Brothers, and playing with W.C. Handy. Settled in New York City (1928), where he toured with his group playing nightclubs and ballrooms; worked with the *Speeding Along* and *Heading for Harlem* revues; played Washington, D.C., nightclubs (1936); recorded the history of jazz, at the invitation of Alan Lomax, for the Library of Congress (1938). Died on July 10, 1941, in Los Angeles, Calif.   Further reading, <u>Gunther Schuller</u>, <u>Early Jazz</u> (1968).

---

on this day in history...

1785,	David Walker, militant abolitionist and theoretician of total African revolt, was born in Wilmington, N.C. (d. 1830).
1829,	David Walker began publishing the anti-slavery pamphlet, *Appeal*.
1987,	The Smithsonian Institute's National Museum of African Art opened in Washington, D.C.

SEPTEMBER 28 MUSICIANS

ROBERT RUSSA MOTON

Educator and lawyer. Born on August 26, 1867, in Rice, Va. Hampton Institute (1890), where he was appointed commandant of the student cadet corps with the title of "major" (1891-1915). Teacher in Cottontown, Va.; received license to practice law (1888); elected president of the National Negro Business League (1900); trustee and secretary of the Board of the Jeanes Fund (1908); toured the South with Booker T. Washington (Miss., 1908; S.C., Tenn., 1909; N.C., 1910; La., 1915), to promote the Hampton-Tuskegee idea of vocational education and biracial cooperation as the best means of advancement. **Principal of Tuskegee Institute** (1915-1935), where he increased the endowment of the school by more than 5 million dollars; adviser on federal appointees to Presidents Wilson, Harding, Coolidge, Hoover, and F.D. Roosevelt; supported the establishment of the Colored Officers Training Camp at Fort Des Moines, Iowa (1917), and secured the appointment of Emmett J. Scott as special assistant to the U.S. secretary of war; toured France (1918), to investigate the treatment of African-American soldiers during World War I; helped found the Commission on Interracial Cooperation (1918); responsible for the building of a veterans hospital for African-Americans (1923), on land donated by Tuskegee Institute; member of the Hoover Commission on the Mississippi Valley Flood Disaster (1927). Chairman of the U.S. Commission on Education in Haiti (1930); received Harmon Foundation Award (1930), for contributions to better race relations; NAACP Spingarn Medal (1932), for his stand on education in Haiti. Died on May 31, 1940, in Virginia. Further reading, Wilson J. Moses, *The Golden Age of Black Nationalism 1850-1925* (1978).

---

on this day in history...

1891,   Nella Larsen, first African-American Guggenheim fellow in creative writing, was born in Chicago, Ill. (d. 1964).

1939,   Barbara-Rose Collins, Michigan 14th District congresswoman, was born in Detroit, Mich.

1946,   Al Green, Grammy Award-winning gospel singer, was born in Forest City, Ark.

1951,   Jesse Leroy Brown, first African-American naval aviator killed in wartime, posthumously received the Medal of Honor.

1963,   Sidney Poitier became the first African-American to receive an Academy Award for best actor (for his role in *Lillies of the Fields).*

SCOTT JOPLIN

Composer and pianist who was known as the **"king of ragtime."** Born on November 24, 1868, in Texarkana, Ark. George Smith College for Negroes in Sedalia, Mo. Left home and traveled throughout the vaudeville circuit, playing in bars and bordellos, absorbing the ragtime music that was being played at the time; performed at the World's Fair (Chicago, 1893); settled in Sedalia, Mo., and began performing in honky-tonks and saloons; started composing music and published *Original Rags* (1899), which marked a turning point in his work and finally revealed a full-fledged artist; published "Maple Leaf Rag" (1899), which sold over a million copies in sheet music, popularized ragtime and started a craze in the United States and Europe that lasted until his death, and made him financially independent after his white publisher agreed to pay him royalties (which was practically unheard of among African-American composers, who would mostly sell their work outright). Moved to St. Louis (1900), where he taught, studied, composed, and formed the Scott Joplin Drama Company; wrote the operas, *A Guest of Honor* (1903), and *Treeminisha* (1907); published the manual, *The School of Ragtime-- Six Exercises for Piano* (1908). Spent the last decade of his life trying unsuccessfully to bring his operas to life on the stage, with his work laying dormant until the phenomenal rebirth of his music in the 1970s; his music was the basis for the movie soundtrack of *The Sting* (1972), his ragtime opera--*Treemonisha* was performed to critical acclaim, and he posthumously was awarded a Pulitzer Prize for his compositions (1976). Died on April 1, 1917, in New York City. Further reading, <u>William J. Shafer</u> and <u>Johannes Riedel</u>, *<u>The Art of Ragtime</u>* (1973).

---

on this day in history...

1875,   The University of Arkansas-Pine Bluff opened.
1934,   Greg Morris, actor, was born in Cleveland, Ohio.
1936,   Don Cornelius, host and executive producer of *Soul Train*, was born in Chicago, Ill.
1967,   The Anacostia Museum opened in Washington, D.C.

SEPTEMBER 27   MUSICIANS

BOOKER TALIAFERRO WASHINGTON

Educator and race leader.   Born into slavery on April 5, 1856, in Franklin County, Va.   Hampton Institute (B.A., 1875); enrolled in the Wayland Seminary in Washington, D.C. (1888).   **Founder and president of Tuskegee Institute** (1881-1915), which he modeled after Hampton Institute; shortly after the passing of Frederick Douglass, he delivered his (what W.E.B. DuBois later called) "Atlanta Compromise" speech at the Cotton States and International Exposition (Atlanta, 1895), indicating his acceptance of the separate but equal doctrine, which made him the unchallenged spokesman for African-Americans from 1895-1906; received an **honorary M.A. from Harvard University (1896), the first African-American to be so honored**; formed the "Tuskegee Machine," a large network of influential African-Americans; **founded the National Negro Business League** (1900); dined with President Theodore Roosevelt at the White House (1901), putting the South into an uproar and making him even more famous; received an honorary D.Lit. from Dartmouth University (1901); wrote an autobiography *Up From Slavery* (1901), which became one of the classic American autobiographies and established him as an international figure; traveled to Europe and was entertained by Queen Victoria of England; secretly financed *Rogers vs. Alabama* (1904), and *Bailey vs. Alabama* (1911), which struck down Alabama black peonage laws. Died on November 14, 1915, in Tuskegee, Ala.   Further reading, <u>Louis R. Harlan</u>, <u>*Booker T. Washington*</u> (1983).

---

on this day in history...

1926,   Moneta Sleet, Jr., Pulitzer Prize-winning photographer for *Ebony*, was born in Owensboro, Ky.

1938,   Gloria Randle Scott, Bennett College president, was born in Houston, Texas.

JIMI HENDRIX

Singer, songwriter, and composer who was regarded as **the most gifted rock musician of the 1960s.**   Born on November 27, 1942, in Seattle, Wash.   Served in the U.S. Air Force; toured with Little Richard, Ike and Tina Turner, King Curtis, the Isley Brothers, and James Brown (1961-1966); played in New York City nightclubs, where he was noticed by British musician Charles Chandler, who invited him to come to England; formed the Jimi Hendrix Experience with Mitch Mitchell and Noel Redding, touring Europe and recording extensively (1966-1967); attracted wide attention for the groups flashy attire, use of electric gadgetry, ear-shattering loud music, and their on-stage antics. Returned to the U.S. and performed at the 1967 Monterey Pop Music Festival and the 1969 Woodstock Festival, which brought him a huge following; some of his best-known recordings included the albums, *Are You Experienced*, *Purple Haze*, and *Band of Gypsies*; honored with *Billboard*'s Artist of the Year (1968), *Playboy Magazine* Artist of the Year (1969), and was inducted posthumously into the Playboy Music Hall of Fame (1971); appeared in the documentary, *Jimi Hendrix* (1973). Died on September 18, 1970, in London. Further reading, <u>Chris Welch</u>, <u>*Hendrix*</u> (1972).

---

on this day in history...

1876,   William Jasper Hale, founding president of Tennessee State University, was born in Retro, Tenn. (d. 1944).
1962,   A. Leon Higginbotham, Jr., became the first African-American member of the Federal Trade Commission.

SEPTEMBER 26   MUSICIANS

WILLIAM TAYLOR BURWELL WILLIAMS

Educator.   Born on July 30, 1869, in Stonebridge, Va.   Hampton Institute; Phillips Academy in Andover, Mass. (1893); Harvard University (B.A., 1897).   Principal of School #24 in Indianapolis (1897-1902). Appointed field agent for: Hampton Institute (1902); the Southern Education Board (1902), studying educational conditions in Virginia and other southern states; the General Education Board (1903), where he worked among the African-American population of the South urging local educational activities and providing assistance to communities eager to improve their schools; the John F. Slater Fund (1906), where he helped establish nearly 400 county training schools for African-American youth in 13 southern states, which relieved many African-American colleges from having to provide elementary and high school facilities; the Anna T. Jeanes Funds (1910), where he was responsible for directing the work of the Jeanes teachers, who supervised primary instruction in the African-American schools of the rural South, organized industrial classes in these schools, and organized and continued community clubs to promote activities for general community improvements. **Came into direct contact with every phase of African-American education in the South** and with leading educators of all races; known throughout the South as the best informed person on African-American education; member of the U.S. commissions on education to Haiti (1922, 1930). Appointed assistant supervisor of vocational training in African-American schools for the Committee on Education and Special Training of the U.S. Department of War (1918); consultant in the teaching-training program at Tuskegee Institute (1919-1927), dean of the college department (1927-1936), and vice president (1936-1947); awarded the NAACP Spingarn Medal (1934), for distinguished service in Negro education; served as National Association of Teachers in Colored Schools president. Died on March 26, 1941, in Tuskegee, Ala.   Further reading, Henry Allen Bullock, _A History of Negro Education in the South_ (1967).

---

on this day in history...

1915,	Walter Edward Washington, Washington's first elected mayor, was born in Dawson, Ga.
1919,	Elizabeth Catlett, "the dean of women artists," was born in Washington, D.C.
1928,	Norma Merrick Sklarek, nation's first licensed woman architect, was born in New York City.
1971,	Samuel Gravely became the first African-American admiral.

APRIL 15

EDUCATORS

WILLIAM CHRISTOPHER HANDY

Composer, cornetist, band leader, educator, songwriter, and publisher who was known as the **"father of the Blues."** Born William Christopher Handy on November 16, 1873, in Florence, Ala. Organized a quartet in Birmingham and played at the Chicago Columbia Exposition--the World's Fair (1893); joined W.A. Mahara's Minstrel as a cornetist, and later as a bandleader (1896-1900, 1902-1903), touring the U.S., Canada, Mexico, and Cuba; music instructor and band master at Alabama A&M College (1900-1902); lived in Clarksdale, Miss. (1903-1908), organizing and leading military and dance bands in the Mississippi Delta region; settled in Memphis (1908), and along with lyricist Harry Pace, established Pace and Handy Music Company; served as a booking agent for other dance bands, therefore controlling the African-American music entertainment industry in the Memphis area. Composed and/or published: "Memphis Blues" (1912), his first published composition, which was originally written for "Boss" Crump's successful Memphis mayoral campaign; "St. Louis Blues" (1914), which became the most widely performed American song in history; "Jo Turner Blues" (1915); "Beale Street Blues" and "A Good Man Is Hard To Find" (1916), which were introduced by Alberta Hunter in Chicago; "Careless Love" (1921), a.k.a. "Loveless Love;" "Aunt Hagar Blues" (1922); "Make Me a Pallet on the Floor" (1923), a.k.a. "Atlanta Blues." Moved to New York City (1918), becoming a **leading publisher of music of African-American songwriters and one of the African-American pioneers in recording;** his collections included, *Blues: An Anthology* (1926), and *Book of Negro Spirituals* (1938); produced a Carnegie Hall show (1928), emphasizing the history of African-American music; author of *Negro Authors and Composers of the U.S.* (1936), and *Unsung Americans Sung* (1944); became one of the most celebrated musicians of his time. Died on March 28, 1958, in Harlem, N.Y. Further reading, W.C.Handy, *Father of the Blues* (1941).

---

on this day in history...

1957,   Ernest Green, Elizabeth Eckford, Gloria Ray, Jefferson Thomas, Melba Pattilo, Carlotta Walls, Minnie Jean Brown, Terrance Roberts, and Thelma Mothershed, escorted by Daisy Bates and federal troops, integrated Little Rock's Central High School.

1962,   Sonny Liston defeated Floyd Patterson for the heavyweight boxing championship.

1965,   Scottie Pippin, Chicago Bulls All-Star, was born in Hamburg, Ark.

SEPTEMBER 25   **MUSICIANS**

PEARL MAE BAILEY

Entertainer, author, and humanitarian. Born on March 29, 1918, in Newport News, Va. Georgetown University (B.A., theology, 1980). Won first prize in an amateur contest at the Pearl Theater in Philadelphia (1933), where she danced and sang "Poor Butterfly" and began her career in entertainment; toured with vaudeville troupes, singing and dancing throughout Pennsylvania coal-mining towns; worked in Washington's elite African-American entertainment district--U Street N.W.; won an Apollo Theater amateur contest; **performed in USO tours (1941-1990)**; toured with Cootie Williams, Count Basie, and Noble Sissle (1943-1944). Debuted as a soloist at the Village Vanguard (1944); worked with Cab Calloway's act at the Strand Theater and Broadway's Zanzibar Nightclub; debuted as an actress in *St. Louis Woman* at Broadway's Marten Beck Theater (1946), where she was hailed as Broadway's best newcomer; appeared in her first Broadway role as a solo star in *House of Flowers* (1954). Played the roles of "Frankie" in 20th Century Fox's *Carmen Jones* (1954), "Gussie" in Paramount's *That Certain Feeling* (1956), "Aunt Hagar" in Warner Brothers' *St. Louis Blues* (1956), and "Maria" in MGM's *Porgy and Bess* (1959). **Held the starring role in David Merrick's all-black production of *Hello, Dolly!* (1967), which has been called the high point of her career** and earned her a Special Tony Award; recorded "Bill Bailey, Won't You Please Come Home," which was about her famous dancing brother; author of *Talking to Myself* (1971), and *Pearl's Kitchen* (1973); received the March of Dimes annual award (1968), the USO "Woman of the Year" Award (1969), and the American Heart Association's "Heart of the Year" Award (1972); **appointed the "Ambassador of Love"** by President Nixon; **special representative in the U.S. delegation to the U.N.** (1975-1990). Died on August 17, 1990, in Philadelphia, Pa. Further reading, Pearl Baily, *The Raw Pearl* (1968).

---

on this day in history...

1862,	The U.S. Senate passed a bill abolishing slavery in the District of Columbia.
1864,	Flora Batson, soprano-baritone known as the "double-voice queen of song," was born in Washington, D.C. (d. 1906).
1864,	Gloria Patton, first African-American woman graduate of Meharry Medical College, was born in Gundy County, Tenn. (d. 1900).
1921,	Marie Maynard Daly, first African-American to earn a Ph.D. in chemistry, was born in Corona, N.Y.
1947,	Lew Alcinder ("Kareem Abdul Jabbar"), NBA all-time leading scorer, was born in New York City.
1952,	Peter J. Westbrook, 11-time national fencing champion, was born in St. Louis, Mo.

APRIL 16   **ENTERTAINERS**

DIZZY GILLESPIE

Trumpeter, conductor, and composer who was known as **one of the founding fathers of modern jazz.** Born John Birks Gillespie on October 21, 1917, in Cheraw, N.C. Lauringburg Technical Institute in North Carolina. Toured: with Fatha Hines, Billy Eckstine, Cab Calloway, and Benny Carter (1930-1944); with the Teddy Hill Band (1937-1939); with his own band and groups (1946-1956); Scandinavia (1948); Iran, Pakistan, Lebanon, Turkey, Greece, Syria, and Yugoslavia (1956-1958), as a goodwill ambassador of the U.S. State Department, which marked the first time in history that the U.S. government had given official recognition to a jazz orchestra; Argentina (1961). Performed at the Juan-Les-Pins Festival in France, Monterery Jazz Festival (1962-1974), Montreux Jazz Festival (1973), and at the Newport Jazz Festival (1973-1976); **co-founder of "The Bop" movement;** composed the songs, "A Night in Tunisia," "Dizzy Atmosphere," "Salt 'n Peanuts," and "Groovin' High;" appeared at the Apollo Theater, Carnegie Hall (1975-1976), Avery Fisher Hall (1975), Radio City Music Hall (1976), and held a command performance at the White House (1978). Honored with a Berlin Film Festival First Prize in soundtrack (1962), degree from Rutgers University (D. Mus., 1970), Institute of High Fidelity's Musician of the Year Award (1975), Grammy (1975, 1976, 1980, and 1989), an invitation to speak before a joint session of the South Carolina State Legislature (1976), Jazzmobile's Paul Robeson Award, National Endowment for the Arts' Jazz Master Award (1982), a place on Philadelphia's Music Walk of Fame (1987), and an induction into the Black Filmmakers Hall of Fame (1988); credited with bringing Afro-Cuban rhythms into jazz, introducing South American samba to the U.S., and with being the first to use electric string bass in the jazz ensemble. Died January 6, 1993, in Englewood, N.J. Further reading, <u>Dizzy Gillespie</u>, <u>*To Be, Or Not to Bop*</u> (1979).

---

on this day in history...

1931,	Cardiss Robertson Collins, Illinois 7th District congresswoman, was born in St. Louis, Mo.
1938,	Mark Edward Warren, Emmy Award-winning director, was born in Harrodsburg, Ky.
1965,	President Johnson issued Executive Order 11246, Title IV, distributing authority among federal agencies for the enforcement of the Civil Rights Act of 1964.
1977,	John T. Walker was installed as the first African-American bishop of the Episcopal Diocese of Washington, D.C.

SEPTEMBER 24

MUSICIANS

JOSEPHINE BAKER

Expatriate entertainer. Born on June 3, 1906, in St. Louis, Mo. Joined a group called the Dixie Fliers and toured on the Theater Owners Booking Association (TOBA) circuit; danced in Noble Sissle and Eubie Blake's production of *Chocolate Dandies* (1924-1925); went to Paris and opened in the American jazz revue *Revue Negre* at the Theatre des Champs-Elysees (1925), dancing the Charleston and singing "Yes, Sir, That's My Baby!", which brought her international fame; opened a nightclub in Paris called the Chez Josephine (1926); embarked on a world tour (1928-1930), traveling through Europe and South America. Starred in: *La Folie Du Jour* at the Folies Bergere (1927), a musical comedy; *Paris Qui Remue* (1930), the revue where she first sang "J'ai Deux Amours;" *La Joie de Paris* (1931), where she performed a ballet number; *Ziegfeld Follies* in New York City (1936), where she had to use the back entrance to get to her St. Moritz hotel suite; *Folies Bergere* (1936). Opened in the Casino de Paris' revue *Paris-Londres* (1939), which coincided with the beginning of World War II, and in Societe des Bains de Mer's *Josephine* (1974-1975), which ran in Monte Carlo and Paris. Recruited by spy Jacque Abtey into the French Resistance (1940-1944), working out of Marseille and serving in Lisbon, North Africa, and Italy; awarded the Medal of Resistance and the French Legion of Honor for her work during the World War II. Toured the U.S. several times after the war, where she was honored by the NAACP as the 1951 "Most Outstanding Woman of the Year," attended the 1963 March on Washington, gave a benefit in New York City for the SNCC, CORE, and the NAACP, and played Carnegie Hall; appeared in the films *Black Shadows* (1923), *La Creole* (1934), *Zouzou* (1934), *Princess Tam-Tam* (1935), *Moulin Rouge* (1944), and the *French Way* (1959). Died on April 14, 1975, in Paris, France. Further reading, <u>Phyllis Rose</u>, <u>*Jazz Cleopatra: Josephine Baker in Her Time*</u> (1989).

---

on this day in history...

1887,   Lawrence Augustus Oxley, special assistant to the U.S. secretary of labor in FDR's "Black Cabinet," was born in Boston, Mass. (d. 1973).

APRIL 17   **ENTERTAINERS**

DUKE ELLINGTON

Jazz innovator, pianist, and band leader who was called **one of the greatest of all jazz composers**. Born Edward Kennedy Ellington on April 29, 1899, in Washington, D.C. Pratt Institute in Brooklyn, N.Y. Studied with classical musician William Marion Cook; wrote his first song "Soda Fountain Rag," while still in high school; formed his first jazz band with three Miller brothers and Chauncey Brown (1919), and a New York City vaudeville group--the Duke's Serenaders (1923); band director of the Washingtonians (1923-1927), performing at the Hollywood Club in New York City; recorded his first songs (1924); wrote the score for the musical *Chocolate Kiddies* (1925); played the famed whites-only Cotton Club in Harlem (1927-1932), which featured African-American performers. Debuted in his (the Ellington Band) first Broadway musical, *Show Girl* (1929), his first of many films, *Check and Double Check* (1930), and embarked on his first European tour (1933); **helped initiate the "Big Band" era and its "swing" music**; brought Billy Strayhorn into his band (1939), and collaborated closely for the next 28 years; inaugurated an annual jazz concert series at Carnegie Hall (1943-1955); held the **first jazz concert performed in a church**--Grace Cathedral Church in San Francisco (1965). Some of Ellington's classic songs and albums, include "Mood Indigo," "Caravan," "It Don't Mean a Thing If It Ain't Got That Swing," "Take the 'A' Train," "In a Sentimental Mood," "Sophisticated Lady," and *Black, Brown and Beige*; composed countless revues, musicals, film scores, compositions, and television productions. Honored with 16 honorary doctorates, the NAACP Spingarn Medal (1959), two Grammy Awards (1959, 1965), the Presidential Medal of Freedom (1969), an induction into the Songwriters and the National Jazz Hall of Fames, and a Duke Ellington Fellowship Program at Yale (1972). Known as the **first authentic jazz "composer."** Died on May 24, 1974, in New York City. Further reading, Duke Ellington, *Music is My Mistress* (1973).

---

on this day in history...

1930,	"Ray Charles" Robinson, Grammy Award-winning musician, was born in Albany, Ga.
1935,	Leslie Coleman "Les" McCann, jazz pianist who founded the Institute of Black American Music, was born in Lexington, Ky.
1972,	The Coalition of Black Trade Unionists was established at a Chicago conference.

SEPTEMBER 23   **MUSICIANS**

LOUISE BEAVERS

One of the most popular character actresses in Hollywood during the '30s and '40s.   Born on March 8, 1902, in Cincinnati, Ohio. Organized and performed with The Lady Minstrels (1923-1926); discovered by an agent for Universal Pictures and debuted in *Uncle Tom's Cabin* (1927); starred in the critical acclaimed *Imitation of Life* (1934); played a loving and concerned mother in *The Jackie Robinson Story* (1950), which allowed her to escape the stereotypical "Aunt Jemima" roles; replaced Hattie McDaniel on the CBS radio and television series "Beulah" (1951-1953); teamed up with Mae West (1954), and played the Congo Room in Las Vegas; inducted into the Black Filmmakers Hall of Fame (1957); member of the Screen Actors Guild. Her film credits included: *Wall Street* (1929), *Up For Murder* (1930), *What Price Hollywood?* (1932), *Her Bodyguard* (1933), *West of the Pecos* (1934), *Annapolis Farewell* (1935), *Bullets or Ballots* (1936), *The Last Gangster* (1937), *Life Goes On* (1938), *The Lady From Kentucky* (1939), *Women without Names* (1940), *Virginia* (1941), *Holiday Inn* (1942), *Good Morning Judge* (1943), *Jack London* (1944), *Delightfully Dangerous* (1945), *Young Widows* (1946), *Banjo* (1947), *For the Love of Mary* (1948), *Tell It to the Judge* (1949), *Girls School* (1950), *I Dream of Jeanie* (1952), *Never Wave at a Wac* (1953), *You Can't Run Away from It* (1956), *Tammy and the Bachelor* (1957), *The Goddess* (1958), *All the Fine Young Cannibals* (1960), and *The Facts of Life* (1961). Died on October 26, 1962, in Los Angeles, Calif.   Further reading, Edward Mapp, *Directory of Blacks in the Performing Arts* (1978).

on this day in history...

1811,	James McCune Smith, the nation's first African-American to receive a medical degree, was born in New York City (d. 1865).
1937,	Robert Dean Hooks, co-founder of the Negro Ensemble Company, was born in Washington, D.C.
1949,	Daniel T. Blue, Jr., North Carolina speaker of the House of Representatives, was born in Lumberton, N.C.
1977,	Alex Haley won a special Pulitzer Prize for his novel *Roots: The Sage of an American Family*.
1978,	Noble M. Johnson, founder of the Nebraska-based Lincoln Motion Picture County, died in Colorado Springs, Colo.
1983,	Alice Walker was awarded the Pulitzer Prize for her novel *The Color Purple*.

APRIL 18   **ENTERTAINERS**

MILES DEWEY DAVIS, III

Jazz trumpeter and composer.   Born on May 25, 1926, in Alton, Ill.   Juilliard School of Music.   Played with Eddie Randall in St. Louis (1941-1943), Charlie Parker, Coleman Hawkins, Benny Carter, Billy Eckstine, and Tadd Dameron (1945-1950); formed his own band, the nine-piece Capitol Band (1948), which contributed to the development of "cool jazz;" appeared at the Paris Jazz Festival (1949), Cafe Bohemia in New York City (1957), Avery Fisher Hall (1974), Carnegie Hall (1975), and at the Newport Jazz Festival (1975); toured with Jazz, Inc. (1952); formed a quintet (1954), which included John Coltrane. Some of his most popular recordings included: *The Complete Birth of the Cool*, which was significant in the development of the "West Coast" bebop style; *Miles Ahead*, which brought him wide recognition as a jazz innovator; *Kind of Blue*, which was a milestone in jazz history; *Bitches Brew*, which was a fusion of jazz, rock 'n roll, and soul elements; *On the Corner*; *A Tribute to Jack Johnson*; *Live at the Fillmore East*. Inducted into the Downbeat Hall of Fame; Grammy Award winner (1960, 1983); influenced such musicians as Herbie Hancock, Cannonball Adderley, John Coltrane, and Chick Corea; **regarded as one of the most influential figures in jazz for more than 25 years,** from the bebop era to the avant-garde of the '70s. Died on September 28, 1991, in Santa Monica, Calif. Further reading, Bill Cole, *Miles Davis* (1974).

on this day in history...

1853,	George Washington Murray, former South Carolina U.S. congressman (1893-1897), was born in Rembert, S.C. (d. 1926).
1915,	Xavier University, nation's first African-American Catholic college, opened in New Orleans, La.
1925,	Eliza Virginia Capers, Tony Award-winning actress, was born in Sumter, S.C.
1928,	James M. Lawson, Jr., a leader of the 1968 Memphis sanitation worker's strike, was born in Uniontown, Pa.
1985,	Michael Spinks defeated Larry Holmes for the IBF heavyweight boxing champion.
1989,	Edward Perkins was named the first African-American director-general of the U.S. Foreign Service.

DOROTHY DANDRIDGE

Actress.   Born on November 9, 1922, in Cleveland, Ohio.   Appeared as The Wonder Kids with her sister Vivian (they later became known as The Dandridge Sisters); won an amateur singing competition on Los Angeles' KNX radio station; invited to perform at the Cotton Club in New York City and became a part of the regular program, which included Cab Calloway, W.C. Handy, and the Nicholas Brothers; made their Hollywood debut in the Marx Brothers' *A Day at the Races* (1937). Began performing solo and appeared in several musical film shorts between 1941 and 1942, which included: *Yes Indeed, Sing For My Supper, Jungle Jig, Easy Street, Cow Cow Boogie,* and *Paper Doll*; appeared with the Desi Arnez Band at the Macombo (1951); became the **first African-American to perform in the Empire Room of New York City's Waldorf-Astoria Hotel** (1951); obtained the lead role in Otto Preminger's all-black musical *Carmen Jones* (1954), which also featured Harry Belafonte, Pearl Bailey, Diahann Carroll, and became the **first African-American woman to be nominated for a best actress Oscar**; appeared in a string of controversial interracial films, including *Island in the Sun* (1957), *The Decks Ran Red* (1958), and *Tamango* (1960). Also appeared in the following films, *A Day at the Races* (1937), *Lady From Louisiana* (1941), *Drums of the Future* (1942), *Hit Parade of 1943* (1943), *Atlantic City* (1944), *Pillow to Post* (1945), *Four Shall Die* (1946), *Ebony Parade* (1947), *The Harlem Globe Trotters* (1951), *Porgy and Bess* (1959), and *Light's Diamond Jubilee*. Died on September 8, 1965, in Los Angeles, Calif. Donald Bogle, *Blacks in American Films and Television: An Encyclopedia* (1988).

on this day in history...

1922,	Richard Henry Boyd, founder of the National Baptist Publishing Board, died in Nashville, Tenn. (b. 1843).
1922,	Enoch Edward Jones, National Baptist Convention of America president, was born in Biloxi, Miss.
1972,	Frederick E. Davison, U.S. Army major general, became the first African-American to lead an army division when he assumed command of the 8th Infantry Division in Germany.
1978,	Max Robinson became the first African-American network news anchor (ABC's *World News Tonight*).

WILLIAM MARION COOK

Violinist, composer, and orchestral director.   Born on January 27, 1869, in Washington, D.C.   National Conservatory of Music in New York City.   Studied with Josef Joachim and Antonin Dvorak; made his solo debut at Carnegie Hall (1895), where, to his dismay, he was reviewed as the greatest <u>Negro</u> violinist in the world; wrote the score for Paul Laurence Dunbar's *Clorindy, or The Origin of the Cake Walk* (1898), which successfully played Broadway's Casino Roof Garden, became the first time an African-American show had played in a major theater and had attracted such wide attention, and established him as a composer and orchestra director. Served as musical director/composer for Bert Williams/George Walker Company's productions of *The Sons of Ham* (1900), *In Dahomey* (1902), *In Abyssinia* (1905), and *In Bandana Land* (1907); **organized the Negro Choral Societies**, lectured on published articles about African-American music, conducted "all-Negro composers" concerts, and collaborated with others to write musicals, which included, *The Casino Girls, Darkeydom, The Traitor,* and *The Cannibal King.* Some of his hit songs and compositions included "Mandy Lou," "Wid De Moon, Moon, Moon," and "Bon Bon Buddy," "Rain Song," "Exhortation," and "Swing Along." Formed Memphis Students jazz band (1905); returned to Carnegie Hall with James Reese Europe's Clef Club (1912), which was highly successful; organized the New York Syncopated Orchestra (1919), touring the nation and playing a command performance for King George V at Buckingham Palace; **helped fill the void in radio's earliest public broadcasting for live music**. Died on July 19, 1944, in New York City.   Further reading, <u>Tom Fletcher</u>, <u>100 Years of the Negro in Show Business</u> (1957).

on this day in history...

1872,	John H. Conyers became the first African-American admitted to the U.S. Naval Academy.
1933,	Clifford L. Alexander, Jr., first African-American U.S. secretary of the Army, was born in New York City.
1943,	Sherman N. Copeland, National Business League president, was born in New Orleans, La.
1974,	The first Black International Tennis Tournament began in Washington, D.C.
1963,	Cecil Fielder, Detroit Tigers All-Star, was born in Los Angeles, Calif.
1967,	Walter Washington was nominated by President Johnson as the first African-American mayor of Washington, D.C.

SEPTEMBER 21   MUSICIANS

SAMMY DAVIS, JR.

Singer, actor, and dancer who was called **"the world's greatest entertainer."**   Born on December 8, 1925, in New York City.   Performed vaudeville acts with the Will Mastin Trio (1930-1948), under the stage name of "Little Sammy;" made his film debut in *Rufus Jones for President* (1931); formed his own production companies, Sammy Davis Enterprise and Altovise Productions; performed on Broadway in productions of *Mister Wonderful* (1956-1957), *Golden Boy* (1964), and *Sammy on Broadway* (1975); appeared in the films, *Porgy and Bess* (1959), *Ocean's Eleven* (1960), *Robin and Seven Hoods* (1964), *A Man Called Adam* (1966), *Salt and Pepper* (1968), *Sweet Charity* (1968), *Save the Children* (1973), *Cannonball Run* (1981), and *Taps* (1989).   Toured extensively on the U.S. and European nightclub circuit, sang on radio and numerous television shows and specials, and recorded "What Kind of Fool Am I," "As Long As She Needs Me," "I've Gotta Be Me" (all for Reprise Records), "Candy Man," "That's Entertainment," "Mr. Bojangles," and "Mr. Wonderful;" member of the famed "Rat Pack," which included Dean Martin and Frank Sinatra; served as a vice president of the Tropicana Hotel in Las Vegas.   Member of the American Society of Magazine Photographers, Operation PUSH, Friars Club, and the United Negro College Fund; served in the U.S. Armed Forces during World War II; awarded the Achievement Freedom Award, Photoplay Gold Medal Award, and a Cannes Film Festival Grand Prix; recorded four Gold Records, and wrote *Hollywood in a Suitcase* (1980).   Died on May 16, 1990, in Los Angeles, Calif.   Further reading, <u>Sammy Davis, Jr.</u>, <u>*Yes I Can*</u> (1965).

---

on this day in history...

1909,	Lionel Hampton, jazz innovator, was born in Louisville, Ky.
1909,	Everette Frederick Morrow, first African-American member of a presidential executive staff, was born in Hackansack, N.J.
1926,	Harriet E. Byrd, Wyoming's first African-American state legislator, was born in Cheyenne, Wyo.
1951,	Luther Ronzoni Vandross, Grammy Award-winning singer, was born in New York City.
1969,	James Earl Jones won a Tony Award for his role in the play *The Great White Hope*.
1971,	The U.S. Supreme Court ruled mandatory school busing constitutional.

APRIL 20   **ENTERTAINERS**

JOHN WILLIAM COLTRANE

Jazz saxophonist who was called the **"father of avant-garde in jazz or the New Black Music."** Born on September 23, 1926, in Hamlet, N.C. Ornstein School of Music and Granoff School of Music in Philadelphia. Served during World War II in the U.S. Navy Band in the Pacific Theater; played alto sax with the Joe Webb Blues King Kolax, Eddie Vinson, and Jimmie Heath bands (1946-1948); played tenor sax with Dizzy Gillespie (1949-1951), Earl Bostic (1952-1953), Johnny Hodges (1953-1954), and with Miles Davis (1955-1956); worked his way up into the upper echelon of American jazz performers and became known by the nickname "Trane." Joined Thelonious Monk and the Five Spot in Greenwich Village in New York City (1957); offered his own exclusive recording contract with Prestige Records (1957); reunited with Miles Davis and recorded *Kinds of Blue* (1958), and along with his own *Giant Steps* (1959), signaled in the beginning of a new direction in jazz, brought him a wide and committed following, and helped him develop into one of jazz's most imitated and influential artists; formed the John Coltrane Quartet and recorded the highly successful, *My Favorite Things* (1960). Also recorded *Africa Brass, A Love Supreme, Ascension, Meditations,* and composed "Alabama" in response to the 1963 Birmingham church bombing; gained international recognition after touring in Europe and Japan; named by *Downbeat Magazine* as the top tenor saxophonist and jazzman of the year (1965); inspired artists in other fields, including poet Amiri Baraka and choreographer Alvin Ailey. Died on July 17, 1967, in Huntington, N.Y. Further reading, Michael Budds, *Jazz in the Sixties* (1990).

---

on this day in history...

1984,   *The Cosby Show* premiered on NBC and soon became a perennially #1 rated show on television.

SEPTEMBER 20   **MUSICIANS**

ELIZABETH TAYLOR GREENFIELD

Educator and singer who became the **first African-American musician to gain recognition**.   Born into slavery reportedly in 1809 in Natchez, Miss.   Began her singing career at a recital before the Buffalo Musical Association (1851), where she was given the nickname **"the Black Swan;"** enlisted J.H. Wood as her manager (1851-1852), and performed at engagements in New York, Massachusetts, Rhode Island, Ohio, Michigan, Wisconsin, Canada, and Vermont; debuted in New York City at the Metropolitan Hall (1853); went to London and debuted at the Stafford House (1853); performed in concert at the Queen's Concert Rooms in Hanover Square (1853), before the Dutchess of Sutherland, the Dutchess of Norfolk, and the Earl and Countess of Shaftesbury; sang in a command performance before the queen at Buckingham Palace (1854). Began her third tour (1856-1857), appearing in New York, Canada, Ohio, Michigan, Wisconsin, and New Jersey; refrained from touring between 1857-1863, because of the turbulence that followed the Dred Scott decision and the outbreak of the Civil War; launched her final tour (1863-1865), singing for audiences in Canada, Michigan, Ohio, and Wisconsin. Sang for the Social, Civil & Statistical Association of Philadelphia (1865), where Frederick Douglass and Frances Harper were speaking; organized the Black Swan Opera Troupe (1862); became active at Philadelphia's Shiloh Church, directing the choir and giving music lessons. Died on March 31, 1876, in Philadelphia, Pa.   Further reading, _Studies in Nineteenth Century Afro-American Music: The Underground Musical Traditions of Philadelphia_ (1983).

---

on this day in history...

1935,   William Adolphus Wilson, founder of the Dance Theater of Boston, was born in Philadelphia, Pa.
1974,   Lee Elder became the first African-American professional golfer to qualify for the Masters Tournament.

APRIL 21   **ENTERTAINERS**

NAT KING COLE

Singer, pianist, and actor.   Born Nathaniel Adams Cole on March 17, 1919, in Montgomery, Ala.   Made his first public appearance in a talent show at the Regal Theater in Chicago (1923); organized his first jazz group, The Musical Dukes, while in high school; made his professional debut as an arranger/music director for the *Shuffle Along* road company (1936); first gained popularity after forming the King Cole Trio with Cole on piano, Oscar Moore on guitar, Wesley Prince on bass, and Lee Young on drums (1937), **becoming one of the first jazz combos and the first African-American instrumental group to have a sponsored radio series** (1948-1949); eventually going solo to concentrate on singing, **becoming one of the first African-American entertainers in modern times to win international recognition as a singer independent of association with an orchestra**. Toured widely at home and abroad, and recording such hits as "Straighten Up and Fly Right," "I Love You for Sentimental Reasons," "Mona Lisa," "They Tried to Tell Us We're Too Young," "Unforgettable," "Smile," "It's Only a Paper Moon," "Nature Boy," "Orange-Colored Sky," and "Route 66;" appeared in a number of films, including *Stars on Parade* (1944), *Make Believe Ballroom* (1949), *Autumn Leaves*,singing the theme song (1956), *St. Louis Blues*, portraying W.C. Handy (1958), and in *Cat Ballou* (1965). Signed with NBC for his own weekly variety show, *The Nat "King" Cole Show* (1956-1957); brutally attacked by three white men while performing on stage in Birmingham, Ala. (1956); Grammy Award winner (1959); recorded over 28 Gold and Platinum records throughout his career. Died on February 15, 1965, in Santa Monica, Calif.   Further reading, Maria Cole and Louie Robinson, *Nat King Cole: An Intimate Biography* (1971).

---

on this day in history...

1865,   Atlanta University was founded.
1944,   Freda Payne, singer, was born in Detroit, Mich.
1989,   The first issue of *Emerge* magazine went on sale.

SEPTEMBER 19   **MUSICIANS**

ALBERTA HUNTER

Composer, nurse, and **one of the first singers to record the blues**.   Born on April 1, 1895, in Memphis, Tenn.   Moved to Chicago and performed at various nightclubs (1911-1922), including Dago Frank's Club, Hugh Hoskins's, Elite Number One, Panama Cafe, De Luxe Cafe, and Dreamland; recorded "Down Home Blues" on the Black Swan label (1921), and also recorded for Paramount, Gennett, OKeh, Victor, Decca, and Bluebird Records; starred with Ethel Waters in *Dumb Luck* (1922); opened in Eddie Hunter's *How Come?* at the Apollo Theater in Harlem (1923), and in his *Struttin' Time* at the Howard Theater in Washington, D.C.; toured Europe (1927-1929), where she opened in the part of "Queenie" in the London production of *Showboat* with Paul Robeson. Returned to Europe (1933-1934), where she was featured in the Cason de Paris revue of *Vive Paris!*, appeared in the film *Radio Parade of 1935*, and performed in Copenhagen; featured in the Heywards' *Mamba's Daughters* (1939), which starred Ethel Waters; wrote a column for the *Afro-American* newspaper called "Alberta Hunter's Notebook" (1942-1943); coordinated African-American talent for the USO, touring and performing in the China-Burma-India theater, Europe, Korea, Japan, Okinawa, awarded the Asiatic-Pacific Campaign Ribbon, and became the **first African-American woman to visit a war zone**; elected as **one of the first African-American woman member in ASCAP** (1952). Performed volunteer work at the Joint Diseases Hospital in Harlem; received her practical nurse's license (1957), and worked at Goldwater Memorial Hospital; returned to show business (1977), performing at The Cookery in Greenwich Village, Newport Jazz Festival, at Carnegie Hall, Kennedy Center, and the White House; received the W.C. Handy Award as Traditional Female Blues Artist of the Year (1979). Died on October 17, 1984.   Further reading, Frank Taylor and Gerald Cook, *Alberta: A Celebration in Blues* (1987).

---

on this day in history...

1928,   Jewel Stradford LaFontant, the nation's first African-American deputy solicitor general, was born in Chicago, Ill.

1935,   Ruth Burnett Love, Chicago Public School's first woman superintendent, was born in Lawton, Okla.

APRIL 22   **ENTERTAINERS**

LULU VERE CHILDERS

Musician who **founded Howard University's School of Music.** Born on February 28, 1870, in Dryridge, Ky. Oberlin Conservatory of Music (1896; B.Mus., 1906). Taught in the Ulrichsville (Ohio) Public School District (1896-1898); teacher and administrator at Wiley College (1898-1900); director of the music department of Knoxville College (1900-1905). Appointed instructor in music at Howard University (1905); director of Howard's music department (1906-1943), where she established college-level courses (including theory, history of music, and music education), enlisted experienced instructors and took the program to school of music status; also established the University Choral Society, Junior Preparatory Department, Orchestra, band, and the Men's and Women's Glee Club. Conducted the University Choral Society's first major production, Mendelsohn's *Elijah* (1907), bringing praise to the department; also conducted Handel's *Messiah* (1912), Pierne's *The Children's Crusade* (1915), Talbert's *Hiawatha* (1919), and the Rankin Chapel's Vested Choir. Produced and directed the following operas, *Mikado* (1923), *Il Travatore* (1939), *Faust* (1940), and *I Pagliacci* (1942); established a concert series, which included Marian Anderson's Easter Sunday Lincoln Memorial performance in front of a mixed crowd of over 70,000 (1939), after being denied the use of the D.C. Board of Education's and Daughters of the American Revolution's facilities. Died on March 6, 1946, in Howell, Mich. Further reading, Walter Dyson, *The Capstone of Negro Education* (1941).

---

on this day in history...

1850,	Congress passed the Fugitive Slave Act.
1895,	Booker T. Washington delivered his "Atlanta Compromise" speech, which soon made him the nation's most famous and powerful African-American, at the Cotton States and International Exposition shortly after the death of Frederick Douglass.
1905,	Edmund Lincoln "Rochester" Anderson, actor, was born in Oakland. Calif.
1990,	Atlanta was named as the site for the XXV Olympiad Summer Games.

SEPTEMBER 18　　　　　　　　　　　　　　　　　　　　　**MUSICIANS**

HATTIE McDANIEL

Singer and actress. Born on June 10, 1895, in Wichita, Kan. Awarded a gold medal by the Women's Christian Temperance Union for excellence in "the dramatic art" for her recital of "Convict Joe" (1910), while attending East Denver High School; made her debut singing with George Morrison's Negro Orchestra in Denver (1915), reportedly becoming the **first African-American to sing on radio**; worked in the traveling production of *Show Boat* (1925); moved to Hollywood (1931), and made her motion picture debut in *The Golden West* going on to appear in over 300 movies; appeared on radio broadcasts, such as KNX Los Angeles' "The Optimistic Donuts Show" as Hi-Hat Hattie (1931-1932), WGAR Cleveland (1940), NBC's "Rudy Vallee Show" with Eddie Carter (1941), CBS' "Blueberry Hill" (1943), "The Beulah Show" (1947-1951), and the "Bing Crosby Philco Radio Time." Criticized by fellow African-Americans for playing "mammy" type roles, in which she replied "I portray the type of Negro woman who has worked honestly and proudly to give our nation the Marion Andersons, Roland Hayeses, and the Ralph Bunches;" **won a best supporting actress Academy Award for her portrayal of "Mammy" in *Gone With the Wind* (1939), becoming the first African-American to win an Oscar**, which she donated to Howard University. Chaired the African-American section of the Hollywood Victory Committee that organized entertainment for African-American troops during World War II; fought for and won an anti-discrimination suit involving her California home; member of the Screen Actors Guild; starred on television's *Beulah* (1951). Died on October 26, 1952, in San Fernando Valley, Calif. Further reading, Carlton Jackson, *Hattie: The Life of Hattie McDaniel* (1990).

---

on this day in history...

1913, The National Urban League was incorporated in New York City.
1936, Thomas Barnes, Gary mayor, was born in Mark Tree, Ark.
1940, Willie Herenton, Memphis' first African-American mayor, was born in Memphis, Tenn.
1947, James A. Hill, Jr., Oregon's first African-American state treasurer, was born in Atlanta, Ga.
1948, Charles R. Johnson, author of the best-selling *Middle Passage*, was born in Evanston, Ill.

APRIL 23   **ENTERTAINERS**

COUNT BASIE

Pianist, bandleader, and composer who became **one of the "Big Band" and jazz orchestra leaders of the 20th century**. Born William James Basie on August 21, 1904, in Red Bank, N.J. Studied organ with Fats Waller, and began playing professionally in Ashbury Park, N.J., and New York City; toured as an accompanist with vaudeville shows; became exposed to the Kansas City sound (1927), where he began playing with Walter Page's Blue Devils and Bennie Moten's jazz bands; formed the Barons of Rhythm, along with Buster Smith (1936), broadcasting live over an experimental Kansas City short-wave station--W9XBY, acquiring the theme song--"One O'Clock Jump," performing under the nickname "Count," and gaining national recognition after jazz enthusiast John Hammond heard one of the broadcasts. Debuted at the Roseland Ballroom in New York City (1936), adding Billie Holiday to the band, and eventually becoming one of the leading groups of the time; played Carnegie Hall in the "From Spirituals to Swing" concert (1938); appeared in the films, *Hit Parade of 1943, Top Man, Cinderfella, Made in Paris,* and *The Last of the Blue Devils*; some of his best known compositions, include "Jumpin' at the Woodside," "Taxi War Dance," "April in Paris," "Good Morning Blues," and "Basie Boogie." Reorganized his band (1952), and toured Europe extensively and frequently; began using his orchestra as a background for prominent vocalists, such as Frank Sinatra, Sammy Davis, Jr., Tony Bennett, and Oscar Peterson. Honored with: a Musicians of America most popular band award (1933), a Grammy Award (1958, 1960, and 1963), an induction into the Down Beat, Ebony Black Music, Newport Jazz, and the Black Filmmakers Halls of Fame (1958, 1975, 1976, and 1978), respectively; the John F. Kennedy Center Performing Arts Award (1981); a star on the Hollywood Walk of Fame (1982); the Presidential Medal of Freedom (1985), posthumously. Died on April 26, 1984, in Hollywood, Fla. Further reading, <u>Ramond Horricks</u>, <u>*Count Basie and His Orchestra*</u> (1957).

---

on this day in history...

1858,	Dred Scott, slave who unsuccessfully sued for his freedom before the U.S. Supreme Court, died in St. Louis, Mo. (b. 1795).
1917,	Jacob Lawrence, one of the most widely-acclaimed African-American artists of the 20th century, was born in Atlantic City, N.J.
1932,	Joseph Woodrow Hatchett, 11th U.S. Circuit appellate judge, was born in Clearwater, Fla.
1970,	The *Flip Wilson Show* premiered on NBC.
1973,	Illinois became the first state to honor the birthday of Martin Luther King, Jr., as a state holiday.
1983,	Vanessa Williams of New York became the first African-American to be crowned Miss America.

SEPTEMBER 17   **MUSICIANS**

OSCAR MICHEAUX

Writer, producer, director, publicist, and a **pioneer in the African-American film industry known as the "dean of black filmmakers**." Born on January 2, 1884, in Metropolis, Ill. Became a Pullman porter on a Chicago-Portland run; purchased some land in Gregory County, S.D., on the Rosebud Indian Reservation (1904), where he began farming and ranching, and expanded his homestead to some 500 acres; published *The Conquest: The Story of a Negro Pioneer* (1913), *The Forged Note: A Romance of the Darker Races* (1915), *The Homesteader* (1917), *The Wind from Nowhere* (1943), *The Case of Mrs. Wingate* (1945), *The Story of Dorothy Stanfield* (1946), and *The Masquerade* (1947). **Founder and president of Oscar Micheaux Corporation** (OMC) in New York City (1919-1947), which produced over 44 films, including the **first African-American silent film**; produced the feature film, *The Homesteader* (1919), OMC's first production; initially enlisted actors from the Lafayette Players Stock Company; introduced Paul Robeson to the screen in *Body and Soul* (1924); released *The Exile* (1931), **the first all-talking motion picture by an African-American company**; produced *The Wind From Nowhere*-inspired *The Betrayal* (1948), **first African-American motion picture to have a Broadway premier**. Some of his other films included *The Hypocrite, Uncle Jasper's Will, The Conjure Woman, The House Behind the Cedars, Harlem After Midnight, God's Step Children, The Notorious Elinor Lee,* and *The Millionaire*. Died on April 1, 1951, in Charlotte, N.C. Further reading, <u>Daniel J. Leab</u>, <u>*From Sambo to Superspade*</u> (1975).

---

on this day in history...

1884, The Medico-Chirurgical Society, nation's oldest African-American medical society, was organized in Washington, D.C.
1886, Augustus Tolton became one of the first Negroes to be ordained into the Catholic priesthood.
1972, James M. Rogers, Jr., became the first African-American to be honored as National Teacher of the Year.

APRIL 24   **ENTERTAINERS**

DANIEL LOUIS ARMSTRONG

Jazz trumpeter who has been called the **greatest jazz performer ever**. Born on July 4, 1900, in New Orleans, La. Played cornet with various local New Orleans Dixieland jazz bands (1917-1922); played with King Oliver's Original Creole Jazz Band in Chicago (1922-1924), making his recording debut; played trumpet with bandleader and arranger Fletcher Henderson in New York City (1924). Began playing independently (1925), forming the Hot Five and Hot Seven Bands; appeared in the Broadway shows, *Hot Chocolate* (1929), *Bottom in Swingin' the Dream* (1939), and performed in the New York Metropolitan Opera House's first jazz concert; **invented the jazz technique of scat singing**, by reportedly accidently dropping his sheet music during a recording session and had to substitute with vocal improvisations until someone picked up his sheet; first toured Europe (1932), where he won the nickname "Satchmo;" also toured Africa, Australia, Canada, South American, New Zealand, Mexico, and Asia. Helped spread the popularity of jazz during the middle part of the 20th century by appearing in motion pictures, including *Pennies from Heaven* (1936), *Every Day's a Holiday* (1937), *Going Places* (1938), *Dr. Rhythm* (1938), *Cabin in the Sky* (1943), *Jam Session* (1944), *New Orleans* (1947), *The Strip* (1951), *The Glenn Miller Story* (1954), *High Society* (1957), *Paris Blues* (1961), *A Man Called Adam* (1966), and *Hello, Dolly* (1969). Recorded such jazz and pop classics as "West End Blues," "When It's Sleepy Time Down South," "Mack the Knife," "Blueberry Hill," and "What a Wonderful Life;" knocked the Beatles from the top of the pop charts with his double-platinum song, "Hello, Dolly;" Grammy Award winner (1964), and became one of the most widely imitated jazzmen in respect to his instrumental and vocal style. Died on July 6, 1971, on Long Island, N.Y. Further reading, George T. Simon, *The Best of the Music Makers* (1979).

	on this day in history...
1925,	Riley "B.B." King, Grammy Award-winning blues great, was born in Itta Bena, Miss.
1934,	Eva Clayton, North Carolina 1st District congresswoman, was born in Savannah, Ga.
1950,	Henry Louis Gates, literary scholar, was born in Keyser, W.Va.
1989,	Debbye Turner, a University of Missouri veterinary student, was crowned Miss America.
1990,	Keenan Ivory Wayans' *In Living Color* won an Emmy for best comedy series.

SEPTEMBER 16   **MUSICIANS**

HARRY PACE

Music publisher, insurance executive, and a **pioneer among African-American record producers**.   Born on January 6, 1884, in Covington, Ga. Atlanta Baptist College [Morehouse College] (B.A., 1903).   Professor of Greek and Latin at Lincoln University in Missouri (1906-1908); worked as a bank cashier in Memphis; founder and president of the **nation's first African-American-owned music publishing company--Pace and Handy Music Company** of Memphis (1908-1913), collaborating with W.C. Handy, with Pace providing the lyrics; left the company to become secretary-treasurer of Standard Life Insurance Company in Atlanta (1913-1918); rejoined Handy when the firm moved to New York City (1918-1921), where they employed Fletcher Henderson as songplugger and pianist, William Grant Still as chief arranger, Fred Bryan and J. Berni Barbour as copyist, and achieved success with their first recording, "A Good Man Is Hard to Find." **Founder and president of the nation's first African-American-owned record company--Pace Phonograph Corporation** (1921-1924), producing records on the Black Swan label, named in honor of Elizabeth Taylor Greenfield; helped pioneer blues recordings by signing artists such as Ethel Waters, Trixie Smith, Henry Creamer, and Alberta Hunter; organized The Black Swan Troubadours (1921), which was composed of Ethel Waters and the Fletcher Henderson-led Black Swan Jazz Masters; recruited William Grant Still as musical director. Sold the Black Swan label to Paramount Records (1924), and **was credited with forcing white recording companies to recognize the vast African-American market for recordings**, to release "race catalogues," and to advertise in African-American newspapers; founded Northeastern Life Insurance Company in Newark (1924), which later became Supreme Liberty Life Insurance, with Pace serving as its first president. Died on July 26, 1943, in Chicago, Ill.   Further reading, Eileen Souther, *The Greenwood Encyclopedia of Black Music* (1982).

---

on this day in history...

1913,	Earl Bostic, jazz alto saxophonist, was born in Tulsa, Okla.
1918,	Ella Fitzgerald, Grammy Award-winning "first lady of song," was born in Newport News, Va.
1932,	Meadowlark Lemon, legendary member of the Harlem Globetrotters, was born in Wilmington, N.C.
1936,	John Daniels, New Haven mayor, was born in Macon, Ga.
1944,	Frederick Patterson, Tuskegee president, founded the United Negro College Fund.
1950,	Chuck Cooper of the Boston Celtics became the first African-American drafted into the NBA.

CHARLES A. YOUNG

Military officer, cartographer, and musician who became the **first African-American to achieve distinction in the military.** Born on March 12, 1864, in Mayslick, Ky. United States Military Academy (1889). Commissioned as a second lieutenant; served as temporary major in command of the 9th Ohio Volunteer Infantry during the Spanish-American War in Virginia, Pennsylvania, and South Carolina (1898-1899); promoted to first lieutenant (1896), captain (1901), major (1915), and lieutenant colonel (1916); served in the Philippines (1901-1902, 1908-1909); became the nation's **first African-American military attache**, serving in Haiti (1904-1907), and Liberia (1912-1915). Accredited with mapping remote and unchartered locations in Haiti, the Dominican Republic, and Liberia; wrote *Military Morale of Nations and Race* (1912); served in the 2nd Division, War Department, and on the General Staff in Washington (1907-1908); commanded the 2nd Squadron at Fort D.A. Russell, Wyo.; worked in the office of the chief of staff in Washington (1912). Awarded NAACP Spingarn Medal (1916), for organizing the Liberian Constabulary and developing roads in Liberia; commanded a cavalry squadron in Mexico (1916-1917); established a school for African-American enlisted men at Fort Huachucha, Ariz.; retired from the Army (1917). Died on January 8, 1922, in Lagos, Nigeria. Further reading, Robert E. Greene, *Black Defenders of America, 1775-1973: A Reference and Pictorial Guide* (1974).

on this day in history...

1889,   Claude McKay, Harlem Renaissance poet, was born in Sunnyville, Jamaica (d. 1948).
1928,   Julian "Cannonball" Adderley, jazz saxophonist, was born in Tampa, Fla.
1940,   Anne Moody, civil rights activist and author of *Coming of Age*, was born in Centreville, Miss.
1945,   Jessye Norman, classical singer, was born in Augusta, Ga.
1963,   Schoolgirls Addie Collins, Denise McNair, Carol Robertson, and Cynthia Wesley were killed in a racially-motivated bombing at the Sixteenth Street Baptist Church in Birmingham, Ala.

SEPTEMBER 15   MILITARY HEROES

BESSIE SMITH

Blues and jazz singer known as **"empress of the blues"** and was reportedly **the first jazz singer**.   Born on April 15, 1894, in Chattanooga, Tenn.   Joined Moses Stokes' traveling show (1912); toured with Ma Rainey in Fat Chappelle's Rabbit Foot Minstrel Show (1915); worked with Pete Werley's Florida Cotton Blossom and the Silas Green Minstrel Shows; produced and starred in *Liberty Belles* (1918-1919), becoming an established blues star in the South; **recorded for Columbia Records (1923-1931), becoming their best-selling artist** after recording her first single "Down Hearted Blues"/"Gulf Coast Blues" and selling over three quarters of a million copies in six months. Left the South and starred in such revues as *How Come* (1923), *Tunes and Topics* (1923), *Yellow Girl Revue* (1927), *Mississippi Days* (1928), *Late Hour Tap Dancers* (1929), and *The Jazzbo Regiment* (1929); **billed as "the greatest and highest salaried race star in the world."** First played with Louis Armstrong (1925), and became a musical mentor to Billie Holiday, Mahalia Jackson, Dinah Washington, and others; purchased an 80-foot Pullman railroad car (1925), to spare herself and her troupe from further indignities they suffered due to "Jim Crow" accommodations; recorded over 150 records, which included "Me and My Gin," "Nobody Knows You When You're Down and Out," "Backwater Blues," and "Do Your Duty;" appeared in her only motion picture, *St. Louis Blues* (1929); posthumously elected into the National Women's Hall of Fame (1984), and the Music Walk of Fame in Philadelphia. Died on September 26, 1937, in Clarksdale, Miss.   Further reading, Gunther Schuller, *Early Jazz: Its Roots and Musical Development* (1968).

---

on this day in history...

1862,   Sarah Boone patented an ironing board,
1886,   Gertrude "Ma Rainey," "mother of the blues," was born in Columbus, Ga. (d. 1939).
1937,   Bob Boozer, Olympic basketball gold medalist, was born in Omaha, Neb.

APRIL 26   **ENTERTAINERS**

HARRIET TUBMAN

Abolitionist, fugitive slave, Underground Railroad conductor, Union scout, spy, and nurse known as **"Moses of her people."** Born into slavery around 1821 with the slave name Araminta [later to go by her mother's name Harriet] in Dorchester County, Md. Escaped to Philadelphia (1849), guided by the North Star and aided by Underground Railroad conductors; made approximately 19 trips back to the South and rescued some 300 Negroes from slavery; outsmarted the Fugitive Slave Act of 1850 and outlasted a $40,000 bounty for her arrest, dead or alive; respected and honored by Frederick Douglass, Susan B. Anthony, and Ralph Waldo Emerson, and despised by southern slaveholders and pro-slavery advocates; severely beaten in Troy, N.Y. (1860), while leading a group that took runaway slave Charles Nalle from the police and marshals; emancipated her parents in a daring 1857 rescue and resettled them in Auburn, New York. First met John Brown in Canada (1858), and approved of his plan to seize the government arsenal in Harper's Ferry, W.Va.; reported to Hilton Head, S.C., and participated in the Civil War as an Union Army cook, nurse, scout, and spy; awarded a mere 20 dollars a month for wartime services after some 30 years of effort; established schools for freedmen in North Carolina, and the Harriet Tubman Home for Indigent and Aged Negroes in Auburn. Died in 1913 in Auburn, N.Y. Further reading, Sarah H. Bradford, *Harriet Tubman, The Moses of Her People* (1961).

---

on this day in history...

1921,   Constance Baker Motley, first African-American woman New York state senator and federal judge, was born in New Haven, Conn.

1964,   A. Phillip Randolph and Leontyne Price were awarded the Medal of Freedom by President Johnson.

1990,   Ken Griffey, Sr., and Ken Griffey, Jr., of the Seattle Mariners, batting third and fourth, hit back-to-back home runs against the California Angels.

SEPTEMBER 14   **MILITARY HEROES**

SARAH VAUGHAN

Jazz singer known as **"the divine one."** Born on March 27, 1924, in Newark, N.J. Winner of the Apollo Theater amateur contest (1942), *Downbeat* magazine's best female singer award (1947-1952), similar awards from Metronome (1948-1953), and Downbeat International Jazz Critics award (1973, 1975-1979); sang with the bands of Fatha Hines (1943-1944), and Billy Eckstine (1944-1945); recorded "Lover Man" with Charlie Parker and Dizzy Gillespie (1945), and "Body and Soul" (1946), which solidified her reputation as a jazz singer; recorded the albums: *The Divine One* (Roulette Records); *Live in Japan* (Mainstream Records); *Lullaby of Birdland, Sassy, Broken Hearted Melody, and Sassy Swings Again* (Mercury Records); *I Love Brazil* and *The Duke Ellington Songbook* (Pablo); *Brazilian Romance* (Columbia). Performed with Oscar Peterson, Ray Brown, the Los Angeles Philharmonic, the National Symphony Orchestra, Duke Ellington's and Count Basie's Orchestras, and at such places as the Fairmont Hotel in San Francisco, Copacabana, Tropicana in Las Vegas, Playboy Hotel in Atlantic City, Symphony Hall in Boston, and the John F. Kennedy Center for the Performing Arts in Washington; participated in the Montreal Jazz Festival (1974), Newport Jazz Festival (1974, 1975), and the Montreal International Jazz Festival (1983). Died on April 9, 1990. Further reading, Dave Gelly, *The Giants of Jazz* (1986).

---

on this day in history...

1927,   Coretta Scott King, founder of the Martin Luther King, Jr., Center for Nonviolent Social Change, was born in Marion, Ala.
1947,   Catherine Liggins Hughes, broadcasting executive, was born in Omaha, Neb.

APRIL 27   **ENTERTAINERS**

ROBERT SMALLS

Civil War naval hero and congressman. Born on April 5, 1839, in Beaufort, S.C. Stole the Confederate dispatch boat, *Planter*, and sailed it out of Charleston Bay surrendering it to a flotilla of the Union blockade (1862); this act convinced the U.S. secretary of war to authorize the recruitment in South Carolina of 5,000 African-American volunteers; officially designated as the pilot and captain of the *Planter*, which was assigned to transport duty for the Union Forces (1862-1865); brigadier general in the South Carolina State Militia. Elected to the South Carolina Constitutional Convention (1868), where he drafted a resolution giving the state its first system of free education; South Carolina state representative (1868-1870), and state senator (1870-1874); South Carolina 5th District Republican congressman (1874-1878, 1882-1886), serving on the Agriculture, Militia, and War Claims Committees; customs collector of the port of Beaufort, S.C. (1889-1912). Died on February 23, 1915, in Beaufort, S.C. Further reading, Okan Edet Uya, *From Slavery to Public Service: Robert Smalls* (1971).

---

on this day in history...

1898,	Albert A. Jones and Amos E. Long patented bottle caps.
1926,	Clifton Reginald Wharton, Jr., first African-American president of a major U.S. university, was born in Boston, Mass.
1948,	Nell Ruth Carter, Tony Award-winning actress, was born in Birmingham, Ala.
1972,	Johnny Ford was elected Tuskegee's first African-American mayor.

SEPTEMBER 13   MILITARY HEROES

DINAH WASHINGTON

Singer who was known as the **"queen of the blues."** Born Ruth Jones on August 29, 1924, in Tuscaloosa, Ala. Became a member of the first all-woman gospel group, the Sallie Martin Colored Ladies' Quartet (1940); won first prize in an amateur contest at the Regal Theater in Chicago (1940), singing "I Can't Face the Music;" began playing in local clubs and gained a reputation as a pianist and singer; landed a job singing upstairs at the Garrick Stage Lounge (1942), where Billie Holiday was performing downstairs on the main stage; changed her name to Dinah Washington and began playing with Lionel Hampton (1943-1946); joined Decca Records (1945), and recorded "Blowtop Blues" with Leonard Feather accompanying. Launched a solo career (1946), and was credited with launching the careers of Patti Austin, Paul Quinichette, Quincy Jones, and Lola Folana; began recording with Mercury Records with her songs regularly appearing on *Billboard*'s new R&B charts; recorded "Harbor Lights" (1949), "Shuckin' and Jivin'" (1949), "I Don't Hurt Anymore" (1954), "What a Difference a Day Makes" (1959), and established herself as a mainstream artist; toured extensively throughout the U.S., with an entourage that included her business manager, hairdresser, companion, seamstress, band, and chauffeur; lifetime member of the Gospel Singers' Convention. Died on December 14, 1963, in Detroit, Mich. Further reading, Donald Bogle, *Brown Sugar; Eighty Years of America's Black Female Superstars* (1980).

---

on this day in history...

1940,   Madge Sinclair, Emmy Award-winning actress, was born in Kingston, Jamaica.
1983,   Gloria Naylor won an American Book Award for fiction with *The Women of Brewster Street*.

APRIL 28   **ENTERTAINERS**

MILTON L. OLIVE, III

War hero. Born on November 7, 1946, in Chicago, Ill. Enlisted in the U.S. Army (1964); was assigned to U.S. Army Training Center at Fort Knox, Ky., U.S. Army Artillery and Missile School at Fort Sill, Okla., U.S. Army Training Center at Fort Polk, La., U.S. Army Infantry School at Fort Benning, Ga., and the 173rd Airborne Brigade in Vietnam. Received the Purple Heart with oak leaf cluster, Armed Forces Expeditionary medal, Combat Infantryman's Badge, Parachutist Badge and the Marksman Badge with qualification bar for rifle. Participated in a search and destroy operation near Phu Cuong, Republic of Vietnam as a member of the 3rd Platoon of Company B, Second Battalion, 503rd Infantry (1965); he saved the lives of his fellow soldiers and sacrificed his own life when he fell on an Viet Cong grenade; **posthumously awarded the Medal of Honor for heroism, becoming the first to receive the nation's highest military honor in the Vietnam War**. Died on October 22, 1965, in the Republic of Vietnam. Further reading, Robert E. Greene, *Black Defenders of America, 1775-1973: A Reference and Pictorial History* (1974).

---

on this day in history...

1935,	Richard H. Hunt, the nation's foremost African-American abstract sculptor and artist of public sculpture, was born in Chicago, Ill.
1944,	Barry White, singer and composer of over 50 gold records, was born in Galveston, Texas.
1973,	John P, Daniels, founder of the Negro Industrial League, died in New York City (b. 1905).
1974,	Eugene Antonio Marino became the nation's first African-American to be consecrated as an auxiliary Catholic bishop.
1992,	Mae C. Jemison, aboard the space shuttle *Endeavor*, became the first African-American woman in space.

ETHEL WATERS

Singer, dancer, and actress known as **"the mother of modern popular singing."** Born on October 31, 1896, in Chester, Pa. Made her singing debut in Philadelphia (1917), becoming the first woman to sing W.C. Handy's "St. Louis Blues" professionally; toured the South playing vaudeville, carnivals, and tent shows; later established herself as one of the leading entertainers of the Harlem Renaissance; performed in *Hello 1919* at the Lafayette Theater in Harlem and first appeared as a name performer in *Oh Joy!* (1922); made her first recording, "New York Glide"/"At The New Jump Steady Ball" for Cardinal Records (1919); hired by Black Swan Records (1921), and recorded "Down Home Blues," "One Man Nan," and the best-seller, "Oh Daddy." Toured with Fletcher Henderson's Black Swan Troubadours; starred in the *Plantation Revue* in Chicago (1924); performed at the Plantation Club on Broadway (1925), where she introduced her song "Dinah," which was the first international hit to come out of an American nightclub; made her first Broadway appearance in the musical *Africana* (1927); appeared in her first movie, *On with the Show* (1929); introduced her song, "Stormy Weather," while appearing with the Duke Ellington Orchestra at the Cotton Club in Harlem (1933). Became the **first African-American to perform in an all-white cast on Broadway** in Irving Berlin's musical, *As Thousands Cheer* (1934), and became **Broadway's highest paid performer**; played Hagar in *Mamba's Daughters* (1939), and **became the first African-American woman to perform the leading role in a dramatic play**; wrote her autobiographies, *His Eye Is on the Sparrow* (1951), and *To Me It's Wonderful* (1972); starred in the television show, *Beulah* (1953), and in *An Evening With Ethel Waters*, becoming the **first African-American woman to have a national televised weekly TV show**; sang with the Billy Graham Crusades (1957-1976). Died on September 1, 1977, in Chatsworth, Ga. Further reading, Sally Placksin, *American Women in Jazz, 1900 to the Present* (1982).

---

on this day in history...

1922,	Parren James Mitchell, Maryland's first African-American congressman, was born in Baltimore, Md.
1926,	Carrie Meek, Florida 17th District congresswoman, was born in Tallahassee, Fla.
1948,	Willi Smith, designer of the Willi Wear clothing line, was born in Philadelphia, Pa. (d. 1987).
1969,	Duke Ellington was presented with the Presidential Medal of Freedom by President Nixon.
1992,	Civil unrest broke out across the nation after not-guilty verdicts were handed down in the Rodney King Beating Trial.

APRIL 29   **ENTERTAINERS**

ULYSSES GRANT LEE, JR.

Educator, army officer, editor, and historian.   Born on December 4, 1913, in Washington, D.C.   Howard University *summa cum laude* (B.A., 1935; M.A., 1936), graduate assistant (1935-1936); University of Pennsylvania; University of Chicago (Ph.D., history of civilization, 1953). Assistant professor at Lincoln University in Pennsylvania (1936-1948); research assistant, consultant, and editor with the Federal Writers' Project (1936-1939); visiting professor at Virginia Union University (1940). Served as first lieutenant assigned to the Army's Information and Education Division during World War II; **staff historian in the Office of the Chief of Military History, Department of the Army** (1946-1952). Elected an alumni member of Howard's chapter of Phi Beta Kappa (1958); taught simultaneously at Morgan State College and the University of Pennsylvania; participated in seminars of the American Society of African Culture (1965), which took him to Nigeria and Sierra Leone; wrote *The Employment of Negro Troops* (1966); served as associate editor of the *Journal of Negro History*. Died on January 7, 1969, in Washington, D.C.   Further reading, Robert E. Greene, *Black Defenders of America, 1775-1973: A Reference and Pictorial History* (1974).

on this day in history...

1927,	William Blackwell Branch, playwright and educator, was born in New Haven, Conn.
1943,	Lola Falana, entertainer who was called "the first lady of Las Vegas," was born in Philadelphia, Pa.
1962,	Thurgood Marshall was confirmed as the nation's first African-American solicitor general.
1977,	Quincy Jones won an Emmy for musical work in *Roots*.

SEPTEMBER 11   **MILITARY HEROES**

BERT WILLIAMS

Entertainer. Born Egbert Austin Williams on February 12, 1874, in Antigua, West Indies. Played the banjo, became a comedian, and sang and danced; teamed with George Walker (1895-1909), in vaudeville acts in San Francisco, New York City, and London; performed in the Broadway musical, *The Gold Bug* (1896), and introduced the old slave dance, the Cakewalk; formed a company and produced *Senegambian Carnival* (1897); produced a series of shows, including *The Policy Players* (1899), *Son of Ham* (1900), *Williams and Walker in Dahomey* (1902-1909), *Williams and Walker in Abyssinia* (1905-1906), and *Williams and Walker in Bandanna Land* (1907-1908), with a repertory company that included Jesse Shipp, Alex Rogers, Will Marion Cook, Ada Walker, and Lottie Williams. Played to a command performance, with George Walker, for King Edward VII of England (1905), becoming the **first internationally famous team of African-American stars in the history of American entertainment**; performed his first solo in the comedy *Mr. Lode of Koal* (1909); became the **first African-American to star in the Ziegfeld's *Follies & Midnight Frolics*** (1910-1919). Recorded songs, such as "Nobody," "Jonah Man," "I'm in the Right Church, but the Wrong Pew," and "Come After Breakfast, Bring Along Your Lunch, and Leave Before Supper;" appeared in the films, *Darktown Jubilee* (1914), and *A Natural Born Gambler* (1916); starred in two Broadway shows developed exclusively for him, *Broadway Brevities* (1920), and *Under the Bamboo Tree* (1922); provided employment and opened doors for scores of African-American entertainers, musicians, composers, lyricists, musical directors, stage managers, and others associated with the stage. Died on March 5, 1922, in New York City. Further reading, Donald Bogle, *Toms, Coons, Mulattoes, Mammies and Bucks, An Interpretive History of Blacks in American Films* (1973).

---

on this day in history...

1931,	William Lacy Clay of Missouri, chairman of the U.S. House Post Office and Civil Service Committee, was born in St. Louis, Mo.
1941,	Lottie Shackelford, Little Rock's first African-American mayor, was born in Little Rock, Ark.
1947,	Bobby Scott, Virginia 3rd District congressman, was born in Washington, D.C.
1961,	Isiah Lord Thomas, III, Detroit Pistons All-Star, was born in Chicago, Ill.
1983,	Robert C. Maynard purchased the *Oakland Tribune*, becoming the first African-American to own a major daily newspaper.

CAMPBELL CARRINGTON JOHNSON

Military officer and social worker.   Born on September 30, 1895, in Washington, D.C.   Howard University (B.S., 1920; LL.B., 1922). Volunteered to serve in World War I and entered the Officers Training Corps at Fort Des Moines, Iowa (1917), where he received a commission as first lieutenant of infantry; **organized and commanded Battery A, 350th Field Artillery at Camp Dix, N.J. (1918-1919), the first battery of field artillery composed of African-Americans**; assisted in organizing Howard University's ROTC unit (1919), and, with the rank of captain, taught military science and tactics; chief of the section in the Bureau of War Risk Insurance, now called the Veterans Administration, which handled insurance and compensation claims of African-American veterans (1919-1923); admitted to the North Carolina and District of Columbia bar (1922), and maintained a law practice in D.C. (1922-1926). Executive secretary of the Anthony Bowen Branch YMCA of Washington, D.C. (1923-1940); director of a training institute for African-American YMCA secretaries in Bordentown, N.J.; founded of Camp Lichtman (1932), a camp for African-American boys from D.C.; member of the Board of Parole of the District of Columbia (1939-1946), and chairman (1946-1947); helped organize the Washington Housing Association; executive assistant to the director of Selective Service in D.C. (1940-1950, 1964-1968); awarded the Army Distinguished Service Medal (1946); appointed a member of the National Capital Housing Authority (1950-1964), where later as vice chairman, secured the passage of resolution ending official segregation in public housing in the Washington. Died on August 22, 1968, in Washington, D.C.   Further reading, Rayford W. Logan, _Howard University: The First Hundred Years, 1867-1967_ (1969).

---

on this day in history...

1888,	John Campbell Dancy, Jr., Detroit Urban League president known as "Mr. Urban League," was born in Detroit, Mich. (d. 1968).
1940,	Ronald J. Temple, City Colleges of Chicago chancellor, was born in Chicago, Ill.
1951,	Albert Wynn, Maryland 4th District congressman, was born in Philadelphia, Pa.

SEPTEMBER 10   **MILITARY HEROES**

EBENEZER DON CARLOS BASSETT

Educator and diplomat.   Born on October 16, 1833, in Litchfield, Conn.   Connecticut State Normal School; Yale College. Principal of a New Haven, Conn., high school; principal of the Institute for Colored Youth in Philadelphia [now Cheyney State University] (1857-1869), where he gave a series of evening lectures on chemistry and natural philosophy; U.S. minister to Haiti and the Dominican Republic (1869-1877), becoming the **first African-American diplomat to represent the U.S. government abroad**; served as dean of the diplomatic corps; elected president of the exclusive "Cercle de Port-au-Prince;" consul general of Haiti in New York City (1879-1888); secretary and interpreter to the minister of Haiti and of the Dominican Republic, and Frederick Douglass (1889-1894); published *A Handbook on Haiti,* a valuable contribution to the geographical knowledge of the island. Died on November 13, 1908, in Philadelphia, Pa.   Further reading, Rayford W. Logan, *The Diplomatic Relations of the United States with Haiti, 1776-1891* (1941).

---

on this day in history...

1901,	Sterling A. Brown, "the folk poet of the new Negro renaissance," was born in Washington, D.C.
1907,	Oliver W. Hill, first African-American elected to public office since Reconstruction (Richmond City Council), was born in Richmond, Va.
1950,	Gwendolyn Brooks became the first African-American to win a Pulitzer Prize (for her poetry book *Annie Allen*).
1991,	Rickey Henderson broke Lou Brock's record when he stole his 939th base against the Yankees.

MAY 1   **GOVERNMENT OFFICIALS & POLITICIANS**

DANIEL JAMES

Military officer and government official nicknamed "Chappie." Born on February 11, 1920, in Pensacola, Fla. Tuskegee Institute (B.S., 1942); Civilian Pilot Training Program (1942). Served as civilian instructor pilot in the Army Air Corps Aviation Cadet Program (1942-1943), entered the program as a cadet and graduated first in his class; commissioned as a second lieutenant (1943), and attended Fighter Pilot Combat Training at Selfridge Field, Mich. Assigned to Clark Field in the Philippines (1949-1950), where he flew 101 combat missions in P-51 and P-80 aircraft during the Korean War; attached to Otis AFB in Massachusetts, as an all-weather jet pilot (1951-1957), where he took charge of the 437th Fighter Interceptors (1954); staff officer stationed at Headquarters U.S. Air Force, the Pentagon, the Royal Air Force Station at Bentwaters, England, and Davis-Mothan AFB, Ariz. (1957-1966); led a combat mission over North Vietnam, in which seven enemy MiG 21s were destroyed, the highest total kill of any mission during the Vietnam War. Served as vice commander at Eglin AFB, Fla. (1967-1968); stationed at Wheelus Air Base in Libya (1969, 1970); deputy assistant secretary of defense for public affairs (1970-1974); vice commander of the Military Airlift Command (1974-1975); promoted to **the U.S. Armed Forces first African-American four-star general** (1975), serving as commander in chief of NORAD/ADCOM and Peterson AFB, Colo. (1975-1978); awarded the George Washington Freedom Foundation Medal (1967, 1968). Died on February 25, 1978. Further reading, Mark R. Salser, _Black Americans in Defense of Their Nation_ (1992).

---

on this day in history...

1806,	Sarah Mapps Douglass, founder of Philadelphia's first school for African-American children, was born Philadelphia, Pa.
1877,	Charles "Buddy" Bolden, originator of the nation's first jazz band, was born in New Orleans, La. (d. 1931).
1912,	Frederick McGhee, civil rights attorney who originated the idea of the Niagara Movement, died in St. Paul, Minn. (b. 1861).
1915,	The Association for the Study of African-American Life and History was founded Chicago, Ill.
1938,	Sonia Sanchez, award-winning poet, was born in Birmingham, Ala.
1968,	Arthur Ashe won the first U.S. Open Tennis Championship at Forest Hills Stadium in New York.

SEPTEMBER 9   MILITARY HEROES

RALPH JOHNSON BUNCHE

Scholar and diplomat.   Born on August 7, 1904, in Detroit, Mich.   University of California at Los Angeles, *summa cum laude* and Phi Beta Kappa (B.A., 1927); Harvard University (M.A., political science, 1928; Ph.D., government and international relations, 1934); Northwestern University; London School of Economics.   Teacher at Howard University for a great part of his career; received Rosanwald Fund fellowship (1932); won the Toppan Prize for his essay on social sciences (1934); Social Science Research Council fellowship (1936); helped found the National Negro Congress (1936), an attempt at racial solidarity; published *Idealogies, Tactics, and Achievements of Negro Betterment and Interracial Organizations* (1940). Became senior social science analyst in the Africa and Far East Section of the Office of the Coordinator of Information (1941); became the **first African-American official in the U.S. State Department** (1944), adviser to the U.S. delegation at the San Francisco conference that drafted the U.N. Charter (1945); director of the Department of Trusteeship and Non-Self Governing Territories (1948-1957); headed the peace-keeping Palestine Commission and negotiated a temporary peace agreement between Egypt and Israel (1949). Awarded NAACP Spingarn Medal (1949), for his distinguished scholarship in Myrdal's study, *The American Dilemma*; **first African-American to received the Nobel Peace Prize** (1950); appointed under secretary-general of the U.N. (1954); trustee of the Rockefeller Foundation (1955-1971); special U.N. representative to the Congo (1960), and Yemen (1963); participated in the Selma to Montgomery March (1965). Died on December 9, 1971, in New York City.   Further reading, <u>Peggy Mann</u>, <u>*Ralph Bunche: UN Peacemaker*</u> (1975).

---

on this day in history...

1920,	The first game of the National Negro Baseball League was played in Indianapolis, Ind.
1925,	Rosco Lee Brown, Emmy Award-winning actor, was born in Woodbury, N.J.
1968,	The Poor People's March on Washington, led by Ralph Abernathy, began.

MAY 2   GOVERNMENT OFFICIALS & POLITICIANS

EDWARD ORVAL GOURDIN

Scholar, athlete, soldier, and judge.   Born on August 10, 1897, in Jacksonville, Fla.   Harvard University (B.A., 1921; LL.B., 1924).   Passed the bar and practiced law in Boston; member of Harvard Student Army Training Corps and was commissioned a **second lieutenant in the Massachusetts National Guard**; inducted into active service (1941), becoming the commanding officer of the Third Battalion of the 372nd Infantry Regiment, with the rank of colonel; oriented, informed, and educated troops in postcollege workshops and seminars in counseling, law, communications, and African-American history (1943-1944); assigned to Fort Huachucha, Ariz. (1944), Fort Lawton, Wash. (1945), and the Pacific Theater (1945). Member of the Mid Pacific Sociology and Psychiatry Board; returned to National Guard status (1946); was member of the U.S. assistant secretary of war's Discharge and Review Board (1946-1947); returned to the Massachusetts National Guard (1947), and served as acting chief of staff, acting judge advocate general, plans and training general staff officer for the defense of Boston, and aide to the governor of Massachusetts; served as assistant U.S. district attorney as chief of the Civil Division, where he handled such cases as immigration, taxation, leases, and contracts; appointed special justice of Roxbury District Court (1952), and to the Massachusetts Superior Court; president of the National Olympic Athletes Association (1965-1966). Died on July 22, 1966, in Quincy, Mass.   Further reading, <u>Mark R. Salser</u>, <u>*Black Americans in Defense of Their Nation*</u> (1992).

---

on this day in history...

1909,	Arthur Courtney Logan, famed Harlem surgeon, was born in Tuskegee, Ala. (d. 1973).
1968,	Sandra Williams was crowned the first Miss Black America.
1990,	Marjorie Vincent of Illinois was crowned Miss America.

SEPTEMBER 8   **MILITARY HEROES**

AMBROSE CALIVER

Teacher, college administrator, public servant, **and an expert on Negro education**.   Born on February 25, 1894, in Saltsville, Va. Knoxville College (B.A., 1915); University of Wisconsin (M.A., 1920); Columbia University (Ph.D., 1930).   Became a high school principal in Rockwood, Tenn. (1916), and an assistant principal of Douglas High School in El Paso; member of the Fisk University faculty (1917-1927), where he developed a training program in manual arts; became Fisk's publicity director (1925), dean of the scholastic department (1926), and **Fisk's first African-American dean** (1927-1930). Specialist in African-American education for the Office of Education (1930-1946); specialist in the higher education of Negroes (1946-1950); assistant to the U.S. commissioner on Education (1950-1955); became chief of the Adult Education Section of the Office of Education (1955). A moving force in the elimination of the lowercase "n" in the spelling of "Negro;" surveyed important educational problems, researched new programs, and wrote bulletins on special phases of African-American education and bibliographies; some of his work included *The Education of Negro Teachers* (1933), *Secondary Education for Negroes* (1933), *Fundamentals in the Education of Negroes* (1935), *Availability of Education to Negroes in Rural Communities* (1936), and *Vocational and Educational Guidance of Negroes* (1938). Responsible for the establishment of the National Advisory Committee on the Education of Negroes (1930), the convening of the National Conference on Fundamental Problems in the Education of Negroes (1934), and the National Survey of the Higher Education of Negroes (1939); appointed director of the Project for Literacy Education (1946). Died on January 29, 1962, in Washington, D.C.   Further reading, Walter G. Daniel and John B. Holden, *Ambrose Caliver, Educator, and Civil Servant* (1966).

on this day in history...

1933,   James Brown, Grammy Award-winning "godfather of soul," was born in Augusta, Ga.

MAY 3   **GOVERNMENT OFFICIALS & POLITICIANS**

HENRY OSSAIN FLIPPER

Military officer and engineer.   Born on March 21, 1856, in Thomasville, Ga.   Atlanta University; **first African-American graduate of the U.S. Military Academy at West Point, N.Y. (1877).**   Commissioned as a second lieutenant in the U.S. Army (1877), **the Regular Army's first African-American officer;** assigned to the all-Negro 10th Calvary Regiment (Buffalo Soldiers), being stationed at Fort Sill, Elliott, Concho, Davis, and Quitman, serving as post engineer; court-martialed and dishonorably discharged, after being accused of embezzlement (1881), posthumously receiving an honorable discharge some 95 years later. Worked as a surveyor for American landowners in Mexico (1881-1886); chief engineer for the Chicago-based Sonora Land Company (1886-1887); opened his own civil and mining engineering company in Nogales, Ariz. (1887); chief engineer of the Altar Land and Colonization Company (1890-1892). Special agent for the U.S. Justice Department's Court of Private Land Claims (1893-1901), researching and translating land-grant claims in Mexican archives, surveying land throughout southern Arizona, providing expert court testimonies in land dispute cases, and preparing the U.S. government's publication, *Spanish and Mexican Land Laws* (1895). Resident engineer for the Balvanera Mining Company in New Mexico (1902-1919); consultant to the chairman of a U.S. Senate subcommittee studying the impact of the Mexican Revolution on U.S. economic interest (1919-1923), and as an assistant to the secretary of the U.S. Department of the Interior; engineer with the Pantepec Oil Company (1923-1930), where he **helped develop the Venezuelan oil industry.** Died on May 3, 1940, in Atlanta, Ga.   Further reading, <u>Henry O. Flipper</u>, <u>*The Colored Cadet at West Point*</u> (1898).

on this day in history...

1800,   James Varick and his followers dedicated Zion Church, New York City's first African-American church.

1941,   Joe Simon, Grammy Award-winning recording artist, was born in Simmesport, La.

SEPTEMBER 7

MILITARY HEROES

FRANCIS LOUIS CARDOZO

Carpenter, minister, educator, and government official. Born on February 1, 1837, in Charleston, S.C. Graduated from the University of Glasgow in Scotland; studied at Presbyterian seminaries in Scotland and England. Became pastor of the Temple Street Congregational Church in New Haven, Conn. (1864); founded Avery Normal Institute in Charleston, S.C. (1865); delegate to the state constitutional convention (1868), where as chairman of the Committee on Education he helped plan the state's public school system; **South Carolina secretary of state** (1868-1872), responsible for bringing the affairs of the State Land Commission back to order; elected state president of the Grand Council of Union Leagues of South Carolina (1870), a Republican-oriented organization. Professor of Latin at Howard University (1871-1872); **South Carolina state treasurer** (1872-1877), where he guarded the state treasury against manipulations of corruptionists; U.S. Treasury Department employee (1878-1884); principal of Washington's Colored Preparatory High School (1884-1891), and its successor M Street High School (1891-1896), where he maintained high academic standards and introduced business courses. Died on July 22, 1903, in Washington, D.C. Further reading, Thomas Holt, *Black over White: Negro Political Leadership in South Carolina During Reconstruction* (1977).

on this day in history...

1897,	Joseph H. Smith patented a lawn sprinkler.
1929,	Jessie Menifield Rattley, Newport News' first African-American mayor, was born in Newport News, Va.
1942,	Nickolas Ashford, singer and songwriter, was born in Fairfield, S.C.
1943,	Norm Rice, Seattle's first African-American mayor, was born in Denver, Colo.
1954,	J. Ernest Wilkins, U.S. Department of Labor, became the first African-American appointed to assistant secretary level.
1969,	Charles Gordone's Pulitzer Prize-winning play, *No Place to be Somebody*, opened in New York City.

MAY 4   **GOVERNMENT OFFICIALS & POLITICIANS**

CHRISTIAN ABRAHAM FLEETWOOD

Editor, army officer, and musician.   Born on July 21, 1840, in Baltimore, Md.   Educated in the home of John C. Brunes; Ashmun Institute [now Lincoln University] in Pennsylvania (1860).   Served in the Union Army as a sergeant major with Company G, 4th Regiment, U.S. Colored Troops (1863-1866), where he saw combat at Fort Harrison, accompanied the Terry expedition, participated in the capture of Fort Fisher and Wilmington, N.C., and performed provost duty at New Bern, N.C., and garrison duty in Washington, D.C.; **awarded the Medal of Honor (1865), for heroism** in the pivotal battle of Chaffin's Farm outside of Richmond, where he seized the colors after two color bearers had been shot down and carried them nobly through the fight. Bookkeeper in Columbus, Ohio (1866-1867); worked in the Freedmen's Bank; member of the District of Columbia National Guard (1880-1892); employed in the U.S. War Department (1881-1892), assuming positions in the Surgeon General's Office, Adjutant General's Office, and Record and Pension Office; organizer and instructor of the Colored High School Cadet Corps of the District of Columbia (1888-1897). Died on September 28, 1914, in Washington, D.C.   Further reading, Robert Greene, _Black Defenders of America 1775-1973: A Reference and Pictorial History_ (1979).

---

on this day in history...

1892,   George Dixon defeated Jack Skelly for the featherweight boxing championship.
1988,   Lee Roy Jones became the first African-American Texas State Ranger.

SEPTEMBER 6   **MILITARY HEROES**

WILLIAM HENRY DEAN, JR.

Educator, economist, government official, and a **straight "A" student throughout his entire secondary and post secondary education**. Born on July 6, 1910, in Lynchburg, Va. Bowdoin College Phi Beta Kappa *magna cum laude* (B.A., 1930); Harvard University economic degrees (M.A., 1932; Ph.D., 1938), dissertation title: "The Theory of Geographical Location of Economic Activity," which was used as a text in economics courses at Harvard and Northwestern University. Harvard University scholar (1930-1931), Henry Lee Memorial fellow (1931-1932), and an Edward Austin fellow (1932-1933). Associate professor of economics and business administration at Atlanta University (1933-1942), where he introduced courses in labor economics; lecturer in economics at the City College of New York (1939); price executive of the Office of Price Administration in the Virgin Island (1942-1944); conducted a survey of 13 cities for the National Urban League (1942-1946); proposed a boycott, until and unless African-Americans were allowed to play on major league baseball teams (1942); director of the Community Relations Project of the National Urban League (1944-1946). Became acting **chief of the U.N. Africa Unit, Division of Economic Stability and Development** (1946), and chief (1949); served as secretary of the U.N. Mission on Haiti (1949); appointed administrative officer of a U.N. Mission to Libya (1949), with the country gaining independence the following year; directed a six-man mission to Italian Somaliland (1951). Died on January 8, 1952, in New York City. Further reading, Rayford W. Logan and Michael R. Winston, *Dictionary of American Negro Biography* (1982).

---

on this day in history...

1883,	Josiah Henson, abolitionist whose life was portrayed in Harriet Beecher Stowe's *Uncle Tom's Cabin*, died in Dresden, Canada (b. 1789).
1905,	The *Chicago Defender* was founded by Robert S. Abbott in Chicago, Ill.
1930,	Douglas Turner Ward, co-founder of the Negro Ensemble Company, was born in Burnside, La.
1969,	Moneta Sleet won a Pulitzer Prize for his photograph of Coretta Scott King and daughter Bernice at the funeral of Martin Luther King, Jr.

BENJAMIN OLIVER DAVIS, SR.

Military officer, educator, and government official. Born on July 1, 1877, in Washington, D.C. Howard University. Commissioned as a first lieutenant in the 8th U.S. Volunteer Infantry (1898-1899); enlisted in the Regular Army as a private, serving with the 9th Cavalry (1899-1901); commissioned as a second lieutenant in the Regular Army (1901), and promoted to first lieutenant (1905), captain (1919), lieutenant colonel (1930), and the **first African-American general in the Regular Army** (1940). Served as military attache to Monrovia, Liberia (1909-1912); commanding officer of the 369th Infantry, New York National Guard (1938-1940); commanding general of the 4th Cavalry Brigade (1941-1944); brigade commander with the 2nd Cavalry Division, assigned to D.C. for duty as assistant to the Inspector General, serving as a special adviser on Negro problems; special assistant to the Commanding General, Communication Zone in the European Theater. Professor of military science and tactics at Wilberforce University (1905-1909, 1929-1930, 1937-1938), Tuskegee Institute (1920-1924, 1931-1937); instructor of the 372nd Infantry, Ohio National Guard in Cleveland. Awarded the Distinguished Service Medal (1944), Bronze Star (1945), and an honorary degree from Atlanta University. Died on November 26, 1970, at Great Lakes Naval Station, Ill. Further reading, Marvin E. Fletcher, *America's First Black General* (1989).

---

on this day in history...

1859, Harriet Tubman's *Our Nig* became the first novel published by a Negro woman.

1936, Alcee Hastings, Florida 23rd District congressman, was born in Altamonte Springs, Fla.

SEPTEMBER 5   MILITARY HEROES

OSCAR JAMES DUNN

Musician, soldier, and politician. Born in 1821 in Louisiana. Apprenticed to learn the plasterer's trade; taught music in New Orleans; enlisted in the first regiment of African-American troops raised in Louisiana, becoming a captain; appointed to the New Orleans City Council by General Sheridan; elected the **nation's first African-American lieutenant governor** (1868), during which his duties included presiding of the Louisiana State Senate. Served as president of the Board of Police Commissioners of New Orleans; member of the board of trustees of Straight University; Grand Master of the all-Negro Free and Accepted Masons of Louisiana; elected presiding officer at the Republican State Convention (1870), putting him in a strong position to become the next governor of Louisiana. Died mysteriously on November 22, 1871, in New Orleans, La., with speculation that he was poisoned. Further reading, Rayford W. Logan and Michael R. Winston, *Dictionary of American Negro Biography* (1982).

on this day in history...

1913,	Richard Austin, Michigan's first African-American secretary of state, was born in Stouts Mountain, Ala.
1931,	Willie Mays, Baseball Hall of Famer, was born in Westfield, Ala.
1960,	President Eisenhower signed the Civil Rights Act of 1960.

MAY 6   **GOVERNMENT OFFICIALS & POLITICIANS**

WILLIAM H. CARNEY

Civil War veteran and Congressional Medal of Honor winner.   Born in 1840 in Norfolk, Va.   Joined the first regiment of Negro troops to be raised in the North by the Union Army, the 54th Massachusetts Infantry (1863), and was soon promoted to sergeant of Company C; accompanied the 54th Massachusetts Infantry to South Carolina (1863), where: the regiment spearheaded an assault on Fort Wagner, just outside of Charleston Harbor; his company suffered heavy losses; he grabbed the Union colors from a soldier who started to fall and carried it forward, while being overwhelmed by a hail of Confederate ammunition for more than an hour; he was wounded and hospitalized, reportedly saying, "Boys, the old flag never touched the ground;" discharged from the Union Army because of disabilities caused by his wounds (1864), as a bonafide **Civil War hero**. Mail carrier in New Bedford, Mass. (1869-1901); participated in ceremonies dedicating a monument to the 54th Massachusetts and its commanding officer Robert G. Shaw in Boston (1897); awarded the Congressional Medal of Honor (1900), for his heroism during the Battle of Fort Wagner; frequently spoke at Boston Memorial Day rallies; messenger in the Massachusetts State House (1901-1908). Died on December 9, 1908, in Boston, Mass.   Further reading, W.F. Beyer and O.F. Keydel, _Deeds of Valor_ (1906).

---

on this day in history...

1865,	Bowie State College was established in Maryland.
1900,	James Madison Nabrit, Jr., president emeritus of Howard University, was born in Atlanta, Ga.
1914,	Jean Blackwell Hutson, historian and Schomburg Collection curator, was born in Summerfield, Fla.
1945,	Ramona Hoage Edelin, president and CEO of the National Urban Coalition, was born in Los Angeles, Calif.

SEPTEMBER 4   **MILITARY HEROES**

GEORGE WASHINGTON ELLIS

Diplomat, lawyer, sociologist, and author.   Born in 1875 in Weston, Mo.   University of Kansas (LL.B., 1893; B.A., 1897); Gunton Institute of Economics and Sociology (1897-1899); Howard University School of Pedagogy.   Admitted to the Kansas bar (1893); passed U.S. Census Board exam (1899); **secretary of the U.S. legation in the Republic of Liberia** (1902-1910), where his reports aided the State Department in developing its policies toward Liberia; elected a fellow of the Royal Geographical Society of Great Britain; declared knight commander of the Order of African Redemption. Opened a Chicago law office (1910), later arguing before the U.S. Supreme Court; wrote *Negro Culture in West Africa* (1914), his most important scholarly work; Chicago assistant corporation counsel (1917-1919). Died on November 26, 1919, in Chicago, Ill.   Further reading, *Who's Who in America, 1918-1919*.

---

on this day in history...

1878,	R.J. Winters patented a fire escape ladder.
1888,	Fenton Johnson, "one of the first Negro revolutionary poets," was born in Chicago, Ill. (d. 1958).
1926,	The first African-American PTA, the National Congress of Colored Parent-Teachers, was founded by Selena Sloan Butler.
1946,	William Hastie was inaugurated as the first African-American governor of the Virgin Islands.

JESSE LEROY BROWN

Naval aviator. Born on October 13, 1926, in Hattiesburg, Miss. Ohio State University School of Engineering (1947). Enlisted in the U.S. Naval Reserve (1946); appointed as an aviation cadet (1947), and trained at the U.S. Navy Preflight School in Ottumwa, Iowa, and Pensacola; won his wings and commissioned as an ensign (1948); assigned to Fighter Squadron 32, Atlantic Fleet at Norfolk. Embarked with his squadron on the *USS Leyte* (1949), which joined the 7th Fleet in combat off the northeast coast of Korea (1950); flew 20 missions and was fatally shot down near the Chosin Reservoir in Korea, **becoming the first African-American naval officer to lose his life in combat**; posthumously awarded the Purple Heart and Distinguished Flying Medal; **first African-American naval officer to have a U.S. Navy ship named in his honor**. Died on December 4, 1950, in Korea. Further reading, Mark R. Salser, *Black Americans in Defense of Their Nation* (1992).

---

on this day in history...

1773,   Thomas Paul, Sr., successor to Prince Hall as head of the Black Masons, was born in Exeter, N.H. (d. 1831).

1838,   Frederick Douglass escaped from slavery disguised as a sailor.

1910,   Dorothy Maynor, founder of the Harlem School of Fine Arts, was born in Norfolk, Va.

1990,   Jonathan A. Rogers became the highest ranking African-American in network television, when he was named president of the CBS T.V. Station Division.

1962,   Michael Darryl Woods, publisher of *AFROMATION: 366 Days of American History*, was born in Omaha, Neb.

SEPTEMBER 3   MILITARY HEROES

JONATHAN C. GIBBS

Minister and state government official.   Born in 1827 in Philadelphia, Pa.   Dartmouth College (B.A., 1852); Princeton Theological Seminary. Became a Presbyterian minister (1854); preached in Troy, N.Y., and Philadelphia; attended the National Convention of Colored Citizens of the United States (Syracuse, 1864), which resulted in the formation of the National Equal Rights League. Sent to the South by the Old Style Presbyterian Church to open churches and schools; attended the Colored People's Convention of the State of South Carolina (Charleston, 1865); worked with freedmen in North and South Carolina (1865-1867); elected to Florida's Constitutional Convention (1868); **Florida secretary of state** (1868-1873); **Florida superintendent of public instruction** (1873-1874), responsible for all public education. Died on August 14, 1874, in Florida.   Further reading, W.E.B. DuBois, *Black Reconstruction in America* (1935).

---

on this day in history...

1862,	Horace W. Bivins, Battle of San Juan Hill Army hero, was born in Pungoteague, Va. (d. 1937).
1910,	Mary Lou Williams, "queen of jazz," was born in Atlanta, Ga. (d. 1981).
1911,	Robert Johnson, legendary Mississippi Delta blues singer, was born in Hazelhurst, Miss. (d. 1938).
1925,	The Brotherhood of Sleeping Car Porters was organized by A. Phillip Randolph.

MAY 8   **GOVERNMENT OFFICIALS & POLITICIANS**

ARTHUR BROOKS

Army officer and an employee of presidents.   Born on November 25, 1861, in Port Royal, Va.   Stabler in the Quartermaster Department (1881); assistant messenger in the U.S. War Department (1881-1885); doorkeeper for the U.S. secretary of war; commander of Company A, Washington Cadet Corps, 6th Battalion of the District of Columbia Militia (1887-1897); commander of the National Guard, 1st Separate Battalion with the rank of major (1897-1912); instructor of Colored High School Cadet Corps of the District of Columbia. Appointed foreman of laborers (1899); member of the House Subcommittee on Colored Visitors during the inauguration of President Theodore Roosevelt (1905); doorkeeper for the White House (1909-1926), where he also served as **presidential valet and custodian of the executive property to Presidents Taft, Wilson, Harding, and Coolidge**; promoted to lieutenant colonel (1912), and retired. Died on July 23, 1926, in Washington, D.C.   Further reading, *Dictionary of Negro American Biography* (1982).

on this day in history...

1833,   Oberlin College, one of the first colleges to admit Negroes, was founded on Ohio.

1912,   Richard Jess Brown, attorney who filed the first civil rights lawsuit in Mississippi, was born in Muskogee, Okla. (d. 1989).

1971,   Cheryl White became the first African-American woman jockey to win a race.

MILITARY HEROES

JOHN PATTERSON GREEN

Lawyer and politician who is known as the **"father of Labor Day."** Born in 1845 in Newbern, N.C. Graduated from Cleveland High School (1869); Union Law School in Cleveland (1870). Apprenticed to learn the bricklayer and plasterer trades; worked as a tailor and a waiter; published *Essays on Miscellaneous Subjects by a Self-Educated Colored Youth* (1866); moved to North Carolina and became a clerk in a grocery store (1870); admitted to the South Carolina bar (1870); elected delegate to the South Carolina State Republican Convention (1872). Returned to Cleveland and was elected Cuyahoga County justice of the peace (1872-1881); elected Ohio state representative (1881, 1890), where he sponsored a bill establishing "Labor Day" in Ohio (with the federal government following suit), supported legislation on civil rights, and served on the turnpike committee; wrote *Recollections of the Carolinas* (1881); elected **Ohio's first African-American state senator** (1892), where he won an appropriation for an industrial department at Wilberforce University. Campaigned for Presidents Harrison, McKinley, and Hoover, and addressed an audience on the subject of "The Relation of Negroes to the Republican Party" (Chicago, 1928); served as Ohio's alternate delegate-at-large at the Republican National Convention (St. Louis, 1896); U.S. postage stamp agent (1897-1905), where he was responsible for supervising the printing and distribution of postage stamps for the entire nation; acting superintendent of finance for the Post Office Department (1905-1906); devoted rest of life to his law practice. Died on August 30, 1940, in Cleveland, Ohio. Further reading, John Patterson Green, *Fact Stranger Than Fiction: Seventy-Five Years of a Busy Life with Reminiscences of Many Great Men and Women* (1920).

---

on this day in history...

1899,   J.A. Burr patented a lawn mower.

1977,   Mabel Murphy Smythe was confirmed as U.S. ambassador to Cameroon.

         GOVERNMENT OFFICIALS & POLITICIANS

MIDIAN OTHELLO BOUSFIELD

Physician, military officer, and insurance executive. Born on August 22, 1885, in Tipton, Mo. University of Kansas (B.A., 1907); Northwestern University School of Medicine (1909). Chicago school health officer and school tuberculosis physician (1914-1916); consultant to the U.S. Children's Bureau and the Chicago Board of Health; **first African-American on the Chicago School Board**; president of the National Medical Association (1934); appointed director of the Negro Health Division of the Rosenwald Fund (1939); member of the White House Conference on Children in a Democracy (1940); member of the board of Provident Hospital. Organizer and commanding officer of the 100-bed Station Hospital #1 at Fort Huachuca, Ariz., during World War II, **first U.S. Army hospital to be staffed entirely by African-American physicians; first African-American colonel in the Army Medical Corps**. An incorporator, member of the board of directors, medical examiner, vice president, medical director, and president of Liberty Life Insurance Company (1921-1929); chairman of the executive committee, vice president, and medical director of Supreme Liberty Life Insurance Company (1929-1948); supporter of the National Association of Colored Graduate Nurses; supervised contributions to African-American medical schools; member of Kappa Alpha Psi fraternity. Died in 1948 in Chicago, Ill. Further reading, *Dictionary of American Medical Biography* (1984).

---

on this day in history...

1947,   Charles S. Johnson became the first African-American president of Fisk University.

1948,   William T. Coleman was appointed the first African-American U.S. Supreme Court clerk.

1970,   Hugh S. Scott of Washington, D.C., became the first African-American superintendent of schools in a major U.S. city.

1979,   Hazel Johnson-Brown became the first African-American woman U.S. Army general.

SEPTEMBER 1   MILITARY HEROES

PATRICIA ROBERTS HARRIS

Lawyer and government official. Born on May 31, 1924, in Mattoon, Ill. Howard University Phi Beta Kappa *summa cum laude* (B.A., 1945); George Washington University (J.D., 1960), where she was a member of the law review, graduated first in her class, and was elected to the Order of the Coif; University of Chicago; American University. Worked for the Chicago YWCA; became executive director of Delta Sigma Theta (1953); admitted to practice law before the U.S. Supreme Court and to the District of Columbia bar (1960); worked on the appeals and research staff of the criminal division of the U.S. Department of Justice (1960-1961). Lecturer in law, associate dean of students, professor of law, and dean of Howard University Law School (1961-1969), becoming the **first African-American woman head of a law school**; delegate to the Democratic National Convention (1964), presidential elector from the District of Columbia (1964), chairman of the credentials committee (1972), and a member-at-large of the Democratic National Committee (1973). Ambassador to Luxembourg (1965-1967), becoming the **first African-American woman ambassador**; alternate delegate to the 21st and 22nd General Assembly of the U.N. (1966-1967); U.S. alternate to the 20th Plenary Meeting of the Economic Community of Europe (1967); partner in the Washington law firm of Fried, Frank, Harris, Shriver, and Kampelman. U.S. secretary of the Department of Housing and Urban Development (1977-1980); U.S. secretary of the Department of Health, Education and Welfare (1980-1981); professor of law in the George Washington School of Law (1983-1985). Died on March 23, 1985, in Washington, D.C. Further reading, J. Clay Smith, Jr., "Patricia Harris," *Notable Black American Women* (1992).

---

on this day in history...

1815,   Henry Walton Bibb, founder of Canada's first Negro newspaper (the *Voice of the Fugitive*), was born in Shelby County, Ky. (d. 1854).

1910,   The National Association for the Advancement of Colored People was incorporated.

1943,   Judith Jamison, artistic director of the Alvin Ailey American Dance Theater, was born in Philadelphia, Pa.

MAY 10   **GOVERNMENT OFFICIALS & POLITICIANS**

LOUIS TOMPKINS WRIGHT

Surgeon, hospital administrator, and civil rights leader.   Born on July 23, 1891, in La Grange, Ga.   Clark College valedictorian (B.A., 1911; D.Sc., 1938); **one of the first African-American graduates of Harvard Medical School** (M.D., 1915); interned at Freedmen's Hospital (1915-1916).   Commissioned a first lieutenant in the U.S. Army Medical Corps at Fort McPherson, Ga., (1917), serving at the Colored Officers Training Camp in Fort Des Moines, Iowa, and Camp Upton, N.Y., where he was assigned to the 367th Infantry Regiment of the 92nd Division; received the Purple Heart (1919). Appointed clinical assistant in the out-patient department of Harlem Hospital, becoming the **first African-American physician appointed to a New York City municipal hospital**; staff member and director of the department of surgery of Harlem Hospital (1919-1949), and president of the Medical Board; **became the first New York City public surgeon** (1929). Treasurer of the NAACP Atlanta branch (1931-1935), and chairman of the national board of directors (1935-1952); admitted to the American College of Surgery (1934), and became a diplomat of the American Board of Surgery (1940); awarded the NAACP Spingarn Medal (1940), for outstanding work in surgery and civic affairs; was a founding member of the American Academy of Compensation Medicine; appointed medical adviser to the director of Selective Service for New York City (1949); appointed to the New York City Committee of the American Cancer Society (1950). Led the fight to build the Negro Veteran's Administration hospital of the North in Harlem, instead of a new "Jim Crow" hospital; **headed the team that first used the "wonder drug" Aureomycin**; advocated a national health insurance policy; regarded as an authority on head injuries and introduced the intradermal method of vaccinating against smallpox. Died in 1952.   Further reading, Charles Organ, Jr., and Margaret Kosiba, *A Century of Black Surgeons: The U.S.A. Experience* (1987).

---

on this day in history...

1907,	Augusta Freeman "Gus" Hawkins, former California congressman (1963-1990), was born in Shreveport, La.
1935,	Eldridge Cleaver, Black Panther Party's minister of information, was born in Wabbaseka, Ark.
1935,	Frank Robinson, first African-American manager in major-league baseball, was born in Beaufort, Texas.
1936,	Marva Delores Collins, founder of Chicago's Westside Preparatory School, was born in Monroeville, Ala.
1955,	Edwin Corley Moses, "greatest hurdler in the history of track and field," was born in Dayton, Ohio.
1979,	Donald McHenry replaced Andrew Young as U.S. ambassador to the U.N.

AUGUST 31

MEDICAL PIONEERS

PERRY WILSON HOWARD

Lawyer and politician. Born on June 14, 1877, in Ebenezer, Miss.   Rust College (A.B., 1898); Fisk University; University of Chicago; University of Illinois (LL.B., 1905).   Taught mathematics at Alcorn A&M College (1901-1905); began his law practice (1907); participated in the Republican National Convention (1912, 1916, 1920, 1924, 1928, 1932, 1936, 1940, 1944, 1948, 1952, 1956, and 1960); appointed by President Harding as special assistant to the U.S. attorney general (1921-1928); served as **chairman of the Mississippi State Republican Committee** (1924-1932); Republican National committeeman from Mississippi (1924-1960), where he became the most senior Republican committeeman, African-American or white, on the national level and chairman of committees at several national conventions. Partner in the prestigious African-American Washington law firm of Cobb, Howard, and Hayes; attended the San Francisco Conference that organized the U.N. as a legal adviser for the Improved Benevolent Protective Order of Elks of the World (1945), to urge all African-Americans to contact their congressmen to demand that the U.N. charter contain safeguards for civil rights of all people. Died on February 2, 1961, in Washington, D.C.   Further reading, Hanes Walton, Jr., *Black Republicans: The Politics of Black and Tans* (1975).

---

on this day in history...

1933,   Louis E. Walcott ("Louis Farrakhan"), national representative of the Honorable Elijah Muhammad, was born in New York City.
1993,   Brenda Council was elected Omaha's first African-American woman city council member.

MAY 11   **GOVERNMENT OFFICIALS & POLITICIANS**

DANIEL HALE WILLIAMS

Surgeon and educator. Born on January, 18, 1856, in Hollidaysburg, Pa. Haires's Classical Academy in Janesville, Wis. (1878); apprenticed under Henry Palmer, the surgeon-general of the State of Wisconsin; Chicago Medical College (M.D., 1883); interned at Mercy Hospital in Chicago. Appointed attending physician at the Protestant Orphan Asylum, to the surgical staff of the South Side Dispensary, clinical instructor at Chicago Medical College, and as surgeon to the City Railway Company. Member of the Illinois State Board of Health (1889-1893), where he worked for the establishment of a bi-racial hospital, where young African-American physician and nurses could intern and train; **founded Provident Hospital & Medical Center** in Chicago (1891), **the nation's first African-American-owned and controlled hospital**, and served as a member of the board of directors (1893-1913). Presented his first major paper, "Appendicitis," at the Gynecological Society Meeting (1893); became the **first surgeon to perform a successful open heart operation** (1893); surgeon-in-chief of Freedmen's Hospital in D.C. (1894-1898), where he established a training school for nurses and first divided the hospital into departments--Medical, Surgical, Gynecological, Obstetrical, Dermatological, Genito-urinary, and Throat and Chest. **Founder and vice president of the National Medical Association**; helped form the interracial Medico-Chirurgical Society of Washington (1895); unsalaried professor of clinical surgery at Meharry College in Nashville; helped establish over 40 hospitals, serving African-Americans across the U.S.; member of the surgical staff at Cook County Hospital (1900-1906); associate attending surgeon at St. Luke's Hospital (1907-1931); charter member of the American College of Surgeons. Died on August 4, 1931, in Idlewild, Mich. Further reading, Lewis H. Fenderson, _Daniel Hale Williams: Open Heart Doctor_ (1971).

---

on this day in history...

1800,	Gabriel Prosser and Jack Bowler led over 1,100 slaves in an attack on Richmond, Va.
1892,	S.R. Scottron patented a curtain rod.
1930,	Xernonia Clayton, TBS vice president of public affairs, was born in Muskogee, Okla.
1931,	Carrie Saxon Perry, Hartford's first African-American woman mayor, was born in Hartford, Conn.
1983,	Guion Stewart Bluford, Jr., aboard the space shuttle _Challenger_, became the first African-American in space.

AUGUST 30   **MEDICAL PIONEERS**

EDWARD AUSTIN JOHNSON

Teacher, lawyer, historian, businessman, and politician. Born into slavery on November 23, 1860, in Raleigh, N.C. Atlanta University; **Shaw University's first law graduate** (LL.B., 1891). Served as principal in the Atlanta Public School system; teacher and principal of Washington High School in Raleigh, N.C. (1885-1891); owned a barbershop; participated in the North Carolina Negro Teachers Association (1886); published a text book entitled *A School History of the Negro Race in America from 1619 to 1890* (1890), to mark the 25 years of freedom for African-Americans and to provide the history of African-American achievements in the U.S. on a level for school children. Law, stenography, and typewriting instructor and dean of Shaw University law department (1893-1907); Raleigh alderman (1897-1899); clerk of the federal district attorney for the Eastern District of North Carolina (1897-1907); North Carolina 4th Congressional District Republican Party chairman; delegate to the Republican National Convention (Minneapolis, 1892; St. Louis, 1896; Philadelphia, 1900). Wrote *History of the Negro Soldiers in the Spanish-American War and Other Items of Interest* (1899), *Light Ahead for the Negro* (1904), and *Adam vs. Ape-Man in Ethiopia* (1931); founding member of the National Negro Business League (1900), and became **one of Raleigh's biggest landowners**; admitted to the New York bar and became **first African-American to be elected into the New York State legislature** (1917-1918). Died on July 25, 1944, in New York City. Further reading, *Journal of Negro History* (October 1944).

---

on this day in history...

1902,   Joe Gans became the first African-American light heavyweight boxing champion.
1926,   Melvin Malcolm Dymally, former California lieutenant governor (1975-1979) and congressman (1981-1993), was born in Cedros, Trinidad.
1967,   H. Rap Brown replaced Stokely Carmichael as chairman of the SNCC.

SUSAN McKINNEY STEWARD

Physician, hospital founder, and women's rights activist.   Born in 1847 in Brooklyn, N.Y.   New York Medical College for Women valedictorian (M.D., 1870), the school's first African-American graduate; Long Island Medical College Hospital (1888).   Practiced medicine in Brooklyn (1870-1896), becoming the **first African-American woman physician in New York State** and attending to both African-American and white patients; organizer, founder, and staff member of the Brooklyn Woman's Homeopathic Hospital and Dispensary (1881-1895). Appointed as a delegate to the New Jersey Homeopathic Society's semiannual meeting (Jersey City, 1889); served on the staff of the New York Medical College for Women in Manhattan (1892-1896); official physician to the Brooklyn Home for the Aged Colored People; college physician at Wilberforce University (1898-1902); one of the founders of the first African-American women's club in New York. Addressed an interracial congress on "Colored Women in America" (London, 1911); read a paper on "Women in Medicine" before the National Association of Colored Women's Clubs (Wilberforce, 1914). Later, practiced medicine in Montana and Valentine, Neb. Died on March 7, 1918, in Wilberforce, Ohio.   Further reading, Hallie Q. Brown, *Homespun Heroines and Other Women of Distinction* (1926).

---

on this day in history...

1917,	Christine Virginia "Isabell" Sanford, Emmy Award-winning actress, was born in New York City.
1924,	Ruth Jones ("Dinah Washington"), Grammy Award-winning singer, was born in Tuscaloosa, Ala.
1945,	Wyomia Tyus, Olympic track champion, was born in Griffin, Ga.
1957,	Congress passed the Civil Rights Bill of 1957, establishing the Civil Rights Commission.
1958,	Michael Joseph Jackson, "the king of pop," was born in Gary, Ind.
1962,	Mel Goode became the first African-American TV news commentator when he began broadcasting on ABC.

AUGUST 29   **MEDICAL PIONEERS**

ERNEST MORIAL

Lawyer, civil rights leader, and city official nicknamed "Dutch." Born on October 9, 1929, in New Orleans, La. Xavier University of New Orleans (B.A., 1951); **first African-American graduate Louisiana State University School of Law** (LL.B., 1954). Attorney for the NAACP Legal Defense and Education Fund, where he filed suits that helped bring an end to segregation in New Orleans public schools, places of public entertainment, municipal facilities, buses, and taxicabs; law partner of civil rights attorney Alexander Tureaud; president of the New Orleans NAACP chapter (1963-1965); **first African-American assistant U.S. attorney in Louisiana** (1965-1967); Louisiana state representative (1968-1970); first African-American to sit on the bench in Louisiana as a judge of the Orleans Parish Juvenile Court (1970); **first African-American to be elected to the 4th Circuit Court of Appeals in Louisiana** (1973-1977); **first African-American mayor of New Orleans** (1977-1985); served as president of the U.S. Conference of Mayors. Died on December 23, 1989, in New Orleans, La. Further reading, Joe Louis Caldwell, "Morial, Ernest N.," *Encyclopedia of African-American Civil Rights* (1992).

---

on this day in history...

1862,	Robert Smalls became the first African-American Civil War naval hero when he confiscated the Confederate dispatch boat *Planter*.
1871,	Alcorn A&M College opened in Lorman, Miss.
1891,	Issac Murphy became the first jockey to win three Kentucky Derbys
1926,	Nathaniel R. Jones, 6th U.S. Circuit appellate judge, was born in Youngstown, Ohio.
1950,	Stevie Wonder, 15-time Grammy Award-winning musician, was born in Saginaw, Mich.
1990,	George A. Stallings was ordained as the first bishop of the African-American Catholic Church.

MABEL KEATON STAUPERS

Nurse and organization executive. Born on February, 27, 1890, in Barbados, West Indies. Freedmen's Hospital School of Nursing [now Howard School of Nursing] with honors (1917). Henry Phipps Institute for Tuberculosis fellow in Philadelphia (1921), where she accepted an assignment at Jefferson Hospital Medical College and learned first hand of the ill-treatment and lack of respect for African-American patients; helped organize the Booker T. Washington Sanitarium (1922); conducted a study of Harlem's health care needs, which led to the establishment and her serving as executive secretary of the Harlem Committee of the New York Tuberculosis and Health Association (1922-1934). **Executive secretary of the National Association of Colored Graduate Nurses** (1934-1946), president (1949-1950), where she collected data, organized state and local nursing associations, advising and counseling African-American nurses, representing them in the larger communities, and organized their bi-racial national council (1928); met with First Lady Eleanor Roosevelt (1944), in an attempt to end the discriminatory policies of the U.S. Army and Navy, which led to the African-American nurses serving in World War II and the integration of the American Nurses' Association. Awarded the NAACP Spingarn Medal (1951), for her contributions to the betterment of African-Americans in the nursing field. Died in 1989. Further reading, Darlene Clark Hine, *Black Women in White: Racial Conflict and Cooperation in the Nursing Profession, 1890-1950* (1989).

---

on this day in history...

1936,   Wayne Morton Washington, first African-American president of the American Meteorological Society, was born in Portland, Ore.

1955,   Emmett Till was kidnapped in Money, Miss., and found murdered four days later.

1963,   The largest single demonstration in U.S. history to date, the "March on Washington for Jobs and Freedom," was held with an estimated 250,000 people hearing Martin Luther King, Jr.'s "I Have A Dream" speech.

1968,   Channing E. Phillips, at the Democratic National Convention in Chicago, became the first African-American to be nominated for president by a major party.

AUGUST 28   **MEDICAL PIONEERS**

P.B.S. PINCHBACK

Soldier, politician, and Reconstruction era leader. Born Pinkney Benton Stewart Pinchback on May 10, 1837, in Georgia. Worked as a cabin boy on canal boats on the Ohio and Mississippi Rivers; captain in the Corps d'Afrique during the Civil War. A **founder and organizer of Louisiana's Republican Party**, and became a member of the state central committee (1867); member of the Louisiana constitutional convention (1867), where he fought for the adoption of a law prohibiting discrimination in public accommodations; delegate to the Republican National Convention (1868). Louisiana state senator (1868-1871); founded the *New Orleans Louisianan* newspaper (1870); founding partner of the Mississippi River Packet County (1870); elected president *pro tempore* of the Louisiana State Senate (1871); lieutenant governor of Louisiana (1871-1872), and later became the **nation's first African-American governor**--Louisiana (1872-1873); elected to the U.S. Senate and to an at-large congressional seat (1872), but both elections were contested with his opponents being seated. Appointed to the Louisiana State Board of Education; delegate to the state constitutional convention (1879), where he sponsored a provision that resulted in the formation of Southern University; surveyor of customs at the Port of New Orleans (1882-1885); studied law at Straight University [now Dillard University] (1885), and was admitted to the bar (1886); U.S. marshal in New York City (1892-1895). Died in December 1921 in Washington, D.C. Further reading, James Haskins, *Pinkney Benton Stewart Pinchback* (1973).

---

on this day in history...

1897, Sidney Bechet, pioneer jazz saxophonist, was born in New Orleans, La. (d. 1959).

1913, Clara Stanton Jones, first African-American president of the American Librarian Association, was born in St. Louis, Mo.

1969, John B. McLendon signed a contract with the Denver Nuggets, making him the first African-American ABA coach.

MAY 14   **GOVERNMENT OFFICIALS & POLITICIANS**

CHARLES BURLEIGH PURVIS

Physician, educator, and hospital administrator. Born on April 14, 1842, in Philadelphia, Pa. Oberlin College, Wooster Medical College [now Case Western Reserve] in Cleveland (M.D., 1865). Worked as a military nurse at Camp Barker in D.C. (1864), and acting assistant surgeon in the Union Army (1865-1869); assistant surgeon at Freedmen's Hospital in D.C. (1869-1881), surgeon-in-chief (1882-1894), **first African-American in charge of an civilian hospital**; instructor of materia medica, therapeutics, botany, and medical jurisprudence at Howard University (1869-1873), Thaddeus Stevens Chair (1871-1872), professor of obstetrics and the diseases of women (1873-1888), professor of obstetrics and gynecology (1889-1907), president of the medical faculty (1899-1900), and professor emeritus (1907-1929). Helped established the National Medical Society of the District of Columbia (1870); secretary and treasurer of Howard University (1873-1896), credited with saving the medical college during the financial panic of 1873; worked at Howard without pay (1873-1906); member of the Howard board of trustees (1908-1926); **first person called to the White House to treat President Garfield, after an assassination attempt at a Washington railroad station** (1881). Lobbied successfully from Congress for an appropriation for a $600,000 building for Freedmen's Hospital (1903); served on the D.C. Board of Education, Board of Health, and Washington Board of Health; admitted to the Massachusetts Medical Society (1904). Died on January 30, 1929, in Los Angeles, Calif. Further reading, Thomas Holt, _A Special Mission: The Story of Freedmen's Hospital, 1862-1962_ (1975).

---

on this day in history...

1884,   Rosalie Virginia McClendon, organizer of the Negro People's Theater in New York City, was born in Greenville, N.C.
1909,   Lester Young, jazz saxophonist nicknamed "Prez" by Billie Holiday, was born in Woodville, Miss. (d. 1959).

AUGUST 27   **MEDICAL PIONEERS**

EMMETT JAY SCOTT

Journalist, administrator, politician, and businessman.   Born on February 13, 1873, in Houston, Texas.   Wiley College.   Reporter for the *Houston Post* (1890-1893); **founder and editor of the *Houston Freeman*** (1894-1897), an African-American weekly newspaper; secretary to Norris Wright Cuney, Texas' leading African-American politician in the late 19th century. **Special assistant to Booker T. Washington** (1897-1915); sent to Liberia as a U.S. commissioner (1909), to study the country's diplomatic and economic problems; secretary of Tuskegee Institute (1912-1919); appointed **special assistant to the U.S. secretary of war in charge of Negro affairs during World War I**; wrote *Scott's Official History of the Negro in the World War* (1919); secretary-treasurer and business manager of Howard University (1919-1932), and secretary (1919-1938). Principal organizer and secretary of the National Negro Business League (1900-1915); member of the Republican Colored Advisory Committee; director of Sun Shipbuilding Company's all-Negro Yard No. 4 in Chester, Pa., during World War II; had business interest in Afro-American Realty Company of Harlem, *Voice of the Negro* magazine, African Union County, Bank of Mound Bayou, and Standard Life Insurance County. Died on December 12, 1957, in Washington, D.C.   Further reading, James E. Waller, "Emmett Jay Scott: The Public Life of a Private Secretary" (M.A. thesis, University of Maryland, 1971).

---

on this day in history...

1940,   Edward T. Lewis, publisher of *Essence* magazine, was born in the Bronx, N.Y.

1942,   The first African-American World War II Army division, the 93rd Infantry, was activated at Fort Huachuca, Ariz.

MONROE ALPHEUS MAJORS

Physician, author, editor, and civil rights leader. Born on October 12, 1864, in Waco, Texas. West Texas College; Tillotson Normal and Collegiate Institute; Central Tennessee College (B.A., 1886); Meharry Medical College (M.D., 1886). Practiced medicine in Austin, Calvert, Texas., Los Angeles, and Waco (1890-1895, 1901), where he established the **first African-American owned drug store in the Southwest** and organized the Colored Hospital (1893), serving as superintendent (1899-1900); also practiced in Decatur, Ill. (1895-1898), Chicago (1901-1903), and in California (1923-1955). Organized the nation's first African-American medical association, Lone Star Medical Association (1886), and served as president of the renamed Lone Star State Medical, Dental, and Pharmaceutical Association (1894); passed the California Board of Examiner (1889); editor of the *Texas Searchlight* (1893-1895); became the **first African-American Texan to practice law**. Lectured in hygiene and sanitation at the Los Angeles Medical College and Paul Quinn College (1891-1894). Edited the *Los Angeles Western News*, where he helped to integrate the police force, city public works, and in the office of the assessor and collectors of taxes; compiled *Noted Negro Women: Their Triumphs and Activities* (1893); associate editor of the *Indianapolis Freeman* (1898-1899), where he published a weekly column "Majors Melange;" editor of the *Chicago Conservator*; published "Ode to Frederick Douglass" (1917), and one of the **first books for African-American children**, *First Steps to Nursery Rhymes* (1921). Died on December 10, 1960, in Los Angeles, Calif. Further reading, J.A. Chatman, *Lone Star State Medical, Dental, and Pharmaceutical History* (1959).

---

on this day in history...

1900,   Hale Woodruff, painter of the "Amistad" murals, was born in Cairo, Ill.
1945,   Melvin Watt, North Carolina 12th District congressman, was born in Steele Creek, N.C.
1960,   Brandford Marsalis, *The Tonight Show* musical director, was born in New Orleans, La.

AUGUST 26   MEDICAL PIONEERS

ROBERT MARA ADGER

Businessman, political activist, and bibliophile. Born into slavery in 1837 in Charleston, S.C. Moved to Philadelphia and attended Bird School, one of the nation's earliest African-American educational institutions. Founded the Benjamin Banneker Institute (1853), a literary-political organization; joined the Black Enlistment Committee and recruited Negro men to fight on the Union Army side during the Civil War; organized the Fraternal Society (1860), a group of refugees from South Carolina concerned with gaining equal rights; delegate to the National Conference of Colored Men (Syracuse, 1864). Benjamin Banneker Institute's delegate to the Pennsylvania Equal Rights League's state conference (Harrisburg, 1865), where he urged "our young colored men to organize among themselves institutions tending to their intellectual and moral elevation;" printed *A Portion of a Catalogue of Rare Books and Pamphlets* (1894); **organized the Afro-American Historical Society** (1897); continued a legacy of preserving materials, which dated back to the Reading Room Society (1828), reportedly the first African-American library. Died on June 10, 1910, in Philadelphia, Pa. Further reading, James G. Spady, "The Afro-American Historical Society: The Nucleus of Black Bibliophiles, 1897-1923," (*Negro History Bulletin,* June/July 1974, pp. 255-56).

---

on this day in history...

1840,	James Milton Turner, U.S. consul general to Liberia, was born in St. Louis, Mo. (d. 1915).
1929,	John Conyers, Jr., of Michigan, chairman of the U.S. House Government Operations Committee, was born in Detroit, Mich.
1966,	Stokely Carmichael was elected chairman of the SNCC.
1966,	Janet Damita Jackson, Grammy Award-winning recording artist, was born in Gary, Ind.

MAY 16

HISTORIANS

MARY ELIZABETH MAHONEY

Nurse, civil rights activist, and suffragist.   Born on May 7, 1845, in Boston, Mass.   Worked at the New England Hospital for Women and Children as a cook, wash, and scrub (1863-1878), and graduated from the hospital's School of Nursing (1879), becoming the nation's **first African-American professional nurse**. Registered with the Nurses Directory at the Massachusetts Medical Library in Boston; employed, mainly, as a nurse in private homes in Massachusetts, New Jersey, North Carolina, and D.C., because most hospitals refused to hire an African-American nurse; became one of the **first African-American members of the American Nursing Association**. Supported the organization of the National Association of Colored Graduate Nurses (1908), and delivered the welcoming address at their first annual conference (Boston, 1909); awarded life membership in the NACGN and was elected national chaplain (1911), where she was responsible for the opening prayers and the induction of new officers, instructing them in their new duties and responsibilities. Moved to New York and headed the Howard Orphan Asylum for Black Children in Kings Park, Long Island (1911-1912); became one of the **first women to register to vote in Boston**, after the ratification of the 19th Amendment (1920). Died on January 4, 1926, in Massachusetts.   Further reading, Mable K. Staupers, _No Time for Prejudice: A Story of the Integration of Negroes in Nursing in the U.S._ (1961).

---

on this day in history...

1925,   The Brotherhood of Sleeping Car Porters was started in the hall of the Imperial Elks in New York City and was described as "the greatest labor mass meeting ever held of, for and by Negro working men."

1927,   Althea Gibson, first African-American woman Wimbledon, French Open, and U.S. Open champion, was born in Silver, S.C.

AUGUST 25   **MEDICAL PIONEERS**

DELILAH ISONTIUM BEASLEY

Journalist and historian.   Born in 1871 in Cincinnati, Ohio.   Wrote for the *Cleveland Gazette* and *Cincinnati Enquirer*; trained as a masseuse in Chicago; studied hydrotherapy, gymnastics, and diagnosis in Springfield, Ohio; **conducted extensive research of African-Americans in the Far West**; became head operator of a bath house at a Michigan family resort. Moved to Berkeley, Calif. (1910), and worked as a nurse; writer for the *Oakland Tribune* (1915-1925), with her own Sunday column called "Activities Among Negroes;" conducted a campaign to persuade San Francisco area editors and elsewhere not to use words such as "darky" and "nigger." Represented the *Tribune* and the Alameda County League of Colored Women Voters at the National Conference of Women Voters (Richmond, 1925), the only African-American woman with press credentials; represented the *Tribune* at the International Council of Women (Washington, 1925); published *The Negro Trail Blazers of California* (1919), which dealt with Spanish exploration and slavery, the earliest African-American settlers and their struggle for civil rights, and the turn-of-the-century conditions. Died in 1934.   Further reading, <u>Richard N. Dillion</u>, *<u>Humbugs and Heroes: A Gallery of California Pioneers</u>* (1970).

---

on this day in history...

1875,	The first Kentucky Derby was won by an African-American jockey named Oliver Lewis riding *Aristides*.
1915,	The National Baptist Convention, the nation's largest African-American organization, was chartered.
1937,	Hazel O'Leary, first African-American U.S. secretary of energy, was born in Newport News, Va.
1954,	The U.S. Supreme Court handed down a decision, in the case of *Brown vs. Brown*, outlawing school segregation.
1969,	Thomas Kilgore was unanimously elected the first African-American president of the American Baptist Convention.

MAY 17   **HISTORIANS**

MILES VANDAHURST LYNK

Physician. Born on June 3, 1871, in Brownsville, Texas. Meharry Medical College (M.D., 1891); Walden University (M.S., 1900); Alabama A&M University; University of Tennessee (LL.B., 1902). Practiced medicine (1891-1901); began publishing of the *Medical and Surgical Observer* (1892), a forum for the expression of medical findings and opinions of African-American physicians, which was the **first medical journal issued by an African-American in the U.S.**; founder and president of University of West Tennessee (1900-1923); **first suggested an organization of African-American physicians, which became the National Medical Association**. Died in 1957. Further reading, Herbert M. Morias, *History of the Negro in Medicine* (1967).

---

on this day in history...

1854,   John Van Surly DeGrasse became the first member of African descent of an American medical association (the Massachusetts Medical Society).

1933,   Lucy Ellen Moton, 37-year principal of Miner Normal School in D.C., died in New York City (b. 1851).

1950,   Edith S. Sampson was appointed the first African-American U.S. representative to the U.N.

1964,   Blair Underwood, actor, was born in Tacoma, Wash.

AUGUST 24   **MEDICAL PIONEERS**

WILLIAM CARL BOLIVAR

Journalist, historical researcher, and bibliophile. Born on April 18, 1849, in Philadelphia, Pa. Bird School; Institute of Colored Youth [now Cheyney State University]. Worked in the War Department in Washington, D.C.; employee of John Ashhurst & County (1866-1914), a Philadelphia banking concern; joined the Benjamin Banneker Institute, an organization responsible for preserving African-American history, which instilled in him the desire to become **one of the most active bibliophiles of the 19th and 20th centuries**; player, publicist, and organizer for the Pythian Baseball Club (1867-1897); helped found the Mutual Baseball League. Began publishing articles on African-Americans, the U.S., Pennsylvania, and Philadelphia for the *Philadelphia Tribune* (1892), using the pen name "Pencil Pusher;" **organizer of the Afro-American Historical Society** (1897), a forerunner of Carter Woodson's Association for the Study of Negro Life; director of the department of Negro history at Downingtown Industrial and Agricultural School in Pennsylvania (1903-1907), where he pioneered teaching Negro history to wide audiences; wrote the booklet *A Brief History of St. Thomas P.E. Church* (1908); elected a corresponding member of the Negro Society for Historical Research in Yonkers, N.Y. (1912). Died on November 12, 1914, in Philadelphia, Pa. Further reading, Henry L. Phillips, *William Carl Bolivar: A Eulogy* (1914).

---

on this day in history...

1946, Reggie Martinez Jackson, baseball's "Mr. October," was born in Wyncote, Pa.

MAY 18   **HISTORIANS**

THEODORE KENNETH LAWLESS

Dermatologist.   Born on December 12, 1892, in Thibodeaux, La.   Talladega College (B.A., 1914); Northwestern University School of Medicine (M.D., 1919; M.S., 1920); Columbia University; fellow of dermatology and syphilogy at Massachusetts General Hospital (1920-1921), St. Louis Hospital in Paris, France (1921-1922), and at Kaiser Joseph Hospital in Vienna, Austria (1922-1924); studied dermatology at the Harvard Pathologist Institute in Freiburg, Germany (1921-1922).   Instructor at Northwestern University School of Medicine (1924-1941); associate examiner in dermatology for the National Board of Medical Examiners; consultant to the U.S. Chemical Warfare Board; operated a dermatology clinic on Chicago's southside; became senior attending physician at Provident Hospital. Winner of the Harmon Award (1929), for outstanding achievements in medicine; **awarded the NAACP Spingarn Medal (1954), for his outstanding work in research of skin and skin-related diseases**; became president of the board of trustees at Dillard University (1959), where he helped secure a $700,000 dormitory building for the school. Died in 1959.   Further reading, Herbert M. Morias, *History of the Negro in Medicine* (1967).

---

on this day in history...

1755,	Jean Baptiste Lislet-Geoffroy became the first member of African descent of the French Academy of Science.
1861,	James Stone became the first Negro to fight for the Union Army during the Civil War.
1892,	O.E. Brown patented the horse shoe.
1900,	The National Negro Business League, led by Booker T. Washington, was formed in Boston, Mass.
1942,	Johnny Ford, Tuskegee mayor, was born in Tuskegee, Ala.
1951,	William Burney, Augusta's first African-American mayor, was born in Augusta, Maine.

MEDICAL PIONEERS

JOHN EDWARD BRUCE

Journalist and historian who was called the **nation's "first Black Nationalist."** Born into slavery on February 22, 1856, in Piscataway, Md. Emancipated (1860), and moved to Washington, D.C.; began to write as a correspondent for African-American newspapers (1874), in Boston, Washington, St. Louis, New York, and Buffalo; founded the *Argus* (1879), *Sunday Item* (1880), and the *Washington Grit* (1884); served as editor of the *Norfolk Republican* (1882), and assistant editor and business manager of the *Commonwealth* of Baltimore (1884); began writing under the column head of "Bruce Grit" for the *Cleveland Gazette* and the *New York Age* (1884); associate editor of *Howard's American Magazine* (1896-1901). Moved to New York and founded the *Chronicle* of New York City (1897), and the *Weekly Standard* of Yonkers (1898); became editor of the *Masonic Quarterly*; worked with the Afro-American League and the Afro-American Council; published *Short Biographical Sketches of Eminent Negro Men and Women in Europe and the United States* (1910). Helped organize the Negro Society for Historical Research (1911); supported Marcus Garvey and the Universal Negro Improvement Association; contributing editor and columnist for the publications the *Negro World* and the *Daily Negro Times*; retired from the New York Port Authority (1922). Died on August 7, 1924, in New York City. Further reading, Robert L. Crowder, "John Edward Bruce: Pioneer Black Nationalist," (*Afro-Americans in New York Life and History* 2, #2, July 1978).

---

on this day in history...

1919,   Malcolm X, founder of the Organization of Afro-American Unity, was born in Omaha, Neb.
1952,   Grace Jones, singer, actress, and model, was born in Kingston, Jamaica.
1991,   Willy T. Ribbs became the first African-American to qualify for the Indianapolis 500.

MAY 19   **HISTORIANS**

WILLIAM AUGUSTUS HINTON

Physician, bacteriologist, educator, and author. Born on December 15, 1883, in Chicago, Ill. University of Kansas; Harvard University (B.S., 1905; M.D., 1912). Taught at Walden University in Nashville, Langston, Okla., Tufts University Medical and Dental Schools, and lectured at Simmons College. Worked in the pathology laboratory, Massachusetts Department of Public Health (1912-1915); director of the Wassermann Laboratory and physician-in-chief of the department of Clinical Laboratories of the Boston Dispensary (1915-1952); instructor in preventive medicine and hygiene at the Harvard Medical School (1918-1921), instructor in bacteriology and immunology (1921-1946), lecturer (1921-1949), and professor of preventive medicine and hygiene (1949-1950), becoming **Harvard's first African-American professor**, and later, professor emeritus (1950-1959). Developed and perfected his world-renowned serological test for syphilis--the Hinton Test (1934), which met the requirements of mass screening, quick results, simplicity, replicability, and unambiguity and was reported to be the best test of its kind by the U.S. Public Health Service; wrote the textbook, *Syphilis and its Treatment* (1936), **first medical textbook by an African-American to be published**. Special consultant to the U.S. Department of Health; consultant to the Massachusetts School for Crippled Children in Boston (1946-1949); elected life member of the American Social Science Association (1948); declined the NAACP Spingarn Medal (1938), the only year that nobody received the medal. Died in 1959. Further reading, James E. Teele, "Hinton, William Augustus," *Dictionary of American Negro Biography* (1982).

---

on this day in history...

1831, Nat Turner began a slave revolt in Virginia.
1917, John Lee Hooker, blues great known as the "Boogie Man," was born in Clarksdale, Miss.
1942, Bill Johnson, first African-American mayor of Rochester, N.Y., was born in Lynchburg, Va.
1989, Huey P. Newton, co-founder of the Black Panther Party, was murdered in Oakland, Calif. (b. 1942).

AUGUST 22   MEDICAL PIONEERS

JOHN WESLEY CROMWELL

Editor, journalist, educator, and historian.   Born into slavery on September 5, 1846, in Portsmouth, Va.   Howard University School of Law (1874).   Emancipated (1851); employed by the Baltimore Association for the Moral and Intellectual Improvement of the Colored People as an agent of the American Missionary Association, and taught in Withersville, Richmond, and Southhampton, Va.; elected delegate and appointed clerk to the first Republican convention (Richmond, 1867); admitted to the bar (1874); organized Alexandria (Va.) *People's Advocate* (1876); chief examiner of the division of money orders in the Post Office Department and register of money order accounts (1874-1885). Elected president of the Washington's Bethel Literary and Historical Association (1881); secretary of the American Negro Academy; **inspired Carter Woodson and others to found the Association for the Study of Negro Life and History**. Published *History of the Bethel Literary and Historical Association* (1896), *The Negro in American History: Men and Women Eminent in the Evolution of the American of African Descent* (1914), "The Aftermath of Nat Turner's Insurrection" (1920), "First Negro Church in the District of Columbia" (1922), and "The Challenge of the Disfranchised; A Plea for the Enforcement of the 15th Amendment" (1924). Died on April 14, 1927, in Washington, D.C.   Further reading, William J. Simmons, *Men of Mark: Eminent, Progressive, and Rising* (1887).

---

on this day in history...

1881,	Mary Elizabeth Branch, first woman president of Tillotson College in Austin, was born in Farmville, Va. (d. 1944).
1890,	John Stephens Durham was appointed U.S. consul to the Dominican Republic by President Harrison.
1923,	Dedication began for the new Abyssinian Baptist Church and Community House in Harlem.
1945,	Harold Eugene Ford, Tennessee 9th District congressman, was born in Memphis, Tenn.

MAY 20   **HISTORIANS**

DOROTHY BOULDING FEREBEE

Physician and educator. Born in 1890 in Norfolk, Va. Simmons College; Tufts Medical School with honors (M.D., 1927), interned in Freedmen's Hospital in D.C. Founder and president of the Southeast Neighborhood House in D.C. (1919-1932), a place for African-American children of working mothers; instructor in obstetrics, director at Howard University Medical School, and head of the Student Health Service (1919-1968); directed the Mississippi Health Project, where she helped treat African-Americans suffering from malaria, diphtheria, smallpox, dental defects, and malnutrition (1935-1942), which turned into the **first African-American hospital in Mississippi**, Taborian [now Mound Bayou Hospital]. Became supreme basileus of Alpha Kappa Alpha (1939); succeeded Mary McLeod Bethune as president of the National Council of Negro Women (1949); became a member of the executive board of the White House's Children and Youth Council and UNICEF; and awarded Tufts University's first alumni achievement award (1959); appointed to the Council for Food and Peace; lectured on preventive medicine in Africa. Served as a special assistant for consumer affairs in the Johnson administration, member of the national board of the YWCA, president of the Medico-Chirugical Society of D.C., and the Washington Urban League. Died on September 14, 1980, in Washington, D.C. Further reading, Rayford W. Logan, _Howard University: The First Hundred Years, 1867-1967_ (1967).

---

on this day in history...

1921,	Wendell Oliver Scott, Sr., stockcar racing's first African-American NASCAR winner, was born in Danville, Va. (d. 1990).
1924,	I. Owen Funderburg, president and CEO of Citizen's Trust Bank of Atlanta, was born in Monticello, Ga.
1931,	Phillipa Duke Schuyler, pianist and composer, was born in New York City (d. 1967).
1932,	Melvin Van Peebles, actor, director, and playwright, was born in Chicago, Ill.
1936,	Wilt Chamberlain, NBA all-time leading rebounder, was born in Philadelphia, Pa.

AUGUST 21   MEDICAL PIONEERS

SARA MARIE DELANEY

Librarian and bibliotherapist.   Born on February 26, 1889, in Rochester, N.Y.   Miss McGovern's School of Social Work.   Librarian at the 135th Street Branch of the New York Public Library (1920-1923), when the Harlem area had shifted from a neighborhood of Irish, Jews, and Italians to one of African-Americans; head librarian at the Veteran's Administration in Tuskegee, Ala. (1924-1958), where she was a **pioneer bibliotherapist** (i.e, the treatment of a patient through selected reading); elected to represent American librarians at a conference (Rome, 1934), where she conducted research at the Vatican library; instructed library students from the universities of Illinois, North Carolina, and Atlanta, and hospital librarians from England and South Africa on her bibliotherapy methods; started a special department for the blind and taught Braille. Councillor for the Hospital Library Division of the American Library Association (1946-1951); founder of the Friendship League of America; instituted the first State Conference for the Blind in Alabama; selected as "Woman of the Year" by the National Urban League (1950); received an honorary doctorate degree from Atlanta University. Died on May 4, 1958, in Tuskegee, Ala.   Further reading, Betty K. Gubert, "Sara P. Delaney," *Notable Black American Women* (1992).

---

on this day in history...

1904,   Thomas Wright ("Fats" Waller), first to use the organ as a jazz instrument, was born in New York City (d. 1943).
1952,   Lawrence Tero ("Mr. T") was born in Chicago, Ill.

MAY 21   **HISTORIANS**

CHARLES RICHARD DREW

Surgeon and scientist. Born on June 3, 1904, in Washington, D.C. Amherst College (B.A., 1926), head football coach at Morgan State College (1926-1928); McGill University in Montreal (Master of Surgery, 1933); Columbia University (Med.D.Sc., 1940), becoming the first African-American to earn a Doctor of Science degree; intern and resident at Montreal General Hospital and Freedmen's Hospital in D.C. Resident in surgery at New York City's Presbyterian Hospital (1938-1940), while a General Education Board fellow; instructor in pathology at Howard University Freedmen's Hospital (1935-1936), instructor in surgery and assistant surgeon (1937-1938), professor and chairman of the department of surgery (1941-1950), professor and chief surgeon (1942-1944), chief of staff (1944-1946), medical director (1946-1948). Published *Banked Blood: A Study in Blood Preservation* (1940); medical director of the "Blood Bank Project" (1940), in charge of collecting and drying blood plasma to be used for transfusions on the battlefield during World War II; **organizer and first director of the American Red Cross Blood Bank** in New York City (1941), and assistant director of the National Research Council, responsible for collecting blood for the U.S. Army and Navy; consultant to the surgeon-general of the U.S. Army (1949). Awarded the NAACP Spingarn Medal (1944), for his work in blood plasma banks, which served as a model for the system of blood banks throughout the world; International College of Surgeons fellow. Died on April 1, 1950, in Burlington, N.C. Further reading, Claude H. Organ, Jr., and Margaret M. Kosiba, *A Century of Black Surgeons--The U.S.A. Experience*, vol. 1 (1987).

---

on this day in history...

1619,	Negro history began in "English America," when a Dutch ship with 20 Negroes arrived at Jamestown, Va.
1941,	William Herbert Gray, president of the United Negro College Fund, was born in Baton Rouge, La.
1942,	Isaac Hayes, Grammy and Academy Award-winning recording artist, was born in Covington, Tenn.
1954,	Quinn Buckner, head coach of the NBA Dallas Mavericks, was born in Phoenix, Ill.

AUGUST 20   **MEDICAL PIONEERS**

WILLIAM LEO HANSBERRY

Historian and pioneer Africanist. Born in 1894 in Gloster, Miss. Atlanta University, where he read DuBois' *The Negro* (1916), and was inspired to go to Boston and study African anthropology; Harvard University (B.S., 1922; M.A., 1931); University of Chicago; Oxford University; Cairo University. Fulbright scholar in Africa (1953-1954), **the first African-American to devote his life exclusively to the study of Africa and its ancient civilizations**; taught history, African archeology, psychology, and sociology at Straight University [now Dillard University] (1921-1922); appointed special and part-time lecturer on ancient African civilizations at Howard University (1922), where he offered the first courses in African history at any American university; co-founded the African-American Institute (1953), Africa House, and the All-African Students Union of the Americas; retired from Howard University as associate professor of history (1959). First recipient of the Haile Selassie I Prize Trust for pioneering work in African history, archeology, and anthropology (1964); Morgan State University honorary (LL.D., 1965); contracted by Random House for a half-million words on African history, which he was working on until his death; *Pillars of Ethiopian History: The William Leo Hansberry History Notebook, Volume I* (1975), published from his private papers. Died on October 17, 1965, in Chicago, Ill. Further reading, Michael R. Winston, *Howard University Department of History 1913-1973* (1973).

---

on this day in history...

1930,	LaSalle D. LeFall, Jr., first African-American president of the American Cancer Society, was born in Tallahassee, Fla.
1940,	Bernard Shaw, CNN anchorman, was born in Chicago, Ill.
1959,	Benjamin O. Davis, Jr., became the first African-American general in the U.S. Air Force.
1970,	Naomi Campbell, international supermodel, was born in London, England.
1989,	Oprah Winfrey received an honorary doctorate in humane letters from Morehouse College.

MAY 22   **HISTORIANS**

JAMES DERHAM

Physician.   Born into slavery on May 1, 1762, in Philadelphia, Pa.   Learned medicine from his masters: John Kearsley, a prominent Philadelphia physician, who taught him how to mix medicines and perform other minor chores; George West, who served as an apothecary with the British forces in America, who allowed him to perform many duties as a doctor; Robert Dow, a New Orleans physician, who employed him in the performance of many medical services. Emancipated (1783); became fluent in French and Spanish; became the **nation's earliest known African-American physician** who secured a license to practice medicine in New Orleans in the 1780s, where he established a successful practice treating African-American and white patients, earning around $3,000 annually. One of his papers, "An Account of the Putrid Sore Throat," was read by Benjamin Rush before the College of Physicians of Philadelphia (1789); treated 50 New Orleans yellow fever victims (1796), losing the fewest patients of any doctor in the city (six); lost only 11 out of 46 patients during a second outbreak of yellow fever (1798), by using a "concoction of garden sorrel and sugar;" restricted from practicing medicine by the commissioners of the New Orleans Cabildo (1801), he soon disappeared from sight.   Further reading, Wilson Armistead, _A Tribute for the Negro_ (1848).

on this day in history...

1954,   Ralph Bunche was named undersecretary of the U.N.

AUGUST 19   **MEDICAL PIONEERS**

ZORA NEALE HURSTON

Anthropologist and folklorist who was known as the **"queen of the renaissance."** Born on January 7, 1901, in Eatonville, Fla. Howard University; Barnard College (B.A., anthropology, 1928). First short story, "John Redding Goes to Sea" was published in Howard University's *The Stylus* (1921); wrote "Drenched in the Light" (1924), "Spunk" (1925), and "Color Struck" (1925), which were published in the National Urban League's *Opportunity* magazine; co-founded the literary organization, Fire (1926), along with Langston Hughes and Wallace Thurman. Wrote her first published novel *Jonah's Gourd Vine* (1934); awarded Rosenwald fellowship (1934), Guggenheim field research fellowship (1935); wrote *Mules and Men* (1938), reportedly the first investigation of voodoo practices among African-Americans. Wrote *Their Eyes Were Watching God* (1937), a love story dealing with African-American relationships; *Tell My Horse* (1938), which dealt with Caribbean folklore; *Moses, Man of the Mountain* (1939), in which she gave Moses a 20th century African-American personality. Sailed to British Honduras (1947), to do research among African-American communities in Central America; member of the American Folklore Society, Anthropological Society, Ethnological Society, New York Academy of Sciences, and the American Association for the Advancement of Science. Died January 28, 1960, in Fort Pierce, Fla. Further reading, Robert Hemenway, *Zora Neale Hurston, A Literary Biography* (1977).

---

on this day in history...

1844,   Charles Edmund Nash, Louisiana's first African-American congressman, was born in Opelousas, La. (d. 1913).

1871,   L. Bell patented a locomotive smoke stack.

1900,   William H. Carney, U.S. Army sergeant and Civil War hero with the 54th Massachusetts Colored Infantry, became the first African-American to receive the Medal of Honor.

1926,   Aileen Clark Hernandez, first African-American president of the National Organization of Women, was born in Brooklyn, N.Y.

1954,   Marvelous Marvin Hagler, boxing great, was born in Newark, N.J.

MAY 23   **HISTORIANS**

ULYSSES GRANT DAILEY

Physician, surgeon, author, and editor.   Born on August 3, 1885, in Donaldsonville, La.   Straight [now Dillard] University; Northwestern University Medical School (M.D., 1906), where he served as assistant demonstrator of anatomy (1906-1908); postgraduate work in London, Paris, and Vienna.   Ambulance surgeon for the Chicago Civil Service (1907-1912); gynecologist in Providence Hospital in Chicago (1907-1912), associate surgeon (1910-1912), attending surgeon (1912-1926), surgeon-in-chief and senior attending surgeon (1926-1932), and senior attending surgeon emeritus (1932-1961); instructor in clinical surgery at Chicago Medical College (1916-1918); attending surgeon at Fort Dearborn Hospital in Chicago (1920-1926); founder and surgeon-in-chief of the Dailey Sanitarium in Chicago (1926-1932). Served as president of the National Medical Association (1916-1917), and editor-in-chief of its *Journal* (1948-1949); wrote more than 40 articles for the *Journal of the National Medical Association*, including "The Future of the Negro in Medicine" (1929), and "Proposals with Reference to the Idea of a Negro College of Surgeons" (1942); co-founder and member of the international board of trustees and fellow of the International College of Surgeons; one of the **first African-American members of the American College of Surgeons**; toured Pakistan, India, Ceylon, the Belgium Congo, Kenya, Uganda, Ghana, Nigeria, Senegal, and Liberia for the U.S. State Department (1953-1954). Died in 1961 in Chicago, Ill.   Further reading, Herbert M. Morias, *The History of the Negro in Medicine* (1967).

---

on this day in history...

1899,	Frank Horne, Harlem Renaissance poet, was born in Brooklyn, N.Y.
1934,	Rayford Johnson, Sullivan Award-winning Olympic decathlon champion, was born in Hillsboro, Texas.
1935,	Gail Fisher, first African-American Emmy winner, was born in Orange, N.J.
1963,	James Meredith became the first African-American graduate of the University of Alabama.
1970,	Malcolm Jamal-Warner, actor, was born in Jersey City, N.J.

AUGUST 18   **MEDICAL PIONEERS**

LUTHER PORTER JACKSON

Educator, historian, and civic leader. Born in 1892 in Louisville, Ky. Fisk University (B.A., 1914; M.A., 1916); University of Kansas; City College of New York; Columbia University; University of Chicago (Ph.D., history, 1937). Staff member at Topeka Industrial Institute in Kansas (1913-1920); teacher and director of the academic department at Voorhees Industrial School in Denmark, S.C. (1915-1918); director of the high school department and teacher of history at Virginia Normal Industrial Institute [now Virginia State University] (1922-1925), associate professor of history (1925-1929), and professor of history and chairman of the history and social science unit (1929-1950). Became **an authority on the Negro in Virginia**; wrote a weekly column "Rights and Duties in a Democracy" for the *Norfolk Journal and Guide* (1942-1948); appointed to the Virginia World War II Historical Commission; wrote *Free Negro Labor and Property Holding in Virginia 1830-1860* (1942), his principal scholarly work. Founded the Virginia Voters League; earned the nickname **"Mr. NAACP,"** for his enthusiasm in local and state fundraising campaigns; published over 61 books, articles, pamphlets, news articles, and brochures that covered history of civic and community activities. Died on April 20, 1950, in Petersburg, Va. Further reading, Earl E. Thorpe, *Black Historians, A Critique* (1969).

---

on this day in history...

1881,	Paul Quinn College was chartered in Waco, Texas.
1940,	Mary Hatwood Futrell, National Education Association president, was born in Alta Vista, Va.
1944,	Patricia Louise Holte ("Patti Labelle"), Grammy Award-winning singer, was born in Philadelphia, Pa.
1951,	The Municipal Appeals Court in Washington, D.C., outlawed segregation in D.C. restaurants.
1954,	Peter Marshall Murray was elected the first African-American president of the New York County Medical Society.

MAY 24

HISTORIANS

ALEXANDER THOMAS AUGUSTUS

Surgeon, medical school professor, and soldier.   Born on March 8, 1825, in Norfolk, Va.   Studied medicine under William Gibson; Trinity Medical College of the University of Toronto (M.D., 1856).   Served as "surgeon of U.S. colored troops" with the Union Army during the Civil War, assigned to the 7th U.S. Colored Infantry at Camp Stanton, Md. (1863-1864), becoming the **first African-American physician to obtain a medical commission** and the highest ranking African-American officer with a rank of major. Became the first African-American head of Freedmen's Hospital in D.C. (1864), where he lectured on dermatology; served as medical examiner of African-American recruits in Benedict, S.C., and Baltimore; worked in the Department of the South (1865-1866), where he headed a hospital in Savannah; breveted a lieutenant-colonel, U.S. Volunteers, for meritorious service (1865), first African-American to attain that rank; discharged (1866). Professor of anatomy at Howard University (1868-1877), the only African-American of the original five member faculty and the **first African-American faculty member of any American medical school**. Died on December 21, 1890, in Washington, D.C. Further reading, Daniel Smith Lamb, *Howard University Medical Department... A Historical Biographical and Statistical Memoir* (1900).

---

on this day in history...

1887,   Marcus Moziah Garvey, founder of the Universal Negro Improvement Association, was born in Jamaica (d. 1990).

AUGUST 17   MEDICAL PIONEERS

RAYFORD WHITTINGHAM LOGAN

Civil rights activist, scholar, and historian. Born on January 7, 1897, in Washington, D.C. Williams College, Phi Beta Kappa (B.A., 1917; M.A., 1929); Harvard University (M.A., 1932; Ph.D., 1936). Professor of history at Virginia Union University (1925-1930); professor of history at Atlanta University (1933-1938); professor of history at Howard University (1938-1942), head of the department of history (1942-1965), and professor emeritus (1965-1982). Editor of the *Journal of Negro History* and *Negro History Bulletin*; consultant to the U.S. State Department and the NAACP; **pioneer in the study of what he called "Negro history,"** and author of *Diplomatic Relations of the United States with Haiti 1776-1891* (1941), *The Negro and the Post-War World, A Primer* (1945), *The African Mandates in World Politics* (1948), *The Negro in American Life and Thought; The Nadir 1877-1901* (1954), and *The Betrayal of the Negro: From Rutherford B. Hayes to Woodrow Wilson*; **co-editor of the *Dictionary of American Negro Biography* (1982), one of the most comprehensive book of historical African-American biographies ever compiled**. Died on November 4, 1982, in Washington, D.C. Further reading, James A. Page and Jae Min Roh, *Selected Black American, African, and Caribbean Authors: A Bio-Bibliography* (1985).

---

on this day in history...

1926, Miles Dewey Davis, Grammy Award-winning jazz great, was born in St. Louis, Mo. (d. 1991).

1932, K.C. Jones, Olympic gold medal-winning basketball champion, was born in Taylor, Texas.

1934, Jesse Owens broke three world records and tied a fourth within 74 minutes at a University of Michigan track meet, which became known as "the greatest single day in the history of man's ahletic achievement."

1943, Eloise C. ("Leslie" Uggams), Tony Award-winning actress, was born in Washington Heights, N.Y.

MAY 25   **HISTORIANS**

NUMA P. ADAMS

Physician, educator, and medical school dean. Born on February 26, 1885, in Delaplane, Va. Howard University *summa cum laude* (B.A., 1911); Columbia University (M.A., 1912); Rush Medical School of the University of Chicago (M.D., 1924), interned at St. Louis City Hospital #2 and Homer G. Phillips Hospital (1924). Taught in public schools in Pennsylvania (1905-1907); instructor, professor, and head of the department of chemistry at Howard University (1912-1919), and the **first African-American dean of Howard's School of Medicine** (1929-1940), which, according to William M. Cobb, "made possible for the first time assumption of the top responsibility in a medical school by Negro physicians to full responsibility for progress and operation of an institution primarily for their development...;" practiced medicine and surgery in Chicago (1925-1929); assistant medical director of the Victory Life Insurance (1927-1929); instructor of neurology and psychiatry in the Provident School of Nursing. Died on August 29, 1940, in Chicago, Ill. Further reading, Herbert M. Morias, *History of Negro in Medicine* (1967).

---

on this day in history...

1902, Wallace Thurman, Harlem Renaissance writer, was born in Salt Lake City, Utah (d. 1934).

1929, Wyatt Tee Walker, first permanent director of the SCLC, was born in Brockton, Mass.

AUGUST 16   **MEDICAL PIONEERS**

DANIEL PAYNE MURRAY

Librarian, bibliographer, and biographical researcher. Born on March 3, 1852, in Baltimore, Md. Personal assistant to the librarian of Congress (1871-1881), **assistant librarian at the Library of Congress** (1881-1923); prepared the eight-page *Preliminary List of Books and Pamphlets by Negro Authors* and the 11-page *List of Colored Inventors in The United States* for a special display on "Negro Literature" for the American Exhibit at the 1900 Paris Exposition; researched, developed, and compiled the Library of Congress' "Colored Author Collection;" wrote articles for the *Voice of the Negro* (1904-1906). Began writing his "Bibliographia-Africania," a compilation of African-American writers and their biographical data; set out to produce "Historical and Biographical Encyclopedia of the Colored Race Throughout the World" (1910), a six-volume encyclopedia created by African-Americans. Produced a book-length manuscript "Bibliography of African-American Literature and Historical Sketch of African-American Authors and Authorship," which included almost 500 biographies of historical African-American figures and more than 250,000 index cards with book titles, background material, and information on events important to African-American people worldwide (1925), and bequeathed his manuscript to the Wisconsin State Historical Society; member of the Philadelphia's American Negro Historical Society. Died on December 31, 1925, in Washington, D.C. Further reading, Rayford W. Logan and Michael R. Winston, "Murray, Alexander Daniel Payne," *Dictionary of American Negro Biography* (1982).

---

on this day in history...

1891,	Julian Herman Lewis, first African-American to earn a Ph.D. in physiology, was born in Shawneetown, Ill.
1907,	Charles W. Anderson of Kentucky, first African-American elected to a southern state's legislature since Reconstruction, was born in Louisville, Ky. (d. 1960).
1938,	Lem Tucker, Emmy Award-winning broadcaster, was born in Saginaw, Mich.
1949,	Phillip Michael Thomas, actor, was born in Columbus, Ohio.

RICHARD WRIGHT

Author, expatriate, and existentialist who was known as the **"greatest African-American novelist."** Born on September 4, 1908, in Roxie, Miss. Moved to Chicago (1927), worked with the Federal Theater Project, The Federal Writers' Project, and the Southside Writers Club; became a member of the John Reed Club, which promoted the publication of his proletarian poetry in *Left Front*, *The Anvil*, and *New Masses*; member of the Communist Party (1933-1942). Moved to New York City (1937), and worked with the Harlem Bureau of the *Daily Worker*; won the *Story Magazine* prize for "Fire and Cloud," and published *Uncle Tom's Children* (1938), a collection of stories about racial tensions and black resistance in the rural South. Author of: *Native Son* (1939), a portrait of northern urban life in the Chicago ghettoes for an African-American youth named Bigger Thomas who was a product of racism and oppression of American capitalism, which brought him national fame and became the **first novel by an African-American to become a Book-of-the-Month selection**; *Twelve Million Black Voices* (1941), a folk history of the African-American; *The Man Who Lived Underground*; *Black Boy* (1941), an autobiography from his early Mississippi childhood until his departure from Chicago, which became an American classic and made him a culture hero; *I Tried to Be a Communist* (1944), an autobiography; *The Outsider* (1953), which dealt with a psychoanalytical theme; *Black Power* (1954); *The Color Curtain* (1956), a firsthand report on the 1955 Bandung Conference; *White Man, Listen* (1957); *Pagan Spain* (1957); *The Long Dream* (1958). Awarded the NAACP Spingarn Medal (1941), for writing one of the best-selling novels of the year, *Native Son*; broke from the Communist Party (1942); helped organize the Congress of Black Writers and Intellectuals (1946); moved to Paris on a self-imposed exile (1947). Died on November 28, 1960, in Paris, France. Further reading, Constance Webb, *Richard Wright: A Biography* (1968).

---

on this day in history...

1875,	Samuel Coleridge-Taylor, composer, was born in London, England.
1935,	Vernon Eulion Jordan, National Urban League director and presidential adviser, was born in Atlanta, Ga.
1938,	Maxine Waters, California 35th District congresswoman, was born in St. Louis, Mo.
1947,	Elihu Mason Harris, Oakland mayor, was born in Los Angeles, Calif.

AUGUST 15   LITERARY FIGURES

JOEL AUGUSTUS ROGERS

Historian and journalist. Born on September 6, 1883, in Negril, Jamaica. Emigrated to U.S. (1906), and became a naturalized citizen (1917); wrote his first book *From Superman to Man* (1917), a fictionalized conversation between a young educated African-American porter and a southern legislator; published *As Nature Leads* (1919), *The Approaching Storm and How It May Be Averted* (1920), *The Maroons of the West Indies and South America* (1921), *The Ku Klux Spirit* (1923), *This Mongrel World; A Study of Negro-Caucasian Mixing Throughout the Ages in All Countries* (1927), and the *World's Greatest Men of African Descent* (1931). Elected to membership in the Paris Society of Anthropology (1930); covered the Italian invasion of Abyssinia for the *Pittsburgh Courier* (1935-1936); author of *100 Amazing Facts About the Negro, with Complete Proof; a Short Cut to the World History of the Negro* (1934), *The Real Facts About Ethiopia* (1936), *Sex and Race* (3 vols., 1940-1944), and *World's Greatest Men of Color* (1940); member of the American Geographical Society and the Academy of Political Science. Died on March 26, 1965, in New York City. Further reading, W. Burghardt Turner, "Joel Augustus Rogers: An Afro-American Historian," (*Negro History Bulletin*, January 1972, pp. 34-38).

---

on this day in history...

1879,	John Jones, Cook County commissioner and Underground Railroad station operator, died in Chicago, Ill. (b. 1816).
1891,	William Hiram Lawson, the nation's first African-American optometrist, was born in Windsor, Ontario, Canada (d. 1966).
1935,	Ramsey Emanuel Lewis, Grammy Award-winning pianist and composer, was born in Chicago, Ill.
1936,	Louis Gosset, Jr., Academy Award-winning actor, was born in Brooklyn, N.Y.
1942,	Dorie Miller was awarded the Navy Cross for being the first American hero of the Pearl Harbor invasion.

MAY 27   **HISTORIANS**

PHILLIS WHEATLEY-PETERS

Poet.   Born around 1753 in Senegal.   Sold into slavery to merchant tailor Jim and his wife Sussanah Wheatley in colonial Boston (1761), as a personal lady's maid; raised with her master's family, educated in the social graces, learned to read and write, and studied Latin. "On the death of Rev. Mr. George Whitefield" (1770), which was her earliest published poem, gained her wide acceptance in middle and upper class Boston; admitted to membership in the Old South Meeting House (1770), which was an exception to their rule of not admitting African-Americans as communicants; fell ill and was emancipated (1773), and sailed off to England to recuperate, where her reputation as a poet preceded her. Her first book of poems, *Poems on Various Subjects, Religious and Moral* (1773), was published in London; returned to Boston as the **nation's first celebrated African-American poet** (1773), to nurse the dying John Wheatley and his daughter Mary Lathrop and manage their affairs. Her poems: "To a Gentleman of the Navy" (1774), which appeared in *Royal American Magazine*; "To His Excellent General Washington" (1775), which appeared in *Royal American Magazine* and Thomas Paine's *Pennsylvania Magazine*; "An Elegy Sacred to the Memory of that Great Divine, the Reverend and Learned Dr. Samuel Cooper" (1784); "Liberty and Peace" (1784). Died on December 5, 1784, in Boston, Mass.   Further reading, <u>Benjamin Brawley</u>, <u>*Early Negro American Wriers*</u> (1936).

---

on this day in history...

1883,   Wade Washington patented a corn husking machine.
1888,   Granville T. Woods patented a galvanic battery.
1938,   Niara Sudarkasa, president of Lincoln University in Pennsylvania, was born in Fort Lauderdale, Fla.
1942,   Lee Smith, Jr. ("Molefi Kete Asante"), "father of Afrocentricity," was born in Valdosta, Ga.
1959,   Earvin "Magic" Johnson, basketball champion, was born in Lansing, Mich.

AUGUST 14   **LITERARY FIGURES**

ARTHUR ALFONSO SCHOMBURG

Bibliophile, curator, and Mason. Born on January 24, 1874, in San Juan, Puerto Rico. St. Thomas College in the Virgin Islands. Emigrated to U.S. (1891), arriving in New York City; researched and read law for law office of Pryor, Mellis and Harris (1891-1896); taught Spanish; became a Mason (1892), master of Lodge El Sol de Cuba No. 38, and grand secretary of the Grand Lodge (1918-1926); messenger to head of the mailing department Bankers Trust Company on Wall Street (1906-1929). **Co-founder of the Negro Society for Historical Research** (1911), along with John Bruce; elected president of the American Negro Academy (1922); wrote *The Negro Digs Up His Past* (1925); compiled a collection of over 5,000 books, 3,000 manuscripts, 2,000 etchings, and several thousand pamphlets that dealt with Negro history; sold his collection to the Carnegie Corporation, who donated it to the New York City Public Library Division of Negro Literature, History, and Prints (1926). Curator of the Negro Collection in the Fisk University Library; curator of New York Public Library Division of Negro Literature, History, and Prints (1932-1938), which now is called the Schomburg Center for Research in Black Culture, containing over 100,000 volumes of Black history, and over 4.5 million artifacts, photographs, magazines, and manuscripts from throughout the world. Died on June 10, 1938, in New York City. Further reading, Donald Franklin Joyce, "Arthur Alfonso Schomburg: A Pioneering Black Bibliophile," (*Journal of Library History*, April 1975).

---

on this day in history...

1940,	Betty Shabazz, director of communications at Medgar Evers College, was born in Detroit, Mich.
1944,	Gladys Knight, Grammy Award-winning singer, was born in Atlanta, Ga.
1957,	William Tucker, III, California 37th District congressman, was born in Compton, Calif.
1980,	Vincent K. Brooks became the first African-American Captain of Cadets at the U.S. Military Academy.

MAY 28   **HISTORIANS**

GEORGIA DOUGLAS JOHNSON

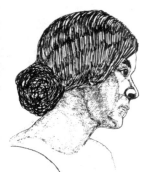

Poet, essayist, educator, government official, and dramatist. Born on September 10, 1877, in Atlanta, Ga. Atlanta University; Oberlin Conservatory of Music; Cleveland College of Music. Taught school in Marietta, Ga., and became an Atlanta assistant school principal; published several books of poetry, including: *The Heart of a Woman* (1918), a book of 62 lyric poems; *Bronze: A Book of Verse* (1922), a book of 56 poems in sonnet, iambic heptameter lines, quatrain, and free verse forms; *An Autumn Love Cycle* (1928), a book of 58 poems chronicling a woman's love affair from beginning to end. Wrote several one-act plays, including: *A Bill to Be Passed* (1922), which showed her advocacy for the passage of the Dyer Anti-Lynching Bill; *And Still They Paused* (1922), which addressed the delay in enactment of the anti-lynching bill; *A Sunday Morning in the South* (1925), which had an anti-lynching theme; *Blue Blood* (1926), which addresses the rape of African-American women by white men after the Civil War and became her first drama to gain public attention. Served as commissioner of Conciliation for the U.S. Department of Labor (1925-1935); **turned her Washington home into a mecca for African-American artists and intellectuals** (1927), with such guests as Sterling Brown, Countee Cullen, W.E.B. DuBois, Alice Dunbar-Nelson, Jessie Faucet, Angelina Grimke, Langston Hughes, James Weldon Johnson, Vachel Lindsay, Alaine Locke, Richard Nugent, Anne Spencer, and Jean Toomer. Wrote the weekly syndicated column, "Homely Philosophy" (1926-1932); organized a correspondence club, the "One World" Washington Social Letter Club (1930-1965); submitted plays to the Federal Theater Project (1935-1939); wrote the poem "Whose Son" during World War II, which was read on the floor of the U.S. Senate and published in the *Congressional Record*. Died on May 14, 1966, in Washington, D.C. Further reading, Gloria T. Hull, *Color, Sex, and Poetry: Three Women Writers of the Harlem Renaissance* (1987).

---

on this day in history...

1881, The first African-American nursing school opened at Spelman College.
1919, Charles Edward Anderson, first African-American to receive a Ph.D. in meteorology, was born in St. Louis, Mo.
1933, Joycelyn Elders, first African-American U.S. surgeon general, was born in Wichita, Kan.
1948, Kathleen Battle, operatic soprano, was born in Portsmouth, Ohio.

AUGUST 13   LITERARY FIGURES

GEORGE WASHINGTON WILLIAMS

Soldier, clergyman, lawyer, and legislator, who was **regarded as "the historian of his race."** Born on October 19, 1849, in Bedford Springs, Pa. Howard University; Wayland Seminary; Newton Theological Institution in Massachusetts (1874); Cincinnati Law School. Served in the Union Army during the Civil War; pastor of the 12th Baptist Church of Boston (1875-1876), New England's oldest and most influential African-American congregation; moved to Washington and became editor of the journal, *The Commoner*, and worked at the D.C. Post Office; installed as the pastor of Cincinnati's Union Baptist Church (1876); worked as a Internal Revenue storekeeper, secretary in the auditor's office of the Cincinnati Southern Railway, and as a columnist for the *Cincinnati Commercial* under the pen name "Aristides." Ohio state representative (1879-1881), serving as chairman of the Committee on State Library and the Committee on Universities and Colleges; author of *History of the Negro Race in America from 1619-1880* in two volumes (1881), first African-American to complete such a comprehensive task. Admitted to the Ohio bar (1881), and the Boston bar (1883); lectured at the World Conference on Foreign Missions (London, 1884); wrote *History of the Negro Troops in the War of the Rebellion* (1887); commissioned to write a series of articles on the Congo in Africa. Died on August 2, 1891, in Blackpool, England. Further reading, John Hope Franklin, "Williams, George Washington," *Dictionary of American Negro Biography* (1982).

on this day in history...

1865, President Andrew Johnson announced his program of Reconstruction.
1958, Ernest Green, eldest of the Little Rock Nine, became the first African-American graduate of Little Rock Central High School.
1973, Tom Bradley was elected Los Angeles' first African-American mayor.
1980, An assassination attempt was made on the life of National Urban League Executive Director Vernon Jordan in Fort Wayne, Ind.
1984, Robert Kimbrough became the first African-American president of the Chicago Dental Society.

MAY 29

HISTORIANS

JAMES LANGSTON HUGHES

Poet, anthologist, translator, playwright, novelist, and columnist who was known as the **"poet laureate of Harlem."** Born on February 1, 1902, in Joplin, Mo. Columbia University; Lincoln University of Pennsylvania (B.A., 1929). His classic early poem, "The Negro Speaks of Rivers" (1921), was first published in the NAACP's *Crisis* magazine; went to the Azores, the Canary Islands, and Africa as a mess steward (1922), to Paris and Genoa (1923), and moved to Washington and worked as a bus boy (1924). Won *Opportunity* magazine's first prize in poetry (1925); some of the more significant works of the **nation's best known African-American poet** included *The Weary Blues* (1926), *Fine Clothes to the Jew* (1927), *The Dream Keeper and Other Poems* (1932), *Shakespeare in Harlem* (1942), *Fields of Wonder* (1947), *One-Way Ticket* (1949), *Montage of a Dream Deferred* (1951), *Ask Your Mama: 12 Moods for Jazz* (1961), and *The Panther and the Lash* (1967); took a poetry reading tour of the South and West (1931-1932). Went to Spain as a correspondent for the *Baltimore Afro-American*, reporting on their Civil War; playwright of *Mulatto* (1935-1937), the **first full-length play by an African-American writer to run on Broadway**; founded three important theater groups (1938-1940), Harlem's Suitcase Theater, Los Angeles' Negro Art Theater, and Chicago's Skyloft Players; wrote two autobiographies, *The Big Sea* (1940), and *I Wander as I Wander* (1956); began writing a column for the *Chicago Defender* (1943), where he first introduced his character "Jesse B. Semple" who was the basis for several of his novels. Visiting professor of creative writing at Atlanta University (1947-1948); poet-in-residence at the University of Chicago Laboratory School (1949-1950); awarded the NAACP Spingarn Medal (1960); elected into the National Institute of Arts and Letters (1961). Died on May 22, 1967, in New York City. Further reading, <u>Arnold Rampersad</u>, <u>*The Life of Langston Hughes*</u> (1986).

---

on this day in history...

1922, The restored home of Frederick Douglass was dedicated in the Anacostia section of Washington, D.C.

1959, Lynette Woodard, Olympic champion and a member of the Harlem Globetrotters, was born in Wichita, Kan.

AUGUST 12   LITERARY FIGURES

CARTER GODWIN WOODSON

Editor, educator, and historian nicknamed **"the father of black history."** Born on December 19, 1875, in New Canton, Va. Berea College in Kentucky (B.L., 1903); University of Chicago (B.A., 1908; M.A., 1908); Harvard University (Ph.D., 1912), dissertation title: "The Disruption of Virginia;" the Sorbonne in Paris, France. Principal of Douglas High School in West Virginia (1900-1903); supervisor of schools in the Philippines (1903-1906); teacher at M Street High School, [now Dunbar High School] (1909-1918); principal of Armstrong High School (1918-1919). The **guiding force in the founding of the Association for the Study of Negro Life and History** in Chicago (1915); director and editor of the *Journal of Negro History* (1916-1950); dean of the School of Liberal Arts and head of the Graduate Faculty at Howard University (1919-1920); dean of West Virginia Collegiate Institute [now West Virginia State College] (1920-1922); organized and became president of the Associated Publishers (1921), which became the most important African-American-owned publishing company for the next three decades; received the NAACP Spingarn Medal (1925), for collecting and publishing the records of African-Americans in America; **inaugurated Negro History Week** (1926), and the *Negro History Bulletin* (1937). Published *The Education of the Negro Prior to 1861* (1915), *A Century of Negro Migration* (1918), *The Negro in Our History* (1922), which became a standard text on African-American history for many years; also published *Negro Makers of History* (1928), and *The Miseducation of the Negro* (1933). Died on April 3, 1950, in Washington, D.C. Further reading, Earl E. Thorpe, *Black Historians* (1971).

---

on this day in history...

1858,   Edward H. Morris, Chicago attorney who built the United Grand Order of Odd Fellows into one of the nation's strongest fraternal organization, was born in Flemingsburg, Ky. (d. 1943).

1943,   James Earl Chaney, civil rights movement martyr, was born in Meridian, Miss. (d. 1964).

1943,   Gale Sayers, Pro Football Hall of Famer, was born in Wichita, Kan.

MAY 30   **HISTORIANS**

ALEXANDER PALMER HALEY

Author and historian.   Born on August 11, 1921, in Ithaca, N.Y.   Elizabeth City Teacher's College in North Carolina. Served in the U.S. Coast Guard (1939-1959), where he was editor of the official publication *Out Post,* and a public relations official at a Coast Guard district headquarters; worked as a free-lance writer; interviewed Malcolm X for *Playboy Magazine* (1962), which turned into *The Autobiography of Malcolm X* (1965), mostly written by Haley and one of the most influential books of the decade. **Author of *Roots: The Saga of an American Family*** (1976), which became a best-seller and the most watched mini-series in television history (1977), sold over 1.5 million copies of the hardback edition (a U.S. record for a first printing), took 12 years of research and writing, was nominated for 37 Emmy Awards by the Academy of Television Arts and Sciences, was translated into 24 languages, and became a sequel (1979); commissioned by Tennessee's governor to write the state's official history; won the Pulitzer Prize (1977). Awarded the NAACP Spingarn Medal (1977), for "his unsurpassed effectiveness in portraying the legendary story of every American of African descent;" author of *Queen*, which also became a mini-series (1993); president of the Kinte Corporation in Los Angeles; established the Alex Haley Roots Foundation in New York City, which provides post-graduate scholarships and course materials for school children. Died on February 10, 1992, in Seattle, Wash.   Further reading, Robert Bain, Joseph M. Flora, and Louis D. Rubin, Jr., *Southern Writers: A Biographical Dictionary* (1979).

---

on this day in history...

1873,   John Rosamond Johnson, composer of the Negro National Anthem--"Lift Every Voice and Sing," was born in Jacksonville, Fla. (d. 1954).
1925,   Carl T. Rowan, first African-American National Security Council member, was born in Ravenscroft, Tenn.
1943,   Kenneth Gamble, "father of the Philadelphia sound," was born in Philadelphia, Pa.
1948,   Amanda Randolph of *The Laytons*, became one of the first African-Americans to appear in a national network television series.
1965,   Six days of rioting began in the Watts section of Los Angeles.

AUGUST 11   **LITERARY FIGURES**

MONROE NATHAN WORK

Sociologist, educator, and **bibliographer**.   Born on August 15, 1866, in Iredell County, N.C.   Chicago Theological Seminary (1898); University of Chicago (B.A., 1902; M.A., 1903).   Ordained as an African Methodist minister; taught English, history, and pedagogy at Georgia State Industrial College in Savannah (1903-1907); director of records and research at Tuskegee Institute (1908-1945); edited and published *The Negro Year Book, Annual Encyclopedia of the Negro* (1912); **compiled *A Biography of the Negro in Africa and America*** (1928), his most comprehensive bibliographical work; initiated the annual Tuskegee Lynching Record. Awarded Harmon Foundation gold medal (1929), for his scholarly research and educational publicity through periodic publication of the *Negro Yearbook*, which supplied factual data on African-Americans and was used in schools and libraries throughout the country and for the compilation of a *Bibliography of the Negro*; received a citation for Public Service from the Alumni Association of the University of Chicago (1942), becoming the first African-American recipient; member of American Sociological Society, Association for the Study of Negro Life and History, and the International Institute of African Languages and Culture; trustee of the National Association of Teachers in Colored Schools. Died on May 2, 1945, in Tuskegee, Ala.   Further reading, Jesse P. Guzman, "Monroe Nathan Work and His Contributions," (*Journal of Negro History*, October 1949, pp. 428-61).

---

on this day in history...

1918,   Lloyd Albert Quarterman, nuclear physicist who worked on the "Manhattan Project," was born in Philadelphia, Pa. (d. 1952).

1931,   Shirley Verrett, operatic mezzo-soprano, was born in New Orleans, La.

1939,   Garland Anderson, playwright and author of the first Broadway play written by an African-American (*Appearances*), died in New York City (b. 1887).

1987,   John Dotson, *Newsweek*'s first African-American reporter, was named publisher of the Boulder (Colo.) *Daily Camera*.

MAY 31   **HISTORIANS**

ANGELINA WELD GRIMKE

Educator, playwright, and poet whose work and style blazed a trail for the Alice Walkers and Toni Morrisons. Born on February 27, 1880, in Boston, Mass. Boston Normal School of Gymnastics (1902); Harvard University. Taught English at Washington's Armstrong Manual Training School and Dunbar High School (1916-1926). Some of her poems and lyrics appeared in the *Norfolk County Gazette's* ("The Grave in the Corner," 1893), *Boston Sunday Globe* ("Street Echoes," 1894), *Boston Transcript* ("El Beso," 1909), *Crisis* ("To The Dunbar High School," 1917), and in *Opportunity* ("The Black Finger," 1923); her poetry also appeared in several anthologies, including Alaine Locke's *The New Negro* (1925), Countee Cullen's *Caroling Dusk* (1927), Otelia Cromwell's *Readings from Negro Authors* (1931), and in Robert Kerlin's *Negro Poets and Their Poems* (1935); author of the short story "The Closing Door," which dealt with a woman who didn't want to bring another child into a cruel world. Playwright of: *Rachel* (1916), a three-act drama that was performed in Washington, New York City, and Cambridge showing how prejudice in the U.S. almost destroyed an African-American family, and according to Alaine Locke, was the **first successful drama written by an African-American and interpreted by African-American actors**; *Mara*, a 190-page four-act drama that dealt with rape, insanity, murder, and lynching, but was never published. Died on June 11, 1958, in New York City. Further reading, <u>Frederick Bond</u>, *The Negro and the Drama* (1940).

---

on this day in history...

1854,   James Farley, first African-American photographer to attain prominence, was born in Prince Edward County, Va.

1880,   Clarence Cameron White, founding member of the National Association of Negro Musicians, was born in Clarksville, Tenn. (d. 1960).

1909,   George William Crockett, Jr., former Michigan congressman (1980-1990), was born in Jacksonville, Fla.

AUGUST 10   **LITERARY FIGURES**

BESSIE COLEMAN

Aviator who was known as "Brave Bessie." Born on January 26, 1893, in Atlanta, Ga. Attended Langston Industrial College [now Langston University] in Oklahoma. Moved to Chicago and worked at the White Sox Barber Shop and managed a chili restaurant; encouraged by the *Chicago Defender*'s Robert S. Abbott, she learned French and went to Europe to study under the chief pilot for Anthony Fokker's aircraft corporation; learned to fly the German Fokker airplane; became the **first African-American woman to earn a pilot's license** (1922). First appeared in the U.S. in an air show, which was sponsored by Abbott and the *Chicago Defender* at Curtiss Field near New York City (1922), performing her barnstorming act before thousands of spectators; repeated the performance at the Checkerboard Airdrome [now Midway Airport] in Chicago six weeks later. Continued performing throughout the U.S.; contracted by Firestone Rubber Corporation to do aerial advertising in California; gave exhibition flights; lectured on the opportunities in aviation at schools and churches; dreamed of starting a school to train African-American aviators. Invited by the Jacksonville, Fla., Negro Welfare League to perform in a Memorial Day air show (1926); a mechanical failure occurred during practicing maneuvers, causing her to fall out of her plane to her death. Died on April 30, 1926, in Jacksonville, Fla. Further reading, William J. Powell, *Black Wings* (1934).

---

on this day in history...

1937,	Morgan Freeman, three-time Oscar nominee, was born in Greenwood, Miss.
1941,	The first African-American tank battalion, the 758th, was activated.
1973,	The first African-American-owned TV station, WGPR-TV in Detroit, was granted a license to operate.

JUNE 1   **INVENTORS & EXPLORERS**

JESSIE REDMON FAUSET

Writer, educator, translator, editor, and critic who was **the most published writer of the Harlem Renaissance**. Born on April 27, 1882, in Camden, N.J. Cornell University, first African-American Phi Beta Kappa and first African-American woman graduate (B.A., 1905); the Sorbonne in Paris, France (1926); University of Pennsylvania (M.A., 1929). Taught at Douglass High School in Baltimore, French and Latin at M Street High School [now Dunbar High School] in Washington (1906-1919), French at the prestigious DeWitt Clinton High School in New York City (1927-1944), and taught at Hampton Institute (1949). **Literary editor of the NAACP's** *The Crisis* (1919-1926), during the height of the Harlem Renaissance; wrote hundreds of the poems, stories, dialogues, biographies, articles, and handled all correspondence and editing for *The Brownies' Book* (1920-1921), a monthly children's publication created by W.E.B. DuBois; encouraged and published the early works of Langston Hughes, Jean Toomer, Claude McKay, George Schuyler, and Countee Cullen, as well as many other lesser known writers; reviewed periodicals and books; evaluated English and French works of fiction, drama, poetry, folklore, journalism, biography, criticism, and literary history; praised James Weldon Johnson's *The Autobiography of an Ex-Colored Man* (1912); wrote poems, articles, travel essays, and reports, such as her coverage of the 2nd Pan-African Congress in Europe (1921), as a Delta Sigma Theta delegate. Wrote several novels, including: *There Is Confusion* (1924), depicting discrimination faced by northern urban African-Americans; *Plum Bun* (1929), which was about a poor African-American girl who looked white; *The Chinaberry Tree* (1931), and *Comedy: American Style* (1933), both classical Greek tragedies. Composed several poems, including "Yarrow Revisited," "This Way to the Flea Market," "Dark Algiers and White," "La Vie C'est La Vie," "Emmy," "The Sleeper Wakes," and "Double Trouble." Died on April 30, 1961, in Philadelphia, Pa. Further reading, Carolyn Sylvander, *Jessie Redmon Fauset, Black American Writer* (1981).

---

on this day in history...

1882,   John Horse, Seminole African-American chief who founded Wewoka, Okla., died in Mexico City, Mexico (b. 1812).

1936,   Jesse Owens won his fourth gold medal of the Olympics in Berlin.

1959,   Kurtis Blow, "father of rap music," was born in New York City.

1963,   Whitney Houston, Grammy Award-winning singer, was born in Newark, N.J.

1987,   Reginald Lewis, of the TLC Group, became CEO of the largest African-American business when his company bought out Beatrice Foods International.

AUGUST 9   **LITERARY FIGURES**

JEAN BAPTISTE POINTE DeSABLE

Pioneer, entrepreneur, trapper, cooper, husbandman, and miller.   Born around 1745 in St. Marc, Haiti.   Worked for the family-owned business, Dessables & Sons, in Haiti. Educated in France and migrated to New Orleans (1765), to find it occupied by Spain; received protection from French Jesuits and escaped to St. Louis; left St. Louis for Peoria after the British took control (1767); settled among the Peoria and Potowatomi Indians; began traveling back and forth between Illinois and Canada (1769), by using the Illinois River and Lake Michigan, frequently stopping at the main portage of Eschikagou. Decided to settle at the mouth of the Illinois River (1774), building a trading post and becoming the **first permanent resident of Eschikagou [now called Chicago]**, which became a major stop for French fur traders passing through on their way back and forth between St. Louis and Canada. Served as a liaison officer between the Indians of the Port Huron region and white officers (1780-1784); returned to Chicago and expanded his trading post by adding a bakehouse, dairy, smokehouse, poultry house, workshop, stable, barn, mill, and other buildings; sold most of his holdings and left Chicago permanently (1800), returning to Peoria; finally settled in St. Joseph, Mo. Died in 1818 in St. Joseph, Mo.   Further reading, Milo Milton Quaife, *Chicago and the Old Northwest 1673-1835* (1913).

---

on this day in history...

1947,   Clarence Page, Pulitzer Prize-winning journalist, was born in Dayton, Ohio.

1951,   Kenneth I. Chenault, president of American Express' Consumer Card and Financial Services Group, was born in Mineola, N.Y.

JUNE 2   **INVENTORS & EXPLORERS**

PAUL LAURENCE DUNBAR

Poet, novelist, and journalist who was called **"the poet laureate of Negro people."** Born on June 27, 1872, in Dayton, Ohio. Dayton Central High School (1891), where he was editor-in-chief of the *High School Times*, president of the literary society, class poet, and the only African-American in his class. Worked as an elevator operator in the Callahan Building on Main Street in Dayton, messenger in the Dayton City Courthouse, and as a clerical assistant to Frederick Douglass who was the commissioner in charge of the Haitian Exhibit at the Chicago World's Fair (1893); delivered a welcome address, with one of his rhymes, to the Western Association of Writers' conference (Dayton, 1892), and was made a member. Published several works of poetry, including: *Oak and Ivy* (1893), his first full-length volume of poetry; *Majors and Minors* (1895), which contains some of his best poems in both Standard English and dialect and was favorably reviewed by the leading literary critic William Dean Howells in *Harper's Weekly*; *Lyrics of a Lonely Life* (1898), which was published in New York and New England and brought him international fame. Helped raise money for Hampton Institute and Tuskegee Institute and wrote Tuskegee's school song; went to Colorado for his health (1900). Published several novels, including: *The Uncalled* (1898), which dealt with the lack of Christianity in churches; *The Love of Laundry* (1900), a love story based on class barriers in white American society; *The Fanatics* (1901), about a pro-Yankee and pro-southern family in Ohio during the Civil War; *The Sport of the Gods* (1901), about a blatant case of southern injustice perpetrated on an innocent and respectable African-American family. Published several collections of short stories, including, *Folks from Dixie* (1898), *Strength of Gideon* (1900), *Old Plantation Days* (1903), and *The Heart of Happy Hollow* (1904). Died on February 9, 1906, in Dayton, Ohio. Further reading, Benjamin Brawley, <u>*Paul Laurence Dunbar, Poet of His People*</u> (1936).

---

on this day in history...

1907,   Bennett Lester Carter, jazz musician, was born in New York City.
1934,   Julian Dixon, California 32nd District congressman, was born in Washington, D.C.
1969,   President Nixon issued Executive Order 11478, which required each federal agency to establish and maintain an affirmative action program of equal employment opportunity.

AUGUST 8   **LITERARY FIGURES**

LLOYD AUGUSTUS HALL

Food chemist and inventor. Born on June 20, 1894, in Elgin, Ill. Northwestern University (Ph.D., 1914; B.S., 1916); Virginia State University (D.S.C., 1944). Sanitary chemist at the Department of Health Laboratories in Chicago (1916-1918); president and chemical director of Chemical Products Corporation in Chicago (1924-1925); consultant to Griffith's Laboratories in Chicago (1925-1929), chief chemist and research director (1929-1946), and technical director (1946-1971). Held more than a hundred patents in the U.S., Canada, and Great Britain and made substantial contributions to the meat-packing industry with his various discoveries of and recipes for curing salts, condiments, spices, and flavors. Member of the board of directors of the American Institute of Chemists; member of Alpha Phi Alpha Fraternity; and the New York Academy of Sciences; **first African-American to hold office in the Institute of Food Chemists**. Died in 1971. Further reading, Louis Haber, _Black Pioneers of Science and Inventions_ (1970).

---

on this day in history...

1884,	Granville T. Woods patented his steam boiler furnace
1942,	Curtis Mayfield, singer, composer, and recording executive, was born in Chicago, Ill.
1943,	Phoebe Beasley, first African-American president of American Women in Radio, was born in Cleveland, Ohio.
1949,	Wesley A. Brown became the first African-American graduate of the U.S. Naval Academy.
1951,	Deniece Williams, Grammy Award-winning singer, was born in Gary, Ind.

JUNE 3   INVENTORS & EXPLORERS

COUNTEE PORTER CULLEN

Poet, novelist, and anthologist.   Born on May 30, 1903, in Louisville, KY.   New York University Phi Beta Kappa (B.A., 1925), where he won the Witter Bynner Poetry Prize; Harvard University (M.A., 1926); the Sorbonne in France. Published several collections of verse, including: *Color* (1925), a collection of poems that made him the **leading poet of the Harlem Renaissance**; *Copper Sun* (1927); *The Ballad of the Brown Girl: An Old Ballad Retold* (1927); *Caroling Dusk* (1927), an outstanding anthology of African-American poets; *The Black Christ, and Other Poems* (1929); *The Medea, and Some Poems* (1937); *On These I Stand: An Anthology of the Best Poems of Countee Cullen* (1947), a selection of his best poems published posthumously. Won *Poetry* magazine's John Reed Memorial Prize (1925); assistant editor of *Opportunity* (1926-1928), the National Urban League's official journal and a leading publication during the Harlem Renaissance; received the Harmon Foundation Literary Award (1927), and won a Guggenheim fellowship (1928), which he used to study abroad; married Nina DuBois, daughter of W.E.B. DuBois (1928), in the major social event of the year in Harlem; taught English and French at New York City's P.S. 139--Frederick Douglass High School in Harlem (1934-1946). Wrote his only novel, *One Way to Heaven* (1932), which was classified as a Harlem-novel and made significant contributions to African-American fiction; published some children's books entitled, *The Last Zoo* (1940), and *My Lives and How I Lost Them* (1942); collaborated with Arna Bontemps in writing the novel *God Send Sunday*, first into a play and then a musical, *St. Louis Woman* (1946). Died on January 10, 1946, in New York City.   Further reading, Alan R. Shucard, *Countee Cullen* (1984).

---

on this day in history...

1945,   Alan Page, Pro Football Hall of Famer and Minnesota State Supreme Court justice, was born in Canton, Ohio.
1989,   Texas Congressman Mickey Leland died in a plane crash in Ethiopia, while on his way to a U.N. refugee camp.

AUGUST 7   **LITERARY FIGURES**

MATTHEW ALEXANDER HENSON

Explorer.   Born on August 6, 1867, in Charles County, Md.   Labored as a cabin boy and able-bodied seaman aboard the merchant vessel *Katie Hinds*, where he traveled through the Straight of Magellan, across the Pacific to the China Sea, across the Atlantic, and into the Baltic Sea; worked as a longshoreman in Boston, bellhop in Providence, laborer in Buffalo, and a coachman in New York City. Met Robert Peary (1887), who hired him as an assistant for his trip to survey a canal route through Nicaragua; accompanied Peary on his trips to the Arctic (1891-1892, 1893-1895, 1896, 1897, 1898-1902, 1905-1906, and 1908-1909), when the expedition finally reached its goal and Henson became the **first person to reach the North Pole** (45 minutes ahead of Peary); published an autobiography, *A Negro Explorer at the North Pole* (1912). Clerk in the New York Customs House (1913-1936); became a life member of the Explorers' Club (1937); received an honorary degree from Howard University (M.S., 1939), and a Gold Medal from the Geographical Society of Chicago (1948); saluted by President Truman in a ceremony at the Pentagon (1950), and honored by President Eisenhower at the White House (1954). Died in 1955 in New York City.   Further reading, J.A. Rogers, *World Greatest Men of Color* (1972).

---

on this day in history...

1905,   S. Bacon Fuller, first African-American member of the National Association of Manufacturers, was born in Monroe, La. (d. 1988).

1922,   Samuel Lee Gravely, first African-American to command a U.S. Navy ship, the *USS Falgout*, and the Navy's first African-American rear admiral, was born in Richmond, Va.

1991,   Frank Robinson was named assistant manager of the Baltimore Orioles.

CHARLES WADDELL CHESNUTT

Author, lawyer, educator, businessman, and the **nation's first great African-American novelist**, whose stories appeared in the leading literary magazines of the time. Born on June 20, 1858, in Cleveland, Ohio. Teacher and principal at State Normal School at Fayettevile, N.C. (1874-1883); stenographer for Dow Jones & Company in New York City; reporter for the *Wall Street Gossip* and the *New York Mail and Express* (1883); legal stenographer in the accounting department of Nickel Plate Railroad; admitted to the Ohio bar (1887); opened a Cleveland law and court reporting office; his first stories, "The Gophered Grapevine" and "Po Sandy," appeared the *Atlantic Monthly* (1887); published his first novel *Rena Walden* (1889). Wrote the novels: *The Conjure Woman* (1899), a collection of short stories narrated by a white northerner; *The Wife of His Youth* (1899), a collection of nine short stories; *The House Behind the Cedars* (1900), which dealt with a young African-American girl attempting to pass as white; *The Marrow of Tradition* (1901), which exposed the misery inherent in a society built on self-deception and untruths; and *The Colonel's Dream* (1905), which dealt with the rebuilding of the South. Member of the general committee of the NAACP and of the Cleveland Chamber of Commerce; **helped found the Playhouse Settlement of Cleveland [now called Karamu House]**; commissioned to write the biography, *The Life of Frederick Douglass* (1899); wrote articles and stories for the NAACP's *Crisis* magazine (1912-1930). Considered as the first serious craftsman among African-American writers, first African-American to be recognized as an undisputed member of the American literati, and the **first to break the color barrier in publishing**; laid the foundation for the Harlem Renaissance with his work. Died on November 15, 1932, in Cleveland, Ohio. Further reading, J. Noel Hermance, *Charles W. Chesnutt; America's First Great Black Novelist* (1974).

---

on this day in history...

1816,	Peter Salem, Revolutionary War Battle of Bunker Hill hero, died in Framingham, Mass. (b. 1750).
1910,	Waldo Willie Emerson Blanchet, Fort Valley State president emeritus, was born in New Orleans, La.
1912,	Bennett McVey Stewart, former Illinois congressman (1979-1981), was born in Huntsville, Ala.
1965,	President Johnson passed the Voting Rights Act of 1965.
1965,	David Robinson, San Antonio Spurs All-Star, was born in Key West, Fla.
1988,	*Yo MTV Raps* premiered on the 24-hour music channel.

FREDERICK McKINLEY JONES

Inventor. Born in 1893 in Cincinnati, Ohio. Became an apprentice mechanic and foreman of an automobile shop in Cincinnati, a pipefitter in Chicago, and a farm machinery mechanic in Hallock, Minn.; served in the U.S. Army during World War I in France as an electrician with the rank of sergeant; mastered electronics through self-study, built a radio station transmitter and a device for combining sound with motion-picture film; worked for Cinema Supplies, Inc., in Minneapolis (1930-1949), where he made sound equipment for theaters in the Midwest; received his first patent (1939), for a ticket-dispensing machine for movie-house tickets. **Designed and patented the first air-cooling unit for food transported to market by trucks** (1940), which made it possible for the first time to transport meat, fruits, vegetables, and dairy products that needed refrigeration over a long distance anytime of the year; co-founded U.S. Thermo Control Company [later called Thermo King] with his former employer (1949), and manufactured air coolers for trains, ships, and airplanes; designed portable cooling units for use in U.S. Army hospitals and on the battlefield during World War II. Received patents for two-cycle gasoline engine, starter generator, and a refrigeration control device; awarded over 60 patents and became the **first African-American member of the American Society of Refrigeration Engineers;** consultant on refrigeration to the U.S. Department of Defense and the Bureau of Standards; posthumously inducted into the Minnesota Hall of Fame (1977). Died on February 21, 1961, in Minneapolis, Minn. Further reading, Robert C. Hayden, *Eight Black American Inventors* (1972).

---

on this day in history...

1929,   Eloise Brown Strand, first African-American chief of the Army Medical Specialist Corps, was born in Stamford, Conn.

1940,   Orlando Patterson, National Book Award-winning author of *Freedom in the Making of Western Culture*, was born in Westmoreland, Jamaica.

1956,   The federal courts ruled that racial segregation on Montgomery buses was unconstitutional.

1956,   The Alabama Christian Movement was organized by Fred Shuttlesworth.

1966,   James Meredith's "March Against Fear" to Jackson began in Memphis, Tenn.

JUNE 5   **INVENTORS & EXPLORERS**

CHARLES EATON BURCH

Educator and literary scholar.   Born on July 14, 1891, in Bermuda.   Wilberforce University (B.A., 1914); Columbia University (M.A., 1918); Ohio State University (Ph.D., 1933), dissertation title: "The English Reputation of Daniel Defoe."   Taught in the academic department of Tuskegee Institute (1916-1917); English instructor at Wilberforce University (1918-1921); Howard University assistant professor (1921-1924), English professor (1924-1936), and **head of Howard's English department** (1933-1948). His "Daniel Defoe's Views on Education" was first published in the *Howard University Record* (1922); took a sabbatical from Howard University and studied with H.J.C. Grierson at Edinburgh University and the National Library of Scotland (1927-1928, 1938); **introduced at Howard University, "Poetry and Prose of Negro Life," one of the first courses at an American university dedicated to Negro literature**; specialist in the field of 18th-century English literature and an expert on the life and works of British author Daniel Defoe. Died on March 23, 1948, in Stamford, Conn.   Further reading, *Directory of American Scholars* (1942).

---

on this day in history...

1879,   William Bailes patented a ladder scaffold support.
1938,   James Hal Cone, theologian scholar, was born in Fordyce, Ark.
1946,   Sherry Ann Jackson, first African-American woman to receive a Ph.D. from M.I.T., was born in Washington, D.C.
1962,   Patrick Ewing, New York Knicks All-Star, was born in Kingston, Jamaica.

AUGUST 5   **LITERARY FIGURES**

PERCY LAVON JULIAN

Chemist and inventor.   Born on April 11, 1899, in Montgomery, Ala.   DePauw University valedictorian and Phi Beta Kappa (B.A., 1920); Harvard University (M.A., 1923); and the University of Vienna (Ph.D., organic chemistry, 1931), dissertation title: "Zur Kerntnis Verschiedener Alkaloids ond uber ein neues Hererocyclishes, Freies Radik." Instructor of chemistry at Fisk University (1920-1922); George and Martha Derby scholar (1924-1925); professor at West Virginia State College (1926-1927); research assistant at Harvard University (1925-1926); associate professor and acting chairman of the department of chemistry at Howard University (1927-1929), professor and chairman (1931-1932); research fellow in organic chemistry at DePauw University (1932-1936); director of research for the Gliden Company's Soya Products Division (1945-1953), director of research of the Vegetable Oil and Food Division (1953-1954), where he successfully developed new processes for paints and perfected a method of extracting sterol from soybean oil for the manufacturing of sex hormones. **Founded and president of Julian Laboratories of Chicago** (1954-1964), which was devoted mainly to the production of synthetic cortisone. Sold Julian Laboratories in 1961 for several million dollars and continued as a consultant; awarded over 125 patents and the NAACP Spingarn Medal (1947), for outstanding contributions to research in chemistry. Served as vice president of the board of directors of Roosevelt College (1948); vice president of the board of trustees of Provident Hospital in Chicago (1948); trustee of Fisk University. Achieved synthesis of physostigmine; produced a synthetic drug for glaucoma; developed an economical way to extract sterol from soybeans; and improved methods of manufacturing cortisone. Died in 1975.   Further reading, <u>Louis Haber</u>, <u>*Black Pioneers of Science and Inventions*</u> (1970).

---

on this day in history...

1826,	Sarah Parker Remond, abolitionist, was born in Salem, Mass.
1869,	Dillard University was chartered in New Orleans, La.
1930,	Barbara Harris, first Anglican female bishop, was born in Philadelphia, Pa.
1934,	Roy Innis, national chairman of the Congress on Racial Eqaulity (CORE), was born in St. Croix, V.I.
1939,	Marian Wright Edelman, founder of the Children's Defense Fund, was born in Bennettsville, S.C.
1949,	Debra McGriff, Detroit Public Schools superintendent, was born in Portsmouth, Va.

JUNE 6   **INVENTORS & EXPLORERS**

BENJAMIN GRIFFITH BRAWLEY

Educator, critic, scholar, and author.   Born on April 22, 1882, in Columbia, S.C.   Atlanta Baptist College [now Morehouse College] (B.A., 1901); University of Chicago (A.B., 1907); Harvard University (M.A., 1908).   English and Latin instructor and professor of English at Atlanta Baptist College (1902-1910); faculty member at Howard University (1910-1912); **professor and dean of English at Atlanta Baptist College** (1912-1920). Performed an educational survey of Liberia (1920); ordained as a Baptist minister (1920), and became the pastor of Messiah Baptist Church in Brockton, Mass. (1921-1922); professor at Shaw University in Raleigh (1923-1931); faculty member at Howard (1931-1939); his historical essays, social commentaries, and book reviews appeared in *The Dail, Lippincott's Magazine,* the *Springfield Republican, The Bookman,* the *Harvard Monthly,* and the *Sewanee Review.* Published *A Short History of the American Negro* (1913), *A Short History of the English Drama* (1921), *Social History of the American Negro* (1921), *A New Survey of English Literature* (1925), a textbook manual for teachers entitled *Freshman Year English* (1929), *A History of the English Hymn* (1932), and *Paul Laurence Dunbar: Poet of his People (1936).* Died on February 1, 1939, in Washington, D.C.   Further reading, Benjamin Brawley, *The Negro in Literature and Art in the United States* (1925).

AUGUST 4   LITERARY FIGURES

LEWIS HOWARD LATIMER

Inventor, engineer, and poet. Born on September 4, 1848, in Chelsea, Mass. Sold copies of the *Liberator* to support his family; served in the Union Army and saw action on the James River aboard the *USS Massasoit* (1863-1865). Learned mechanical drawing while working for a Boston patent solicitor, Crosby & Gould, and was **contracted by Alexander Graham Bell to make the patent drawings for the first telephone (1876)**; began working at the United States Lighting Company in Bridgeport, Conn., (1880), and invented carbon filaments for the Maxim electric incandescent lamp and an inexpensive method of making the filament; worked as an engineer, chief draftsman, and expert witness on the Board of Patent Control in gathering evidence against the infringement of patents held by Westinghouse and General Electric. Began his association with Thomas Edison (1883), served as engineer for the Edison Company during the installation of the electric light systems in New York City, Philadelphia, Montreal, and London. Wrote the text, *Incandescent Electric Lighting: A Practical Description of the Edison System* (1890); taught mechanical drawing to immigrants at the Henry Street Settlement in New York City (1906); became the **only African-American member of the "Edison Pioneers;"** privately published a 25-page booklet, *Poems of Love and Life* (1923). Died on December 11, 1928, in Flushing, N.Y. Further reading, Aaron E. Klein, *The Hidden Contributors: Black Scientists and Inventions in America* (1971).

---

on this day in history...

1917,	Gwendolyn Brooks, first African-American Pulitzer Prize winner (for *Annie Allen*) was born in Topeka, Kan.
1943,	Yolande Cornelia "Nikki" Giovanni, "princess of black poetry," was born in Knoxville, Tenn.
1959,	Roger Nelson ("Prince"), Academy Award-winning recording artist, was born in Minneapolis, Minn.
1987,	Lloyd Richards won a Tony Award as best director for the August Wilson play *Fences*.

JUNE 7   **INVENTORS & EXPLORERS**

WILLIAM STANLEY BRAITHWAITE

Poet, anthologist, and critic. Born on December 6, 1878, in Boston, Mass. Educated at home; became an apprentice typesetter at Ginn & Company; published his first volume of poetry, *Lyrics of Love* (1904); literary editor and columnist for the *Boston Evening Transcript* (1908-1929); publisher of the *Poetic Journal of Boston* (1912-1914); editor of *Poetry Review* (1916-1917); **founder and editor of B.J. Brimmer Publishing Company** (1921-1927); member of the editorial board of *Phylon*. Served as editor of several collections of verse, including: *The Book of Georgia Verse* (1908); *The Book of Restoration Verse* (1909), which showcased the early American poets, including Carl Sanburg, Edgar Lee Masters, and Vachel Lindsay; *Anthology of Magazine Verse* (1913-1939, 1958-1959), which made him a nationally known anthologist. **Professor of creative literature at Atlanta University** (1935-1945); awarded the NAACP Spingarn Medal (1918), for outstanding literary achievements by an African-American; wrote his autobiography, *The House Under Arcturus* (1941); his essays and poems were published in *Atlantic Monthly, North American Review,* and *Scribner's*; praised the novels of Jessie Fauset and Jean Toomer' *Cane*, but denounced Claude McKay for his militant poem "If I Must Die;" received honorary degrees from Talledega College and Atlanta University (1918); published *Selected Poems* (1948). Died on June 8, 1962, in New York City. Further reading, Benjamin Brawley, *The Negro in Art and Literature* (1918).

---

on this day in history...

1908,   Allen Allensworth filed site plans in the Tulare County recorder's office for the all-black town of Allensworth, Calif.

1937,   Roland W. Burris, Illinois' first African-American state attorney general, was born in Centralia, Ill.

AUGUST 3   **LITERARY FIGURES**

ELIJAH McCOY

Inventor and engineer whose inventions were called "The Real McCoy."   Born on May 2, 1844, in Colchester, Ontario, Canada.   Learned mechanical engineering as an apprentice; worked on the Michigan Central Railroad, which led him to **develop a lubricator for steam engines--a first of its kind**; received his first patents (1872, 1873, and 1874), and assigned away a majority of his rights to capitalize McCoy Manufacturing Company in Detroit. Invented and patented a lubricator for air-brake pumps, steam dome for locomotives, lubricants for slide valves and locomotive cylinders, lubricator for improving engines where steam was used to aid in feeding oil to the cylinders, dope cup lubricator, sight-feed chamber connected with the lubricator, lubricator for heavy oils, lubricator for locomotive engines, and an oil cup with support and sight-feed arm. His lubricating devices were quickly adopted by major industries using heavy equipment, such as stationary engines and locomotives, steamships on the Great Lakes, trans-Atlantic liners, and machinery in many factories; also invented and patented folding ironing board, folding scaffold support, buggy top support, tread for tires, lawn sprinkler, and a vehicle wheel tire. His over 40 patents yielded millions of dollars for others. Died in 1929 in Eloise, Mich., a comparatively poor man.   Further reading, Robert C. Hayden, *Eight Black American Inventors* (1972).

---

on this day in history...

1928,   Edward Joseph Perkins, United Nations diplomat, was born in Sterlington, La.

1939,   Bernie Casey, actor, was born in Waco, Texas.

JUNE 8   INVENTORS & EXPLORERS

ARNA WENDELL BONTEMPS

Writer, poet, educator, librarian, historian, curator, and playwright who was a central figure in the discovery, dissemination, and preservation of African-American literature. Born on October 13, 1902, in Alexandria, La. Union Pacific College (B.A., 1923), University of Chicago (M.A., 1943). Moved to New York City (1924), where he first met Langston Hughes and became **one of the most outstanding figures of the Harlem Renaissance**; won *Opportunity* magazine's Alexander Pushkin Award for poetry twice for his poems "Golgotha is a Mountain" (1926), and "The Return" (1927); won first prize in NAACP's *Crisis* magazine poetry contest for his poem "Noctrine at Bethesda." Taught at Oakwood School in Huntsville, Ala. (1930-1932); appointed to the Illinois Writers Project (1932); **head librarian at Fisk University** (1943-1965); authored *God Sends Sunday* (1931), which he and Countee Cullen adapted into *St. Louis Woman* for Broadway (1946); edited *The Poetry of the Negro 1746-1949* (1949), and collaborated with Langston Hughes on *The Book of Negro Folklore* (1958); received a Jane Addams Children's Book Award (1956), for his *Story of the Negro*. Served as director of university relations at Fisk (1965), taught English at the University of Illinois (1966), and served as curator of the James Weldon Johnson Memorial Collection of Negro Arts and Letters at Yale University (1969-1972); writer-in-residence at Fisk (1972-1973), where he worked on his autobiography. Wrote *You Can't Pet a Possum* (1934), *Block Thunder* (1936), *Drums at Dusk* (1939), *Golden Slippers: An Anthology of Negro Poetry for Young People* (1941), *George Washington Carver* (1950), *Frederick Douglass: Slave, Fighter, Freeman* (1959), *American Negro Poetry* (1963), *Famous Negro Athletes* (1964), and *The Harlem Renaissance Remembered* (1972). Died on June 6, 1973, in Nashville, Tenn. Further reading, Wilhelmena S. Robinson, *Historical Negro Biographies* (1969).

---

on this day in history...

1945,   Jewel Jackson McCabe, National Coalition of 100 Black Women president, was born in Washington, D.C.

AUGUST 2   **LITERARY FIGURES**

RONALD ERWIN McNAIR

Astronaut and physicist. Born on October 21, 1950, in Lake City, S.C. Lake City's Carver High School valedictorian (1967); North Carolina A&T State University *magna cum laude* (B.S., 1971); E'cole D'ete Theorique de Physique in Les Houches, France; Massachusetts Institute of Technology (Ph.D., 1976). Picked cotton and cucumbers and cropped tobacco in his early life; developed some of the earliest chemical and high-pressure lasers and was recognized nationally for his work in laser physics; physicist at Hughes Research Laboratories in Malibu, Calif. (1976-1978). Mission specialist for the National Aeronautical and Space Agency (1978-1986); selected as one of 35 applicants from a pool of 10,000 for the astronaut program (1978), and became the second African-American to fly in space; orbited the earth 122 times aboard *Columbia* (1984), launching a $75 million communications satellite. Became a member of the National Society of Black Professional Engineers and was a sixth degree black belt in karate. Died aboard the space shuttle *Challenger* 91 seconds after liftoff from Cape Kennedy, Fla., on January 28, 1986. Further reading, Richard Lewis, Challenger: The Final Voyage (1988).

on this day in history...

1888, Peter Marshall Murray, first African-American to hold high office in the American Medical Association House of Delegates, was born in Houma, La.

1933, Richard E. Artison, first African-American sheriff of Milwaukee County, Wis., was born in Omaha, Neb.

1934, Jackie Wilson, entertainer who was known as "Mr. Excitement," was born in Detroit, Mich. (d. 1984).

1978, Larry Holmes defeated Ken Norton for the WBC heavyweight boxing championship.

1992, William Pinkney became the first African-American to circumnavigate the globe solo via a South Atlantic route, when he sailed into Boston Harbor aboard the *Commitment*.

JUNE 9   **INVENTORS & EXPLORERS**

JAMES BALDWIN

Writer, playwright, and civil rights advocate. Born on August 2, 1924, in New York City. A boy preacher in Harlem's storefront churches; later became a Pentecostal preacher; worked in the defense industry; moved to New York City's Greenwich Village to work at becoming a writer; wrote articles that were published in the *Nation*, *New Leader*, and *Commentary*; moved to Paris to write around the beginning of the civil rights movement, because of overwhelming racism in America. Wrote the novels: *Go Tell It on the Mountain* (1953), a semi-autobiographical account of his early years wrestling with religion; *Giovonni's Room* (1956), which was set in Paris; *Another Country* (1962), which was a critical and commercial success; *Tell Me How Long the Train's Been Gone* (1948). Wrote the plays: *Blues for Mister Charlie*, based on the Emmett Till murder case; *Amen Corner* (1964), about a Pentecostal preacher. Published several collections of essays including: *Notes of a Native Son* (1955), which brought him critical acclaim; *Nobody Knows My Name* (1960), which established him as a major force in American literature; **the best-selling, *The Fire Next Time* (1963), which was regarded as one of the most brilliant essays written in the history of the African-American protest**. Returned to the U.S. to help in the civil rights movement and served as a member of the national advisory board of the Congress of Racial Equality; received a Eugene Saxton fellowship, Rosenwald fellowship (1948), Guggenheim fellowship (1954), *Partisan Review* fellowship (1956), National Institute of Arts and Letters Award (1956), and Ford Foundation grant-in-aid (1959). Died on December 1, 1987, in New York City. Further reading, William Weatherby, *James Baldwin: Portrait of a Writer* (1989).

---

on this day in history...

1918,	Theodore Judson Jemison, Sr., National Baptist Convention USA president, was born in Selma, Ala.
1925,	The National Bar Association was organized in Des Moines, Iowa.
1931,	Lucien E. Blackwell, Pennsylvania 2nd District congressman, was born in Whitset, Pa.
1932,	Henry Frye, North Carolina State Supreme Court justice, was born in Richmond County, N.C.
1941,	Ronald H. Brown, first African-American U.S. commerce secretary, was born in Washington, D.C.

AUGUST 1   **LITERARY FIGURES**

JAN EARNST MATZELIGER

Inventor and businessman. Born on September 15, 1852, in Paramaribo, Surinam. Sailor aboard an East Indian vessel (1871-1873), disembarking in Philadelphia and eventually settling in Lynn, Mass.; found employment in a shoe factory operating a McKay sole sewing machine, a heel-burnisher, and the button-hole machine; attended evening classes, maintained a personal library on scientific and practical works, and gave lessons in oil painting. Patented a shoe lasting machine (1883), after almost 10 years of development and the assigning of two thirds of his invention to raise the needed capital; performed the first public test of his invention (1885), which was successful and **revolutionized the U.S. shoe industry and made Lynn, Mass., the shoe capitol of the world**; sold all rights to his patent to Consolidated Lasting Machine Company, which began to manufacture his device for a block of stock (1885)--it later became the largest shoe manufacturing concern in the nation, United Shoe Machinery Corp. Patented a "Mechanism for Distributing Tacks, Nails, etc." (1888), "Nailing Machine" (1890), and a "Tack Separating and Distributing Mechanism" (1890); posthumously awarded the Gold Medal and Diploma at the Pan-American Exposition in 1901. Died on August 24, 1889, in Lynn, Mass. Further reading, Lou Haber, _Black Pioneers of Science and Inventions_ (1970).

on this day in history...

1854,   James Augustine Healy was ordained as the first African-American Catholic priest at Notre Dame Cathedral in Paris, France.
1898,   Hattie McDaniel, first African-American Academy Award winner, was born in Wichita, Kan. (d. 1952).
1940,   The Cotton Club of New York City, whose clientele were called the "Aristocrat of Harlem," closed.
1972,   Barbara Jordan, Texas state senate president _pro tem_, became the nation's first African-American woman governor "for a day."

JUNE 10   INVENTORS & EXPLORERS

BUTLER ROLAND WILSON

Lawyer and civil rights leader. Born on July 22, 1860, in Greensboro, N.C. Atlanta University (1881); Boston University School of Law (LL.B., 1884). Practiced law with Archibald Grimke and George Ruffin (1884-1887), later practiced independently, specializing in criminal law and became one of the most respected lawyers in New England; attorney for Moorfield Storey, who was a white Boston lawyer, American Bar Association president, and first president of the NAACP. Helped Archibald Grimke edit, *The Hub*; appointed master of chancery in Boston (1898); member of the Boston "Radicals;" **original endorser of the call for the Niagara Movement** (1905); helped organize the Boston branch of the NAACP (1912), executive secretary of the Boston branch (1912-1926), president (1926-1936), and counsel and member of the NAACP national board of directors; protested against the segregated YMCA, the showing of *Birth of a Nation*, the segregated African-American Army officer training post at Fort Des Moines, Iowa (1917), the Pan-African movement, and a Massachusetts law banning interracial marriages (1924); argued that the African-American problem must be fought on American soil. Became the **first African-American member of the American Bar Association** (1912); member of the Massachusetts Board of Appeals on fire insurance rates (1917-1939); helped prepare, along with James Weldon Johnson, the papers that resulted in the first of the Atlanta University Publications, *Mortality Among Negroes in Cities* (1896). Died on October 31, 1939, in Boston, Mass. Further reading, Charles Flint Kellogg, *NAACP,* vol. 1 (1967).

---

on this day in history...

1874, Patrick Francis Healy was inaugurated as president of Georgetown University, becoming the first African-American to head a predominantly white university.

1960, Elijah Muhammad called for the creation of a separate black state.

1962, Wesley Snipes, actor, was born in Orlando, Fla.

1988, Willie Stargell, Pittsburgh Pirates champion, was inducted into the Baseball Hall of Fame.

GARRETT AUGUSTUS MORGAN

Inventor, editor, and entrepreneur. Born on March 4, 1875, in Paris, Ky. Moved to Cleveland and began working as a sewing machine adjuster for a clothing manufacturer, which was the beginning of a lifetime of entrepreneurial achievements; developed his first invention, a belt fastener for sewing machines (1901), and sold it for $150; began repairing and selling sewing machines (1907); opened a tailoring shop, which manufactured coats, suits, and dresses (1909); and started G.A. Morgan Hair Refining Company, where he **introduced the first human hair straightening process** (1913). **Patented a safety helmet "breathing device," or gas mask** (1914); after a Cleveland waterworks tunnel disaster trapped municipal workers 250 feet below Lake Erie (1916), Morgan was called upon to bring his experimental gas mask, and he and his brother helped rescue over 20 men from a tunnel filled with smoke, natural gases, dust, and debris; his masks were worn by fire fighters throughout the U.S. and protected American soldiers in the battlefield from deadly chlorine gas fumes during World War I. **Awarded American, Canadian, and British patents for his three-way automatic traffic signal invention** (1923), and sold the rights to General Electric for $40,000. Founded and published a weekly African-American newspaper, the *Cleveland Call* (1920-1923); served as treasurer of the Cleveland Association of Colored Men; awarded First Grand Prize Golden Medal by the National Safety Device Company at the Second International Exposition of Safety and Sanitation for his gas mask (1914); given honorary membership in the International Association of Firefighters; posthumously cited by the U.S. government (1963), for inventing the first traffic signal. Died in 1963 in Cleveland, Ohio. Further reading, James C. Williams, *At Last Recognition in America: A Reference Handbook to Unknown Black Inventors and their Contribution to Black America* (1978).

---

on this day in history...

1920,   Hazel Dorothy Scott, pianist-singer and wife of Adam Clayton Powell, Jr., was born in Port of Spain, Trinidad (d. 1981).

1926,   Amalya L. Kearse, 2nd U.S. Circuit appellate judge, was born in Vaux Hall, N.J.

1930,   Charles Bernard Rangel, New York 15th District congressman, was born in New York City.

JUNE 11   INVENTORS & EXPLORERS

GEORGE BOYER VASHON

Lawyer, educator, and writer. Born on July 25, 1824, in Carlisle, Pa. **Oberlin College's first African-American graduate** (B.A., 1844). Became secretary of the first Juvenile Anti-Slavery in America (1838); taught school in Chillicothe, Ohio, where he taught John Mercer Langston; studied law under Judge Walter Forward in Pittsburgh; admitted to the New York State bar (1848), becoming the **first African-American lawyer in the state of New York**; taught at the College Faustin in Port-au-Prince, Haiti (1848-1850); practiced law in Syracuse (1850-1854). Wrote the poem, "Vincent Oge" (1853); professor of belle-lettres and mathematics in New York Central College in McGrawville, N.Y. (1854-1857), where he was one of the first African-American teachers in a white school in the antebellum era; teacher and principal in the Pittsburgh colored school system (1858-1863), and at Avery College (1864-1867); **first African-American teacher at Howard University** (1867-1868). Served as solicitor for the Freedmen's Bureau in Washington (1867); delegate from Rhode Island and chairman of the committee on credentials at the National Convention of Colored Men of America (Washington, 1869), joined the national executive committee (1870); taught at Alcorn University (1874-1878). Died on October 5, 1878, in Mississippi. Further reading, Benjamin Brawley, _Early Negro American Writers_ (1935).

---

on this day in history...

1822,	James Varick became the first bishop of the African Methodist Episcopal Zion Church.
1961,	Larry Fishburne, Emmy Award-winning actor, was born in Augusta, Ga.
1988,	The first National Black Arts Festival opened in Atlanta, Ga.
1993,	Eugene Willis Skinner, Omaha's first African-American full-time public school teacher, principal, and administrator, died in Omaha, Neb. (b. 1915).

ROBERT A. PELHAM, JR.

Inventor, politician, journalist, and government official. Born on January 4, 1859, in Petersburg, Va. Served in the military (1877-1880); subscription department head at the *Detroit Post* (1880-1884), and as, an independent contractor, distributed the newspaper (1884-1891); helped found *The Venture* newspaper (1879), and the *Plaindealer*, which, as managing editor and business manager, he built it into one of the leading African-American newspapers in the Midwest (1883-1891). Temporary chairman of the Michigan Colored Convention and represented Detroit at the National Colored Men's Convention (Pittsburgh, 1884); founded the Michigan Club (1884); co-founded the Afro-American League (1889); appointed clerk of the office of Detroit's collector of internal revenue (1884), and oil inspector for the State of Michigan (1887); delegate to the Republican National Convention (1888), a sergeant-at-arms (1896); member of the Afro-American Bureau of the Republican National Committee. Received an honorary degree from Howard University (LL.B., 1904); clerk in the U.S. Customs Bureau (1900-1937), where he **received patents for a tabulation machine (1905), and a tallying device (1913), for use in the bureau**; publisher and editor of the African-American weekly, *Washington Tribune* (1939-1941); founded an African-American news agency, the Capitol News Services, Inc. Died on June 12, 1943, in Washington, D.C. Further reading, William J. Simmons, *Men of Mark* (1887).

---

on this day in history...

1930,	Barbara Harris, first African-American woman Anglican priest, was born in Philadelphia, Pa.
1963,	Medgar Evers, Mississippi NAACP field secretary, was assassinated in Jackson, Miss.
1972,	The National Black MBA Association was incorporated.

JUNE 12   INVENTORS & EXPLORERS

ROBERT HENDERSON TERRELL

Judge and educator. Born on November 27, 1857, in Charlottesville, Va. Harvard University *magna cum laude* (B.A., 1884); Howard University (LL.B., 1889; LL.M., 1893). Taught in the District of Columbia public schools (1884-1889); became chief clerk in the office of the auditor of the U.S. Treasury (1889); married Mary E. Church (1891); practiced law in Washington (1892-1898); became teacher of the M Street High School in Washington (1898), and later principal; served on the Washington Board of Trade. Appointed justice of the peace in the District of Columbia (1901); delivered an address, *A Glance at the Past and Present of the Negro*, at Robert R. Church's Auditorium before the Citizen's Industrial League of Memphis (1903); served as **judge of the Municipal Court of the District of Columbia** (1910-1925); faculty member of Howard University Law School (1910-1925); served as Grand Master for the Grand United Order of Odd Fellows of the District of Columbia; charter member of Epsilon Boule of Sigma Pi Phi fraternity (1911), which included some of the nation's most distinguished African-Americans. Died in 1925 in Washington, D.C. Further reading, Mary Church Terrell, *A Colored Woman in a White World* (1940).

---

on this day in history...

1909,   Chester Bomar Himes, author of *Cotton Comes to Harlem*, was born in Jefferson City, Mo.

1914,   Dovie Hudson, community activist in rural Mississippi, was born in Carthage, Miss.

1942,   William Dean, Jr., proposed a boycott until or unless African-American were permitted to play on major league baseball teams.

NORBERT RILLIEUX

Inventor and engineer.   Born on March 17, 1806, in New Orleans, La.   Studied engineering at L'Ecole Centrale in Paris (1830).   Became an instructor in applied science; **invented, developed, and patented evaporating pan called the multiple effect vacuum pan evaporator,** which increased the efficiency of sugar refining and the production capabilities of sugar plantations; his sugar refining invention was later used in Cuba and Mexico and was called "the greatest invention in the history of American chemical engineering." Designed and developed a sewage-disposal system for New Orleans; returned to Paris (1854), and resumed teaching and became headmaster at L'Ecole Centrale; became interested in Egyptology and made important contributions to the deciphering of hieroglyphics. His evaporator played a significant role in revitalizing the Louisiana region economy after the Civil War and the multiple-effect principle was applied to the production of soap, gelatin, glue, and waste-recycling processes in paper mills and other industries. Died on October 8, 1894, in Paris, France.   Further reading, Aaron E. Klein, *The Hidden Contributions: Black Scientists and Investors in America* (1970).

on this day in history...

1893,	T.W. Stewart patented a mop.
1937,	Eleanor Holmes Norton, D.C. delegate to Congress, was born in Washington, D.C.
1950,	Jesse Binga, Chicago millionaire banker, died in Chicago, Ill. (b. 1865).
1951,	Anna Perez, former First Lady Barbara Bush's press secretary, was born in New York City.
1955,	Leah J. Sears-Collins, Georgia's first African-American woman state Supreme Court justice, was born in Heidelberg, Germany.
1967,	Thurgood Marshall was appointed the first African-American justice to the U.S. Supreme Court by President Johnson.

DAVID AUGUSTUS STRAKER

Lawyer, politician, educator, judge, lecturer, author, and newspaper publisher. Born in 1842 in Bridgetown, Barbados. Howard University law degree (1871). Teacher and principal of St. Mary's Public High School in Barbados; taught former slaves in Louisville (1868-1896); served as clerk of the U.S. Post Office (1871-1875); moved to South Carolina and became a member of the law firm of Elliott, Dunbar, Stewart, and Straker (1875). Won a seat representing Orangeburg County in the South Carolina House of Representatives (1876); inspector of customs in Charleston (1880-1882); **dean of the new law school at Allen University in Columbia** (1882-1887); received wide recognition for his work as defense counsel in a murder case, *Coleman vs. State* (1884), in which he unsuccessfully used the new criminal defense of transitory insanity. Moved to Detroit (1887); admitted to the Michigan bar and developed a prosperous mixed practice; lectured on the "New South" and wrote, *The New South Investigated* (1888); successfully appealed to the Michigan State Supreme Court the case of *Ferguson vs. Gies* (1890), a case dealing with discrimination in public places, which set a precedent for civil rights cases from the turn of the 20th century. First African-American elected circuit court commissioner for Wayne County, Mich. (1893-1897); compiled, *The Circuit Court Commissioner's Guide, Law and Practice* (1897); argued for the right of all American citizens to vote, hold public office, obtain an education, live where one pleases, work at whatever job fits one's talents, and to have equal access to all public facilities. Organizer and first president of the National Federation of Colored Men (1895), a forerunner to the NAACP, which sought remedies against lynching, fraudulent elections, and disenfranchisement; wrote articles for the *Detroit Advocate* (1901-1908), and for the *AME Church Review*. Died on February 14, 1908, in Detroit, Mich.   Further reading, Dorothy Drinkard-Hawkshawe, "Straker, David Augustus," *Dictionary of American Biography* (1982).

---

on this day in history...

1917,   10,000 African-Americans, led by W.E.B. DuBois and James Weldon Johnson, marched down New York City's Fifth Avenue in a silent parade to protest racial indignities across the U.S.

LEWIS TEMPLE

Inventor.   Born in 1800 in Richmond, Va.   Began operating a whale craft shop on Coppin's Wharf in New Bedford, Mass. (1837-1845), a center for the whaling industry; operated a blacksmith shop (1845-1854), becoming prosperous from the manufacturing and sale of iron. From an idea that came to him at his barber shop, he **invented a whaling harpoon** called the Temple Toggle (1848), which was said to be "the single most important invention in the history of whaling." Died in May 1854 in New Bedford, Mass.   Further reading, Robert C. Hayden, *Eight Black American Inventors* (1972).

---

on this day in history...

1918,	Leroy Walker, first African-American president of the U.S. Olympic Committee, was born in Atlanta, Ga.
1941,	John Edgar Wideman, author of *Philadelphia Fire*, was born in Washington, D.C.
1946,	Margaret Bradley ("Marla Gibbs"), actress, was born in Chicago, Ill.
1970,	Cheryl A. Brown won the Miss Iowa Pageant, becoming the first African-American to compete in the Miss America Pageant.
1989,	Pennsylvania Congressman William Gray was elected House Democratic Whip, the highest level of leadership ever held by an African-American in Congress.

JUNE 14   **INVENTORS & EXPLORERS**

T. McCANTS STEWART

Lawyer, pastor, author, educator, and editor. Born in 1854 in Charleston, S.C. University of South Carolina valedictorian (B.A., 1875; LL.B., 1875). Became a partner with Congressman Robert Brown Elliott in the Charleston, S.C., law firm of Elliott, Dunbar, Stewart and Straker (1875); professor of mathematics in the South Carolina State Agricultural College at Orangeburg; ordained as an AME minister (1877), becoming the pastor of Bethel AME Church in New York City; went to Liberia as a Charles Sumner Professor of Belles Lettre, at the College of Liberia. Lobbied the State of New York to adopt a law to prevent insurance companies from determining premiums by race; wrote editorials for the New York *Freeman*; member of the Brooklyn Board of Education, where he reportedly had the word "colored" removed from the school district. Moved to Honolulu (1898); established the weekly Portland, Ore. *Advocate* (1903); **returned to Liberia and served as associate justice of the Supreme Court** (1906-1915); lived in England (1915-1921); founded the African-Progress Union (1918), to promote the solidarity of African-Americans and Africans; moved to St. Thomas, V.I. (1921), where he was a member of a delegation from the Virgin Islands to the U.S. (1922). Died on January 7, 1923, in St. Thomas, V.I. Further reading, August Meier, *Negro Thought in America 1880-1915* (1963).

---

on this day in history...

1880,   A.P. Abourne was awarded a patent for his coconut oil refining process.
1979,   The first body was found in what was later called the "Atlanta Child Murders."

JULY 27   **LAWYERS & JUDGES**

GRANVILLE T. WOODS

Inventor nicknamed **the "Black Edison."** Born on April 23, 1856, in Columbus, Ohio. Studied electrical and mechanical engineering (1876-1878). Served as an engineer on a long tour aboard the British steamship, *Ironsides* (1878); engineer on the Danville & Southern Railroad (1882-1884); invented and patented a steam boiler furnace, which provided a better method of combustion and economized fuel (1884), and a telephone transmitter (1884), which was bought by American Bell Telephone Company. Owner of Woods Electric Company in Cincinnati (1884-1890), which manufactured and sold telephone, telegraph, and electrical instruments; invented the Multiplex Railway Telegraph (1887), a device for informing engineers about trains immediately in front of and behind them, thus ensuring safer rail travel; invented the overhead conducting system for electric railways (1888), which led to the development of the elevated railway systems in metropolitan areas throughout the world. Challenged unsuccessfully by Thomas Edison over patent rights; patented a galvanic battery (1888), automatic cut-out for electric circuits (1889), electric railway system (1891), incubator (1899), automatic circuit-breaker device (1900), and railway break apparatus (1904). Died on January 30, 1910, in New York City. Further reading, M.A. Harris, *The Black Book* (1974).

on this day in history...

1877,   Henry Ossain Flipper became the first African-American graduate at the U.S. Military Academy at West Point.
1921,   Besse Coleman became the first African-American woman to receive a pilot's license.
1927,   Natalie Leota Hinderas, first African-American artist to gain prominence in the field of classical music, was born in Oberlin, Ohio.
1949,   Johnnie B. "Dusty" Baker, San Francisco Giants manager, was born in Riverside, Calif.

JUNE 15   **INVENTORS & EXPLORERS**

ALTHEA T.L. SIMMONS

Lawyer, lobbyist, organizational official.   Born on April 17, 1924, in Shreveport, La.   Southern University (B.S., 1945); University of Illinois (M.B.A., 1951); Howard University School of Law (1956); University of California at Los Angeles; American Society of Training Development; American Management Association; New School for Social Work in New York City; National Training Laboratory.   Became an associate with the W.J. Durham law office (1956-1961). Served as executive secretary of the Texas State Conference of NAACP branches and chairperson of the executive committee of the Dallas branch; field secretary out of the NAACP subregional office in Los Angeles (1961-1964); NAACP secretary of training (1964-1974), where she was responsible for compiling and distributing all training manuals and materials, as well as planning and implementing training and executive development programs for the NAACP's national office, in the field, and for the executive secretaries of branches; director of the NAACP's National Voter Registration Drive (1964); NAACP educational director (1974-1977), developing handbooks, pamphlets, programs, and other instructional materials designed to uplift African-American youth; associate director of branch and field services (1977-1979), where she supervised the NAACP's nationwide network of branches, field staff, and the Membership, Youth, and College Division. Coordinator of the Evers family relocation (1963), after the assassination of Medgar Evers; succeeded Clarence Mitchell as **director of the Washington Bureau and chief lobbyist for the NAACP** (1979), helping bring about extensions of voting rights, passage of Fair Housing Act, and the bill to establish a Martin Luther King, Jr., national holiday. Member of the National Manpower Advisory Committee, U.S. Department of Labor (1969-1974), executive board of Delta Sigma Theta (1976-1990), General Board of Pensions of the United Methodist Church; vice president of NOW Legal Defense and Education Fund (1974-1977). Died on September 13, 1990, in Washington, D.C.   Further reading, Jessie Carney Smith, *Notable Black American Women* (1992).

---

on this day in history...

1865,   Patrick Francis Healy, while at Yale, became the first African-American to earn a Ph.D.
1948,   President Truman issued Executive Order 9981, directing the Armed Forces to provide "equality of treatment and opportunity for all personnel without regard to race, color, religion, or national origin."

ROBERT SENGSTACKE ABBOTT

Newspaper editor and publisher. Born on November 28, 1868, in St. Simon's Island, Ga. Chaflin University; Hampton Institute (1896); Kent College of Law in Chicago (LL.B., 1898). Practiced law in Topeka, Kan., and Gary, Ind.; **founded the *Chicago Defender* (1905),** which he called "The World's Greatest Weekly;" peddled the newspaper door-to-door on Chicago's South State Street, while serving as editor, business manager, and as the entire staff. President and treasurer of Robert Abbott Publishing Company (1905-1940), where he built the weekly circulation to over a quarter of a million copies and turned the *Defender* into one of the most influential African-American newspapers of its day; he attacked discrimination, segregation, and lynching, and encouraged African-Americans to migrate from the South. Strongly opposed Marcus Garvey's Universal Negro Improvement Association; named a member of the Chicago Commission on Race Relations (1922), following "The Red Summer" of 1919; pressed for the passage of the Dyer Anti-Lynching Bill (1922), and for the confirmation defeat of John J. Parker to the U.S. Supreme Court (1930). Board member of the Wabash Avenue branch of the Chicago YMCA (1923-1933); supported of the Chicago Urban League by campaigning for the improvement and employment of African-American workers in white-owned and operated businesses in the African-American community (1928-1931); served as national president of the Hampton Alumni Association; member of the Ancient Order of Foresters, Thirty-third Degree Mason. Died on February 29, 1940, in Chicago, Ill. Further reading, Roi Ottley, *The Lonely Warrior: The Life and Times of Robert S. Abbott* (1955).

---

on this day in history...

1947,   Eddie Levert, lead singer of the O'Jays, was born in Canton, Ohio.
1970,   Kenneth Gibson of Newark was elected the first African-American mayor of a northeastern U.S. city.
1975,   Adam Wade became the first African-American to host a nationally televised game show (*Musical Chairs*).

JUNE 16   **JOURNALISTS**

EDITH SPURLOCK SAMPSON

Lawyer, U.N. official, and judge.   Born on October 13, 1901, in Pittsburgh, Pa.   New York School of Social Work; University of Chicago School of Social Service Administration; John Marshall Law School (LL.B., 1925); Loyola University of Chicago (LL.M., 1927), **first woman to receive the LL.M. degree from the university**.   Admitted to the Illinois bar (1927); worked with the YWCA and the Illinois Children's Home and Aid Society; operated a law practice on South State Street in the heart of Chicago's "Black Belt" (1924-1942), specializing in criminal law and domestic relations and becoming a kind of clinic for thousands of poor people; referee for the Juvenile Court of Cook County, Illinois (1925-1942); became one of the **first African-American women to be admitted to practice before the U.S. Supreme Court** (1934). Became chairwoman of the executive committee of the National Council of Negro Women; elected president of the World Town Hall Seminar. Appointed, as a substitute for Eleanor Roosevelt, **the first African-American U.S. delegate to the U.N.** (1950), as an alternate to the fifth regular session of the General Assembly; began traveling abroad addressing the status of the African-American population (1951); reappointed alternate delegate and a member-at-large of the U.S. Commission for UNESCO (1952). Became an assistant corporation counsel for Chicago (1955); member of the United States Citizens Commission on the North Atlantic Treaty Organization (1961-1963); elected associate judge of the Municipal Court of Chicago, Branch Forty-one (1962-1964), **becoming the first elected African-American woman judge**; member of the Advisory Committee on Private Enterprise in Foreign (1964-1966); elected associate judge of the Circuit Court of Cook County (1964). Died in 1979.   Further reading, Marianna W. Davis, *Contributions of Black Women to America,* vol. 1 (1982).

---

on this day in history...

1921,   Liberty Life Insurance Company, now called Supreme Life Insurance Company, was founded by Frank L. Gillespie.
1951,   Douglas H. Palmer, Trenton's first African-American mayor, was born in Trenton, N.J.

CLAUDE ALBERT BARNETT

Journalist. Born on September 16, 1889, in Sanford, Fla. Tuskegee Institute engineering degree (1906). Moved to Chicago and became a postal clerk and an advertising salesman for the *Chicago Defender*; started a mail-order business (1913), distributing African-American portraits between Chicago and California; co-founder and advertising manager for Kashmir Chemical Company; **founder and president of the Associated Negro Press** (1919-1964), which began exchanging national news releases to publishers for advertising space, while supplying national and international news to African-American newspapers around the country; it also offered a special news service for African news in French and English. Served as consultant to the U.S. Department of Agriculture (1930-1953), advising Agriculture Secretaries Henry A. Wallace, Claude R. Wickard, and Charles F. Brannon on means of assisting the nation's African-American farmers; married Etta Moten (1934), a well-known actress, singer, and radio personality; worked as an advertising adviser for Poro Beauty College. Served as president of the board of directors of Chicago's Provident Hospital (1938-1942); Tuskegee board of trustees member; member of the board of directors of Chicago's Supreme Life Insurance Company, New York City's Liberia Company, the Chicago chapter of the National Red Cross, Phelps-Stokes Fund in New York City, President Truman's Committee for the Physically Handicapped, and a life member of the Art Institute of Chicago; served as a Star of Africa commander of Liberia and an Order of Honor and Merit chevalier of the Republic of Haiti. Died on August 2, 1967, in Chicago, Ill. Further reading, Lawrence D. Hogan, *A Black National News Service, The Associated Press and Claude Barnett, 1919-1945* (1984).

on this day in history...

1775,	Peter Salem shot and killed British commander Maj. John Pitcairn, becoming the hero of the Battle of Bunker Hill.
1849,	Thomas Ezekial Miller, former South Carolina congressman (1889-1891), was born in Ferbeeville, S.C. (d. 1938).
1880,	Carl Van Vechten, Harlem Renaissance writer and photographer, was born in Cedar Rapids, Iowa (1964).
1966,	Stokely Carmichael called for the Black Power Movement at a Greenwood, Miss., rally.
1972,	Frank Wills discovered a break-in at the Watergate Complex.

JUNE 17

JOURNALISTS

EDWARD H. MORRIS

Lawyer and fraternal leader.   Born on May 30, 1858, in Flemingsburg, Ky.   St. Patrick's College (1874).   Read law in the office of Edward A. Fisher in Chicago; admitted to the Illinois bar (1879); sustained the right of the county, as Cook County attorney, to tax insurance companies; argued before the Illinois Supreme Court (1889), resulting in Illinois' first civil rights law (in the case of *Baylies vs. Curry*); member of the Illinois General Assembly (1890-1892, 1902-1904), where he was responsible for school teachers receiving pensions and the legalization of slave marriages for purpose of rights of inheritance. Began a private practice (1904), serving as a consulting attorney for railroad and corporate interests; following the Chicago Race Riot (1919), he was appointed to the Chicago Commission on Race Relations, which produced the report *The Negro in Chicago*; member of the Illinois Constitutional Convention (1920-1921); named receiver for the State of Illinois when the Jesse Binga State Bank collapsed (1930). Joined the United Grand Order of Odd Fellows (1882); served as deputy grand master (1884-1888), grand master (1888-1903, 1910-1943), making it one of the strongest fraternal orders in the nation; traveled to Australia and Great Britain as an Odd Fellow representative. Died on February 3, 1943, in Washington, D.C.   Further reading, *Chicago Defender National Edition* (February 6, 1993).

---

on this day in history...

1914,	Kenneth B. Clark, co-founder of the Joint Center for Political and Economic Studies, was born in the Panama Canal Zone.
1929,	Cornelius H. Charlton, Korean War hero, was born in East Gulf, W.Va. (d. 1951).
1963,	Karl Malone, Utah Jazz All-Star, was born in Summerfield, La.
1964,	Barry Bonds, San Francisco Giants and National League MVP, was born in Riverside, Calif.
1993,	Reginald F. Lewis, Boston Celtics captain, died in Waltham, Mass. (b. 1966).

HENRY ALLEN BOYD

Publisher, banker, and church leader. Born on April 15, 1876, in Grimes County, Texas. Became **San Antonio's first African-American postal clerk**; appointed secretary of the denomination's Home Mission Board for the National Baptist Convention (1896); **co-founded the National Baptist Publishing Company in Nashville** (1896), where they printed and distributed national Baptist literature and became an influential force among 20th-century publishers of religious material; ordained as a Baptist minister (1904); managed the National Baptist Church Supply Company, which manufactured and distributed pews, benches, and other church furniture, and the National Negro Doll Company, which produced African-American dolls and sold them nationwide. **Co-founded and managed the *Nashville Globe*** (1905-1959), created in response to a streetcar boycott by the African-American community protesting newly-enacted "Jim Crow" laws and initiated several local and statewide race reforms and campaigns; lobbied for the creation of the Tennessee Agricultural and Industrial State Normal School in Nashville (1911) [now Tennessee State University]. President of One Cent Savings Bank and Trust Company of Nashville [later changed to Citizens Savings and Trust Company] (1922-1959), where he invested in a Jacksonville real estate project, Atlanta's Standard Life Insurance Company, and Supreme Life Insurance Company of Chicago. Organizer and corresponding secretary of the National Negro Press Association; trustee of Meharry Medical School and Fisk University; board of directors emeritus of Supreme Life. Died on May 28, 1959, in Nashville, Tenn. Further reading, Lester C. Lamon, *Black Tennesseans 1900-1930* (1977).

---

on this day in history...

1937,   Barbara Ann Teer, founder of the National Black Theater, was born in East St. Louis, Ill.
1939,   Lou Brock, Baseball Hall of Famer, was born in El Dorado, Ark.
1942,   Bernard W. Robinson became the first African-American to earn a naval commission.
1966,   Samuel Nabrit became the first African-American to serve on the Atomic Energy Commission.
1991,   Wellington Webb became Denver's first African-American mayor.

JUNE 18   **JOURNALISTS**

CLARENCE M. MITCHELL, JR.

Lawyer, administrator, and lobbyist who was known as the **"101st senator."** Born on March 4, 1911, in Baltimore, Md. Lincoln University (B.A., 1932); University of Maryland Law School (LL.B., J.D.); University of Minnesota; Atlanta University. Admitted to the Maryland bar; became reporter for the Baltimore *Afro-American*; served as director of the St. Paul (Minn.) Urban League; NAACP labor secretary (1945-1950), planning and directing the drive to bring about fair employment practices for government employees; testified before the Civil Service Commission about racial discrimination in post offices (1948), which led to sweeping reforms. Served as director of the NAACP Washington bureau (1950-1979), becoming the **nation's top civil rights lawyer**; legislative chairman of the Leadership Council on Civil Rights; awarded the NAACP Spingarn Medal (1969), for his meaningful contributions to the cause of civil rights; urged Congress to pass the Civil Rights Bill of 1957, which created the U.S. Commission on Civil Rights. Lobbied for the passage of the Civil Rights Act of 1964, Voting Rights Act of 1965, Fair Housing Act of 1968, extension of the Voting Rights Act's ban against literacy tests for five years, and enforcement powers for the Equal Employment Opportunity Commission; awarded the "Medal of Freedom" by President Carter (1984). Died in 1984. Further reading, W. Augustus Low and Virgil A. Clift, *Encyclopedia of Black America* (1981).

---

on this day in history...

1868,	The 14th Amendment was ratified, granting citizenship to all Negroes.
1889,	W.A. Martin patented the lock.
1947,	Spencer Christian, ABC's *Good Morning America* weathercaster, was born in Charles City, Va.
1967,	The deadliest riot of 1967 began at an afterhours club on Twelfth Street in Detroit, Mich.
1984,	Suzette Charles of New Jersey replaced Vanessa Williams as Miss America.

MARY SHADD CARY

Editor, abolitionist, and suffragist who was the **first woman in North America to publish and edit a newspaper**.   Born on October 9, 1823, in Wilmington, Del.   Howard University (LL.B., 1883).   Taught in Wilmington, West Chester, New York City, and Norristown; moved to Canada West (1850), after the passage of the Fugitive Slave Act and became a schoolteacher in Windsor; edited *Notes on Canada West* (1852), to inform fugitive slaves on what they might expect once they reach the border; publishing agent and **editor of *Provincial Freeman*** (1853-1858), a journal serving the fugitive slave community; contracted as the official printer for the Chatham Town Council. Lectured throughout the Midwest (1855-1856), attacking African-Americans and whites who were compromising in anyway on the issue of slavery or who were preparing to accept second class status; supported the True Band Society of Amherstburg, a militant group who preferred settling internal African-American disputes through African-American arbitration boards; helped Osborne P. Anderson (one of John Brown's assistants) prepare his notes for the publication, *A Voice from Harpers Ferry* (1861); became a naturalized British subject (1862); taught in Michigan (1862), and for the American Missionary Association in Chatham; appointed a recruiting officer for African-American volunteers to the federal armies in Indiana during the Civil War. Moved to Washington (1865), and became a public school principal and wrote for Frederick Douglass' *New National Era* and John W. Cromwells' *The People's Advocate*; joined the National Women's Suffrage Association. Died on June 5, 1893, in Washington, D.C.   Further reading, <u>Robin W. Winks</u>, <u>*The Blacks in Canada*</u> (1971).

---

on this day in history...

1865,   Juneteenth Day was first celebrated, commemorating the week that slaves in Texas found out about their emancipation.
1953,   African-Americans protesting discriminatory treatment in Baton Rouge began a bus boycott.

JUNE 19   **JOURNALISTS**

FLOYD BIXLER McKISSICK

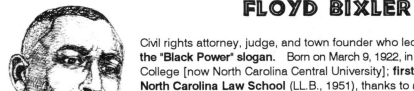

Civil rights attorney, judge, and town founder who led the Black Power movement during the 1960s and **popularized the "Black Power" slogan.** Born on March 9, 1922, in Asheville, N.C. Morehouse College; graduate of North Carolina College [now North Carolina Central University]; **first African-American student and graduate of the University of North Carolina Law School** (LL.B., 1951), thanks to a law suit filed by McKissick and the NAACP ordering the school to integrate. U.S. Army sergeant during World War II (1941-1944), winning a Purple Heart; served as youth chairman of the North Carolina NAACP; participated in the Congress of Racial Equality (CORE) Journey of Reconciliation (1947), which traveled throughout the South testing new federal laws prohibiting segregated services in interstate transportation, which became one of the first non-violent direct action campaigns; Durham attorney in private practice (1951-1963), defending thousands of demonstrators who were brought to trial for conducting sit-ins at "white only" lunch counters, theaters, beaches, swimming pools, bus station waiting rooms, etc. National chairman of CORE (1963-1966), where he warned "white America" of an impending nationwide outbreak of violence (i.e., Watts, Chicago, Detroit, Newark race riots), if they ignored nonviolent African-American protests; helped plan and organize the monumental demonstrations and negotiations of North Carolina's "Freedom Highways" campaign, which led to the desegregation of a major hotel chain; **national director of CORE (1966-1968)**, bringing the organization into the Black Power movement; author of *Three-Fifths of a Man* (1968). Formed the Warren Regional Planning Corporation, awarded federal funds from the New Communities Act, and **launched the model town of Soul City, N.C.** (1968), where he envisioned a metropolitan area ran by African-Americans with business and industrial opportunities; served as pastor of the First Baptist Church of Soul City; North Carolina 9th District Court judge (1990-1991). Died on April 28, 1991, in Durham, N.C. Further reading, August Meier and Elliott Ruwick, *CORE: A Study in the Civil Rights Movement, 1942-1968* (1973).

---

on this day in history...

1902,   Asa Spaulding, first African-American to serve on the board of a major U.S. corporation, was born in Columbus County, N.C. (d. 1990).

1939,   Jane Bolin became the nation's first African-American woman judge.

1961,   Milton A. Francis, first African-American specialist in genitourinary diseases, died in Washington, D.C. (b. 1882).

ALICE ALLISON DUNNIGAN

Educator and pioneering journalist. Born on April 27, 1906, outside of Russellville, Ky. Kentucky State College (B.A., 1926); West Kentucky Industrial College (1932); Howard University. Taught school in Kentucky (1926-1942), while working for the Work Progress Administration to support herself during the five months when schools were not in session; passed a civil service Grade 2 examination (1942), and began working for the Labor Board in Washington, and later, as an economist in the Office of Price Administration. Wrote a local news column for the *Owensborough Enterprise*, and articles, poems, and small stories for other Kentucky newspapers; chief of the Washington Bureau of the Associated Negro Press (1947-1961), where she became the **first African-American woman to be an accredited White House correspondent**; received credentials from the White House Press Association, State Department Press Association, and a Metropolitan Police Pass of Washington. Accompanied President Truman on a campaign trip to California by train (1948), as one of only two women; member of the Washington Press Club and the Capital Press Club; traveled to Canada for Expo '67, Israel for an anniversary celebration, South America, Africa, Mexico, the Caribbean, as well as extensively throughout the U.S.; campaigned for President Johnson (1960); appointed education consultant to the President's Committee on Equal Employment Opportunity (1961), where she worked for the passage of the Civil Rights Act of 1964; information specialist for the U.S. Department of Labor (1966-1967); editorial assistant for the President's Council of Youth Opportunity (1967-1970). Wrote *The Fascinating Story of Black Kentuckians: Their Heritage and History* and assembled a weekly column for the *Louisville Defender*; awarded the Capital Press Club's Newsman's Trophy (1951); received a Kentucky Colonel commission (1962); inducted into the Journalism Hall of Fame at the University of Kentucky (1982). Died in 1983 in Washington, D.C. Further reading, Alice Dunnigan, *A Black Woman's Experience--From Schoolhouse to White House* (1974).

---

on this day in history...

1926,	Mordecai W. Johnson became the first African-American president of Howard University.
1946,	Andre Watts, internationally-renowned concert pianist, was born in Nuremburg, Germany.
1949,	Lionel Richie, Grammy Award-winning recording artist, was born in Tuskegee, Ala.
1960,	Harry Belafonte became the first African-American to win an Emmy (for his variety special, *Tonight With Harry Belafonte*).

JUNE 20   **JOURNALISTS**

THURGOOD MARSHALL

Lawyer, judge, and civil rights leader.   Born on July 2, 1908, in Baltimore, Md.   Lincoln University in Pennsylvania *cum laude* (B.A., 1930), as a pre-dental student; Howard University Law School (1933), at the top of the class.   Operated a private practice in Baltimore (1933-1938); assistant to his mentor Charles H. Houston at the NAACP legal office (1936-1938); appointed special counsel of the NAACP in New York City (1938); director of the NAACP Legal Defense & Educational Fund (1939-1961). Traveled throughout the South and argued a variety of cases including: *Smith vs. Allwright* (1944), in which he fought and won the right for African-Americans to vote in Texas; *Morgan vs. Virginia* (1946), which signaled the end of segregation on interstate passenger carriers in Virginia; *Shelley vs. Kraemer* (1948), which held state enforcement of restrictive housing covenants to be unconstitutional; *Sweatt vs. Painter* (1950), which resulted in the admission of African-American students to the University of Texas School of Law; *Brown vs. Board of Education of Topeka* (1954), which overthrew the 19th-century *Plessy vs. Ferguson* "separate but equal" ruling and began the slow progress of school desegregation. Awarded the NAACP Spingarn Medal (1946), for his contributions as a lawyer before the U.S. Supreme Court; 2nd Circuit Court of Appeals judge (1961-1965), writing over 100 opinions; **first African-American U.S. solicitor general** (1965-1967); first **African-American U.S. Supreme Court justice** (1967-1991). Died on January 24, 1993, in Bethesda, Md.   Further reading, Carl T.Rowan, *Dream Makes, Dream Breakers: The World of Justice Thurgood Marshall* (1992).

---

on this day in history...

1896,	The National Organization of Colored Women was organized by Mary Church Terrell in Washington, D.C.
1903,	George Thomas Downing, founder member of the Grand United Order of Odd Fellows, died in Newport, R.I. (b. 1819).
1934,	Edolphus Towns, New York 10th District congressman, was born in Chadbourn, N.C.
1940,	Jim Clyburn, South Carolina 6th District congressman, was born in Sumter, S.C.
1950,	The 24th Black Infantry Regiment scored the first victory of the Korean Conflict.
1969,	Alfred Daniel King, younger brother of Martin Luther King, Jr., was killed in a swimming pool accident at his Atlanta home.

JULY 21   LAWYERS & JUDGES

TIMOTHY THOMAS FORTUNE

Journalist, freelance writer, and civil rights leader nicknamed **"the dean of African-American journalists"** and best known as **"the most militant and articulate race spokesman in the North."** Born into slavery on October 3, 1856, in Marianna, Fla. Howard University. Learned the printer's trade; worked for the *People's Advocate* in Washington; moved to New York City (1879), and worked as a printer; became part owner of the weekly tabloid *Rumor*; editor of the *New York Globe* (1881-1884). **Founded and edited the *New York Freeman* [later called the *New York Age*]** (1884-1907), in which he condemned racial discrimination and demanded full equality for African-American citizens through his militant editorials; it became a leading African-American newspaper. Wrote *Black and White: Land and Politics in the South* (1884); denounced the Republican Party for its betrayal of southern African-Americans; supported the Prohibition Party (1887); founding member of the National Afro-American League (1890), whose objectives and philosophies paved the way for 20th century civil rights movements; called for the conference (Rochester, 1898), that organized the National Afro-American Council; initiated a platform emphasizing suffrage and civil rights, which helped shape some of the goals of the NAACP; **first advocated the term "Afro-American" instead of "Negro."** Wrote editorials and stories for the *New York Sun*, the *Boston Transcript*, and the *Norfolk Journal and Guide*; special agent of the U.S. Treasury Department (1903), studying race and labor conditions in Japan, Hong Kong, and the Philippines; became editor of Marcus Garvey's and the Universal Negro Improvement Association's *Negro World* (1923). Died on June 2, 1928, in Philadelphia, Pa. Further reading, Lou Thornbrough, *T. Thomas Fortune, Militant Journalist* (1970).

---

on this day in history...

1927,	Carl Stokes of Cleveland, first African-American mayor of a major U.S. city, was born in Cleveland, Ohio.
1947,	Jimmie Walker, actor known as "the Black Prince," was born in the Bronx, N.Y.
1951,	William Thompson was posthumously awarded the Medal of Honor, first African-American recipient since the Spanish-American War.
1964,	James Earl Chaney and two other civil rights workers disappeared near Philadelphia, Miss.

JUNE 21   **JOURNALISTS**

CHARLES HAMILTON HOUSTON

Lawyer, civil rights advocate, and educator whom Thurgood Marshall called **"the first Mr. Civil Rights."** Born on September 3, 1895, in Washington, D.C. Amherst College Phi Beta Kappa and valedictorian (B.A., 1915); Harvard University *cum laude* and **first African-American editor of the *Harvard Law Review*** (LL.B., 1922; D.J.S., 1923), becoming the **first African-American to earn a Doctor of Juridical Science**; University of Madrid (D.C.L., 1924). English instructor at Howard University's College of Arts and Science (1915-1916), instructor on the commercial department faculty (1916-1917), law instructor (1924-1929), associate professor and vice dean at the School of Law, where he taught Thurgood Marshall (1929-1935), and general superintendent of the Law School Library; enlisted in the U.S. Army and trained at the Colored Officers' Training Center in Fort Des Moines, Iowa, and was commissioned as a lieutenant in the Infantry during World War I; taught English at Dunbar High School in Washington, D.C. (1919). Admitted to the District of Columbia bar (1924), and became a member of the law firms of Houston & Houston, of Houston & Hastie, and of Houston, Bryant & Gardner (1924-1950); prepared a report entitled "The Negro and His Contact with the Administration of Law" (1927-1928), under a Laura Spelman Rockefeller Memorial grant; member of the Washington Board of Education (1933-1935). Retained by the American Fund for Public Service and the NAACP (1934-1935), to direct a campaign of legal action and public education against racially unequal apportionment of public education funds and discrimination in public transportation; NAACP special counsel (1935-1940); argued in the case of *Missouri ex. rel. Gaines vs. Canada* (1938), his first major case before the U.S. Supreme Court; member of the NAACP National Legal Committee (1940-1948), chairman (1948-1950); vice president of the National Lawyers Guild and the American Council of Race Relations. Died on April 20, 1950, in Washington, D.C. Further reading, <u>Genna Rae McNeil</u>, *<u>Groundwork: Charles Hamilton Houston and the Struggle for Civil Rights</u>* (1983).

---

on this day in history...

1954,	Freeman Bosley, Jr., St. Louis' first African-American mayor, was born in St. Louis, Mo.
1967,	The first National Conference of Black Power opened in Newark, N.J.
1973,	The first African-American-owned and operated news network, the National Black Network, began operations.
1988,	Presidential candidate Jesse Jackson received over 1,200 delegate votes at the Democratic National Convention.

ROBERT MAYNARD

Publisher.   Born on June 17, 1937, in Brooklyn, N.Y.   Wrote for the *New York Age-Defender*, while in high school; hired as a reporter by the *York (Pa.) Gazette & Daily* (1961-1967), after sending out over 300 applications to papers around the country; became a leader of the movement to integrate the U.S. newspaper industry; Harvard University Neiman fellow (1966). *Washington Post* reporter (1968-1972), associate editor and ombudsman (1972-1974), and editorial writer (1974-1977); *Oakland Tribune* editor (1977-1983); purchased the *Oakland Tribune* for $22 million, serving as president and editor (1983-1992), **orchestrating the first management-leveraged buyout of an American newspaper and becoming the first African-American owner of a major U.S. daily;** co-founder of the Institute for Journalism Education at the University of California at Berkeley, an organization whose primary mission was to create opportunities for minority journalists in American newspapers. Member of the board of trustees of the Rockefeller Foundation and the Foundation of American Communications; member of the board of directors of the Bay Area Council, Associated Press, and of the Pulitzer Prize; member of the Council of Foreign Relations and the Sigma Delta Chi Society of Professional Journalists. Died on August 17, 1993, in Oakland, Calif.   Further reading, *Oakland Tribune* (August 18, 1993).

---

on this day in history...

1909,	Katherine Dunham, "grand dame of American dance," was born in Glen Ellyn, Ill.
1937,	Joe Lewis became the heavyweight boxing champion of the world by defeating James Braddock.
1941,	Ed Bradley, Emmy Award-winning reporter, was born in Philadelphia, Pa.
1949,	Ezzard Charles defeated Jersey Joe Walcott for the heavyweight boxing championship.
1962,	Clyde Drexler, Portland Trailblazer All-Star, was born in New Orleans, La.

WILLIAM HENRY HASTIE

Educator, lawyer, judge, and government official. Born on November 17, 1904, in Knoxville, Tenn. Amherst College (B.A., 1925); Harvard University (LL.B., 1930; S.J.D., 1933). Admitted to the District of Columbia bar and joined the firm of Houston and Houston; Howard University faculty member (1930-1937), and professor and dean of the Law School (1939-1940, 1943-1946); assistant solicitor for the Department of the Interior (1933-1937); judge of the U.S. District Court for the Virgin Islands (1937-1939), becoming the **first African-American federal judge** and the youngest; civilian aide to the U.S. secretary of war (1940-1943), where he protested the continued segregationist practices of the U.S. Army and Army Air Corps. Awarded the NAACP Spingarn Medal (1943), for his distinguished career as a jurist and an uncompromising champion of equal justice, who resigned from his position as civilian aide to the U.S. secretary of war in protest against discriminatory treatment of African-Americans in the Armed Forces; appointed the first African-American governor of the Virgin Islands (1946). Served as judge for the U.S. Court of Appeals for the 3rd Judicial Circuit (1949-1971), becoming the **first African-American U.S. appellate judge**; aided the attempt of Thomas Hecutt to enter the University of North Carolina; argued cases involving salary equalization in North Carolina and Maryland, and fought employment and discrimination. Died on April 14, 1976, in Philadelphia, Pa. Further reading, <u>Gilbert Ware</u>, <u>*William Hastie: Grace Under Pressure*</u> (1984).

---

on this day in history...

1948,   Phylicia Rashad, actress, was born in Houston, Texas.
1979,   Patricia Harris was named U.S. secretary of health and human services.

JULY 19   **LAWYERS & JUDGES**

ETHEL LOIS PAYNE

Journalist who was called **"the first lady of the Black press."** Born on August 14, 1911, in Chicago, Ill. Crane Junior College; Garrett Institute; graduate of Medill School of Journalism at Northwestern University. Began her journalism career working in Tokyo (1949), where she was director of an army club and kept a journal about discrimination against African-American soldiers serving in the Korean War; hired by *Chicago Defender* as a Washington correspondent and became the **first African-American woman to join the White House press corps** (1953-1973), where she gained immediate recognition by asking President Eisenhower why the Howard University choir had been turned away from a Republican Lincoln Day celebration, received an apology from the President becoming the main story of the day. Covered her first international conference in Bandung, Indonesia (1956); interviewed Chinese Premier Chou En-Lai and Ugandan dictator Idi Amin; also covered Capitol Hill, U.S. Department of Labor, U.S. Department of Housing and Urban Development, U.S. Department of State, Equal Employment Opportunity Commission, and the U.S. Information Agency; served as staff writer of the AFL-CIO Committee on Political Education; as regular columnist for the *Afro-American, Miami Times, Miami Herald, St. Louis Sentinel, Chicago Defender, Michigan Chronicle*, and *Pittsburgh Courier*. Became the **first African-American woman war correspondent in the Vietnam War** (1967); president of Capital Press Club (1970-1973); named by Fisk University as the first recipient of the Ida B. Wells Distinguished Journalism Chair (1973); commentator of "Matters of Opinion" on WBBM, CBS, in Chicago (1978-1982). Died on May 28, 1991, in Washington, D.C. Further reading, <u>Dorothea W. Slocum</u>, <u>"Ethel Payne,"</u> *Notable Black American Women* (1992).

---

on this day in history...

1893,	Willie Sims, the wealthiest jockey of his time, won five races on six mounts at Sheephead Race Track in New York.
1904,	Willie Mae Ford, "mother of gospel music," was born in Rolling Fork, Miss.
1934,	Jesse White, Jr., founder of the Jesse White Tumblers, was born in Alton, Ill.
1938,	Charles McDew, SNCC organizer of Orangeburg lunch counter sit-ins, was born in Massillon, Ohio.
1940,	Wilma Rudolph, Olympic track champion, was born in Clarksville, Tenn.
1948,	Clarence Thomas, U.S. Supreme Court associate justice, was born in Pin Point, Ga.

JUNE 23   **JOURNALISTS**

ARCHIBALD HENRY GRIMKE

Lawyer, editor, author, civil rights leader, and diplomat. Born into slavery on August 17, 1849, near Charleston, S.C. Lincoln University in Pennsylvania (B.A., 1870; M.A., 1872), where he worked as their only African-American librarian while a student; Harvard University (LL.B., 1874). Helped organize the Ashum Presbyterian Church (1867); admitted to the Suffolk County bar (1875), and was law partner of Butler Wilson; **founded and published New England's first African-American newspaper,** *The Hub* (1883-1886); president of the Massachusetts Suffrage League; leader of the Negro Independents and the Boston "Radicals," which was a group of well-educated African-Americans who protested all forms of segregation and discrimination. Alternate delegate to the Republican National Convention (1884); wrote articles for the *Herald and Traveller* in Boston; published *William Lloyd Garrison, the Abolitionist* (1891), *The Life of Charles Sumner, the Scholar in Politics* (1892); trustee and secretary of the board of the Westborough Insane Asylum; consul to Santo Domingo in the Dominican Republic (1894-1898); president of the American Negro Academy (1903-1916); served as treasurer of the Committee of Twelve (1904), an organization of African-Americans designed to end the growing rivalries in racial ideologies. Member of the original Committee of Forty (1909), which helped pave the way for the formation of the NAACP; attended the Amenia Conference (1916); awarded the NAACP Spingarn Medal (1919), for his notable achievements in behalf of African-American rights. Died on February 25, 1930, in Washington, D.C. Further reading, Charles Flint Kellogg, *A History of the National Association for the Advancement of Colored People 1990-1920* (1967).

---

on this day in history...

1863,	The 54th and 55th Massachusetts Negro Regiments were involved in the first major battle of the Civil War, the Battle of Fort Wagner.
1899,	Leonard C. Baily patented a folding bed.
1941,	Martha Reeves, Motown Records secretary who formed her own group "The Vandellas," was born in Detroit, Mich.
1943,	Calvin Peete, professional golfer, was born in Detroit, Mich.

JULY 18   **LAWYERS & JUDGES**

WILLIAM PICKENS

Editor, civil rights leader, orator, and educator who was known as "Dean" Pickens and recognized by Langston Hughes as **"one of the most popular platform orators in America."** Born on January 15, 1881, in Anderson County, S.C. Talladega College; Yale University (B.A., 1904). Taught classics at Talladega College (1904-1914), Wiley University (1914-1915), and Morgan State University (1915-1920); became a member of the Committee of One Hundred (1910); wrote for the Niagara Movement's *Voice of the Negro*; helped establish the Louisville branch of the NAACP, advocated the colored officers' training camp at Fort Des Moines, Iowa, and attacked "Jim Crow" laws in Memphis. **A contributing editor of the Associated Negro Press** (1919-1940); field secretary and director of branches of the NAACP (1920-1942), where he was responsible for recruiting, establishing new branches, fundraising, and investigating; joined with the Committee of Eight in demanding the imprisonment of Marcus Garvey (1922); lectured for the Federal Forum Project (1937-1938), a national network of adult education centers; served as director of the Interracial Section of the Treasury Department's Savings Bonds Division (1941-1950). Died on April 6, 1954, in Jamaica. Further reading, Sheldon Avery, "Up From Washington: William Pickens and the Negro Struggle," Schomburg Center for Research in Black Culture.

---

on this day in history...

1896,	Booker T. Washington became the first African-American to receive a honorary degree from Harvard University.
1933,	Mitilda Sissieretta Jones ("Black Patti"), singer, died in Providence, R.I. (b. 1869).
1939,	Harold James Melvin, leader of the R&B singing group "The Bluenotes," was born in Philadelphia, Pa.
1943,	Georg Stanford Brown, actor and director, was born in Havana, Cuba.
1949,	*Billboard* magazine replaced the term "Race Records" on its record charts with "Rhythm & Blues."

JAMES ADLAI COBB

Lawyer, educator, judge, and civil rights leader.   Born in 1876 in Arcadia, La.   Fisk University; Straight University [now Dillard]; Howard University (LL.B., 1899; LL.M., 1900; B.P., 1902).   Admitted to the bar in Washington, D.C. (1900); practiced law and was known as a constitutional lawyer (1900-1926); **senior partner in the most prestigious African-American law firm in Washington--Cobb, Howard & Hayes** (1935-1958); special assistant in the U.S. Department of Justice (1907-1915), where he gained a national reputation in prosecuting cases under the 1906 Pure Food and Drug Act. Faculty member of Howard University School of Law (1916-1938), serving as vice dean (1923-1929); admitted to the bar of the U.S. Supreme Court (1917); associate counsel in *Buchanan vs. Warley* (1917), *Nixon vs. Herndon* (1927), and *Nixon vs. Condon* (1932); delegate to the Republican National Convention (Chicago, 1920), and alternate-delegate (Cleveland, 1924). Municipal Court for the District of Columbia judge (1926-1935); chairman of the District of Columbia Selective Service Appeals Board; trustee of the Washington Public Library; director of the NAACP, National Urban League, and the National Council of Jews and Christians; member of Epsilon Boule of Sigma Pi Phi fraternity, which was composed of some of the most distinguished African-Americans in Washington. Died on October 14, 1958, in Washington, D.C.   Further reading, Rayford W. Logan, "Cobb, James Adlai," *Dictionary of American Negro Biography* (1982).

---

on this day in history...

1935,	Carol Johnson ("Diahann Carroll"), actress, was born in New York City.
1944,	Over 200 African-Americans were killed in an explosion at an ammunition depot in Port Chicago, Calif.
1960,	George Washington Carver National Monument, first to honor an African-American, was dedicated in Missouri.

JULY 17   LAWYERS & JUDGES

MAX ROBINSON

Broadcast journalist.   Born on May 1, 1939, in Richmond, Va.   Oberlin College; Virginia Union University; Indiana University.   Newsreader at WTOV-TV in Portsmouth, Va. (1959), where he had applied for a "whites only job," read the news from behind a screen, and was fired after removing the screen one night so the family could see him on the air; cameraman and first African-American reporter at WTOP-TV in Washington, D.C. (1965), performing mainly traffic reports; first African-American on-air reporter at WRC-TV in Washington, D.C. (1965-1969), covering the riots following the assassination of Martin Luther King, Jr., 1968 national elections, and anti-Vietnam War demonstrations, winning several journalism awards. Associate professor at Federal City College in Washington, D.C. (1968-1972); **first African-American anchor in Washington, D.C.** (1969-1978), co-anchoring the coveted 6 p.m. and 11 p.m. newscast on D.C.'s #1 news station--WTOP-TV (now WUSA-TV); hired by Roone Arledge as correspondent and the **first African-American network news anchor**, *ABC World News Tonight* (1978-1983), which featured Peter Jennings in London, Frank Reynolds in Washington, and Robinson in Chicago; journalist in residence at William & Mary College (1981); first African-American anchor at WMAQ-TV in Chicago (1983-1985); worked as a freelance journalist (1985-1988). Won a Regional Emmy (1967), for a documentary on African-American life in Anacostia, *The Other Washington*; honored by the president of Liberia with the Star of Africa (1972), the city of Washington with a Max Robinson Day, with an Emmy Award for his coverage of the 1980 national elections, and by the National Association of Black Journalists for his fight to portray African-Americans in news stories from their viewpoint; made his last public appearance at Howard University's School of Journalism (1988). Died on December 20, 1988, in Washington, D.C.   Further reading, <u>Chicago Tribune</u> (December 21, 1988).

---

on this day in history...

1876,	Isaiah Dorman, Sioux Indian interpreter who accompanied George Custer, was killed in the Battle of Little Big Horn.
1933,	James Howard Meredith, first African-American student at the University of Mississippi, was born in Kosciusko, Miss.
1942,	Willis Reed, New Jersey Nets vice president of basketball operations, was born in Bernice, La.
1942,	President Roosevelt issued Executive Order 8802, abolishing discrimination in all government departments, armed services, and national defense jobs.

SADIE T. M. ALEXANDER

Lawyer and civil rights activist. Born on January 2, 1898, in Philadelphia, Pa. University of Pennsylvania (B.S., 1918; M.A., 1919; Ph.D., 1921; LL.D., 1927), becoming the **first African-American to receive a Ph.D. in economics and first African-American woman graduate of the University of Pennsylvania School of Law**, dissertation title: "Standards of Living Among 100 Negro Migrant Families in Philadelphia." Assistant actuary of the North Carolina Mutual Life Insurance Company in Durham (1921-1923); elected the first president of the Grand Chapter, Delta Sigma Theta; became the **first African-American woman to be admitted to the Pennsylvania bar** (1927); member of Raymond Pace Alexander's law office (1927-1959), specializing in estate and family law; **first African-American assistant city solicitor of Philadelphia** (1927-1931, 1936-1940); secretary of the National Bar Association (1943-1847). Member of the Philadelphia Fellowship Commission (1946-1965), where she served as chairperson of a special committee to ensure that Philadelphia's new city charter would contain provisions that would guarantee equal treatment and equal opportunity in the city's administration; fought against discrimination and segregation in Philadelphia hotels, restaurants, and theaters, which led to an appointment to the President's Committee on Civil Rights (1947); member of the board of the Philadelphia Commission on Human Relations (1953-1968); practiced law independently (1959), handling domestic relations, divorces, adoptions, civil and probate, and juvenile care cases; served as counsel to the law firm of Atkinson, Myers, and Archie. Chairperson on the White House Conference on Aging (1978-1981); member of the American Civil Liberties Union, NAACP, and Philadelphia Housing Authority; received honorary degrees from the University of Pennsylvania, Drexel University, Lincoln University, Spelman College, and Swarthmore College. Died on November 1, 1989, in Philadelphia, Pa. Further reading, Theresa Snyder, "Sadie Alexander," *Notable Black American Women* (1992).

---

on this day in history...

1904, Harold Dadford West, first African-American president of Meharry Medical College, was born in Flemington, N.J.
1934, Donald Milford Payne, New Jersey's first African-American congressman, was born in Newark, N.J.
1947, Alexis M. Herman, first African-American woman to serve as CEO of the Democratic National Convention, was born in Mobile, Ala.

JOHN BROWN RUSSWURM

Journalist, publisher, editor, abolitionist, colonizationist, and Liberian government official.   Born into slavery in 1799 in Port Antonio, Jamaica.   Bowdoin College in Brunswick, Maine (1826), becoming **one of the first African-American graduates of an American college.**   Moved to New York City (1826), a center for free Negroes in the U.S. at the time; met with other African-Americans leaders in New York City at the home of M. Crummell (1826-1827), and agreed to launch a newspaper; **founded and edited the first African-American newspaper in the U.S.,** *Freedom's Journal* (1827-1829), with Samuel Eli Cornish, as senior editor; became sole editor later that same year; an early Black Nationalist, later converting to colonization in Africa and changing the name of the paper to *The Rights of All*. Migrated to Monrovia, Liberia (1829); editor of the *Liberia Herald* (1830-1835); served as superintendent of education in the Monrovia colony (1830-1836); became the **first African-American colonial agent of the American Colonization Society** (1834-1836); appointed as governor of Maryland in the Liberia Settlement (1836), becoming the **first African-American to hold the rank of governor in Africa**; encouraged agriculture and trade, built a jail and fort, took a census, and established a court with presiding justices. Died on June 9, 1851, in Liberia.   Further reading, Mary Sagrin, *John Brown Russwurm, The Story of Freedom's Journal* (1970).

---

on this day in history...

1893,   William Lee Conley ("Big Bill Broonzy"), blues great, was born in Scott, Miss. (d. 1958).
1934,   Roy Wilkins replaced W.E.B. DuBois as editor NAACP's *Crisis* magazine.

JUNE 26   **JOURNALISTS**

WHITNEY MOORE YOUNG, JR.

Civil rights leader.   Born on July 31, 1921, in Lincoln Ridge, Ky.   Kentucky State College (B.S., 1941); Massachusetts Institute of Technology; University of Minnesota (M.A., sociology, 1947).   Served in World War II; St. Paul Urban League director of industrial relations and vocational guidance; executive director of the Omaha Urban League (1950-1953), where he was instrumental in ending segregation in Omaha's public housing; dean of the Atlanta University School of Social Work (1954-1960); accepted a Rockefeller grant to study at Harvard University (1960). **Executive director of the National Urban League** (1961-1971), transforming it into a socioeconomic organization; proposed a domestic Marshall plan to assist African-Americans in catching up called, *To Be Equal* (1963), which was the foundation for President Johnson's War on Poverty; key organizer of the March on Washington (1963); under his reign, the NUL expanded to over 80 branches and an annual multi-million dollar budget. Died on March 11, 1971, in Lagos, Nigeria, while attending a conference of American and African leaders.   Further reading, <u>Guichard Parris</u> and <u>Lester Brooks</u>, <u>*Blacks in the City: A History of the National Urban League*</u> (1971).

---

on this day in history...

1968,	Ellen Holly became the first African-American in daytime television when she appeared on ABC's *One Life To Live*.
1970,	James McGhee was sworn in as Dayton's first African-American mayor.
1985,	Claude Harris became Seattle's first African-American fire chief.

JULY 15   **LABOR & MOVEMENT LEADERS**

ERA BELL THOMPSON

Journalist and writer. Born on August 10, 1906, in Des Moines, Iowa. North Dakota State University; Morningside College (B.A., 1933); Medill School of Journalism at Northwestern University. Worked at the Settlement House, Work Projects Administration, Chicago Relief Administration, Chicago Board of Trade, Illinois State Employment Services, and as a waitress, elevator operator, and a housekeeper (1933-1945); received a Newberry fellowship (1945), and wrote her autobiography, *American Daughter*; served as **managing editor of John H. Johnson's *Negro Digest* (1947-1951), co-managing editor of *Ebony* magazine (1951-1964), and international editor (1964-1986)**. Member of the board of directors of Hull House (1960-1964); member of the North Central Manpower Advisory Commission (1965-1967); honored as Iota Phi Lambda Outstanding Woman of the Year (1965). Died on December 29, 1986, in Chicago, Ill. Further reading, Ann Shockley and Sue Chandler, *Living Black American Authors* (1973).

---

on this day in history...

1901,   Harry V. Richardson, founder and first president of the Interdenominational Theological Center, was born in Jacksonville, Fla.

1937,   Frederick Jones patented a ticket dispensing machine.

1972,   Patricia Harris was named chairwoman of the Democratic National Convention.

WILLIAM SAXBY TOWNSEND

Labor leader. Born on December 4, 1897, in Cincinnati, Ohio. University of Toronto; graduate of the Royal Academy of Science; Blackstone College of Law in Chicago (LL.B., J.D.). Served in World War I in an all-black stateside unit; elected vice president of an American Federation of Labor red cap local (1936); organized red caps across America; president of the International Brotherhood of Red Caps (1937), which became the United Transport Service Employees of America (1940); led the UTSEA out of the AFL into the Congress of Industrial Organizations (1942), becoming a member of the CIO's executive board, making him the **first African-American vice president in organized labor**. Lecturer on human and industrial relations at Seabury Western Theological Seminary in Evanston, Ill.; awarded the Arthur Schomburg Collection of the New York Public Library's Race Relations Leadership Award (1942); served as the international representative of labor to conferences in Cuba, Mexico, Japan, and German; served as a member of the Committee of the World Federation of Trade Unions (1952), studying conditions in the Pacific Rim; wrote the handbook, *Trade Union Practices and Problems* (1952), after traveling to Japan, where he addressed the Japanese Diet and was honored with a monument; **vice president of the newly merged the AFL-CIO** (1955-1957), becoming one of their highest ranking African-American officers. Died on February 3, 1957, in Chicago, Ill. Further reading, Rayford W. Logan, *What the Negro Wants* (1944).

---

on this day in history...

1888,	The *Indianapolis Freeman*, nation's first illustrated African-American newspaper, was founded by Edward Cooper.
1891,	J. Standard was awarded a patent for a refrigerator.
1934,	Lee Elder, professional golfer, was born in Washington, D.C.

JULY 14   LABOR & MOVEMENT LEADERS

WILLIAM MONROE TROTTER

Businessman, editor, and militant civil rights leader.   Born on April 7, 1872, in Chillicothe, Ohio.   Harvard University (A.B., 1895; M.A., 1896), **first African-American elected to Harvard's Phi Beta Kappa Society.**   Insurance and mortgage broker in Boston (1897-1906); **founded and edited the *Boston Guardian*** (1901-1934), a protest newspaper that demanded full citizenship and equal rights for all African-Americans; became the leader of the "Boston Radicals" and launched a campaign against Booker T. Washington and his "Tuskegee Machine," which led to the Niagara Movement (1905-1907), the first national organization of militant African-Americans; organized a group of about 30 people to disrupt Washington's speech to the Boston Negro Business League at the African Methodist Episcopal Church (1903), which resulted in Trotter receiving a 30-day jail sentence and the local media calling the incident the "Boston Riot." Founded the National Equal Rights League (1908), which he described as "an organization of the colored people and for the colored people and led by the colored people" in comparison to the NAACP; attended a peace conference (Versailles, 1919). Lived out the rest of his life in Boston, where he died in 1934, on his 62nd birthday.   Further reading, Stephen R. Fox, *The Guardian of Boston: William Monroe Trotter* (1970).

---

on this day in history...

1874,	The Freedmen's Savings & Trust Company, because of mismanagement, closed its doors causing over 60,000 African-American depositors to lose their investments.
1936,	Major Odell Owens, New York 11th District congressman, was born in Memphis, Tenn.
1949,	Don Baylor, Colorado Rockies' manager, was born in Austin, Texas.
1964,	Malcolm X founded the Organization of African Unity in New York City.
1978,	The U.S. Supreme Court handed down a decision in the case of *Bakke vs. The Regents of the University of California*, stating that the university system's special minority admission policy was unconstitutional.

JUNE 28   **JOURNALISTS**

BAYARD RUSTIN

Civil rights theoretician, organizer, and strategist who **helped unite the peace and civil rights movements.** Born on March 17, 1912, in West Chester, Pa. Cheyney State College; Wilberforce University. Organizer for the Young Communist League (1936-1941); joined the Fellowship for Reconciliation (1941), which organized interracial fellowship conferences, developed nonviolent protest tactics to combat racism, mediated potentially volatile racial situations, registered African-American voters, and led to the establishment of the Congress of Racial Equality; joined with A. Phillip Randolph in planning the March on Washington movement (1941), in response to employment discrimination at the beginning of World War II; sentenced to prison as a conscientious objector against the war (1942). Became field secretary for CORE (1947), leading the first "Freedom rides" in North Carolina, which resulted in him being sentenced to a chain gang; became executive secretary of the War Resisters League (1953); **special aide to Martin Luther King (1955-1962), helping to guide the Montgomery bus boycott, and drafting the original plan for the Southern Christian Leadership Conference** (SCLC); organized civil rights demonstrations at the Democratic and Republican National Conventions (1960); served as the **master planner of the 1963 March on Washington.** Organized the New York City public schools boycott (1964); executive director of the A. Phillip Randolph Institute in New York City (1964-1987), which as a part of the AFL-CIO, served as a bridge between the African-American community and organized labor; helped organize the Memphis sanitation workers (1968); became an early leader in the gay rights movement. Died on August 24, 1987, in New York City. Further reading, David J. Garrow, *Bearing the Cross: Martin Luther King, Jr., and the Southern Christian Leadership Conference* (1986).

---

on this day in history...

1928, Robert N.C. Nix, Jr., of Pennsylvania, first African-American state Supreme Court chief justice, was born in Philadelphia, Pa.

JULY 13 **LABOR & MOVEMENT LEADERS**

ROBERT LEE VANN

Lawyer, editor, publisher, civil rights leader, and government official.   Born on August 27, 1879, in Ahoskie, N.C.   Wayland Academy in Richmond, Va. (1903); Western University of Pennsylvania [now the University of Pittsburgh] class poet (B.A., 1906; LL.D., 1909), where he became the first African-American editor-in-chief of the school newspaper (1904-1906).   Admitted to the bar (1909); served as **editor, treasurer, and legal counsel of the *Pittsburgh Courier*** (1910-1940), which he built into the nation's largest African-American newspaper of the era, crusaded against segregation and discrimination, and demanded more recognition of African-American in the white press. Appointed fourth **assistant city solicitor in Pittsburgh (1918-1921), the highest position held by an African-American in municipal government**; founded a monthly magazine *The Competitor: The National Magazine* (1920); joined the Associated Negro Press (1925); published columns by George Schuyler, Joel A. Rogers, and Walter White; used the services of syndicated Washington correspondent, Louis Lautier, and cartoonist and photographer, Wilburt Holloway. Supported A. Phillip Randolph's attempts to gain acceptance of the Brotherhood of Sleeping Car Porters (1925); opened a larger printing plant on Pittsburgh's Central Ave. (1929); reported on the Italian invasion of Ethiopia, Joe Louis, and Jesse Owens' four gold medals; increased the nationwide circulation to over a quarter of a million (1938); supported the Committee on Participation of Negroes in the National Defense Program. Special assistant to the U.S. attorney-general and a member of President Roosevelt's "Black Cabinet" (1932-1936); helped obtain the enactment of a Pennsylvania state equal rights law (1935). Died on October 24, 1940, in Philadelphia, Pa.   Further reading, Andrew A. Buni, *Robert L. Vann of the Pittsburgh Courier: Politics and Black Journalism* (1974).

---

on this day in history...

1869,	William Henry Hunt, U.S. consul to Madagascar, was born in Hunt's Station, Tenn. (d. 1951).
1886,	James van der Zee, "the dean of Harlem photographers," was born in Massachusetts.
1922,	Lloyd Richards, Tony Award-winning director of *A Raisin in the Sun*, was born in Toronto, Canada.
1926,	Julius W. Becton, first African-American director of the Federal Emergency Management Agency, was born Bryn Mawr, Pa.
1941,	Stokley Carmichael, civil rights activist and leader of the Black Power Movement, was born in Port-of-Spain, Trinidad.

ASA PHILIP RANDOLPH

Labor leader and socialist who was called **"one of the most progressive labor leaders in America."** Born on April 15, 1889, in Crescent, City, Fla. City College of New York. Moved to New York City and worked as a porter, railroad waiter, and elevator operator; **co-founder and president of the socialist newspaper, *The Messenger: "The Only Radical Negro Magazine in America"*** (1917-1928), in which he spoke out against World War I, favored women having the right to vote, cheered the Russian Revolution, and prompted the U.S. Justice Department to call him and Chandler Owen "the most dangerous Negroes in America." **Organized the first African-American trade union--the Brotherhood of Sleeping Car Porters** (1925), after being invited by Ashley L.Totten to speak to sleeping-car porters at a special organizing meeting; organized Brotherhood offices from Omaha to Oakland and from Chicago to New York City; brought the Brotherhood into the American Federation of Labor (1929); elected the first president of the National Negro Congress (1936); **negotiated the first collective bargaining agreement ever between an African-American union and a large American company--the Pullman Company** (1937), making him the nation's most popular African-American political figure. Achieved acceptance of Brotherhood as full international member of the AFL; influential in getting President Roosevelt to form the Fair Employment Practice Committee (1941), after threatening a massive march on Washington; awarded the NAACP Spingarn Medal (1942), for his leadership in labor; founded the League for Nonviolent Civil Disobedience in the Armed Forces (1947); appointed to the New York Housing Authority (1955); elected vice president of the AFL-CIO (1957); founder and president of the Negro American Labor Council (1960-1966); initiated the March on Washington (1963); founder of the A. Phillip Randolph Institute (1965). Died on May 16, 1979, in New York City. Further reading, Sarah Wright, *A. Phillip Randolph: Integration in the Workplace* (1990).

---

on this day in history...

1849,   William Hooper Councill, first president of Alabama A&M University, was born in Fayetteville, N.C. (d. 1909).

1899,   Edgar Daniel Nixon, Alabama NAACP president who bailed out Rosa Parks and co-founded the Montgomery Improvement Association, was born in Montgomery, Ala. (d. 1987).

1938,   William Henry "Bill" Cosby, actor, comedian, author, philanthropist, and child psychologist, was born in Philadelphia, Pa.

1949,   Frederick M. Jones patented an air conditioning unit.

1976,   Barbara Jordan became the first African-American and woman keynote speaker of the Democratic National Convention.

JULY 12   **LABOR & MOVEMENT LEADERS**

IDA BELL WELLS-BARNETT

Educator, journalist, lecturer, suffragist, and **anti-lynching crusader**. Born on July 6, 1862, in Holly Springs, Miss. Rust University. Taught school in and near Memphis (1884-1891); wrote for a Memphis African-American weekly, *Living Word* (1891); became half-owner and head of the editorial department of the *Memphis Free Speech* and launched her anti-lynching crusade (1892); her office was destroyed that same year by an angry white mob after she investigated the lynching of three of her friends and reported her findings; fled for her life to New York and briefly worked for the T. Thomas Fortune's *New York Age*. Traveled to Europe (1893, 1894); edited a pamphlet, protesting the exclusion of African-Americans from the World's Columbian Exposition in Chicago (1893); organized a Chicago woman's club (1893), which led to the formation of the Federation of Colored Women's Clubs; **edited the pamphlet, *A Red Record* (1895), the first serious treatment of the tragedy of lynching**; founded the Negro Fellowship League. Served as secretary of the National Afro-American Council (1898-1902), condemning mob violence, criticizing President McKinley for his indifference to the rights of African-Americans, calling for reduction of southern representation in the House, and opposing U.S. imperialism; chairperson of the Anti-Lynching League, attending the meeting of the Niagara Movement (1906); member of the Committee of Forty (1909), which led to the founding of the NAACP; active member of the NAACP Executive Committee (1910-1912). Served as probation officer for the Chicago Municipal Court (1913-1916); **founded the first African-American women's suffrage club, Alpha Suffrage Club of Chicago**; attended the Versailles Peace Conference (1918); served as director of the Cook County League of Women's Clubs. Died on March 25, 1931, in Chicago, Ill. Further reading, Alfreda Duster, *Crusade for Justice* (1970).

---

on this day in history...

1917, Lena Horne, Tony Award-winning singer, was born in Brooklyn, N.Y.
1926, Mordecai Johnson was elected Howard University's first African-American president.
1949, William Hinton, bacteriologist and immunologist, was appointed Harvard University's first African-American professor.
1966, Mike Tyson, the youngest heavyweight champion in boxing history, was born in Brooklyn, N.Y.

JUNE 30   **JOURNALISTS**

CHANDLER OWENS

Socialist, journalist, and publicist.   Born on April 5, 1889, in Warrenton, S.C.   Virginia Union University (1913); New York School of Philanthropy; Columbia University.   Received the first National Urban League fellowship; met A. Philip Randolph and together joined the Socialist Party (1916); ran an unemployment bureau, edited an African-American hotel-workers' newsletter, and **published a Marxist-oriented newspaper, *The Messenger*** (1917-1928); played a major role in the deportation of Marcus Garvey and analyzed the racial status quo during the World War I era. Became managing editor of the *Chicago Bee*; paid columnist for the *Chicago Daily News*; speechwriter and publicity chairman of the Negro division of Wendell Wilkie's presidential campaign (1940); during World War II he became a publicist for the Anti-Defamation League of B'nai B'rith; race relations consultant for the Office of War Information and **wrote its pamphlet, *Negroes and the War*** (1942), with over five million copies distributed to soldiers and civilians; campaigned for Thomas Dewey (1948), Robert Taft and Dwight Eisenhower (1952), Gov. William Stratton and Senators Everett Dirksen, Barry Goldwater (1964). Died in November 1967.   Further reading, George S. Schuyler, *Black and Conservative* (1966).

---

on this day in history...

1905,	The Niagara Movement meetings began in Buffalo.
1925,	Mattiwilda Dobbs, pioneering African-American operatic singer, was born in Atlanta, Ga.
1945,	Richard Earl Wesley, writer of *Uptown Saturday Night* and *Let's Do It Again*, was born in Newark, N.J.

THOMAS MONROE CAMPBELL

Government official and historian. Born on February 11, 1883, in Elbert County, Ga. Tuskegee Normal and Industrial Institute (1906); Iowa State University. Employed by U.S. Department of Agriculture, based out of Tuskegee Institute (1906-1953); **first African-American demonstration agent**, (1906-1909), traveling the South in a wagon called the Jesup Agricultural Wagon or "Movable School" being the first to bring scientific agricultural techniques to African-American farmers in the fields; USDA district agent (1909-1918), responsible for supervising and instructing other agents; USDA field agent (1918-1953), conferring, advising, cooperating, and working with state extension directors, land grant college presidents, and farm and civic organizations on matters pertaining to African-American farmers, farm families, and students in Alabama, Georgia, Florida, Louisiana, Mississippi, Oklahoma, and Texas; pressured the USDA to hire more African-American extension agents, who by his retirement totaled 800. Honored by the Harmon Foundation (1930), for distinguished service in the field of farming and rural life; Tuskegee Institute honorary (M.S., 1936); member of the Eugene Field Society of the National Association of Authors and Journalists; began a collection of Negro folk traditions (1936), as told to him by former slaves that he met on his rural circuit; served as a consultant in the Southern States War Committee of World War II; traveled to Liberia, Sierra Leone, Ghana, Nigeria, and Cameroon on a three-member commission to survey their methods of preparing soil, planting, and cultivating crops (1944), which resulted in the publication, *Africa Advancing*; received the Length of Service and Superior Service Awards of the USDA (1947); retired, as the **nation's oldest active Extension Service worker** (1953). Died on February 8, 1956. Further reading, Thomas Campbell, *The Movable School Goes to the Negro Farmer* (1936).

---

on this day in history...

1870,	James Webster Smith became the first African-American appointed to the U.S. Military Academy.
1899,	Thomas Andrew Dorsey, "father of gospel music," was born in Villa Rica, Ga.
1926,	Arthur Lewis, Nobel Prize-winning economist, was born in New York City.
1929,	John Hope became the first president of the new Atlanta University, the nation's first African-American post-graduate school.
1935,	Charles Houston became the NAACP's first paid full-time special counsel.
1976,	Kenneth Gibson, Newark mayor, was named the first African-American president of the U.S. Conference of Mayors.

JULY 1

LABOR & MOVEMENT LEADERS

ISSAC MYERS

Pioneer labor leader and Mason.   Born on January 13, 1835, in Baltimore, Md.   Apprenticed to an African-American ship caulker James Jackson, becoming a skilled worker supervising the caulking of clipper ships (1860-1865), until he was driven from the Baltimore shipyard by striking white caulkers; proposed a union of African-American caulkers to cooperatively operate their own shipyard and railway. **Became president of the Colored Caulkers' Trade Union Society of Baltimore**; issued stock, borrowed capital, secured a mortgage, purchased a shipyard and railway, and took possession of Chesapeake Marine Railway and Dry Dock Company (1866), which employed over 300 African-Americans; served as delegate to the National Labor Union annual convention (Philadelphia, 1869); **president of the Colored National Labor League (1869-1871), nation's first such national organization**. Detective for the Post Office Department (1872-1879); Baltimore coal yard owner (1879-1882); U.S. gauger (1882-1887); organizer and president of the Maryland Colored State Industrial Fair Association, the Colored Business Men's Association of Baltimore, the Colored Building and Loan Association of Baltimore, and the Aged Ministers Home of the AME church (1887-1891); grand master of the Maryland Masons and author of a *Mason's Digest*. Died on January 29, 1891, in Baltimore, Md.   Further reading, Philip S. Foner, *Organized Labor and the Black Worker, 1619-1973* (1974).

---

on this day in history...

1889,	Noble Sissle, bandleader and founder of the Negro Actor's Guild, was born in Indianapolis, Ind. (d. 1975).
1927,	David Dinkins, New York City's first African-American mayor, was born in Trenton, N.J.
1933,	Richard Gordon Hatcher of Gary, first African-American mayor of a major U.S. city, was born in Michigan City, Ind.
1945,	Harold A. McRae, Kansas City Royals manager, was born in Avon Park, Fla.
1949,	Frederick M. Jones patented a starter generator.
1989,	Bertram Lee and Peter Bynoe purchased the Denver Nuggets, becoming the first African-Americans to own a major professional sports franchise.

JULY 10   **LABOR & MOVEMENT LEADERS**

PETER HUMPHRIES CLARK

Educator, historian, abolitionist, civil rights leader, and the descendant of William Clark of the Lewis and Clark Expedition. Born in 1829 in Cincinnati, Ohio. Apprenticed to printer Thomas Varney; schoolteacher in Ohio (1949-1950); assisted slaves on the Underground Railroad; served as national secretary of the Colored Convention (Rochester, 1853); drafted the constitution for the National Equal Rights League (1853); attended the National Convention of Colored People (Syracuse, 1853); operated a grocery store. Became editor of the *Herald of Freedom* (1853); helped Frederick Douglass in publishing the *North Star* (1856); early Republican Party member (1856-1872); wrote *The Black Brigade* (1869), a story of an African-American home guard unit during the Civil War; was the first principal of Cincinnati's Gaines High School and **superintendent of Cincinnati's colored public schools** (1865-1887). Served as a trustee of Wilberforce University; became member of the Workingmen's Party of the U.S., spoke to the Cincinnati Workingmen's Society on "Wages, Slavery and Remedy," and became known as the **nation's first African-American socialist**; nominated on a socialist ticket for state superintendent of schools in Ohio (1877); moved to St. Louis (1887), and taught at St. Louis' Sumner High School (1887-1908). Died on June 21, 1925, in St. Louis, Mo. Further reading, Wendell P. Dabney, *Cincinnati's Colored Citizens, Historical, Sociological and Biographical* (1920).

---

on this day in history...

1822, Denmark Vesey, slave insurrectionist leader, was hanged in Charleston, S.C.

1922, Aaron Henry, director of the Freedom Summer of 1964, was born in Dublin, Miss.

1925, Medgar Wiley Evers, slain civil rights leader, was born in Decatur, Miss. (d. 1963).

1930, Fritz Jones ("Ahmad Jamal"), jazz pianist, was born in Pittsburgh, Pa.

1935, Ed Bullins, Black Panther Party's minister of information and playwright, was born in Philadelphia, Pa.

JULY 2   **LABOR & MOVEMENT LEADERS**

ELIZABETH DUNCAN KOONTZ

Educator and organization official. Born on June 3, 1919, in Salisbury, N.C. Livingstone College (B.A., 1938); Atlanta University (M.A., 1941); Columbia University; Indiana University; North Carolina Central University. Taught at Harnett County Training School in Dunn, N.C.; Aggrey Memorial School in Landis, N.C. (1941-1942); special education classes at Price High School in Winston-Salem, N.C. Became active in the National Educational Association (1952); **first African-American president of the National Education Association's Department of Classroom Teachers** (1965-1966); developed a film strip for the National School and Industrial Supply Corp., *The Negro American Citizen*; received Livingstone College honorary (Ph.D., 1967); **first African-American president of the National Education Association** (1968-1969), bringing a change from traditional conservative ideas to liberal activism. **First African-American director of the U.S. Department of Labor Women's Bureau** (1969-1973); deputy assistant secretary for Labor Employment Standards, designated as a special counselor on women's programs under the U.S. secretary of labor; coordinator of nutrition programs in the North Carolina Department of Human Resources (1973-1975); assistant superintendent for teacher education in the North Carolina Department of Public Instruction (1975). Died on July 6, 1989, in Salisbury, N.C. Further reading, *Current Biography Yearbook* (1969).

---

on this day in history...

1893, Daniel Hale Williams performed the world's first successful heart operation at Chicago's Provident Hospital.
1942, Richard Roundtree, actor, was born in New Rochelle, N.Y.
1947, Orenthal James Simpson, Pro Football Hall of Famer, was born in San Francisco, Calif.
1955, E. Frederic Morrow of the Eisenhower administration became the first African-American White House executive staffer.

JULY 9   **LABOR & MOVEMENT LEADERS**

FRANK RUDOLPH CROSSWAITH

Editor, author, and radical labor organizer.   Born in 1892 in Fredericksted, Danish West Indies [now the U.S. Virgin Islands].   Organized African-American elevator operators, motion-picture operators, mechanics, laundry workers, drugstore clerks, and grocery clerks; elected executive secretary of Trade Union Committee on Organizing Negro Workers (1925), whose slogan was "Union Hours, Union Conditions and Union Wages for Negro Workers in New York City." Became a full-time organizer for the Brotherhood of Sleeping Car Porters; general organizer of the International Ladies' Garment Workers' Union; elected chairman of the Harlem Labor Committee (1934); **organized the "first African-American Labor Conference"** that was held at the auditorium of Harlem's Renaissance Casino (1935), where he and A. Phillip Randolph called for the solidarity of African-Americans and whites, the 30-hour work week, condemnation of the failure of the New York state legislature to ratify the child labor amendment, adoption of a comprehensive amendment to the Constitution of the U.S. covering nearly all the goals of organized labor, and the urging of African-American clergymen and press to recognize and promote genuine labor unions; chairman of the Negro Labor Committee, which established the Harlem Labor Center. Served as vice chairman of the American Labor Party and member of the state executive board of the Liberal Party; lecturer for the Socialist Party and the League of Industrial Democracy; committee member who made plans for the March on Washington (1941), which led to the establishment of the Committee on Fair Employment Practices; board member of the New York Housing Authority (1942-1947). Died on June 17, 1965, in Chicago, Ill.   Further reading, Charles Lionel Franklin, _The Negro Labor Unionists of New York_ (1936).

---

on this day in history...

1776,	Prince Hall established the first lodge of masonry for men of African descent in Boston, Mass.
1920,	Wade Hampton McCree, Jr., appellate judge and U.S. solicitor general, was born in Des Moines, Iowa (d. 1981).
1962,	Jackie Robinson became the first African-American to be inducted into the National Baseball Hall of Fame.

LABOR & MOVEMENT LEADERS

EUGENE KINCKLE JONES

Civil rights leader, educator, and organization founder.   Born on July 30, 1885, in Richmond, Va.   Virginia Union University (B.A., 1906); Cornell University (M.A., 1908). Served as social science instructor at State University, Louisville, Ky. (1908-1909), taught at Louisville's Central High School (1909-1911); **founder and was one of the first initiates of Alpha Phi Alpha, the first African-American college fraternity** (1906), as a trustee secured the incorporation (1908), president of the Alpha chapter (1907), member of the committee that designed their pin, organized Beta chapter at Howard University, and the Gamma chapter at Virginia Union University. Became the National Urban League's first field secretary (1911), helping expand the organization to over 40 branches; associate chief executive of the National League on Urban Conditions among African-Americans (1912-1917); **National Urban League executive secretary** (1917-1941), giving league support to the struggle to organize unions and to gain collective bargaining rights; general secretary, National Urban League (1941-1950). **Established** *Opportunity: Journal of Negro Life* (1923-1948), a publication that served as an outlet for African-American writers of the Harlem Renaissance; served as race relations adviser to the U.S. Department of Commerce during the New Deal era, the "Black Cabinet" (1934-1937); helped establish the Schomburg Center for Research in Black Culture in Harlem. Died on January 11, 1954, in New York City.   Further reading, Nancy J. Weiss, *The National Urban League, 1910-1940* (1974).

---

on this day in history...

1914,   William Clarence "Billy" Eckstine, a pioneer in defining the role of African-American solo jazz singers, was born in Pittsburgh, Pa. (d. 1993).

1935,   Constance Berry Newman, first African-American director of the U.S. Office of Personnel Management, was born in Chicago, Ill.

1943,   Mildred Brown founded Nebraska's first African-American newspaper, *The Omaha Star*.

1943,   Alice Faye Wattleton, Planned Parenthood president, was born in St. Louis, Mo.

JULY 8   **LABOR & MOVEMENT LEADERS**

BENJAMIN JEFFERSON DAVIS, JR.

Lawyer, Communist leader, and politician. Born on September 8, 1903, in Dawson, Ga. Morehouse College Academy (1920); Morehouse College; Amherst College (B.A., 1925); Harvard University (LL.B., 1929). Practiced law in Atlanta (1932-1935), where he defended Angelo Herdon, a young African-American Communist who was arrested for leading a protest demonstration, which carried the death penalty in the state of Georgia; based his defense on the unconstitutionality of the state insurrection statue, the exclusion of African-Americans from the jury, the right of citizens to assemble to petition their government, and the many other rights denied to common working people; Herndon was found guilty, sentenced to 20 years in prison, which was later reversed bringing Davis international prominence. Moved to New York City and was appointed editor of the Communist Party's African-American oriented *Liberator*; joined the *Daily Worker* (1936), serving as writer, music critic, and editorial board member; elected to Adam Clayton Powell, Jr.'s vacated New York City Council seat (1943-1945), where he specialized in African-American affairs, demanding investigations into segregated housing, police brutality, overcrowding at Harlem Hospital, inadequate fire protection, and major league baseball's color barrier; elected to the New York City Council on the Communist Party ticket (1945-1949); expelled from the City Council (1949), for violating the Smith Act of 1940, which outlawed the teaching of or advocating the overthrow of any government in the U.S. by force. **Served as Communist Party national secretary, national committee member, chairman of the Harlem region, and chairman of the New York State District**, the Party's largest; defended the Soviet intervention in Hungary (1956). Died on August 22, 1964, in New York City. Further reading, <u>Wilson Record</u>, *<u>The Negro and the Communist Party</u>* (1951).

---

on this day in history...

1881,	Tuskegee Negro Normal Institute opened in Tuskegee, Ala.
1892,	Arthur G. Gaston, Sr., *Black Enterprise's* "entrepreneur of the century," was born in Demoplis, Ala.
1922,	Damon J. Keith, 6th U.S. Circuit appellate judge, was born in Detroit, Mich.
1963,	Ralph Bunche and Marian Anderson became the first recipients of the Medal of Freedom.
1991,	The National Civil Rights Museum officially opened at the Loraine Motel in Memphis, Tenn.

JULY 4   LABOR & MOVEMENT LEADERS

THOMAS ARNOLD HILL

Author and civil rights leader.   Born on August 23, 1888, in Richmond, Va.   Richmond Business College (1907); Virginia Union University (B.A., 1911).   Served as National Urban League assistant executive secretary (1914-1916), and western field secretary responsible for organizing western branches; **Chicago Urban League organizer and executive secretary** (1917-1925), where he played an active role in restoring order after the Chicago race riots of 1919; **National Urban League director of industrial relations** (1925-1940), where he emphasized greater opportunity for African-Americans in employment, the right of collective bargaining, and better education of workers in industry. Acting executive secretary (1933-1936), while Eugene Kinckle Jones was on leave in Washington; published the column "Labor" in the National Urban League's *Opportunity: Journal of Negro Life*; member of the President's Emergency Committee on Employment (1930), President's Conference on Home Building and Home Ownership (1932), and vice president of the National Conference of Social Work (1937). Consultant to National Youth Administration director Aubrey Williams; author of *The Negro and Economic Reconstruction* (1937); assisted Gunnar Myrdal in his research on African-Americans (1945-1946), by contributing studies on the NUL and its branches; served as a consultant to schools, colleges, and other institutions. Died in 1947 in Cleveland, Ohio.   Further reading, Arvrah Strickland, *Chicago Urban League* (1966).

---

on this day in history...

1781,   James Lafayette Armistead infiltrated the headquarters of British General Cornwallis seemingly as a servant hired to spy on the Americans, but in reality was a Patriot spying on the British.

1904,   Leroy Robert "Satchel" Paige, "the greatest pitcher of all time," was born in Mobile, Ala. (d. 1982).

JULY 7   **LABOR & MOVEMENT LEADERS**

JAMES WILLIAM FORD

Labor unionist and Communist leader.   Born in 1893 in Pratt City, Ala.   Fisk University (B.A., 1920).   Served in France with the 92nd Division of the 325th Signal Corps as a radio engineer during World War I; parcel post dispatcher with the post office in Chicago (1919-1927), where he joined the Postal Workers Union. Joined the Communist Party through the Trade Union Educational League and the American Negro Labor Congress (1926); became an organizer and leader of Negro workers in Africa and West Indies; elected delegate of the Trade Union Educational League to the 4th World Congress of International Labor Union (Moscow, 1927); attended the 6th World Congress of the Communist International (Moscow, 1928), and 7th (1935); delegate to the 2nd World Congress of the League Against Imperialism (Frankfurt, 1929), where he called for the independence of Ethiopia. Became head of the International Trade Union Committee of Negro Workers (1929), the Negro department of the Trade Union Unity League, and helped organize the American Negro Labor Congress and the League of Struggle for Negro Rights; **organizer of the First International Conference of Negro Workers** (Hamburg, 1930); spoke to a conference on African children sponsored by the League of Nations (Geneva, 1931). Communist Party vice presidential candidate (1932, 1936, 1940), the **first African-American to run for national office; became leader of the Harlem section of the Communist Party** (1933); advocated the philosophy of a "United Front" with the NAACP, National Negro Congress, National Urban League, and other African-American organizations (1937); regular contributor to the *Daily Worker*, the *Communist*, the *Communist International*, and wrote *The Negro and the Democratic Front* (1938). Died on June 21, 1957, in New York City.   Further reading, Wilson Record, *The Negro and the Communist Party* (1951).

---

on this day in history...

1809,	Thomas Paul, Sr., founder of the Abyssinian Baptist Church in New York City.
1892,	Andrew J. Beard patented a rotary engine.
1912,	Clarence William Wright, co-founder of the National Institute of Science, was born in Thomasville, Ga. (d. 1968).
1975,	Arthur Ashe became the first African-American to win the Wimbledon Men's Singles title.

JULY 5   **LABOR & MOVEMENT LEADERS**

LESTER BLACKWELL GRANGER

Civil rights leader and educator. Born on September 16, 1896, in Newport News, Va. Dartmouth College (B.A., 1918); New York University; New York School of Social Work. Served as artillery lieutenant during World War I; taught at Slater Normal School (1919-1920), St. Augustine's College, Tulane University, Dillard University, Rutgers University, Morehouse College, Hampton Institute, Atlanta University, Parks College, Loyola University, and Texas Southern University. Industrial secretary with the Newark Urban League; director of extension at the New Jersey state vocational school in Bordentown. National Urban League educational secretary (1934-1938); worked for the Welfare Council of New York City (1938-1940); National Urban League assistant executive secretary (1940-1941), and **executive director of the National Urban League** (1941-1961). Served as chairman of the Federal Advisory Council on Employment Security as special adviser to the Secretary of the Navy James Forrestal during World War II, as the architect of the policy established by the U.S. Navy for ending segregation, and helped to fight discrimination within the ranks of organized labor; received the U.S. Navy's Distinguished Civilian Service Medal (1946), and the President's Medal for Merit (1941). Edgar B. Stern distinguished visiting professor at Dillard University (1962-1966), and visiting professor of urban sociology (1966-1976); named honorary president of the International Council of Social Welfare (1964); served on the board of directors of the Council of Social Work Education. Died on January 9, 1976, in New Orleans, La. Further reading, Jesse Thomas Moore, Jr., _A Search for Equality: The National Urban League, 1910-1961_ (1981).

---

on this day in history...

1864,	John Wesley Gilbert, archeologist and Miles College president, was born in Hepzibah, Ga. (d. 1923).
1932,	Deloreese Patricia Early ("Della Reese"), actress and singer, was born in Detroit, Mich.
1957,	Althea Gibson became the first African-American to win a Wimbledon Singles title.
1960,	Valerie Brisco-Hooks, Olympic track and field champion, was born in Greenwood, Miss.
1965,	Patricia Harris was sworn in as ambassador to Luxembourg, becoming the first African-American woman U.S. ambassador.
1968,	Elizabeth Koontz was elected the first African-American president of the National Education Association.

JULY 6 **LABOR & MOVEMENT LEADERS**

For Reference

Not to be taken from this room